oh! sex education!

Oh!
SEX
EDUCATION!

MARY BREASTED

PRAEGER PUBLISHERS
New York · Washington · London

My thanks to Norma Morrison, Charles Baker, Wesley McCune, Jerome Bakst for providing information, to Robin Reisig and Joseph Morello for their editorial help, to Margaret Pepper and David McGranahan for all their fine suggestions. And many thanks to my editor at Praeger, William J. Weatherby, and his assistant, Norman Folsom, and Norman MacAfee, for their help in getting the book done. And to Ross Wetzsteon for the title.

Grateful acknowledgment is also made for permission to quote from the following sources:
Part of the chapter "Saving It for the Back Seat," which first appeared in *The Village Voice*, copyright The Village Voice, Inc., 1969.
"Sexuality and Sexual Learning in Early Childhood" by James Elias and Paul Gebhard, *Phi Beta Kappan*, 1969.
"Is the Schoolhouse the Proper Place to Teach Raw Sex?" by Gordon V. Drake, copyright Christian Crusade Publications, 1968.
"Normal Socio-sexual Development" by Carlfred B. Broderick in *The Individual, Sex, & Society*, The Johns Hopkins Press, Baltimore, 1968.
The *Playboy Forum*, *Playboy* magazine, October, 1969, copyright © 1969 by HMH Publishing Co. Inc.
Family Life and Sex Education: Curriculum and Instruction by Esther D. Schulz and Sally R. Williams, Harcourt, Brace and World, Inc.
A statement by Dr. Mary Calderone appearing on pages 3 and 4 of a reprint of an article in the November 25, 1968, *Medical Economics*, copyright © 1968 by Medical Economics, Inc., a subsidiary of Litton Publications, Inc., Oradell, N.J. Reprinted by permission. None of this material may be reproduced, stored in a retrieval system, or transmitted in any form or by any means (electronic, mechanical, photocopying, recording, or otherwise) without the prior written permission of the publisher.
Parts from *On Becoming a Woman* by Mary McGee Williams and Irene Kane by permission from Dell Publishing Co. Inc., copyright © 1958, Dell Publishing Co. Inc.

PRAEGER PUBLISHERS

111 Fourth Avenue, New York, N.Y. 10003, U.S.A.
5, Cromwell Place, London S.W.7, England

Published in the United States of America in 1970
by Praeger Publishers, Inc.

© 1970 by Praeger Publishers, Inc.

Library of Congress Catalog Card Number: 78–101655

Printed in the United States of America

To Mother and Father

Contents

one

Sex Education and I

"I had been told the usual lies about the Stork . . ."

Sex Education and I

Not long after I had begun the research for this book, I realized that I was a subject of some interest to my sources. There seemed to come a point during each interview when they would start asking me the questions. Now, a certain amount of inquiry is normally carried on by the sources of any story. They like to ask you a few questions about yourself at the end of an interview to show you that they, too, can listen. They ask you harmless little questions, like, "Where did you go to school?" or "When did you start to write?" But you know that you are not required to go on at length about yourself, that these questions merely constitute a small, courteous closing gesture almost like a parting handshake.

But the questions from the sources for this book were altogether different. Oh, there would be a few of the harmless ones at first. But there would be more than two or three of these. And gradually I would realize that my sources were indeed curious about me. They would keep on asking questions. They would make little jokes about my name. And often they would ask me just where I stood on this sex education question.

Eventually I learned to volunteer a little autobiographical sketch before the questions started. For eventually I learned what they all really wanted to know. The bolder ones had made it quite clear. Sometimes the most courageous of them would ask the essential question right off. And occasionally, they would not even bother to ask it very gently. "How did you get into *this?*" was one way they would put it. "Why did you decide to do a book on *sex* education?" was another version. And in their faces, I thought I could perceive faint traces of suspicion, as if they were thinking that I had suffered some terrible sexual trauma or that I harbored secret and strange sexual cravings or, worse still, that I was ruthlessly mercenary and had hardheadedly selected sex education as my topic because everybody knew that sex would sell a book. There

3

was probably a little truth in all their assumptions, but I always had the urge to tell them that an editor at Praeger had discovered my name in a phone book and decided right then and there that I was the one to produce their volume on the sex education controversies.

Nevertheless, all this special attention taught me that a person who chooses to write about sex in our land of Ultra-Brite toothpaste and mini skirts will inevitably arouse strange curiosities. And having learned that, I concluded that my book would have to begin with a little essay on Myself, and How I Got Into *This*.

It all started in what the current occupants of the White House might call a low-key fashion. One of my friends on the staff of *The Village Voice* had just signed a contract with Praeger Publishers to do a book on military justice. During conversations with his editor, my friend discovered that the editor was looking for someone of our generation to do a book on a sex education controversy. My friend, who knew that I was not making enough money to keep myself alive, suggested my name. So the editor, who had read my *Voice* articles, called me, and with much trepidation, I said, yes, I might like to do the book.

The thought of putting out a whole book terrified me. I had a school girl's awe-struck notions about authors. And I kept telling my editor that I didn't understand why he had picked me to do the thing. I worried a little, privately, about the topic. It wasn't exactly my area of expertise. I had written stories about politics and narcotics programs and small city-problems. And although I thought that the sex education controversies just had to be producing a wealth of interesting material, I wondered whether a high school teacher or a sociologist or even a historian might not be the proper type to do a book about them. But the more I expressed these doubts, the more confident my editor seemed to be that he had selected the right person to do the book.

I committed myself irrevocably to the task in mid-July of 1969, and after signing the contract, I began to have trouble falling asleep. The Book would not let me rest. I began writing it in my head:

Sex is the central American anxiety. We are the most puritanical country in the West, and yet our bookstores are stocked with anti-Puritan volumes of every sort, sexual reassurance for the masses, erotic rejuvenation books for tiring married couples, great thick statistic-packed volumes that tell us what percentage of our women have orgasm and how frequently our men spill their seed, soothing clinical paperbacks for frigid women and impotent men; and beside all these, the fake Victorian pornography with its long, drawn-out foreplay scenes, guaranteed to turn her or him on. It is no wonder that *Portnoy's Complaint* was an instant best seller.

Thus would begin the great essay on America's sexual schizophrenia, composing itself each night in my head. And each time it began, another voice would critically interpose, "You can not say such things. You have not lived long enough or read enough to be able to tell anybody just what the central American anxiety is. It could be the race question, or it could be the war, or even the dread thought of nuclear annihilation. You had better just stick to the facts and keep away from all those exalted generalizations."

During my days this kind of internal debate was suspended, and I spent them on fitful fact-hunting missions, sandwiched in between deadlines for my *Village Voice* articles. One of the best discoveries was a *National Observer* article that had appeared in a June issue.

"A Fight Rages over Sex Education," the article was headed, and it told me, among other things that:

"*National Observer* correspondents across the nation report that opinion runs deep in almost every state, that the issue has brought on major public fights in at least 30 states. . . . The controversies have evoked public rallies, petition campaigns, and long, tempestuous school board meetings.

" 'Teach students to read, not breed,' is a common slogan. Citizens organizations have adopted names such as Sanity on Sex (SOS), Mothers for Moral Stability (MOMS),"—I liked that name—"Illinois Council for Essential Education (ICEE), Parents for Orthodoxy in Parochial Education (POPE), and Parents Opposed to Sex and Sensitivity Education (POSSE)."—I liked the last two acronyms, too. They were simple and to the point and seemed almost parodies of the god-fearing law-and-order slogans that their authors probably lived by. I began to think that writing about the people who had thought up those acronyms should be more fun than plugging out stories on the city's library crisis or even the Mayoral race.

"The anti-sex-education explosion—called a 'sexplosion' by the National Education Association (NEA), itself a principal target of the opponents—erupted throughout the nation only within the past few months," I read further. "The NEA points to 'extremist organizations of the far Right' as the cause."

That brought me up short, that last bit about " 'extremist organizations of the far Right.' " I could not remember having met an extremist from the far Right, and I was sure I would not know how to interview one. I had seen some extremists at peace demonstrations. They were tough-looking men with Very Short Hair, and they had been known to pounce on demonstrators, the mere sight of whom seemed to infuriate them.

I had long hair myself. I began imagining the hostile faces of women in MOMS refusing to answer my questions. They would identify me immediately as The Enemy, I decided. They could tell by looking at me that I was an advocate of sexual freedom, believed in Women's Rights (although also, paradoxically, prone to nervousness around men I admired), hated the Vietnam war, had been a Vista Volunteer, and had spent four years of my life in that hotbed of pinko liberalism that was Cambridge, Massachusetts. They might even ask me cruel questions about my own long discarded chastity, and I was not sure how I would answer those.

I began to reflect upon my own sex education, which had been none too good. I had been told the usual lies about the Stork, and then later my mother had thought up a story closer to the truth in which the father would produce a seed and plant it in the mother's garden. Hearing this, I concluded that one became pregnant by eating a special food from this garden, and I began doggedly asking my mother where I could get this special food. My older brother and sister, being just about like everybody else's older brother and sister, would hear me bothering my mother on this theme, and thinking themselves vastly superior, equipped as they were with the facts, they would laugh at me. Finally, they decided to be magnanimous and let me in on the secret. They decided it, as I recall, on my ninth birthday, which is the kind of day you remember. With much giggling and some rather graphic hand gestures, they gave me a rudimentary understanding of the sex act. Full of what then struck me as the awful truth—for I had also been taught that the ultimate humiliation was to be derived from being spied naked by a boy—I marched angrily to my mother, demanding to know why I had been told a lie and declaring firmly that I would never do *that*. My poor mother was by this time having difficulty restraining her own impulse to laugh, but she nobly tried to reassure me with pious statements about the wonderful "rosy glow" which, she claimed, surrounded a woman engaging in The Act.

Somehow, I couldn't really find all kinds of psychologically significant elements in that incident. It didn't seem to have affected me any more or less than a million other fragments of my childhood, which altogether had given me that semirelaxed puritanism of a middle-class child. It was the kind of puritanism which still rejected sex for its own sake and respected fidelity, but saw no particular. purpose in chastity or even marriage—for people who weren't planning to have children.

There was a sex scandal during my sophomore year of college, which seemed to interest the people in Boston more than it interested the students. The thing was started when a psychiatrist from the Harvard Health Center passed around a report on female patients who—he thought—had become disturbed as a result of their sexual experiences. Just at that time the Radcliffe student government was pushing for a liberalization of our parietal hours, and the psychiatrist wanted to lobby against this liberalization with his report. Somehow the *Boston Globe* or the *Herald* got hold of the report. The resulting stories were sometimes quite interesting, but we wondered whether they were true. We didn't know anybody who had been to an orgy.

Still, we were pretty shocking to our parents and our parents' friends—until the magazines started telling everybody what we were doing. Then our parents decided that if we wanted to live with our boyfriends during the summers, they could at least console themselves with the thought that all our friends were doing likewise. And as long as we didn't get pregnant, they just quietly tolerated our goings on. We were, after all, as domesticated as they. We just weren't quite so quick to sign social contracts.

We were, in fact, allowed to pass so easily into nonmarital wifehood that we began to sound like wives among ourselves. We talked about our men in those faintly maternal tones of domesticated women. And when we complained about them, we did it with the kind of resignation that descends upon people who realize they are indeed committed for better or for worse.

We prided ourselves on our defiance, nevertheless, telling each other that *we* would never end up as mindless housewives, that we weren't even sure we wanted to get married. Because we were not about to move to some godforsaken place on account of Him. We were going to be English professors and novelists and psychoanalysts, and it would be just too bad if He got a job in a small college up in New England the same year that we got a job in San Francisco.

Meanwhile, we would spend our summers diligently keeping house for our men.

And so it was only natural that by our junior year we should discover the Woman Question. We had noticed, by that time, that there just *weren't* any female professors at Harvard. Oh, we had heard about one over in the Chemistry department or someplace equally obscure. But we were, most of us, English majors, and there weren't any women in our department—unless you counted the female teaching assistants, and there were only a few of those. We noticed all right. And we noticed, too, that our men had a tendency to forget that *we* were just as serious as *they* were about choosing occupations. They would get very contrite when we reminded them, however, and they were by no means the worst offenders. The worst ones were to be found among the young graduate students and tutors, who liked to tell us that we would make good librarians. We told ourselves that they were idiots with secret fears of intelligent women. But we read Doris Lessing and Virginia Woolf, and we worried. Because Doris Lessing's neuroses weren't exactly inspiring, and we weren't sure whether we were ready to follow Virginia Woolf's fine vision right to the bottom of a river, either.

By the time the Women's Liberation Movement started burning bras at the Miss America contest, I was in Vista, and most of my friends were in graduate school. We were all trying to ignore our old dilemma, telling ourselves that the world would just have to take us on our own terms. Today we hover around the fringes of the Women's Liberation happenings, admiring and fearing the defiance of the more militant women, signing petitions for repeal of the abortion laws, and wondering whether our curious reluctance to join the Movement full-time is a sign that we have been partial domestics all along.

But here I was, assigned to write a book about the strange sex education battles, battles that seemed to me so outdated, so remote, and curiously irrelevant to the concerns of my friends that I wondered whether I would be able to understand the people who were involved in them. I then read the arguments of educators who offered convincing statistics, which showed that woefully small percentages of children got their first sexual information from their parents. And I read counterarguments by the opponents of sex education—some of them psychiatrists of rather strong right-wing political persuasions—which contained fewer statistics but many anecdotes illustrating the ill effects of sex education in the schools. The opponents seemed to think that sex was such an emotionally charged subject that no educator could teach it without communicating his own anxieties and values to his pupils. And because most of the opponents were of the opinion that educators were, on the whole, more permissive than they, the opponents argued that the entire subject should be left out of the curriculum, or at the most, included in a high school biology class.

I thought I could sympathize with their concern from my detached and faintly superior vantage point. If I was more Advanced than they were, I told myself, it was only because of an accident of birth. And perhaps they ought to be allowed to say something about the manner in which their children learned the facts of life. Maybe it didn't really matter how children learned those things; maybe what mattered was the degree to which their parents felt the schools were accountable to them.

I read many more extravagant theories thought up by the opponents, theories about how sex education was part of a Communist plot, and about how it would produce a generation of hippies, but I was willing to overlook these or at least to set them aside while I looked into the more serious questions about parental rights, which the opponents had also raised. I suspected that what they said about teachers communicating their own anxieties and values to their students was correct. Yet I couldn't really believe that students were profoundly affected by their teachers' attitudes. .It was now almost universally accepted by behavioral scientists that a child's deepest sexual traits were irrevocably fixed by the time he was five and that his values were pretty well established by the time he was ten. These scientists had determined beyond all reasonable doubt that the ineluctable molding of the child was thus the parents' or the earliest guardian's doing and that their marks would be upon him to the grave. And the more careful social scientists had even questioned the whole notion of a "generation gap," asserting that even the hard-driving businessman who sees his adolescent son turn on him and on his profit motive is really viewing resurrected elements of his own dormant conscience. These theories of social determinism I had read and believed, primarily because they were supported by my own and my friends' experiences. So I began to wonder, as I made my internal efforts to sympathize with the sex education opponents, what slight effect a teacher could manage with his late and far less potent touch.

There were ponderous questions involved in this odd controversy, I decided. They were questions that worried me, for I knew that men had spent their lives, serious, disciplined lives paced out in laboratories and prisons and mental wards, trying to answer them. They were interesting questions, which at least had the power to make me take the whole controversy seriously. But I wondered whether I ought to allow myself to stray beyond the story itself and into those murky areas of social science. It would be safer to just Stick to The Facts.

And what were the facts? Already in June, if the newspaper accounts were to be believed, there had been sex education battles in thirty states. A Congressman from Louisiana had begun introducing a series of anti-sex education articles into the Congressional Record. An old employee of the ultraright-wing Liberty Lobby had set up his own outfit in Washington called the American Education Lobby, and he was busy printing up copies of a pamphlet headed, "Sex Education: Assault on American Youth." The John Birch Society had embarked on a nation-wide crusade against sex education and all the other subversive elements its members saw in the American public schools. The Society's crusade had started in January of 1969, and by April of that year its Movement to Restore Decency (MOTOREDE) committees had proliferated across the land, prompting one jubilant Birch coordinator to write in a memo to Birch chapter leaders and section leaders:

"Interest in establishing functioning MOTOREDE Committees has been increasing by leaps and bounds. If this enthusiastic interest is properly directed and used to create understanding, it could be the greatest boost to recruiting (for the John Birch Society) that we have ever had."

An outfit called the Christian Crusade, which had lost its tax exemption in 1966 for mixing a little too much politics with the fundamentalist religion it was selling, had started knocking sex education way back in the summer of 1968. The Crusade's then educational director, Gordon V. Drake, had published a pamphlet with the thrilling title, "Is the Schoolhouse the Proper Place to Teach Raw Sex?" toward the end of that summer, and, as it had sold rather well, Dr. Drake began accompanying the Crusade's leader, the Reverend Billie James Hargis, on his revival tours. Together they had organized countless decency committees.

In December of 1968, "Let Freedom Ring!" the dial-a-diatribe telephone network, brain child of a Birchite physician in Sarasota, Florida, had begun relaying messages inspired by Dr. Drake's booklet. Sample: "Is the schoolhouse the proper place to teach *raw sex?* The Bible and Christian morality are now out of our schools, but sexology is definitely in. . . ."

For five weeks in a row during the spring of 1969, the right-wing radio broadcaster Dan Smoot, who had nine and a half years of FBI service behind him and probably knew a good Commie when he saw one, had told his listeners how the sex educators were "debauching" the young. And a January, 1969, headline in the Phoenix, Arizona, monthly *Free Enterprise* ("Action News for Anti-Communists") had screamed, "SOCIALISTS USE SEX WEDGE/In Public Schools to Separate Children from Parental Authority."

It seemed that every right-wing pamphleteer, radio preacher, committee organizer, and free-lance Commie-hater of indeterminate stripe had taken up the standard of all-American decency. Their numbers were staggering, and they put out material at such a rapid rate that I despaired of consuming it all. Even the Anti-Defamation League, with its scores of researchers doing nothing but collecting and filing the publications of the God, Country, and Motherhood types, could not fit every last pamphleteer into its books on the radical Right.

And the right wing, as I discovered on my fact-hunting forays, was only half of it. There was the whole field of sex education with its audio-visual aids and old textbooks and new textbooks and college professors and marriage counselors and high school teachers and forward-looking superintendents. There was a woman named Evelyn Duvall, who seemed to have been around longer than anyone else or at least wrote that way because her books for teenagers didn't seem to offend anyone. There was a man named Wardell B. Pomeroy, a real sexologist, who seemed to be hated by a good number of people because he had helped Kinsey write his reports and because he had recently written a book called *Boys and Sex*, intended for adolescents and containing such blasphemous statements as: "Masturbation in private is an acceptable way of releasing sexual tension, and an important part of growing up. Fear, anxiety and guilt are the only enemies." There was a man named Lester A. Kirkendall, who taught Family Life and Sex Education at Oregon State University and who had drawn the fire of the better-informed sex education opponents because he had studied the association between "premarital intercourse and interpersonal relationships" in the thinking of 200 college-level males and had published his conclusions in a book with that title.

And there was, above all, the Sex Information and Education Council of the United States, with an acronym that the opponents liked to hiss out as if in imitation of the great Serpent himself: SIECUS. SIECUS was a voluntary health organization with a rather broad and ambitious purpose—to establish "sexual sanity" in America. It was headed by a woman who, I had decided, must be quite extraordinary. Her name was Dr. Mary Calderone, and very early in my fact-finding missions, I had discovered stinging attacks on Dr. Calderone. She had been called "the high priestess of sex education," which wasn't such a terribly bad title, but the opponents hadn't been satisfied with mere titles. They had tried to imply that Dr. Calderone was a Communist by digging out some old McCarthy era records of a SIECUS board member's performance before the Senate Internal Security Sub-committee. The man's name was Isadore Rubin, and he was sus-pect in the eyes of the anti–sex education people because he had declined to tell the subcommittee whether or not he had ever been a member of the Communist Party. Rubin was the editor of a magazine called *Sexology*, which did nothing to help him in the opinion of the sex education opponents; *Sexology* had rather erotically suggestive cover pictures—although its contents were serious, studied articles on human sexuality, the sort that you might find in any scholarly journal.

I imagined myself saving Dr. Calderone and Isadore Rubin from these cruel Communist smears, presenting them in such a favorable light that any reasonable reader would have to admire their good works and laugh at their critics. I was to learn, however, that neither of them felt in need of rescue. I would find that Dr. Calderone, in fact, considered me a sort of nuisance, or at least treated me as one, and that Rubin seemed to view me with gentle and kindly condescension, as an amateur lost in a realm of experts.

By the middle of August, I had become convinced that the Sex Education Controversy in microcosm was something I could not possibly master by the December first deadline I had set my-self. A man at the Washington headquarters of the National Edu-cation Association (NEA) had given me a list of over 100 anti–sex education committees. I had read through thick files of newspaper clippings and had consumed stories from all the major cities in the Midwest, not to mention all the right-wing literature I had de-voured. And I had not yet been able to find anyone who could tell me how many public schools *had* sex education programs.

But worst of all, no one could tell me whether sex education had had any measurable effect on the youngsters who had been exposed to it.

Sticking to the facts, it appeared, would not be any simple mat-ter. For the facts were too numerous in some areas and too scarce in others. Even the NEA man could not estimate the magnitude of the movement to oppose sex education, for that was what it seemed to be, a movement backed by the organized right wing. And if he didn't know how many schools were offering sex edu-cation—and he was, after all, in a position to know—then how would I find out?

Each time I had begun an article for *The Village Voice*, I had been afflicted with self-doubts, but none like the kind that haunted me as I tried to plan out my approach to this book. Months later, after I had gathered more material than I could use, I was to veer dangerously in the other direction, to begin regarding myself as a bit of an expert on: The Right Wing, Sex, Sex Education, The Professionals In the Field, and Life in General. But back in the middle of August, I fretted over itineraries and outlines and the Central American Anxiety.

Despite my fears, or perhaps because of them, I formulated a plan. I would take two or three towns where the sex education battles had been intense, and I would study them. I would try to pick towns that were not similar so that the danger of misrepresentation would be lessened. I would, in other words, gather and present the story in microcosm and leave the absolute exact tabulations for the real social scientists. I selected, in the end, one town, but I explored events in several other towns for purposes of comparison. I selected the town that had become a symbol to the people involved on both sides of the controversy and that was, in a sense, where it all really began. The town was Anaheim, California, where one of the most advanced sex education programs in the country had been operating since 1965. I spent two weeks there during late September and early October of 1969, and those just happened to be the two weeks when the local sex education opponents were at an all-time high point. I came away from Anaheim with more material than I could use. I had rented a Volkswagen with brakes that sounded as though they had been manufactured in Detroit instead of Wolfsburg, Germany, and I had driven nearly one hour past Anaheim down the San Diego Freeway because, as I soon learned, the towns in southern California are not often marked as such. The people there must find the towns by plotting their way among the freeways, as with coordinates on a graph, for the signs tell them which road they are passing, not, usually, which town. But I had charted my way into Anaheim and found myself a cheap little motel that was renting to what appeared to be the town's only Negro, black, Afro-American (he worked strange hours and never told me which noun he preferred). It was a place with a clientele so poor that they had to do without phones in their rooms but still enjoyed those California essentials, the swimming pool and the TV.

I had arrived three days after the Reverend Billy Graham came to town for his Twentieth Anniversary Crusade, which I had considered great good luck and perhaps even a sign that the fates were arranging to have all the god-fearing folk perform their very best Bible-Thumping for my Book. I had arrived nearly two weeks after an article on the Chicago anti–sex education convention, by me, had appeared in *The Village Voice*. I had not been very kind to the "Antis," as I had begun to call them, in that piece, and I had afterwards reflected that publishing my views so early might not have been very smart. So I had begun my work in Anaheim with a generous amount of fear. The Word might have gotten out on me, I had imagined. Right-wingers, I had heard, wrote to each other constantly.

As it turned out the Anaheim right-wingers didn't get The Word on me until weeks after I had left, and then one of them wrote me an indignant letter to tell me that I was "a fake." Which was, strictly speaking, true. For I had tied my hair back in a secretarial fashion and worn my longest skirts and listened sympathetically to a number of right-wingers and their children. I had lied to the chairman of the school board, to protect my sources, which, my journalism school professors had taught me, was what you sometimes had to do in keeping with that higher ethic, The Pursuit of the Truth. I had listened to the children who had taken the Family Life and Sex Education course and liked it, and I had listened to the ones who said they didn't. I had listened to the newspaper editor who thought there would really be a Second Coming. And I had interviewed a sex education teacher who wasn't making any grand predictions but still said grace at dinner.

I had come away with something like a dozen tapes, several filled notebooks, what felt like ten pounds of literature, a dollar-sized wooden disk that said, right on its side, that it would turn into money when sex education was taken out of the schools, and a stomach disease from a diet of tacos and take-out coffee. I knew, by the end of my stay, which radio stations played "Abbey Road" before they were playing it back East and which ones played the faith-healer Reverend A. A. Allen and at what times of the day or night.

Before and after my visit to Anaheim, I did visit other towns, interview educators, follow the short and happy career of Gordon Drake, enjoy the momentary glory of watching two congressmen summoned from the House floor to speak with me, attend the National Council on Family Relations Convention in Washington, and go to that national convention of the Antis in Chicago. But it was at some point during my stay in Anaheim that I had begun to think that I knew what the sex education battle was all about. I would keep amending my conclusions long after I left Anaheim, and I was to write that it was about many things, some of which probably contradicted each other. But contradictions ceased to bother me about halfway through the book because I had decided by that point that no one really fully understood the controversy and hence it would be misleading to present one rigid theory about it. One thing did seem certain, however. Anaheim lay at the exact point where the two contending forces were concentrated. It was as if the radio preachers and disk jockeys had themselves elected to orchestrate the battle well in advance, as if they had both agreed to saturate the airwaves right there in the heart of Orange County and fight out on that very spot a contest between the Now generation and the Hereafter tradition of America's aging backwoods metaphysics.

two

•

Anaheim

"Conservative sexual attitudes seem, in fact, so
common in Anaheim and the towns that surround
it that it is difficult to understand how any Orange
County high school superintendent could have for a
moment entertained the thought of putting sex education into his public schools. But the famed Orange
County conservatism seems to have been exaggerated by the news media. . . ."

From Prussia to Disneyland

There was once a time when you could start out from
Los Angeles on a horse in the morning and by evening—if you
were traveling down the old missionary trail—reach a prosperous,
self-contained, little German settlement on a bank of the Santa
Ana River. This was the original Anaheim. A tiny grape-growing
cooperative established by a group of liberty-loving Germans, some
of whom had had to get out of the old country in a hurry. There
were draft dodgers and free thinkers among them, and these
hadn't been popular types in Prussia around 1848. But they had
made it to San Francisco, some before, and some after the Revolution of 1848, and there they had pooled their money to buy up a
plot of good farmland south of Los Angeles. They started moving
their families onto this land in 1858, and each of them took an
equal portion of the collective property for himself. The grape
vines they planted died of a mysterious blight after twenty years
and were replaced with orange trees. Their original cooperative,
the Los Angeles Vineyard Society, was dissolved long before the
grapes died. Indeed, the pride of private ownership is said to
have taken over soon after they settled on their individual lots.
In 1886, their community, which they had very early named Anaheim, became permanently incorporated as a town. It was a thrifty
and you could almost say ungenerous community, for in 1876 its
citizens had refused to give the Southern Pacific Railroad a sub-
sidy to bring its line down to their area, and they later let the citizens of Santa Ana carry the burden of getting the railroad line
extended on down the coast.

There are a few good stories about the first citizens of Anaheim
locked in a glass case in the Mother Colony Room of the Anaheim
Public Library. (Anaheim is considered to have been the mother
colony for all of Orange County, and some of its present-day citizens spend their patriotic energies on projects like the Mother
Colony Room.)

The best story is the tragedy of poor Theodore Schmidt, who lost his beautiful wife to the richest man in the territory. She must have been something because Schmidt stopped off in New Orleans (on his way to California) long enough to marry her, and then several years later a man named August Langenburger was so taken with her that he decided to woo her away from poor Theodore. Langenburger was a very wealthy man by the standards of that period, and he convinced the beautiful Mrs. Schmidt to break her solemn vows and marry him. Actually, the story in the library—it's a little character sketch in a thesis—doesn't say just who did the convincing, but it does say that Mrs. Schmidt divorced poor Theodore all right. It must have broken his heart, because he left town just before she went through with it, and he didn't come back for many years.

Which should have been a warning right then to the good burghers of Anaheim that the god who ruled over their town loved either reckless passion or free enterprise or both. Because today the town's divorce rate is about equal to its marriage rate, and free enterprise has done so well there that the land those original settlers bought for about $2 an acre is now worth thousands of dollars an acre. (Land near prime tourist areas goes for about $75,000 an acre.)

Today you can drive to Anaheim from Los Angeles in one hour, but without the aid of the freeway exit signs and the view of the simulated Matterhorn jutting out of Disneyland to guide you, you would have no way of knowing you had reached the town. It is indistinguishable from Fullerton, Cypress, or Garden Grove, from any of those Orange County towns that surround it and that are, in turn, indistinguishable from the outskirts of Los Angeles. Where once you would have come upon a distinct entity, a neatly organized set of vineyards, houses, and public buildings, you now find shopping centers, gas stations, drive-in banks, roadside mortuaries, residential tracts, and one-story office buildings spreading and spilling out in all directions under a harsh ozone-sharpened glare.

Anaheim today has no main street worthy of the name, although it does have a central thoroughfare lined with banks and old hotels and a graying City Hall. But every wide street in Anaheim looks like a central thoroughfare and like every other wide street in the neighboring towns. Indeed, the same streets with the same names extend from Anaheim out into those surrounding towns. The whole western half of Orange County, in which Anaheim lies, is one vast network of four-lane boulevards and six-lane freeways. No one can survive there without a car.

Shopping centers like little colonies of plastic casing spring up everywhere along the roads. And in front of each is a huge oil-stained parking lot. There is no place to linger in all that asphalt, and no one stays at a shopping center for very long. If you walk to one, the people peer at you strangely, looking for your car, as if, without it, you appear to them incomplete. They are, those shopping centers, set up in odd places at odd distances from the belated center of town. It is as if the car itself had planned them, as if it felt a need to be forever on the move between those great, flat, oil-spattered parking lots like a dumb beast roaming and searching for fine grazing land.

There is no more devastating form of punishment available to Anaheim parents than the withdrawal of driving privileges. Anaheim children do their courting in cars, and it is not just the final secret and passionate back seat fumbling that their parents dread. In Anaheim the car is not merely a portable trysting place. It is the essential equipment for flirtation. There is an area up near the high school football stadium that serves as a weekend cruising ground for the town's unclaimed young. They come in their souped-up Volkswagens and raised-body Mustangs, two girls in one car, two boys in another, and they travel a strip along La Palma Avenue between two drive-in eating spots. Volkswagens, with their pert, round bodies, are popular with the girls. The boys, in longer-bodied models, pursue them up and down the avenue, around this corner, into that lane, veering and double-clutching and flooding their engines at the intersections for all the world as if the cute-assed VWs, and not the girls inside them, were their prey. These youngsters can so skillfully transmit coyness and urgency through their machines that in their hands the cars *look* animate and eager for the ancient chase.

The Anaheim Chamber of Commerce people call their town the "Family Capital of the World." They invented this wholesome-sounding title after Walt Disney built his incredibly lucrative Magic Kingdom south of Anaheim's center. Disneyland is advertised as a treat for the whole family, and in case that kind of appeal is not enough, it is also billed as "The Happiest Place on Earth." What Disney built (in 1955) was a vast collection of story-book settings, quaint little fake old-fashioned streets, and random temptations such as the ride down the simulated Matterhorn or the submarine cruise among captured tropical fish. The place brings huge summertime and weekend crowds to Anaheim that keep the town's myriad motels in business. And Disney's creation inspired a number of other local entrepreneurs as well as the City of Anaheim to try their own methods of attracting the tourist trade. In nearby Buena Park, there is now a Movieland Wax Museum and a Japanese Deer Park. In Anaheim the newest goodies are the baseball stadium (home stadium for the California Angels) and the Convention Center.

There is one tourist attraction in Buena Park that has been around a good deal longer than Disneyland and could itself have been Disney's inspiration. This is Knott's Berry Farm and Ghost Town, which contains a hodgepodge of trinket shops, scenes from the Old West, and a real brick-by-brick replica of Independence Hall. Walter Knott, the owner, has been building it up ever since 1928, the year he first decided to branch out from the berry farm- ing and build a tea room where his wife could sell her berry pies.

But it was Disneyland that stimulated the development of a tourist industry in Anaheim and gave it its reputation as a "family town." Yet anyone walking through Disneyland and hearing the whines of children who are desperately trying to take in the whole overpriced place could be tempted to conclude that the Magic Kingdom is a fabulous enticement to fratricide or at least that it puts a heavy strain on filial bonds. There is something irritatingly saccharine about the whole extravagant fantasyland with its real live cartoon characters deployed to greet the visitors throughout the grounds. It has the passionless, cheery-cheery quality of the duller children's stories, stories in which the heroes are always perfect and innocent and asexual. The female Disney tour-guides themselves look as though they were picked from the pages of old family magazines, with their inoffensive skirt lengths, modest hair- dos, and permanent smiles. And it is Disneyland policy to turn away customers who are "not neat in appearance," which trans- lated means that you can't get in there if you are a female past puberty wearing a see-through blouse or a mini skirt or if you have wildly unkempt hair. Nor can you get in if you are a male without a shirt or with your own kind of wild hairdo.

Outside Disneyland, the Family Capital of the World strikingly fails to live up to its title. Couples divorce each other there at a rate of about 15 per cent a year. And even the families that stay together often don't stay in Anaheim for long. They come there from Los Angeles as people from Manhattan have gone to the Bronx. It is the first move out on their way to the fancier suburban communities, those expensive and precariously built homes in the foothills and canyons beyond the brief coastal flatlands. Many families that settled in Anaheim within the last fifteen years have migratory histories, for their breadwinners are retired military men with jobs in the area's new aeronautics and weapons industries. A good number of Anaheim's children can rattle off a long list of the names of widely scattered military bases where their fathers have worked. And Anaheim has a healthy portion of divisions of the firms that get the juiciest defense contracts—firms like Lear-Siegler, Inc., and North American Aviation. The Anaheim-based Lionel-Pacific Corporation has made profits as high as 1,403 per cent on its contracts with the air force.

But weapons and space industries have built branches all over Orange County. (It was a Long Beach company that in the fall of 1969 outbid Dow Chemical for the Defense Department's napalm contract.) And throughout Orange County there are people with migratory histories and broken or second marriages. There is a restless spirit in the people of that area, which gives them a childlike charm and at the same time sends them into foolish business schemes, makes them susceptible to sudden religious conversions, and spurs them to strange, quick moves on to other towns. They are a people of wild extremes who are capable of buying the newest, best-equipped swimming pools in the country and flocking to hear the oldest and least tenable spiritual myths in the country thundering over the most modern of amplifying systems.

It was Orange County that produced the California Citizens Committee to draft Goldwater in 1964. It was Orange County that sent a Bircher to the state legislature. It was Orange County that for ten days in the early autumn of 1969 packed the Anaheim Stadium every night of Billy Graham's Twentieth Anniversary Crusade. It was Orange County that sent James B. Utt to the House of Representatives, he having been the kind of Republican who told his constituents:

The Beatles and their mimicking rock-and-rollers use the Pavlovian techniques to produce artificial neuroses in our young people. Extensive experiments in hypnotism and rhythm have shown how rock-and-roll music leads to a destruction of the normal inhibitory mechanism of the cerebral cortex and permits easy acceptance of immorality and disregard for all moral norms.

There are men and women in Orange County who have long suspected that a network of cold and calculating Communists has been responsible for all the things that they, the patriotic citizens, do not like about their government and their society. Their vision is not altogether unlike that of some left-wing radicals who have seen an equal and comparable conspiracy of military industrialists at work behind nearly everything they, the leftists, dislike about their government and their society. However disparate the goals of these two groups, they have shared this almost metaphysical certitude: that American political events are not the products of accident, bumbling, compromise, or even the *independent* efforts of powerful interest groups; American political events are part of a consciously executed Grand Design.

What has distinguished the two radical factions from each other —aside from their aforementioned goals—is their unequal display of imaginative talent. Here the radical Right has had a distinct advantage, for its members have been capable of sensing the Communist menace in the most unlikely places, places where the radical leftists would never have thought to look for signs of creeping Imperialism. Take your city's water system, for instance. The radical rightists will tell you that if your water has been fluoridated, you can be certain that there are some Communists or Communist pawns at work in your city government. The radical Left may tell you that your democratic rights are still intact only because the repressive tolerators at the top have cleverly chosen to allow you some outlets for your political frustration—to prevent you from getting so angry at them that you start fomenting revolution. It's a kind of don't-trust-*anything*-the-power-structure-does reasoning that can seem far-fetched, but it doesn't come anywhere near the Commie-menace-in-the-water-system theory for sheer paranoid genius.

In Orange County the right wing has perceived the Communist menace, or something dangerously close to it, in pornography, atheism, the United Nations, rock-and-roll music, and John Hershey's book *Hiroshima*. That last item was removed from the County's school libraries in January, 1969, at the bidding of the County school board, one of whose more patriotic members explained that he thought the book presented a one-sided view of the United States' use of the atomic bomb against Japan.

Decency ranks high on the list of right-wing causes all over the County. In November, 1969, the county government passed a law prohibiting topless and bottomless shows, but the law was declared unconstitutional just eleven days after its passage. At Knott's Berry Farm, where a foundation called the Americanism Education League is based, there is a bookstore that has been selling antipornography pamphlets for years. (The store also sells just about every right-wing tome that has ever been printed, and the pamphlet selection there is a veritable Bircher's treasure trove.)

"Printed Poison," is the title of a pamphlet you might pick out if you wandered into the store's antipornography section. This particular one is copyrighted 1960 and was written by a man named James Shea.

" 'My son is a pervert,' " the text of it begins. " 'I blame those books and pictures mostly. . . .'

"This flat statement could not express the anguish of the mother's tears and heartache," you learn if you read further, "but it speaks volumes about the depths of naked evil in the printed filth that claims countless victims every year." and it goes on like that for thirty pages, leading you, in the end, to a group called Citizens for Decent Literature.

In Anaheim itself, the city council tried to evict some topless dancers from Melodyland, a theater opposite Disneyland, but a local court thwarted their efforts by declaring that the topless show was legitimate theater. And soon after my visit to the town, the local newspaper, the *Anaheim Bulletin*, began running front-page stories about local stores that sold pornography. The stories touched off a new decency campaign, and the Mayor of Anaheim began publicly denouncing both the stores and the town's one adult movie theater.

Conservative sexual attitudes seem, in fact, so common in Anaheim and the towns that surround it that it is difficult to understand how any Orange County high school superintendent could have for a moment entertained the thought of putting sex education into his public schools.

But the famed Orange conservatism seems to have been exaggerated by the news media, for when the adult population of the Anaheim Union High School District was polled in 1963, the results showed that over 90 per cent of the people there were in favor of sex education. Of course, just because they told poll-takers that they were in favor of sex education, it did not necessarily follow that the district parents would also rouse themselves from their swimming pool patios and ranch house living rooms to go cast votes for pro–sex education school board candidates. Out of some 100,000 eligible voters, about 85,750 stayed home on the day of the crucial April 1969 school board election. And on that day two anti–sex education candidates won seats on the District Board of Trustees. Even in Anaheim proper, the mother colony, which contains about 42 per cent of the district's eligible voters, the turnout for that election was a little over 14 per cent.

The Anaheim Union High School District encompasses all the elementary school districts in Anaheim, Cypress, and Los Alamitos, includes much of the territory in La Palma, Rossmoor, and Stanton, and extends into parts of Buena Park, Garden Grove, Fullerton, and Orange. It covers over forty square miles of Orange County, and they happen to be the forty-odd square miles upon which the most rapid development in almost the entire United States has occurred during the past two decades. In the nineteen years previous to that crucial school board election, Anaheim itself had changed from a town of about 14,500 people into a small city with a population of approximately 168,000. And in the period between 1955 and 1969—the post-Disneyland period—the number of eligible voters in the Anaheim Union High School District had increased tenfold.

One of Anaheim's oldest residents, a man who asked to be referred to as a "long-time interested citizen" (he is much better qualified to offer expert opinions about the town's politics than that phrase would indicate), told me he thought that the area's rapid growth and its voter apathy were directly related. He offered this analysis of the Anaheim Union High School District's politics:

New voters evidence great political potential in small areas, but so far it has not functioned coherently in any large areas. Their jobs are so varied and take them to Long Beach, Santa Ana, Los Angeles, etc. This and their cars make them stranger[s] to even the folks in their block. Most of them seldom come to downtown Anaheim, or if they do, they seldom seem to stop there. They are not known by those who operate there. Those of them who have aspired to office have had no extensive following so [they have] had little chance to win it. The present Mayor, Clark, had to run several times for councilman and get on advisory committees before he became known well enough to win downtown votes and a seat on the council. He is the first from the new areas to be elected.

Mayor Clark himself ascribed his victory to the fact that he had emphasized his "small businessman" status during his campaign. He also said that he thought his campaign speeches on behalf of "the little R-1 or residential small property owner" had helped to put him in office. The owner of a gas station, Clark was wearing a Mickey Mouse watch in the fall of 1969, and he avoided both sex education and partisan politics in his remarks for this volume. But he did go on a bit about the terrible smut stores and the wonderful homeowners.

You don't become Mayor in Anaheim by a direct vote from the people. You are chosen by your fellow city councilmen for a one-year term. All five of the city's councilmen are elected at-large in nonpartisan contests, but it doesn't hurt them to be in the good graces of the local Republican leaders—who are, generally speaking, conservative. The five councilmen don't appear to do much beyond deploring the growth of the local pornography trade and planning the still rapid development of the Family Capital of the World.

There is one unique element in the Anaheim city government, an element left over from the very first governmental structure established in the mother colony. The town's earliest settlers established something called the Anaheim Water Company to manage their affairs. And today the Anaheim city government owns the town's water system and public utilities as well as a golf course, the Angels' stadium and the Convention Center. All of these holdings bring in enough money to keep the homeowners' taxes relatively low, a factor that seems more important to most of the townspeople than the reflection that they are living under a mild form of socialism.

Still, Anaheim and its environs have attracted a considerable number of capitalists, 3,000 of whom were reported to have joined the John Birch Society by 1966 (according to *Newsweek*). And there is no doubt that the area's conservative and radical right-wingers are the most consistently active people in the local politics. Just why conservatism is so highly concentrated in Orange County, no one seems to know. But certainly the fact that the area's most powerful figures have been conservative Republicans must have had some influence on the hearts and minds of the local citizens. There was the vast Irvine family ranch, which as late as 1967 comprised about 20 per cent of the land in the county. There was Knott's establishment. And, more recently, there was, of course, Disneyland. The owners of all three establishments just couldn't help thinking that good old American free enterprise looked pretty fine from atop their respective money piles, and they were all staunch defenders of decency and the American flag.

Yet the very prosperity those three families promoted in Orange County has attracted a population that is overwhelmingly middle class and whose children are very much like the children of the middle class in any suburban community. Thus, hard by the shadow of Disneyland's Matterhorn, there have appeared some signs and portents of the county's entry into the Aquarian Age.

Not long after I had left the area, a high school student-body president in the town of Orange announced that he would not perform the traditional duty of his office—leading his fellow students in the pledge of allegiance. "It is just by happenstance that I happened to be born here," he stated in an article, which appeared in the student newspaper. "I don't feel I owe this country any particular allegiance." He might be "just as happy" as a citizen of any other country, he explained, save those that were "Communistic, socialistic, or under strict government controls."

Robert Gumpertz is the young man's name, and after the publication of his article, it was a name familiar to all readers of the *Anaheim Bulletin*. The *Bulletin*, which belongs to the Freedom Newspapers chain, went on a kind of campaign against young Gumpertz, and soon the conservative California Citizens Committee had entered the fray. It developed that the high school "mascot," a cute little blonde named Valerie Spencer was not your typical Aquarian child, and she challenged Gumpertz to a debate. Miss Spencer's mother just happened to be a member of the California Citizens Committee who thought Gumpertz had made "a calculated and contrived insult to every man who has sacrificed for his country."

In the end Miss Spencer was given a place on an evenly divided six-man panel along with Gumpertz. Soon after the debate was held, a large majority of the student body voted to retain Gumpertz as their president. And the Orange County Teachers Association passed a resolution in support of him, calling it support for "the concept of individual freedom and right of dissent."

There had been other, earlier signs of a new student political assertiveness in Orange County. In March of 1969, students from high schools throughout the county had gathered at the Disneyland Hotel for a one-day conference on student concerns. This group had come up with a grand total of eighty-nine recommendations for changes and improvements in school policies, teaching techniques, dress codes, and student government. (They had also voiced support for sex education.) And they had later presented their list of recommendations to their respective district boards.

In early October of that year, the former president of the Anaheim High School student body told me that the district boards could expect trouble if they did not act on the student recommendations. In late September, the Anaheim district board had relaxed the school dress codes, but the students feared that the state superintendent's office or the California legislators might establish a state-wide high school dress code. If that happened, the rather unmilitant former student president said, the students might "do something ridiculous" such as holding a "protest." He said that there had been "a lot of commotion" over the summer, and when pressed to explain that phrase, he vaguely brought out:

"Just commotion in and among the kids about the quote Establishment unquote and all of this SDS stuff and what SDS is gonna do and how their rights have been infringed upon by saying that they must come to school wearing certain things and they can't wear certain other things, and all *that* commotion."

SDS and drugs and costumes out of *Hair*, and "all *that* commotion" have come to the Anaheim Union High School District. Up around the cruising strip, drugs—marijuana and amphetamines, that is—are as easy to cop, say the youngsters, as they once were only in the hippie havens. And if you tune into one of the area's hipper radio stations, you can hear irreverent political satire in between the Beatles songs, little radio skits sandwiched into the space of a minute or so with very good imitations of Richard Nixon and Spiro Agnew trying to figure out how to break the bad news to General Hershey or of similar conversations we would all like to have heard. On virtually the same frequency several hours later, you may hear an old lady telling about the day her son fell on the picket fence and pierced his side so badly that she thought for sure he was going to die until she brought out her prayer handkerchief and placed it over his wound and saw right then and there a miracle, a piece of ragged flesh knitting itself together again under the sweet cloth of the Lord, oh, thankyoujesus, thankyoujesus, thankyoujesus, thankyoujesus, thankyoujesus.

With such contrasts are the sounds of Orange County issuing forth into the delicate poisons of its once fine, dry desert air.

So picture Anaheim as a huge, sprawling semiurban, virtually all-white (except for a few peaceful Mexicans) community with a good number of mini-skirted or maxi-skirted long-haired children, with the latest revivalist minister's church of the real and true Jesus Christ right next door to four gas stations, with the signs that advertise unbe*liev*ably cheap swimming pools, with too many motels and hundreds of low-slung homes, with palm trees and tropical sunsets and the Los Angeles Smog. Picture it as if it were simply an extension of the first makeshift towns of the prospectors and escaped criminals and maddened preachers and rejected second-blooming or third-blooming dames who had come a long way in quest of something and weren't likely to stop just because they'd reached the ocean. For in parts, it looks as if their towns had just slowly oozed out along the highways and the old coach roads and the new beach roads till they had filled in all the empty spaces in between but kept the character of overnight stops along the roads themselves, where now you see the fueling places and the one-night havens for the latest motel- and trailer-nurtured migratory breed.

James Townsend and the One-World Child

"This thing goes a lot deeper than what it appears to be on the surface," James Townsend was explaining. And with a look that seemed to say, "Brace yourself," he paused to let his words take effect. Then he gave me the awful truth about the Anaheim sex education program.

"This is a UNESCO-conceived, SIECUS-directed program," he solemnly brought out. Apparently I failed to show the proper amount of amazement, for he soon added:

"When we sent our representative to the UNESCO convention —and I believe that was in 1948—we accepted, without a dissenting vote, UNESCO in toto, in other words, without reservations.

"As usual our representatives were extreme left-wing liberals —I'm being kind now. These people all believed in the one-world government concept, and they've worked ever since as diligently as possible to turn this nation into a state of the United Nations."

James Townsend, father of two, devout Catholic, and admirer of Senator Barry Goldwater, had lived in Anaheim since his high school days. His family had migrated there from rural Kentucky, and he still retained a soft trace of that region's accent in his speech. He had fought in World War II, and later he had tried to set up a baked-goods delivery business in Yuma Arizona. But he had spent most of his life in Anaheim, and his friends there were the sort of people who, in the early fifties, had exacted a promise from the school board that the UNESCO booklet series *Toward World Understanding* would never appear on the shelves of the public school libraries.

Mr. Townsend could not claim credit for having thought up all on his own his theories about the improbable places where Communists were at work, but at least he had shown a receptiveness of mind for those theories as they emerged from the truly original

right-wing thinkers. Thus he had come to believe what Robert
Welch, the founder and chairman of the John Birch Society, had
unequivocally stated and what the Christian Crusade's Gordon
Drake had strongly hinted: Sex education was part of the Communists' Grand Design. And for three hours of a hot September
day, he told me just where sex education fitted into that Grand
Design and what he had been doing to snuff it out.

He started talking in the coffee shop of an Anaheim bowling
alley, drinking cup after cup of coffee and speaking very slowly
so that his every word could be recorded. He continued talking
all the way back to his Fullerton office—he said he was a financial
consultant for real estate companies—and he kept on with his
monologue long after he was settled back at his desk.

In his office was a stack of copies of a newspaper that he had
started publishing, a tabloid called *The Educator*, which carried
news of the sex education battles in various parts of the country
and which he hoped would attract a national readership. His
office was listed in the literature of the California Citizens Committee (which he had helped to found) as the headquarters of
that committee, and he was currently one of its state chairmen.

On the wall near the entrance of his office were two posters.
One contained a pop art picture of Lyndon Johnson and Hubert
Humphrey dressed in Batman and Robin suits, accompanied by
the words "Dynamic Duo Exposed." The other displayed a large
photograph of a black man in a Black Panther outfit hanging
from a telephone pole. Below him were the words:

Register Your Gun
Be A Real Swinger.

But back to Mr. Townsend's monologue.

"We know from our studies that certain people in government
and education are trying to create the one-world child," he was
saying, by now into the thirty-third page of my steno-sized notebook. "Sex education is only a part of a total program. And there
are things far worse, for example, sensitivity training and the new
social sciences.

"The new social sciences are again a UNESCO-conceived program to create the one-world child, to change his thinking."

"Are UNESCO materials used in the Ananheim District
classes?" I cut in.

"Oh, certainly!" he told me. "I can't recall offhand [which textbooks include them], but you will find that they have eliminated

the deep beliefs—that used to come from the schoolroom—of America first. They no longer play up our history. . . .

"But, you see, sex education is the emotional vehicle that we have used to focus attention on the whole darn school programs.

"We readily agree that health and biology and physiology could be very helpful. But we see absolutely no reason for these courses to go into the vivid details. Each conceivable detail goes into [the Family Life and Sex Education course], all kinds of perversions right into a how-to-do-it.

"The SIECUS crowd said that they were changing attitudes, and they thought that sex should start at three years old. These people stated that the parents should bathe with a young child, that they should even invite 'em into the bedroom. They wanted to make sex as common as a drink of water, and they said that morals have no place in sex. . . .

"Now, in the Anaheim program. It was being used as a pilot program [for school districts] all over the United States. They used the Anaheim program as an example of sex education, to sell it to other districts. . . .

"Our school superintendent, Paul Cook, acquired national recognition as a result of the Anaheim sex ed—sex *instruction* program, we call it. He received write-ups in national magazines, national news media. He was sought out as a lecturer and was the only high school superintendent in the United States that was ever mentioned on a national level in regards to sex education. Paul Cook was ridin' mighty high. . . .

"Anyway, Anaheim being responsible for this program going into other areas made us realize that inasmuch as it had stated here that it would have to end here."

The Anaheim Family Life and Sex Education (FLSE) program, which Mr. Townsend and his allies had indeed brought to an end, had been introduced into the district's junior and senior high schools on a limited scale in the spring of 1965. The following fall it was offered to all the Anaheim District's students in the seventh through twelfth grades (except in those schools where there were not yet enough sex education teachers to staff the six levels). Until the summer of 1969, when the California State Legislature passed a law barring from a sex education class any child who did not bring with him written permission from his parents, the Anaheim District administration had allowed only those children whose parents sent negative notices to be withdrawn from the course. The law had merely established a subtle difference. For before its passage, it had been possible for a child in the district who liked the course—but knew his parents did not—to quietly attend it, hoping they would never find out. In the fall of 1969 about 80 per cent of the district pupils came to school with parental notices saying they could take the course. In previous years, nearly 99 per cent of the students had failed to bring the negative notices. So the new state law (and perhaps also the local controversy) had brought about a reduction in prospective enrollment of nearly 20 per cent.

As it turned out, 100 per cent of the Anaheim District's pupils got no formal sex education in the fall of 1969, notices or no notices. There was no sex education course being offered in the Anaheim District during the fall of 1969. And that was due to Mr. Townsend's efforts and the efforts of a few hard-working mothers.

The course that the unlucky 80 per cent would have gotten was an ungraded, four-and-a-half week session covering the facts of reproduction, pregnancy, birth, and, in the lower grades, physical changes during puberty. Class sessions had been conducted largely in the form of group discussions in previous years, and the students had been encouraged to bring up questions that troubled or interested them. Each class had contained a question box for unsigned questions which students might not dare to ask out loud.

The course was called Family Life and Sex Education because much of it had been devoted to family and social adjustment problems. On any given day of the four and a half weeks, the seventh-graders were more likely to have seen a film about peer group pressures, for example, than they were to have seen one on the physical aspects of puberty. The latter sort of film would be shown to them at some point, but the emphasis of the seventh-grade sessions was placed on youngsters' social problems. Similarly, the twelfth-graders would learn more about the problems of raising a family than they would about sexual intercourse.

In fact, everything in the FLSE program had been designed to produce good family members. Whether or not that was what the course actually *had* produced, the curriculum guide said that "a family with strong bonds of affection, loyalty and cooperation" was its *intended* product. And Mr. Townsend couldn't quarrel with that.

What he could and did object to was the manner in which the course had been conducted, with its free floating discussion groups that had looked to him like sensitivity training sessions. Certainly, there had been elements of what might be called sensitivity training in the style of presentation, the circular seating, the nondirective teacher, the use of role playing, and the sanctioning of group decisions about questions under discussion. All of these techniques were employed in the Anaheim sex education program, and all of them are used by sensitivity trainers. But the term "sensitivity training" has been used as a label for such a variety of styles of group therapy, group "encounters," and group touch-ins that the term has ceased to have any precise meaning.

The Anaheim school administrators were to tell me that the FLSE program discussion groups had been intended to encourage students to make their own moral judgments about sexual and social behavior. Teachers, they said, had been allowed to offer their own opinions, but they had been trained to show respect for the opinions of their students. Both the district superintendent and the former director of the FLSE program, Sally Williams, said they thought such a teaching method would produce morally responsible students more readily than an extensive use of precepts or moralizing. In the introduction to the FLSE curriculum guide, their general philosophy is clearly stated. It reads in part:

The curriculum is concerned with developing effective interpersonal relations and attitudes to serve as a specific basis for making meaningful moral judgements. It is directed towards helping the student to determine his solutions to problems in the light of his own goals and philosophy within the context of the community's goals and values.

James Townsend and his friends did not think that the Anaheim students should be making up their own minds about anything related to sex. The philosophy upon which the FLSE program had been based was simply counter to their own. It would later develop that they also emphatically disapproved of what the FLSE curriculum guide said about masturbation ("Masturbation will not impair the mind. It will not interfere with the successful performance of the sexual function under normal conditions. Any harm resulting from masturbation, according to the best medical authorities, is likely to be caused by worry or a sense of guilt due to misinformation.") and that they just as emphatically objected to the fact that the guide even mentioned homosexuality. The guide had been, of course, written for teacher consumption, but the teachers were expected to cover both topics in their classes.

Until the summer of 1968, the course drew no harsh criticism from the community. Then, abruptly, the California Citizens Committee mobilized itself for a crusade. At a late August school board meeting, a woman named Mrs. Eleanor Howe stood up to ask whether she and her friends could give a special presentation of their views on the FLSE program. The board did not grant her request at that meeting. But after it became obvious that a considerable number of parents—who appeared at every subsequent school board meeting—wanted the special session, the board scheduled a "workshop," as they called it, for the group, which was soon dubbed simply, "the Antis."

Mrs. Howe was the star of that event, which took place on October 17th and featured such well-known experts on sex education as the Birchite State Senator John Schmitz and the imaginative physician Dr. Melvin Anchell. Mrs. Howe had prepared a slide show and a tape-recorded narration to go with it. She had apparently put a lot of work into it, because her narration included points that could be found in all the right-wing materials on sex education. She had lifted whole passages out of Gordon Drake's pamphlet, "Is the Schoolhouse the Proper Place to Teach Raw Sex?" without giving him credit for them. And she had apparently read that Frank Capell article on SIECUS, which had been reprinted in the Congressional Record. She quoted passages from a *Saturday Evening Post* article on sex education, which mentioned SIECUS (and contained somewhat misleading statements about the Anaheim program's connections with SIECUS), and a similar *Redbook* article. She tried to show how the whole Anaheim program had been masterminded by SIECUS with a slide of an Orange County family life and sex education conference program that was dated February, 1968. The program listed Sally Williams among the participants and indicated that she was a SIECUS board member. She was, but she had joined the SIECUS board *after* the Anaheim program was developed. SIECUS did not exist when the original Anaheim curriculum was planned.

At the next regular school board meeting, held a week later, James Townsend made it clear that he and the other members of the California Citizens Committee had not spoken their all during that special three-hour session. Accompanied by a sizable number of Antis, who had vowed to go to every board meeting until the FLSE program was removed, Townsend was apparently feeling quite effusive. For his remarks take up a good deal of space in the transcript of this board meeting. Several board members and Paul Cook, the district superintendent, challenged him often. Yet, despite their disagreements and despite the presence of a hostile group, the board members exchanged views with Townsend in tones that were generally casual and suggestive of the easy familiarity of a New England town meeting. This section of the transcript conveys those friendly tones—along with the obvious moments of exasperation:

MR. TOWNSEND: I say that this Board does not have the vaguest idea what goes on in those classes, that you only know what you've been told. I doubt if any of you have ever sat in any one of these programs and sat through it to know what's going on—

MR. PICKLER [a board member]: Mr. Chairman, . . . that is not a specific pertaining to the program—

MR. TOWNSEND: Specifically, SIECUS is behind this program. . . . One.

MR. PICKLER: I got that message last week, Jim, you don't have to tell me again.

MR. TOWNSEND: Two: I charge that my taxpayer's portion of money is being spent for the sex education program in which I deny it should be spent. It costs this District X number of dollars a year to present this program. There are numerous people—and you say you can get a thousand letters, Mr. Cook? I'll challenge you to a contest of letters if you want to have a pro and con. . . .

MR. COOK: We're not going to have any contest.

MR. PICKLER: Jim, there is one way of removing this program from the schools. We have five board members here. Three of them come up for election in the month of. . . . what?

MR. MARTEN [the board chairman]: April.

MR. PICKLER: April. All you have to do is get three members, three people who are in opposition to our thinking right now, and you can change the sex education course. We haven't got much longer to go.

MR. TOWNSEND: Well, you know, this is an old, old story. If I come down here, and I make a charge there's three members on this board coming up and we'll remove them, now, I'm pressuring the board. Now, I'm not trying to pressure the board by threatening to kick you off the school board. That's not the point.

MR. ALMAND [another board member]: Mr. Townsend, you made a remark there that I want to elaborate on—I would like you to elaborate on. Now, you said you bet—if I may repeat you—that this board, or the board members, has not reviewed this program. Is that correct?

MR. TOWNSEND: Yes, I did. I said I thought you didn't know what was going on in the classes.

MR. ALMAND: All right, all right, I'll accept that. Now, may I ask, have you ever sat in my living room in your life?

MR. TOWNSEND: No, sir.

MR. ALMAND: Then how can you say I have not done anything in review of this program?

The demagogue-weary board members tended to get off in little personal exchanges like that as Paul Cook seemed to be worrying

about protecting the image of his program. A little further on
in the transcript, you can read his long impassioned defense. He
launched into it soon after Townsend had remarked:

"We must believe when we see people like Mrs. Williams
quoted in a national publication that she hurries over to the
coach to find out what the latest locker-room lingo is so that she
can convey this to these classes, we must believe that she knows
what she's talking about. We must believe when we don't see this
board denying that this is a SIECUS showcase—"

"Oh, we denied that. Now, Jim, don't. Jim, let's stick to the
facts," Royal Marten, the chairman, had cut him off. But Townsend wouldn't be silenced because Townsend apparently believed
that *Saturday Evening Post* article, which had called the Anaheim program a "SIECUS showcase" (a phrase which falsely
conveyed the impression that SIECUS had planned the Anaheim
FLSE program—when actually SIECUS people had initially
asked the Anaheim educators for information about sex education
programs and could only be said to have cooperated with them
through a natural sharing of mutual concerns, long after the
Anaheim program had been planned).

Cook, who had obviously read the magazine articles in which
the Anaheim program was mentioned, began here his lengthy
rebuttal:

Jim, let me point out to you, you must be sophisticated enough to
know that when you're quoted in—as we were quoted—in *Time*
magazine and in a number of other magazines, some of the things
they said were complete fabrications. Including the statement, including the statement that Mrs. Williams went to the coaches to find out
the latest dirty words. That is an utter and complete fabrication. In
Time magazine it said that we bandied the four-letter words around in
the school. I deny that and say it is a complete and utter fabrication,
from beginning to end.

Now, this is the point we're making: We are more than willing to
investigate anything. I can't say that at some time some teacher has
not said one word that was out of line. I can't deny that. They're
human beings. But . . . basically, we have done exactly as we have
said and as Mr. Almand has said. We have literally thousands of
statements from students who have gone through the course and we
have hundreds of parents who have gone through the [parent orienta-
tion] course, and as far as we know we're doing and telling you exactly
—now, you may very well disagree, which I see you do, but, for instance, we have repeatedly explained to you people the fact that
SIECUS was, could not have been a part (of the Anaheim program
development). It actually got its charter in May of '64. . . . It is

SIECUS that wrote this board and asked to use its material. It is not this board that wrote to SIECUS to use anything.

We do not—I have seen *Sexology* as a magazine on the stands all my life. I've never read it. We've never used it in our classes. . . . Whether our teachers have ever seen it, I don't know. But here these sorts of things are being bandied about by this group of people. They are not trying to check on things.

Jim, we could have answered all these questions. I could see very well how you could disagree with the things that we're doing in class. . . . You may think, as this gentleman thinks ["This gentleman" was a Mr. Bonnell, who would later emerge as an anti–sex education school board candidate], it's terrible to mention masturbation. But the fact of the matter is that it does occur among humans, and it's a very common practice. And the problem is that this is a part of the things that we think young children need some protection and help in.

Now, the point I'm trying to make is that we're struggling. But to say, as you have said, as this Mrs. Howe has said repeatedly, that this board or any of its employees ever had any direct communication with SIECUS or took any direction from SIECUS is a complete and utter fabrication.

"And yet," Mr. Townsend came back, "we can take you right over here in your classrooms and show you twenty-six publications that are either used as textbooks or supplementary textbooks— they are written by members of the board of SIECUS, the so-called experts with a long Ph.D. degree behind them that doesn't necessarily signify that they're qualified to drive a jeep across the street."

The transcript continues on for six more pages with Mr. Townsend's quotes liberally sprinkled throughout. We may as well part with it here, however, and leave Mr. Townsend echoing George Wallace, who likes to say that the "so-called intellectuals" are not capable of riding a bicycle across the street.

As for Townsend's notion that there were twenty-six publications written by members of the board of SIECUS in the Anaheim District classrooms, it must have been derived from the fact that many of the SIECUS board members had written textbooks that were widely used—before that infamous organization was founded.

The Anti Ladies and the Unsung Hero

Before last year, if you'd mentioned Anaheim, Calif., most people would have thought of Disneyland, the huge amusement park that's located there. Today, Anaheim (pop. 160,000)* has another kind of notoriety. From Darien, Conn., to Renton, Wash., opponents of sex education point to Anaheim as a community where, it is alleged, venereal disease and illegitimacy run rampant because of a pioneering curriculum in Family Life and Sex Education. In literature circulated by the Birch Society and Hargis' Christian Crusade, Anaheim is depicted—along with Sweden—as a swamp of juvenile immorality, Exhibit A of the results of sex education.—From Look *magazine, September 9, 1969.*

Two weeks before I arrived in Anaheim, the anti–sex education forces completed the destruction of the Union High School District's Family Life and Sex Education program. They had persuaded the district board to withdraw all but five of the program's books and all but two of the FLSE films from the district schools and libraries. (The curriculum guide for the program listed forty-four films, nineteen film strips, one tape recording, one slide set, thirty-four books, and twenty pamphlets as materials available for classroom use. All save the acceptable five books and two films had been packed away by early October, 1969.) And the board had passed a ruling forbidding all school employees to discuss the FLSE program with community groups. The board chairman made it clear that they were also forbidden to talk with the press.

Paul Cook was still superintendent of the district—in name. But he had been deprived of his powers and duties, and the district board was dealing instead with his assistant, a more compliant man named Kenneth Wines. Cook had decided to resign

---

* Anaheim Chamber of Commerce publications state 168,000.

and was staying on only to negotiate the terms of his retirement with the board.

Sally Williams, the former director of the FLSE program, had been back in her old position as school nurse since June of 1969. And although she was in demand all over the country as a speaker and consultant to groups interested in setting up sex education programs, she had been told by the district board that she would be fired if she were to accept one of these invitations. Two local colleges that had previously invited her to teach their education students had recently withdrawn those offers. It was Mrs. Williams's understanding—gleaned from members of her professional association—that any attempt on her part to challenge the board's restrictions would bring reprisals from them, reprisals directed not against her but against the FLSE program. (For although the program had been halted, the board had indicated that it would probably be resumed in the spring in a modified form.)

Several weeks after I left the area, the board ruling about school employees talking with the press was withdrawn on the advice of counsel. But while I was there that ruling was in effect, and it created extraordinary problems for Sally Williams and Paul Cook, both of whom wanted to be heard. It also created problems for me because it meant that I could find only one sex education teacher—a man who was no longer working in the district—who would speak to me. Mrs. Williams and Mr. Cook agreed to see me, realizing that their statements would be published many months later. But they were both nervous about having others learn that I was interviewing them. Mrs. Williams told me not to phone her at work, and Paul Cook would not submit to an interview until the day before I was to leave Anaheim.

One could almost say that early October, 1969, was the period of an all-time low for the Anaheim liberals, but that might not be precisely true. For although the board's restrictive directive about publicity was soon to be canceled, the bitterness that the sex education controversy had spawned in the school system lingered on for many months, and at least one source was later to tell me that it had gotten progressively worse.

The most publicized point in the Anaheim controversy was that April, 1969, board election, in which two out of three available board seats (there were five altogether) had been won by sex education opponents. That election had shaken the confidence of sex educators all over the country. Townsend had been quite correct when he said that the Anaheim program had served as a model for programs in other districts, and thus when educators began reading about how the community rose up and repudiated that there model program in an election, they began to hold conferences about ways to deal with the national Antis. Meanwhile, the Antis were proudly broadcasting the Anaheim election results in far away places to whatever set of worried parents they could find.

Nowhere had that election been more devastating to sex education proponents than in Anaheim itself, however. "The results of this go far beyond sex education," Paul Cook had told *Look* magazine. "You don't turn off hatred just like that. It spreads and spreads. People in the community have stopped talking to each other. People come to school board meetings now and question our textbooks on other subjects. Where will it all stop?"

What puzzled me, as I read about Anaheim's troubles, was the way that all observers and participants in that town seemed to have taken the sex education fight so very seriously. The Antis had, after all, only won two out of five seats on the board. And the vote itself had constituted no great victory for them. Roughly 14 per cent of the local voters had gone to the polls and a good portion of them had pulled the levers for the three incumbent board members (one of them was re-elected and the other two finished fourth and fifth in the race). Yet Paul Cook had made it sound as though the Yahoos were taking over the country's school systems, starting in Anaheim. And back east the sex education experts and the people at the National Education Association had been telling writers for *Look*, *Redbook*, and the *National Observer* that there were indeed other Anaheims throughout the land, communities in which school administrators had begun to shiver at the mention of Dr. Gordon V. Drake's name.

When I arrived in Anaheim, my bafflement was, for the first few days, quite overwhelming. For I realized right off that the protagonists in the local controversy had taken it all even more seriously than the magazine articles and eastern experts had indicated. Only gradually would I sense the power of this issue behind which the vital and meaty heart of so many anxieties was really pumping away. But at first I approached it like some luckless and green detective, who had been assigned to solve a crime the nature of which he did not even wholly understand. I asked myself what had really sparked the controversy. And who was involved in it for political reasons and who for personal ones? Why were the three sex education supporters on the board making so many concessions to the two Anti representatives? What was

there to fear in sex education? What was so bad about a school
system without sex education? Had the whole Anaheim battle
been masterminded by the Christian Crusade? Or were all the
Antis plagued by potent sexual fears that the sex education program had somehow magnified? And did they *really believe* it was
all a Communist plot?

Such questions kept me scattering in all directions for those
first few days, writing down Townsend's every last word, rushing
to his house to hear his children, reading about Anaheim's period
of Klan rule up in the Mother Colony room, going up to the
Celebrity Suite of the Grand Hotel where Mrs. Howe was putting
on a kind of anti-sex education show. By a form of oversaturation,
I was learning that right-wingers loved to talk, that the *Anaheim
Bulletin* loved to print their letters, that their children looked
like ordinary middle-class adolescents and hadn't found sex education as alarming as their parents had, that the controversy had one
unsung hero, and that religion and social class created more profound divisions in America than I had realized.

Before taking the plunge into the thick of it all, I had read a
statement written by Paul Cook called, "How It All Began,"
which included a history of the sex education program as well as
a list of questions that had been raised by the Antis. Cook had
written it shortly before the April, 1969, school board election,
and the whole thing had been printed in the *Anaheim Bulletin.*
In the historical section, he had stated:

In the summer of 1962 a group of adults appeared at a meeting of the
Board of Trustees of the Anaheim Union High School District to
criticize the use of a film in which a coach discussed the problem of
masturbation and attempted to quiet some of the fears that young
boys ordinarily have concerning this practice. In addition, these people were concerned about the moral problems involved in sex education and, further, felt that it was improper to introduce any reference
to sex in the public schools. This group made statements [to the
effect] that a majority of the people in the community would be
violently opposed to such a program if they knew about it.

Two weeks later, the same group appeared with a few additional
adherents and requested that all reference to sex education be taken
from the school's program, one small coterie even demanding that any
reference to sex be removed from the Biology curriculum.

While the Board of Trustees did not intend to ignore the need for
sex education, it suspended all such teaching in the district's schools
in order to consider the whole subject in detail. The Board considered
its position and decided to develop a blue-ribbon citizens' advisory
committee which would thoroughly investigate the teaching of sex

education in the public schools. Twelve organizations in the community were asked to appoint a member from each of their groups who would be willing to work on such a committee. Representing the organizations were two physicians, a police sergeant from the juvenile division, a probation officer, two ministers, a priest, a rabbi, and representatives from parent-teacher organizations, the local Chamber of Commerce, a boys' club, a women's club, and the American Association of University Women.

Cook had gone on about the advisory committee's work, telling how the group had finally decided to do an opinion survey among the adults of the district, a survey which was to reveal that over 90 per cent of them favored sex education "in both junior and senior high schools." And in what would later sound like an inflated claim, he had concluded, "THIS OVERWHELMING SUPPORT HAS BEEN THE FOUNDATION OF THE SUCCESS OF OUR FAMILY LIFE AND SEX EDUCATION PROGRAM IN THIS DISTRICT [his emphasis] because no matter what anybody said, no matter what was printed in the newspapers or magazines, we knew that the majority of parents would continue their support, provided we did a good job."

Following the history, Cook had written a careful set of answers to his series of typical Anti questions, denying that the students were taught "the techniques of sex" in the FLSE classes, that the course drove "a wedge between parent and student," that students who stayed out of the classes would be subject to ridicule, or that his administration had ever used "films or filmstrips showing humans or animals engaged in sexual intercourse." He also explained that students had been "encouraged" to take their textbooks and "instructional materials" home and to discuss them with their parents. He conceded that " 'barnyard' terminology" was sometimes used "at the beginning of these classes," but claimed that some children simply knew no other terms for "sexual matters" when they entered the course. And he tried to explain the difference between what the Antis saw as instruction in masturbation and what the FLSE teachers considered a necessary presentation "of the most modern medical opinion" on that troublesome activity.

Three of the questions Cook posed for himself and then answered in this section of the statement I was to hear repeatedly during my two weeks in Anaheim. Cook's answers, which all of the Antis must have read, for they all subscribed to the *Anaheim Bulletin*, had obviously failed to win them over.

To the question, "Why can't parents teach their children about sex?" he had responded:

They can. But many parents have told us that there is a lack of communication and understanding between them and their children which makes discussions relating to sex unsatisfactory. Others have been frank to admit that their own information about sex is inadequate, that they do not know the proper terminology, and that they feel embarrassed. In those families where open communication exists, parents can and do teach their children about sex. Unfortunately, the pressures of earning a living and the present tendency of the family to spend less time together in a learning situation, makes it difficult for many parents to establish the atmosphere necessary for a fruitful discussion of sex.

To the question "Doesn't teaching children about sex make them more likely to engage in premarital sex activities?" he had replied:

No. On the contrary, the discussion of the hazards of premarital sex activities tends to develop the understanding and awareness young people need to manage their physical desires. Our program teaches young people about the basic differences between married love and premarital experimentation. We encourage continence and we provide the children with sound, logical, and understandable reasons why premarital sex is a dangerous and self-defeating activity.

Although it was difficult to understand why the Antis had not found that last answer reassuring, I had already read enough of the sociological material that some of those evil SIECUS people had written to know that Cook was straying a little from the data there. No one had proved that "the discussion of the hazards of premarital sex activities" could help young people learn "to manage their physical desires." Of course, no one had proved that discussing the "hazards of premarital sex" with youngsters would send them into the hay fields any earlier than they were already going without the benefit of such warnings.

Cook's claims for the deterrent powers of such warnings were not supported by any scientific material that I had seen. But that struck me as somewhat irrelevant to the purpose of his statement. For he had made it quite clear that his administration considered premarital sex "a dangerous and self-defeating activity." And why the Antis hadn't been reassured by *that* disclosure was altogether a mystery to me.

It would later become clear that the Antis had simply chosen to ignore that section of Cook's statement, that they had focused their alarmed attention on another portion of it altogether, this being his lengthy reply to the question "Do we teach morals in the course?"

This question is often asked in the context of religious morality [Cook had written here]. The Supreme Court decision relating to the separation of church and state forbids the teaching of religion in the public schools. Our students come from a variety of religious backgrounds. Some have little or no religious training and no connection with any established church. Some, in fact, are not Christians. Even if it were not forbidden by law, it would be impossible to teach religious morality without involving the schools in a controversy over which particular religion's approach to morality should be taught.

Our solution to the problem has been to provide the student with a framework for deciding to do the morally correct thing in any of the varied situations which will face him throughout his life. We do this by suggesting a basis for moral judgment and we think this is worth stating in its entirety:

We tell the student that those decisions, actions and attitudes which:
———increase trust among people
———result in greater integrity in personal relationships
———dissolve barriers separating people
———produce better cooperation
———enhance self-respect and produce an appreciation of the worth of personality
will produce right moral actions.

Conversely, we say, those actions, decisions and attitudes which:
———increase distrust
———lead to deceit and duplicity in relationships
———erect barriers between persons and groups
———produce uncooperative attitudes
———diminish self-respect and result in the exploitation of others for one's own gratification
will produce wrong, immoral actions.

It was not very difficult to perceive the importance of the Moral Question in the Anaheim struggle. But to understand *why* it was so important in an area where 90 per cent of the citizens had said they favored sex education, now, that was another problem altogether. And it could become more of a problem after a reading of that statement by Paul Cook followed by a session with James Townsend. Because James Townsend talked as though he had never read Cook's statement or had never allowed one word of it to penetrate and jar those neat conspiracy theories, which seemed to surround him like a great plastic shield, warding off the 1960's and the end of the Cold War. Townsend could just as easily have been talking about water fluoridation. His overdependence upon right-wing rhetoric gave me no clue, no unmistakable sign, that would explain why water fluoridation had in fact been replaced by sex education as the number one manifestation of the Commie plot.

Setting out, then, to cover all points of view in no particular order—the Anti Ladies, their children, and a former *Anaheim Bulletin* reporter (the unsung hero)—I was continually searching beyond the obvious. It could not all be a simple clash of beliefs, I kept telling myself. There had to be something frightening in the FLSE program. Something terrible must have happened in a sex education class. One of the Antis' children must have tried to rape his mother. Or perhaps the sex education teachers were all strange, breathy creatures whose peculiar lusts were warmed by a classroom full of teenagers discussing dating problems.

* * *

Ralph and Cecelia Townsend sat beneath a huge picture of Jesus, whose saintliness radiated out in all directions on the canvas. Ralph, who was a twenty-year-old, did not live with his parents, but he spent a good deal of time at home. Cecelia, a sixteen-year-old girl enrolled in the eleventh grade, still lived at home under the care and protection of her quiet, dark-haired mother and her garrulous father. On this particular occasion, Mrs. Townsend sat with them in her spacious living room, listening to her children's criticisms of the Anaheim sex education program. She sat quietly and with a pleasant expression on her face, looking as if she were proud of her offspring. And only rarely did she interrupt to correct them or remind them of some detail. In her dining room a huge stack of anti–sex education literature was visible, piled up on the table as if ready to be served out to the senior Townsend's hungry followers.

It turned out that the Townsend children were friends with the Howe boys, the twin sons of Mrs. Eleanor Howe, who had organized the Antis' October 17, 1968, presentation for the school board. The Howes and the Townsends were members of the same Catholic church that had protested the use of the sex education film in 1962. The priest who had led that initial protest, Father Paul Peterson, was gone, but his successor apparently encouraged the same stern views among his parishioners.

Cecelia and Ralph seemed to have little to add to what their father had already said about the FLSE program itself. But Mr.

Townsend had indicated that he thought his children had been pressured and ridiculed by the teachers and students in retaliation for his own involvement in the controversy. So I asked Cecelia and Ralph whether this was true.

Cecelia, a striking blonde with baby blue eyes and pretty, delicate features, answered with a cheerful assurance as if the incidents she described had strengthened rather than weakened her confidence.

"Well, last year—I don't know if this was planned or not," she began, "but, um, we did—we were playing volleyball and we did form groups to go into. And it's usually your friends go into the, you know, same group or team. And then after that was over, it seemed like after we'd all become very good friends, it was like the teacher said, 'All right, these are the kids that are gonna go into sex education.' And she just read off the names. And the way to get out of sex education is you had to, uh, have a note to get out of it, not to get into it. And it was like, almost every one of my friends was in there. And, of course, you'd wanta be in there with all your friends. You wouldn't want to stay behind with the kids you didn't know particularly. And it was my first year in public school, so I didn't know very many kids at the time.

"And so a lot of my friends went into the class, and I said I wasn't going in. 'Cause I didn't know that much about sex education. All I knew was my parents wanted [me] to stay out of it at the time.

"And one of my friends turned to me, and they said,

" 'You don't know everything about sex.'

" 'Well, I know that, but, you know, the questions I do have, I feel I can go to my parents, you know, for . . .' " Cecelia said, imitating her own reply to her friend.

"They were all trying to get me to go in there," she went on. Her friends told her that her parents did not have to know she was attending the course, she said, but she had replied:

" 'Well, it'd be kinda hypocritical if I went into the class after my parents have been fightine it.' " (Southern California children frequently pronounced "ing" as if it were spelled "ine.") " 'And I don't like to do it behind their backs.'

"So I tried to find out as much as I could about the course itself. And some of my girlfriends were saying that they would just talk frankly about the male organs in the class. And this embarrassed a lot of my girlfriends. . . . And the kids . . . they're all afraid to get out of it. None of 'em wanted to. 'Cause all their friends were in there."

Cecelia attended Anaheim High School, where several other children of the Antis went to school. But she didn't seem to think that their presence had been much comfort. It was her theory that most of the children who willingly attended the course did so because they could get out of the gym class that way.

Ralph Townsend had attended Anaheim High School for three years, and, hence, he had been exposed to the FLSE program before his parents became involved in the controversy. And during his tenth-grade year, he had attended the full four-and-a-half week session of the course.

"I thought the class was very boring through the whole class," he said, apparently meaning throughout the tenth-grade session. "Really, they didn't teach you anything that you already didn't know. The teacher was just as informed as any other parent and probably less at that time because he was a young teacher.

"At one time we had a—the males were separated from the females and, uh, the males talked to the nurse about all the questions they had, like sixty-nine and stuff like that, all this. And the girls talked to the teacher, the male teacher.

"But, uh, the class was very boring, and I disliked it very much," he repeated without a change of expression.

"Did you have the feeling that most of the students knew more than the teacher could tell them or as much as the teacher could tell them?" I asked.

"Well, the teacher never really told anything that had anything to do with, uh, you know, sex education. . . . You learned just as much in the streets as you did through the teacher."

Ralph offered most of his criticisms in a dull, deadpan voice and with an implacable, unflinching expression on his face. He looked strikingly like his father. They both had flat faces with high prominent cheek bones and large round hollows under their eyes. Ralph sat, during the whole interview, almost motionless, with one arm bent across his lap as if in an unconscious gesture of modesty.

His account was a little confused. He said that he had taken the sex education course during the tenth grade at Anaheim High School and then dropped out of it after a few days in the eleventh grade. But later, he mentioned an incident in a twelfth-grade FLSE class, so apparently he dropped back into the course for a few days during his senior year. And an incident during one of the twelfth-grade sessions had shocked him out of the course again.

"The teacher asked us, 'Can I be frank?' " he began, recalling the incident. "And everybody said, 'Sure.' And he goes, 'All right. I don't want anybody squealin' on me.' And everybody agreed on this.

"And, uh, so then he wrote the four-letter word on the black-board."

"What teacher?" I asked.

"Mr. Dearth," said Ralph.

"Is he still teaching in the school?"

"Uh, yes, he is," said Ralph. (Actually, the teacher, Paul Dearth, was *not* teaching in the district that fall. He was teaching a graduate course at Long Beach State College and working on his doctorate at UCLA. He was later interviewed and given a chance to defend himself.)

"He said to the class, 'I don't want anybody squealing on me'?" I asked.

"Yes," said Ralph, and then amended this after a pause, "Uh, well, maybe not in those exact words. But—I can't think if it was 'squealing' or 'telling on me,' " and, considering for a moment, he thought of still another version: " 'Don't go to your parents and tell them that I said this four-letter word.' And it was not the four-letter word," Ralph went on, "it was any other cussword you could possibly think of. And, this is what 'frank' meant to him.

"And he wrote it on the chalk board, and then he looked over to this boy . . . and I distinctly remember this because he looked at him, and he goes, 'Would you do'—and then he used the four-letter word, uh—'to your wife?' And the kid looked at him [and said], 'Of course.' He [the teacher] goes, 'Well, I won't. I, I love my wife.'

"And right there he made the kid feel about two feet high."

"Was the kid married?" I asked.

"Oh, no," said Ralph.

"He was planning to get married," Mrs. Townsend interjected.

"No, he wasn't planning to get married or anything," Ralph told her. "It just popped out of the air, you know. He just, anybody, he just happened to ask this question, and, uh, . . . I got very upset because I, I was always brought up to respect a woman and not curse in front of 'em or anything like this. . . . Now, if it was a all-male class, it would never bother me at all. I could cuss just as bad as they could if I wanted to. But some of the questions were embarrassing, and I didn't like the class.

"So I ditched for a week. 'Cause I couldn't stand it, and then I went to my parents and I asked 'em to give me a note to get me out. Gym was twice as much fun as that lousy class!"

Ralph said that his gym teacher had needled him a little for getting out of the class, but he seemed to have been left alone after the first day in gym. It was his impression that several of his friends thought the class was "a big joke." But most of them "didn't have much of a point of view" about it, he said. Sometimes they would "ditch" with him, and sometimes they would stay in the class.

Chatting at random after each of them had summarized his and her views, Ralph and Cecelia both mentioned the FLSE program material on masturbation.

"They've [anonymous authorities] proven that masturbating [can cause harm]," Cecelia said quite matter-of-factly. "And after they get married [people who masturbate] might not be able to have normal sex. Now, how can they ["they" being the school administration, at this point] teach that?"

"What I got was, it's all right to masturbate," said Ralph. "What I've been taught, that's about as low as you can get."

"My children were brought up to believe in the ten Commandments and [that] these things were wrong," Mrs. Townsend added gently.

"And there's one other thing I wanted to say," Ralph went on, "I was listening to a KRLA radio program. And this one boy said his name and then he goes, 'Without sex education'—oh, he said he was fourteen years old—'Without sex education, I might be playing poker on my honeymoon with my wife.'"

"People have lived for centuries and centuries and they've never had sex education," Ralph solemnly opined. "They didn't play poker on theirs, I'm sure, because I'm here," he said, looking vaguely in his mother's direction. "So far's I'm concerned, sex education is just a, a waste of time. Because what they're teaching is nothing."

*   *   *

Henry Davis, whom everyone called "Hank," was the sole school employee who was authorized to speak with the press in early October, 1969. He was, in fact, in charge of press relations at the district administration offices, and he seemed eminently qualified for the job. He had spent much of his life working as a sports reporter for *Stars and Stripes*, the military newspaper, and he had collected a reporter's pile of facts on every prominent Anti from the area. So he was an invaluable source. But beyond that, he was also a man who had taken considerable risks for his own principles during the Anaheim controversy. And he spoke with a wizened, folksy jauntiness that made him sound like a character out of "Gunsmoke." With relish, he would announce that he had "libellous" things to say about the Antis, and he would soon make good on this boast. Not your ordinary press relations man, Hank Davis even looked a bit like a Gunsmoke character, perhaps "Doc," and he was refreshingly blunt.

The story of his journey from the *Anaheim Bulletin* to the offices of the Anaheim Union High School District headquarters was in itself an example of his odd independence. It made him, in my eyes, the unsung hero of the Anaheim controversy, and later events did nothing to change that view.

"I had been assigned on the Family Life and Sex Education story," Davis began his account of his *Anaheim Bulletin* days, his eyes showing how he savored the tale. "And I had gone to Los Angeles and done a lot of research on the thing, and I was unable to find anything in the material that I went through which convinced me that sex education was a, a Communist plot to demoralize the youth of the United States. I discovered that sex education had been attempted in the United States ever since 1905, and that was even before the existence of a Communist Party [which is not strictly true, but it was before the existence of the Communist Party as we know it today], so the argument didn't make sense. And, uh, I came back pretty well convinced ,that the schools were doing a pretty good job with what they had to work with.

"And I wrote this, and it was rejected. There was a great deal of rewriting done on what I had turned in. It made Sam [Campbell, the editor] very unhappy, and we quarreled a bit about this and went around in circles. And I was just generally unhappy about the whole setup, and I would have quit if I had [had] guts enough. But, you know, it was a question of hangin' onto a job that was better'n no job at all."

Davis paused here, gathering himself up for what he knew to be the best part of the story. He seemed the sort of man who ought to be telling it all on an old porch or perhaps in a saloon, not in a clean, overlighted school administration office.

"So I was disgruntled, and I went around and did my work and tried to stay away from this sex education thing as much as I could. And then one day, Mrs. Burns and Mrs. Kelly [two of the Anti mothers] came up to the office. You've been up in the *Bulletin*. You know how it is, just one big room. And they were standing behind my desk talking to John Steinbacher [an anti–sex

education columnist], and they were asking him for the tape recorder. . . .

"I gathered that they were intending to go out to the schools
and, uh, do some secret recording in one of the classrooms. And
then I figured this is just, uh, dirty pool—and not only that, but
it's against the law in the state of California. The law very
specifically states that nobody shall take a concealed tape recorder
into a room.

"So I just blew the whistle on 'em. I picked up the telephone
and called the schools and told 'em that Mrs. Burns and Mrs.
Kelley were on their way out to one of the schools with a tape
recorder, and I didn't know which school.

"And, as it happened, they weren't admitted to the school. But
somebody must have put two and two together, seen me calling
about this time and concluded that I had blown the whistle on
Kelly and Burns. So Sam asked me about it, and I said, yes. And
he started to ask me whether I thought this was, uh, fair. And I
told him,

" 'Oh, Sam, I don't want to discuss it. Let's just call it *off!*' I
said, 'I'll—you can take it as two weeks' notice, or I'll quit now.'

"And Sam said, 'Well, you leave now, and I'll pay you to the
end of the week.'

"And that," said Davis smiling," was the end of *that*. And far's
I'm concerned, it was good riddance."

Davis explained the history of the Anaheim controversy much as
those eastern educators had done, as it paralleled the chronology
of the Christian Crusade's national campaign against sex education. But the Anaheim district board had held out for many
months after it all started, he said, and on January 30, 1969, they
had publicly announced their continuing support for the FLSE
program. Nevertheless, the Antis had persisted, and when the
two new board members took over in July of that year, it had
seemed inevitable that the program would be revised.

"What they have come up with now is a program which has
nothing left to it," said Davis. "They've eliminated all the tape
recordings, all of the film slides, all of that sort of material. Even
the highly elaborate, very expensive models of pregnant women
have been taken out of the program. So right now we have a program which is back on almost the birds and bees level. And it
isn't in operation because the board has been unable to agree on
a time to conduct it."

Davis knew so much about the history of the controversy, about the various stands of the board members, about the many arguments of the local Antis, that I assumed he would also know where all those pro–sex education parents had been hiding themselves. Well, they had shown up for one meeting in early January, 1969, he said. It was the counterpart to the meeting that the Antis had run on October 17, 1968. But since then there had been precious few supporters at the board meetings—and not a great number of favorable letters to the *Anaheim Bulletin*.

"It's strange that people don't want to come to the board and say anything in favor of the program," Davis mused. "But if you could see the way these individuals *act* towards anybody that approves the program, you'd understand why decent individuals hesitate to appear. They are booed and shouted at and threatened. They get telephone calls in the middle of the night and letters, and literature is thrown around their houses. And ordinary people just don't wish to become involved in—with this poor white trash type that causes all this disturbance."

"Have you ever had calls in the middle of the night?" I asked.

"No, I haven't," he replied. "Mr. Cook and Mrs. Williams have had calls. And some of the most atrocious things have been said about Mr. Cook and Mrs. Williams. You just wouldn't believe it —the hints and suggestions that—what's going on and how it goes on—are just awful. People have the dirtiest minds," he concluded with a wise chuckle. "Really. It's astonishing."

*   *   *

The Burns family lived in the town of Cypress. You got to their house by traveling Anaheim's Lincoln Avenue westward past innumerable shopping centers, which, at some imperceptible point, stopped being Anaheim shopping centers and became Cypress shopping centers. The Burns house was on a street called Vista Real, and they had been living in it for a little over a year. Before my session with her was over, Mrs. Burns was to remark that she wished they had never bought the house.

She was a woman of medium height and a fairly well-preserved shape. She wore her hair quite short and straight in what looked like an overgrown pixie cut, and it was a dull reddish blond color that appeared faintly artificial. She was clad in brown and white checkered slacks and a brown shirt on this particular afternoon. She looked as though she liked to dress with functional taste, without frills or impractically delicate fabrics.

During the long interview, her fifteen-year-old daughter, Darlyn, sat listening—except at those points when her mother asked her to tell of her own experiences in the FLSE course. Darlyn was a frail-looking blonde ("rinsed" blonder, her mother said), who wore a neat, dark sleeveless dress of modest length. Her hair was pulled severely back from her forehead, and she had a faintly visible birthmark on the side of her face which seemed to gain prominence from the tension that her taut hairdo put upon her skin. When she spoke, Darlyn sounded much younger than her years; she had a child's faint lisp, and she seemed quite ill-at-ease when discussing the more graphic material her mother urged her to divulge. As she spoke, her birthmark took on heightened color, seeming to signal her alarm.

Mrs. Burns had two other children, a five-year-old boy who appeared only briefly, and a twenty-one-year-old married daughter who sat listening through much of the afternoon but remarked once or twice that *she* hadn't had sex education and she thought she had made out well enough. Mrs. Burns said her own age was thirty-eight, which meant that she had borne her oldest daughter at age seventeen.

"We moved to Cypress in August of 1968," she began, her voice even and clear. "And we weren't even aware we were in the Anaheim Union High School District until we moved in. And then, after we became aware, then we found out they had a Family Life and Sex Education program, but we still weren't aware of what it was. But one day Darlyn came home from school, and she said,

" 'Mother, I didn't have to dress for gym today. We were put in a Family Life class.'

"I said, 'What did you talk about?'

"She said, 'Well, one of the things the teacher told us was she likes to swim in the nude with her husband.' And [Darlyn said] that mostly it was review because she hadn't been a student there last year. They had reviewed some basic physiological facts.

"And then I thought, 'Well, I had better check into this.' So I called my sister practically the same day and talked to her about it. She told me that she had just the night before been to an orientation meeting at her school on the Family Life program— she has a son the same age as Darlyn—and that a gentleman had stood up and he had demanded that the school nurse read from this book, *Attaining Womanhood*, a description of intercourse. And that it was so vivid that she was shocked, and most of the parents were very upset. And that this was being used in the seventh grade, which would be twelve-year-old children. And she asked me that if I went up to the school—I told her I was planning on going up to the school and looking over the books—she said if I went to the school to look for this book."

(*Attaining Womanhood* was listed as a supplementary text for *eighth* graders in the FLSE curriculum guide.)

Mrs. Burns said that she did go to her daughter's school to meet her sex education teacher and look over the books. The teacher had told her, she claimed, "Well, if we didn't like the class, why didn't we just take our child out of it and forget about it? And I told her, well, I would take my child out of it, but I intended to see what was going on here anyway as a taxpayer and an interested parent of the community."

Mrs. Burns had taken her child out of the class all right, but she hadn't forgotten about it in the year since then, and she didn't sound as though she would be letting it slip from her mind anytime soon.

"I object to twelve-year-old children discussing how a boy gets an erection because a girl is kissing him and going into details of how an erection happens in a mixed classroom," she said with some spirit. "And this is what they were doing. I object to them making masturbation an approved thing. And all of our books and films go along with, 'Everybody masturbates, so why fight it? Go ahead and do it, and don't feel guilty. That's the worst thing you can do is feel guilty when it comes to sex. You should never feel guilty.' Like, the class my niece was in. We got quite a bit of information out of that classroom, and this class decided in a discussion, . . . they decided that all boys should have premarital sex. Because at least one partner should know what they're doing. And they decided that for today's dating standards, that fondling a girl's breasts was fine, that this isn't going too far, this is all right."

Back in the fall of 1968, however, Mrs. Burns hadn't known much about the free-floating discussions in the FLSE classes. And at that time she had concentrated on the reading materials. She had xeroxed passages from two books she claimed to have found in her daughter's sex education classroom. One was *He and She*, by a British educator named Kenneth Barnes (Beaconsfield: Darwin Finlay Son, 1962); and the other was one called *Dating, Mating and Marriage*, by Jessie Bernard, Helen E. Buchanan, and William M. Smith, Jr. (Cleveland: Howard Allen, 1958). (Neither book was listed as a student text in the curriculum guide, and Sally Williams later said that the first had been read and rejected by her staff. The second one had been kept in the professional

library, she said, and only the teachers had been allowed to read
it.)

The passage from *He and She* that Mrs. Burns had xeroxed
went as follows:

When I talk to boys about the sex act I have to answer numerous
detailed questions. *How long does it take?* The answer is anything
from a few minutes to, say, half an hour. In the course of years people
can develop a power of control that will delay the orgasm for a long
time, and this enables them to enjoy a prolonged intimacy in which
there may be long periods of stillness. *How often does it happen?*
There are great variations in this. . . . Between normally vigorous
people who are eager to have a baby, or who use birth-control, it may
be several times a week when they are first married. In middle life,
especially when people are carrying heavy responsibilities in the outside world, it may be once a week or less. These are only rough
averages. *Are there several positions in which the act can take place?*
Yes. The commonest is one in which the woman lies on her back
with her legs apart and the man lies between her legs and over her
body, resting his weight on his elbows. But the positions can be
reversed and the woman can lie or kneel astride the man. They can
also lie on their sides facing each other. It is entirely normal and
wholesome for people who love each other to experiment with every
possible variation; indeed it would be just plain dull to allow habit to
take charge so that it was always done the same way in the same
position.

The next two sentences had been underlined, apparently by
Mrs. Burns, and they read, "It need not always take place at night
nor always in bed. It can take place with great exhilaration, in
lonely places out of doors."

The passage from the second book, *Dating, Mating and Marriage Today*, that Mrs. Burns had xeroxed was a series of anonymous quotes on remembered adolescent reactions to kissing. A
few samples were:

"I went on my first 'date' when I was 15 years old. I took this girl to
a movie in our local theatre and then walked her home. I had sat in
the same seat with this girl and also other girls previously to this
when the band or basketball team went on trips. Because I didn't kiss
this girl 'goodnight' she would not go out again with me." . . .

"Fellows who neck with a girl on the first date usually don't have
the proper respect for her. I feel that if you don't kiss a girl until
your third or fourth date, she will know that you aren't just taking
her out to see how far you can get." . . .

"High school also was the signal for sex education. My mother
began telling me about men who hired boys to go into hotels with

them. Here I developed the concept that sex was dirty, and men were 'animals.' . . . It was fortunate that my first experience with sex was an enjoyable one. The first time I was kissed, I was greatly surprised. He was kind, gentle, and quite nice. I would wake in the middle of the night wanting to be kissed again following this experience."

Mrs. Burns explained that she had taken the "objectionable" books to the school board on October 17, 1968, and at that meeting she had become acquainted with the other Antis. It was interesting that she first approached the board on that date because the October 17th meeting was *not* held on the night of the regularly scheduled board meeting. Those take place twice a month, and someone not familiar with the controversy could have been expected to attend one of them. However, Mrs. Burns claimed that she knew nothing of the organized opposition until she attended that special meeting. But from that day on she had joined their crusade to halt the FLSE program.

"Would you say that your involvement in this is generally in keeping with your politics? Is this unusual for you?" I asked her.

"It's real unusual for me because, to begin with, I was a Democrat. And I'm still a registered Democrat, and I *thought* I was a liberal, but I really don't understand the meaning of the word," she said.

"And I've never been involved politically in anything other than just to go up and vote when it's time to vote. . . . I've just been concerned with my family . . . up until the time that this came up, and then I realized that somebody had better do something. And mighty doggone fast. Because I didn't like, I don't like what's going on in the schools. "I'm *very* concerned about it."

"Do you feel that Communism is involved in this in any way?"

"I didn't in the beginning," Mrs. Burns hesitantly brought out. "But I have been shown so many detailed documents, and, uh—"

"By whom?" I quickly inquired.

"Well, some of the stuff that's coming out of UNESCO," said Mrs. Burns, either misinterpreting the question or choosing to ignore it. "And the fact that Isadore Rubin is an identified Communist, and . . . Kirkendall isn't a Communist, but he's a Humanist, and the Humanist religion, which—I think that's the only thing you can call it—leans toward, if they aren't Communistic, they certainly help the Communistic plan, even if they aren't intending to help the Communists. . . .

"And another thing, it's too big. This is going on all over the

United States. When I thought it was just a local problem, I didn't believe it was a Communistic plot. But now, when you see the same sales job being sold to every city across the United States and the same people, you would think that there are thousands and thousands of people promoting this sex program. . . . Like Mary Calderone has been to practically every state in this union. She is the major saleswoman for their program. It hasn't been a large number of people. The public hasn't been demanding the program, that I can see."

(James Townsend had given me a booklet that could have been one of the sources of Mrs. Burns's political views. Printed up to accompany the film *Pavlov's Children*, which Mrs. Howe was busy showing in the Grand Hotel, the booklet bore the same title.

Among the pieces of undeniable proof of the Commie plot behind sex education in this twenty-six page glossily finished pamphlet were two pictures that had allegedly been taken from the pages of *Nude Living* magazine, a product of the Elysium Institute. One picture showed two nude young nubiles kissing each other with apparent passion and squeezing one another's breasts. The editors of "Pavlov's Children" had blocked out crucial areas such as nipples, but had cleverly left enough breast visible so that the of course shocked and repulsed reader could see what was going on. The other picture showed a lot of legs and buttocks and enough else to allow the reader to comprehend that it was a photograph of two females and one male homo sapiens going at it.

The Elysium Institute never confirmed the source of these pictures. And their connection to school sex education was, if they *had* actually appeared in *Nude Living* magazine, tenuous at best. But the fact that some of Elysium's publications carried an "Elysium Institute Directory," which listed a number of legitimate sex research and/or information outfits, including SIECUS, was apparently enough to convince the editors of "Pavlov's Children" that SIECUS would soon be putting pictures of girls squeezing each other's breasts into our nation's classrooms.

Nevertheless, the Townsends and the various other contributors to this pamphlet [which carried a sizable Knott's Berry Farm ad] soon reissued it with more Commie plot theories and much duller pictures.)

Darlyn, who sat patiently through much of her mother's talk, needed a little gentle encouragement from her mother before she squared her little shoulders to give her own report on the evils of the Anaheim sex education program. She and later also a neighbor's child related some interesting little tales of the frictions that had developed between the Antis' children and the sex education teachers. Both girls said that one female teacher had, as one of them put it, "flipped us off" ("She gave us the finger.") in the school yard. That teacher could not be reached for comment, but Sally Williams was later to tell me that such a gesture would have been wildly uncharacteristic from that particular teacher.

Another incident, which both Darlyn and her friend, a dark-haired girl named Deborah Johnson, described with some indignation revealed the odd polarizing effect that the controversy seemed to have had on the two of them. For as they told their respective versions of the event, it was clear that they had come to think of every sex education teacher as a kind of enemy, as someone who could never be trusted.

Darlyn related it as follows:

"One day over the loud speaker they said everybody should come in and see these Dickenson Models they have on display. [These were the models of pregnant women, which Davis had mentioned.] So my two girlfriends who also had been, had a note written on them so they couldn't go see, go in the Family Life class, we decided that we'd go up and see if she [the teacher] would let us in. Because we weren't 'sposed to be in. So we got up to the door, and we were getting scared, and so we were about to turn around to walk away. And she comes out of the door and she invites us in." This last sentence Darlyn pronounced in an injured tone.

"And she knew perfectly well that we weren't supposed to be in there," Darlyn continued, not stopping to consider that perhaps she and her friends had also known perfectly well that they weren't supposed to be, as she put it, "in there."

"She invites us in," Darlyn went on in her faint, childish voice, "so we just went on in. And she starts explaining these models of the birth of babies. And she's telling how great they were and how interesting they were and [how] they should get some good discussions on 'em.

"And so we went out, and we told our mother that she invited us into the class."

Deborah Johnson told much the same story. She said that the three girls had decided to approach the room containing the models "outa curiosity." The teacher, she said, knew that the three of them "weren't allowed in the sex class, you know, because we had a big controversy over it, and my mom gonna take, uh, she said the next time that she'd sue or take 'em to the board or sumpthin' if they let us go into the sex class. So out of curiosity, [another girl, who shall remain nameless], Darlyn and I, we went up to the sex class. And instead of [the teacher] saying, 'I'm sorry, you're not allowed in,' she pulled us in!"

Both Darlyn and Deborah seemed proud of this tale, as if it were the story of a heroic foray behind enemy lines. And they seemed to have belonged to a minority in their junior high school the previous year (they were both attending a senior high school in the fall of 1969), for they both described the social styles in that school as if these had been alien to their own.

"Before we moved out to Cypress, we lived in Downey," said Darlyn, "and there was nothing wrong. . . . There wasn't anything like there is here. . . . Here everybody's really—there was just a couple of good ones at our [junior high] school. The majority of 'em were wild ones who all they did was talk about sex and smoke pot. Got drunk every day. . . ."

The legal drinking age in California is twenty-one. Perhaps Darlyn exaggerated a little. But Deborah seemed to agree with her, adding that the junior high school had served "like a hangout at night" for the Anaheim District's youngsters.

After the two girls had completed their tales of wrong goings-on, Mrs. Burns displayed a willingness to continue on indefinitely with her own shocked reminiscences. A reading of old school board meeting transcripts would later reveal that her energies had not failed her over the long months of debate. Her comments appeared frequently in those records. She had stood up to offer lists of textbooks she wanted banned; she had asked about Sally Williams's involvement with SIECUS, and on one occasion she had told the board that she knew of a tenth-grade girl—whose name she would not divulge—who had begun to masturbate after exposure to the FLSE program. Her husband's name appeared in none of the transcripts that I read, and Mrs. Burns's critics were to tell me that they had never seen him. (He worked as a machinist in one of the local engineering plants, Mrs. Burns told me.)

On a later occasion I asked Mrs. Burns about the alleged incident with the *Anaheim Bulletin* tape recorder. She said that Mrs. Kelly (who could not be reached for comment) had made the remark about taking it—hidden—into an FLSE class. But, said Mrs. Burns, "she was kidding. . . . She would no more break the law. . . ."

     * * *

The Pippingers lived in Los Alamitos, another of the amorphous Orange County towns near Anaheim. Their house, a low-slung ranch-style building with the large windows so common in southern California, was, by some supreme irony, located on Cherry Street. In front of it the Pippingers had placed a sign which bore the numbers of their street address and the words, "OUR DREAM." A small American flag was discreetly pasted in a corner of their front picture window.

The Pippingers were soon to give up their dream, however, for they had decided to sell their house (which had a bright blue swimming pool out back) and move closer to a local Baptist school—so that their children need never face the infidel public school teachers again. Mrs. Jan Pippinger had asked the Lord whether he liked this idea, or rather, she had asked him to send her a buyer, and she had taken it as a sign of the Lord's approval of her plan that the first man who came to look at the house said he would take it.

She was a trimly built attractive woman, who wore a tightly fitted light green dress on the afternoon of the interview. When I saw her later at a school board meeting, she wore a knitted outfit that was similarly flattering to her figure. She wore her blond hair in a soft bouffant style, which gave her an airline stewardess's sort of cuteness. Much later I was to dub her "Mrs. Sex Education," for it would turn out that she was the best looking Anti woman I encountered. When I first arrived at her house, she was chewing gum at a rapid rate, which added to her youthful cuteness but detracted from the solemnity of her religious statements. And although she said that she and her husband had lived in Phoenix, Arizona, before they had moved to Orange County, she spoke in the accents of the Midwest, which was where she had grown up.

Her husband, whose first name was Fon, worked as the manager of a meat storage center for the Lucky Food Stores chain. He was dressed in work clothes and fiddling with various things around the house during much of my visit, and he looked so much older than his wife that I took him for a repair man at first. Mrs. Pippinger did not introduce him for some time, and she seemed at first oblivious to his presence. Later, she consulted him on Biblical points, and when asked how old she was, she turned to him to ask his age, then subtracted nineteen years and divulged her own. He was fifty-seven, she thirty-eight. They had three children, two little blond girls, ages seven and ten, and a seventeen-year-old dark-haired boy named Gary.

The two girls had just arrived home from school when I appeared, and they were complaining to their mother that their library cards had been rescinded. Mrs. Pippinger glanced a little sheepishly over at me, and then, turning back to her daughters, said, yes, she would go pay for "that book," and then they could get their library cards back.

"I had a book," she said, turning again to me, "and the offensive pages were torn out. So I have to go down and pay for the book."

"Who tore out the pages?"

"They just got removed," said Mrs. Pippinger in an arch tone. "The pages of animals and all that jazz."

(I had heard about "that book." It was a volume called *How Babies Are Made,* which had been written for young children and published by Time-Life, Inc. The book was everywhere used as a shocker by anti–sex education crusaders, for it contained two cartoon illustrations of animals copulating, a pair of dogs and a pair of chickens. The cartoon pictures did not show any genitals, but merely showed the two dogs and the two chickens mounted atop one another in separate couplings.

On another page of the book there was a cartoon picture of a man and a woman in bed together. The pair was almost entirely covered by a sheet, but it was possible to discern that the cartoon man was lying over the cartoon woman. On the woman's face was a happy smile. The text by this picture said, "You have already learned how a father's sperm meets and fertilizes a mother's egg to create a new baby."—which you had, if you had read the first part of the book—"To do this they lie down facing each other. Unlike plants and animals, human mothers and fathers share a very private and beautiful love in this way.")

Whatever had driven Mrs. Pippinger into fighting sex education—she said it was the day her son had come home from school and told her about the class, remarking afterwards, "What are we, mother, animals?"—it was clear that she had somewhere acquired an acute sense of mission. This was evident as she described her religious conversion or "call to Christ," as she called it.

She had had two conversion experiences, really. The second and more formal one had occurred eight years before. The first seemed to have been, as she described it, merely a moment of strange existential terror, in which somewhere her sense of sin seemed to have been lurking.

"I drank a lot," she said. "We lived a gay life, so to speak. We went night-clubbing. And I began to drink quite a bit.

"I used to have all these books—because it puzzled me, if there was a god, why all the heartache in the world?" The books, she indicated, were psychology books.

"When I was pregnant with Terry Lee twelve years ago [she lost one child, and this must have been the one], I quit drinking. I would go with them [her family and friends], but I wouldn't drink. It made my friends very angry with me. Made my uncle furious. They could not stand to be around me not drinking. . . .

"So I went downstairs by myself. . . . I just looked up at the sky and said, 'I need help. I don't know where to turn.' And this marvelous peace came over me. I couldn't let go of it."

Eventually she had become a member of the Nazarene Church, whose members neither drank nor smoked nor danced nor went to movies—and Mrs. Pippinger had recently decided that it was not consistent with her religion to watch television. She claimed to doubt not one word of her thick, dog-eared Bible, which sat, except when she consulted it, prominently before her on the dining room table. She also claimed that the Lord himself communicated with her by means of an "inner voice," the nature of which she could not pin down precisely. But she had, nevertheless, been encouraged by a number of outer voices, the Reverend Billy Graham's being the latest of these. (He was reported to have said, "The schools got into trouble when they took God out and put sex in," on the first night of his Anaheim crusade.) Mrs. Pippinger had been going every night to the Anaheim Stadium to sing in the 2,000-or-so-man choir for Billy Graham.

Yet however strongly she declared her spiritual motivation, Mrs. Pippinger had done nothing to halt the FLSE program until after Townsend's group had started its organized crusade. She said that her son had asked to be removed from the course way back in 1966, yet, according to her own account, she had not become actively involved in the struggle until after the January 30th board meeting, the meeting at which the old board had announced its unanimous (and continued) support for the program.

After that meeting, Mrs. Pippinger said she printed up her own set of flyers and personally placed them on teachers' cars all over the district. She also wrote letters to the school board and on one occasion handed the board members copies of a religious poem entitled, "Let the Stranger Speak." The poem was printed beside a picture of a giant Christ figure standing by the UN Secretariat building, his hand raised as if poised to knock. The poem's message, needless to say, was that Christ, not the men in the UN, could bring peace.

Mrs. Pippinger's complaints about the Anaheim District's sex education program were generally similar to those voiced by Mrs. Burns, although she did not list the sexual details Mrs. Burns had so matter-of-factly catalogued. But Mrs. Pippinger's theory about the plot behind the sex education program was much more thoroughly developed than the hesitantly outlined Communist conspiracy theory of Mrs. Burns.

"I believe it's Satan," said Mrs. Pippinger. "I believe it's a satanic plot. It's coming right from the Devil. And he's using the Communists.

"This is all leading up to the Anti-Christ one-world government. And you know who—it's the Illuminati. It's them."

You did really have to know who the Illuminati had been before you could fully appreciate her peculiar alarm.

"Illuminism," the historian Richard Hofstadter writes in *The Paranoid Style in American Politics and Other Essays* (New York: Knopf, 1965):

had been founded in 1776 by Adam Weishaupt, a professor of law at the University of Ingolstadt [in Bavaria]. Its teachings today seem to be no more than another version of Enlightenment rationalism, spiced with anticlerical animus that seems an inevitable response to the reactionary-clerical atmosphere of eighteenth-century Bavaria. A somewhat naïve and utopian movement which aspired ultimately to bring the human race under the rules of reason, it made many converts after 1780 among outstanding dukes and princes of the German states. . . . Although the order of the Illuminati was shattered by persecution in its native principality, its humanitarian rationalism appears to have acquired a fairly wide influence in Masonic lodges. . . . Americans first learned of Illuminism in 1797, from a volume published in Edinburgh (later reprinted in New York) under the title, *Proofs of a Conspiracy Against All the Religions and Governments of Europe, carried on in the Secret Meetings of Free Masons, Illuminati, and Reading Societies.*

The star anti–sex education reporter on the *Anaheim Bulletin*, John Steinbacher, had written a book about Robert Kennedy (*The Man, the Mysticism and the Murder*) in which he put forth the theory that the Illuminati were still alive and doing well and plotting the destruction of American democracy. Which was something you had to bear in mind as Mrs. Pippinger gave out her own theories.

"Satan is also using the Illuminati," she went on. "And that isn't just John Steinbacher's theory. That is hundreds of us that know. Billy Graham mentioned it, that the world is being psychologically conditioned for the Anti-Christ. You'll have a number on your forehead or your hand, all this. Data processing. It's going on now."

Soon she was saying that she would "just as soon" that her children "dug a ditch" as see them go to "liberal arts colleges. Because you don't find all this trouble in the colleges that are teaching the kids how to do something.

"To me, higher education has become America's god," she said gravely. "People are inclined to think that if you have a Ph.D., you're a god. We don't have to know the answers to everything. Satan had to know everything, too. That's why he rebelled."

Mrs. Pippinger had been combatting the influence of the local satanic forces with her leaflets and by helping the California Citizens Committee do its organizing. She said that she had even called a rally of her own, and although she had been unable to enlist the help of the John Birch Society—help she almost gleefully said she had requested—for that event, she had been able to convince one of her old friends to come tell everyone about the Communist menace. Her friend, Bea Dockins, claimed to have once been a member of the Communist Party, and she had told Mrs. Pippinger that the Communists had scheduled their great revolution for 1970. "And they were gonna use the colored people to get things all stirred up," said Mrs. Pippinger, her eyes alight. "They were given sensitivity training. That's how they keep Communists in the Communist Party."

Another of Mrs. Pippinger's divinely inspired projects had been an automobile trip around the country, undertaken the previous summer. She had gone through countless towns, seeking her political kin, telling them about Anaheim, gathering shock material from their communities, and getting as far as Washington, D.C., where she had visited sympathetic Congressmen. She described a strange weariness, which she said had descended upon her in the capital as she lost her way among that city's maze of traffic circles. After Washington, she said, she had avoided the big cities, and there was about her a vaguely perceptible sheepishness as she revealed this fact. She seemed to be a woman who was especially troubled by chaos—and she seemed to know this and to consider it a little shameful, like a child who is already old enough to know that his fear of the dark is not reasonable but cannot yet go to sleep without a light beside his bed.

When Mrs. Pippinger related the tale of her own childhood, her odd vulnerability, her childlike hunger after certitude, seemed more readily understandable. She said that her mother had died when she was five, and, as her father was ill at the time, she had been sent to live with a seventy-five-year-old great-aunt and from there to a Methodist orphanage and then into a series of foster homes that had never seemed to work out. "The women that have this desire to help children like myself were lovely," she said, "but they aren't always aware of their husbands' intentions. A girl who is placed in a home like this, she has to be awfully careful of how she conducts herself." Earlier she had said that she had not gotten her own sex education in the best of ways.

Her story was quite engaging, and, as she brought it up to her late adolescence—after she had graduated from a high school near Chicago and was working for U.S. Steel—I anticipated the happy ending. So I tried to prompt it from her with a question like "So, when did you meet your husband?" or "When were you married?"

Mrs. Pippinger quickly changed the subject. I made a mental note of that and asked the question again at another point. Again, she changed the subject. Hence, I gathered that it was not a subject that one went into at the Pippinger household—which should be of no concern to anyone else, and yet it was worth noting, after all, because Mrs. Pippinger had figured so largely in a struggle for all-American decency.

But Mrs. Pippinger wanted to talk about the horrors of the Anaheim sex education program and her various sufferings in her battle to eliminate them. She told me that she thought the district board had laughed at her when she had handed them copies of that poem, "Let the Stranger Speak." And she wanted me to see a copy of a letter she had written to a teenage girl from her own church. She and the girl had an argument, and she had later written the letter as a kind of peace offering.

From the text of the letter, it seemed pretty clear that Mrs. Pippinger's zealous attacks on the sex education program had sparked her argument with the girl (whose name was Karen) but that her quarrel with the girl had not centered on that topic for long. In the heat of passion, Mrs. Pippinger had apparently told Karen that her skirt was too short; Karen had started to cry; one of Karen's relatives or friends had told Mrs. Pippinger that *her* skirts were too short and furthermore she wore too much lipstick.

The next day (September 22, 1969), Mrs. Pippinger had written Karen the apologetic letter to explain that she would not have lit into Karen quite so vigorously if Karen's relative or friend had not lit into *her* in front of all her children.

It was quite a revealing letter, for it showed Mrs. Pippinger's acute sensitivity to ridicule. The thing went on for several pages, covering all the outrages of sex education and the Grand Satanic Conspiracy. Throughout it Mrs. Pippinger seemed to have been propelled by her sense of injury. It was as if her quarrel with Karen had reminded her of every other painful moment in her struggle against sex education. She had even described for her young friend the way she had been slighted by the people at the headquarters of the Nazarene Church in Kansas. She had run across a Nazarene minister in Columbus, Ohio, she wrote, and he had not agreed with her stand. Thus she had tried to report him to the church's general headquarters and had been given a kind of brushoff. The headquarters people had told her not to mention any names, and (as she also described the incident to me) they had treated her with an air of humiliating condescension, almost as if she were a child. Subsequently, she told Karen, she had discovered that the man in charge of training the young Nazarene ministers had gone through a counseling institute that was "SIECUS recommended." (She did not name the institute.)

Mrs. Pippinger was a prolific crusader. She had written several letters to the *Anaheim Bulletin,* and in one of these she had reported on the state of sex education as she had found it in Columbus, Ohio, the scene of her run-in with the Nazarene minister. A widowed father had told her that his daughter had come home "upset." The girl had been told to write an essay on "The Act of Sexual Intercourse," Mrs. Pippinger claimed. At the same school, Lynden McKinley, there was mixed P.E., and the students were told to wear their bathing suits, "bikinis O.K.," Mrs. Pippinger reported. This man's daughter had allegedly refused, and the school (according to Mrs. Pippinger) threatened not to pass her. The girl was also allegedly told to have a ballet costume for mixed dancing classes during P.E. Mrs. Pippinger added that this was against the family's religious convictions, "especially when they force the colored and white students to dance with one another."

Hank Davis had written to an administrator at the Lynden McKinley School, enclosing a copy of Mrs. Pippinger's letter. The administrator described the allegations as "completely false."

There was a sex education course at the school, but it had been well received until the widowed father came, wrote the administrator. His daughter was not asked to write on the act of sexual intercourse; she "wanted to." The students were only occasionally in mixed physical education classes, and this was for volleyball or some similar activity. No one wore either bathing suits or bikinis, he wrote, adding that there had been a modern dance unit for which students were invited to wear appropriate costumes. The administrator added that "no black or white student has ever been forced to dance with a member of the opposite race."

If Mrs. Pippinger had ever doubted the veracity of the stories she had gathered on her trip, she did not say so. And she had told some stories of her own about Anaheim. Sex education and sensitivity training, promoted by SIECUS, "has been incorporated into nearly all subjects taught in Anaheim," she told the *Daily Oklahoman*. She also said that all the lights had once been turned off in an Anaheim classroom while "wild African music" was played and special colored lights were flashed around the room. "Many of the students reported having experienced 'strange sexual feelings' while this was going on," she told the newspaper.

(No such incident was reported to me during my stay in Anaheim.)

Mrs. Pippinger's seventeen-year-old son, Gary, a solemn-faced, closely shorn boy, had accompanied her on her trip around the country, and he, too, had written to the *Anaheim Bulletin*. His letter was a defense of his mother, written in response to someone who had called her an extremist. Mrs. Pippinger had spoken proudly of his religious fervor during the early part of my session with her. She said that he had never been on a date, and that when he went to the beach, he would say to her—amidst the scantily clad young damsels—"Mom, I don't know where to look!" He later offered some brief comments of his own about sex education, and he was quite noticeably less vehement in his criticisms than his mother had been.

"Do you feel that there should be any sex education in the schools?" I asked him at one point.

"Yes," he said, "because I feel that kids need to know certain things. They need to know certain consequences like venereal disease. . . . They need to be faced with a decision of what they really want to do, what the consequences of their action now will do to their lives later. I think too many kids just do what they feel on impulse."

Gary sounded as though he might even have absorbed some of the thinking of the Anaheim sex education teachers. For his comment about the "need to be faced with a decision" was quite similar to an idea expressed in the introduction to the FLSE curriculum guide: "Students are faced with many decisions in this area and it has been proven that it is more fruitful and meaningful for them to make decisions in relation to personal values."

But then Gary added, "As far as discussing all the deviate . . ."

"What do you consider deviate?" I asked.

"I don't think heavy petting is appropriate," he said and, pondering this, added, "I wouldn't call it deviate." He did not say exactly what he would call deviate.

I asked him whether he had been pressured to return to the class after he withdrew from it.

"No, no, I didn't get any pressure at all from the teachers," he said. "A couple of kids asked me [about it]. I just told them I'd rather be in P.E."

Gary also said that he thought "a lot of kids" had been embarrassed during the FLSE classes in the junior high school grades, but that in his senior high school, he "didn't see any adverse effect at all."

After he left, Mrs. Pippinger resumed her discourse. She, like Mrs. Burns, appeared driven by a need to vent an unrelenting furor, some lust for spiritual overkill that had sprung up in her at the sight of those copulating cartoon dogs or perhaps the first edition of the "Pavlov's Children" booklet.

She kept talking long after I had stopped recording her words. She talked as she rummaged through her boxes and stacks of literature, searching for undeniable proof of the Grand Design. She talked as she handed me two paperbacks about fictional experiments in coed living. She talked as she handed me: a mimeographed copy of selections from the book, *Brainwashing,* by Major William E. Mayer, M.D. ("based on his experiences as chief neuro-psychiatrist of the U.S. Army in charge of the Task Force in Tokyo responsible for rehabilitation of returned American prisoners of war from Korea"); a xeroxed copy of an essay entitled, "The Principal: A Machiavellian Guide for School Administrators," by Laurence E. Ely, a professor of education at Trenton (New Jersey) State College; a copy of the poem "Let the Stranger Speak"; a copy of an essay called, "Values in the Social Studies," by a Dr. Thomas Grotelueschen from Wisconsin State University, at Whitewater; three typewritten statements by herself; and, finally, a mimeographed copy of a piece by a Long

Beach woman entitled, "Why I Resigned as President of Millikan PTA" which was dated November 24, 1964, and contained such essential educational questions as: "Why does the PTA never take a stand for the prompt dismissal of teachers of doubtful loyalty and character?"

Mrs. Pippinger talked as I backed step by step to her front door. She kept talking as I stumbled backward along her front walk. Talking about Christ and conspiracy and social conditioning and Christ and conspiracy and social conditioning. She might have kept talking for another three hours or more. But that would have meant she would miss hearing Doomandsalvation pronounced over something like twenty huge loudspeakers in the Anaheim Stadium. "There's enough power in this stadium tonight to change America and reverse the trend that is leading us to destruction," she would learn that night. And she would be told how to "reverse the trend," for Rev. Billy Graham could give you rules for almost everything. "The apostle Peter says, 'Abstain from fleshly lusts which war against the soul,'" he would say. "You bring your body under the discipline of Christ. . . . It means when they [the unbelievers] lie, you don't lie. It means when they cheat, you don't cheat. It means when they engage in sex, you don't engage in sex. . . . He will give you supernatural powers to say *no*. . . . There's the security [of absolute faith]. . . . You know why you're here. . . . And when you die you know where you'll go."

*   *   *

While Mrs. Pippinger was being told over and over again that she could be sure where she would go if she would just take a step forward for Jesus, Mrs. Eleanor Howe was up in the Celebrity Suite of the Grand Hotel telling her small audiences (almost entirely female) that they could be sure where their children would go if they did not take a step forward against sex education.

Mrs. Howe was giving continuous showings of the *Pavlov's Children* film, and before and after each one, she would make a little speech. "Now, those of us that are here probably don't have anything to worry about," she would say, "but what about our children? . . . What would look like something . . . that is Orwell's 1984 . . . is happening today."

Up in the front of the room, just under the small movie screen, her audiences could read a poster that said:

The Pavlovians
Who are they?

Where do they get their money?
Why are they invading the classrooms?

The film itself was actually a series of still shots accompanied by a narrative that was the crudest kind of political propaganda—about on a par with the products of the Red Chinese. The general message was that the Russians had decided to use Pavlovian techniques to condition America's young into a receptiveness for life under a totalitarian Communist regime. And, of course, the vehicle for this conditioning was—you guessed it—sex education.

The Communists wanted the "faceless masses of an atheistic world tyranny," said the voice, and the voice did not sound as though the man it belonged to was kidding. "World thought control is the goal of the UNESCO change agents," was one of the film's many grim warnings. And onto the screen would flash a cartoon picture of a tiny man in the posture of someone seized with terror. Over the tiny man loomed a dark sky, and in front of him the earth appeared to be splitting apart. "A nightmare world," the voice said at this point, "without hope or love or joy."

At a later point a woman's voice was heard—allegedly the voice of someone who had worked in support of UNESCO, but her name was never disclosed. "I worked for peace," she said, as the picture on the screen showed a woman walking across what appeared to be a battlefield, "and to think that I have [helped to build] a creature who would wrench my child from me. This shall not be." The film's message was basically that contained in the two editions of the "Pavlov's Children" booklet: the UN and the Communists are behind it all, plotting to transform your children into spineless beings. "Every mother's child helpless in her arms is tomorrow's Pavlovian experiment," was the closing line of the narration. The shot accompanying it was a touching picture of a young mother holding an infant.

Lillian and William Drake had produced the film, and Mrs. Drake was up in the Celebrity Suite with Mrs. Howe when I arrived. The Drakes, I later learned, owned a publishing outfit called Impact Publishers, and they had allied themselves with the most extreme elements of the right wing. William Drake had become a contributing editor with *American Mercury* magazine sometime within the previous year. And *American Mercury* magazine, which once printed the works of men like H. L. Mencken, its founder, had fallen into the hands of the most reactionary right-wingers in America, men like Col. Curtis B. Dall, of the Washington-based Liberty Lobby, and E. Merrill Root, who made his living writing articles for the Birch Society's *American Opinion* magazine and "evaluating" textbooks for an organization called America's Future, Inc., located in New Rochelle, New York.

In fact, the Liberty Lobby itself had planned a "Symposium on Sex" for its followers in the Los Angeles area, and I would see Mrs. Drake and Mrs. Howe there displaying their irrefutable proof of the Communist Conspiracy behind sex education (UNESCO booklets on population control along with nudist magazines, SIECUS newsletters, and random shockers such as the special *Look* magazine issue on the Woodstock rock festival) not far from the White Citizens Council display table with its Wallace buttons and its bumper stickers that said, "I'M ALL WHITE—AND ALL AMERICAN."

But for three days, Mrs. Howe and Mrs. Drake were running their own show, and although the *Anaheim Bulletin* reported that they were drawing "packed audiences," I never saw more than about fifteen people gathered in the Celebrity Suite. Of course, I visited the place only two times, so it was possible that I had come during the slack periods.

Mrs. Howe was interviewed during little snatches of time as her audiences watched the film and she drank cups of coffee in the bedroom next door. She was frequently interrupted by concerned mothers from other towns or by friends who would drop in to see how her fight for America's survival was coming along. John Steinbacher, of the *Anaheim Bulletin*, came by at one point, and he quickly joined in the spirit of the crusade, calling up the California Marriage Counselors (who were about to begin a conference in another part of the hotel—and were considered to be nearly as evil as sex educators by the ladies in the Celebrity Suite) to invite them to a showing of *Pavlov's Children*. The two ladies were all aflutter because they expected a contingent from Billy Graham's own staff, his piano player among them, and they were worried that they might not be able to seat the entire group.

In this atmosphere, came snatches of Mrs. Howe's history and of her opinions on sex education. She had silvery hair, which appeared to have been dyed that color. She wore the sort of glasses that remind one of those winglike protuberances on the larger car models of the early sixties. She had a face that showed determination, a face with a pointed chin and a jaw that seemed to be permanently set against potential attackers. Mrs. Howe wore a flowered dress with a full and rather long skirt, and her shoes were the sort that were stylish in the early sixties, with spike heels and sharply pointed toes.

Mrs. Howe said that she was forty-seven years old and that all four of her children had graduated from Anaheim High School. Her two youngest children, the eighteen-year-old twin boys, had alerted her to the dangers of sex education, she said.

"One night at dinner one of the boys said, 'Mother, would you please write a letter and get me out of sex.' And I was shocked. I said, 'I don't know what you're talking about.' I didn't really believe what they said about what went on in the classroom. I couldn't sleep all night."

Then, she said, in September of 1968, a teacher asked her son Rick "a real embarrassing question. The teacher asked him, 'What would you do if you came home and found your twelve-year-old son masturbating?' My son said, 'Well, at the age of twelve, if he didn't know that that was wrong, I'd probably have spanked him.' "

Her son's answer had apparently been considered a bit stodgy by the other students, and—at least according to Mrs. Howe—he had decided then that he wanted out. She said she subsequently invited a few youngsters over for an evening and discovered that they all disliked the course. There had been about fourteen of them, she said, and "I had from many of the girls, 'I'm so embarrassed sometimes I just wanta die! I don't know where to look.'

"So then I wrote a letter to the school board," Mrs. Howe went on, "and I waited a month. I still didn't get an answer." Finally, she said, she wrote a letter to the *Anaheim Bulletin*, and she claimed that during the first three days after it was printed she received sixty-eight phone calls from disgruntled parents. Eventually she got a call from someone in MOMS, and she began to work with that group. But she also said that she had been working with the California Citizens Committee for some time. And, after working with MOMS for an indefinite period, she had become frustrated; she "felt that the organization wasn't doing anything." Then she thought of requesting a board hearing for the Antis.

She did not specify exactly when she had decided to give herself over to a full-time struggle against sex education, but she did say that she had eventually resigned from her receptionist's job ("I'd rather not name the company") to free herself for the fight.

"My life is now completely—something that I never dreamed of really. Something that as a housewife, someone who loved to go out and dance, have a drink with my husband, play golf—"

she said, leaving the sentence incomplete, as if she could find no words to describe the terrible burdens placed upon her by the hectic schedule of her campaign.

She had spoken to groups all over Orange County. She had been invited to speak to a group called Sanity on Sex (SOS)— expenses paid—in Oklahoma City. She had just returned from a ten-day sojourn in Washington, D.C., where she and the William Drakes had shown *Pavlov's Children* to interested legislators. She had spent so much of her time battling sex education that the Anaheim school officials liked to speculate that she was being paid by one of the wealthier right-wing organizations, the Birch Society or the Christian Crusade.

But Mrs. Howe liked to point out that the Birch Society had not taken up the issue of sex education until January of 1969, and she had been involved in the struggle since the middle of 1968. She did say that Gary Allen, a frequent contributor to the Birch Society's *American Opinion* magazine, had visited her home and made use of her files for one of his articles on sex education (and the Communist conspiracy).

As for Dr. Gordon Drake of the Christian Crusade (no relation to the William Drakes), why, Mrs. Howe said she "didn't use any of his material" and had not even been aware that it existed until several months after she had become involved in the controversy. She said that Drake and Hargis had visited the Anaheim area "shortly after" she'd returned from Oklahoma City. She had been in Oklahoma City in early December, 1968. (The Oklahoma City newspapers also said she had been there in early December of 1968.) She said that Drake and Hargis were honored at a dinner at Knott's Berry Farm and that she had been present at that occasion. She said that some other woman had arranged the dinner and that a number of the anti–sex education people had attended it.

Mrs. Howe kept telling me that she couldn't remember dates well. Her life had been so cluttered during the last few months, she indicated, that events had become blurred in her memory.

Events must have been quite severely blurred in her memory, for much of what she told me did not conform with the versions gathered from other sources. Dr. Drake later told me that he had dined at Knott's Berry Farm on October 18, 1968. The Knott's Berry Farm public relations office confirmed Drake's version. Mrs. Howe had placed the dinner at sometime in January or February of 1969. That was a big difference, and a significant one. For the great Antis' production before the board had taken place only a day earlier. And that meant that the Anaheim Antis knew something about Gordon Drake before they staged their three-hour extravaganza. Dr. Drake told me that he and Hargis had spent the whole first two weeks of that October in California organizing the state-wide anti–sex education organization (California Families United) that held its first meeting in early November, 1968. And Drake read off the names of towns he'd been in during those two weeks from an old date book he had kept. Before and after October 17th, he had visited southern California towns. "Incidentally, Mrs. Howe has been writing to us right straight through," Drake told me.

And when I read through the transcript of the Antis' October 17, 1968, presentation, I discovered that Mrs. Howe had lifted whole passages out of Drake's pamphlet, "Is the Schoolhouse the Proper Place to Teach Raw Sex?" When I later confronted Mrs. Howe with this fact, the guardian of American decency said, "Whatever I used I think it was probably available at the time." Drake's pamphlet was copyrighted. Had she asked his permission at that time? "I didn't think to ask him for permission at that time." Ah, then she did admit she had used portions of it. Just why hadn't she wanted to say that she had used his material during the first interview? "Very emphatically, I have forgotten."

Mrs. Howe's less than perfect memory seemed to have failed most strikingly in relation to her own children's experiences with the FLSE program. Her twin sons were interviewed at home one afternoon while she was off carrying on her mission. She had encouraged me to interview her sons because, she had said, they had gotten her into the controversy.

Rick Howe: "When my mom first started it an' she went on TV about it an' everything, I was really embarrassed, an' I never became interested in it or nothin'. I, I hated what she was doin'."

Rob Howe: "I was embarrassed just as he was, you know, I was. . . . An' kids would come up to me, you know, an' they'd ask me, uh, 'What's your mom really think about it?' you know. An' I'd just go, 'Well, I don't know. It's—she's doin' what she wants to do, you know.' That's what I'd say."

In all fairness to the Howe boys, it must be said that they defended their mother's right to fight for what she believed in. And Rick said that after reading some of the sex education material which had been sent to her by various worried parents in different parts of the country, he had come to believe that some sex education courses were harmful. And both he and Rob said that they had not approved of the teaching methods used in the Anaheim FLSE class. They had both graduated from Anaheim High School in the spring of 1969.

As Mrs. Howe had said, Rick *had* dropped out of the FLSE course after his teacher had asked him a question which embarrassed him. But Rick claimed that the question, which he would not repeat, had had something to do with "a natural problem for women." He said he thought it was a question "that you'd ask a girl in some private class," and that he had refused to answer it. "I knew about that. I mean, it's no big deal," he said. "But he [the teacher] just came out, right out, and asked me what the word meant, you know. And I didn't feel like answering in front of boys and girls and everybody's lookin' at you and everything, and I just refused. So I left the class for that—"

"That's when my mom came in," his brother Rob cut in.

"The school took you out instead of your mother taking you out?" I asked Rick.

"Yeah. Well, that's because I refused to participate. I just—it just wasn't worth it to me for that," Rick said.

"Well, did your mother have to send a letter to get you out?" I persisted.

"No. Uh, see, I went up to the office . . . I hadda go up n' sit for the rest of the period. And then he [the teacher] came up there after the period and talked to me, and I just said no, and he said, 'Okay, I'll get you outa the class. You just go to gym tomorrow.' And that's all I ever heard about it, you know."

Rick said that this had occurred sometime during his junior year—which would have been the 1967–68 school year—but he could not recall the exact time of year when it had taken place. His mother had placed the incident in September, 1968, which would have been during Rick's senior year. (The FLSE courses, being so short, were given to various sections of each class at different times during the school year.)

Paul Cook later told me that it was quite possible that Rick had been dropped from the class without the note from his parents. Cook said that when students were especially unhappy in the class, they were allowed to drop out of it without going through the formality of obtaining such a note.

Rob Howe said that he hadn't dropped out of the course until his senior year. And he said that he had done so then partly because his mother had *asked* him to drop out of it. He said that the FLSE teacher had also discouraged him from wanting to remain in the course. He claimed that the teacher had made playful references to his mother—who was by the fall of 1968 deeply involved in the Anaheim controversy.

Neither one of the Howe boys had much praise for the FLSE course, and they were not exactly young radicals. But they both wore their hair long enough to pass among the Anaheim young with a touch of Aquarian cool, and Rick kept remarking that they were not "goody-goodies" and knew how to have a good time when they wanted to. Both of them made numerous remarks in defense of their mother. And Rick said that he had often exchanged angry words with schoolmates who had teased him about her activities.

"You know, people write my mom . . . thankin' her for the great job she's done," said Rick, "an' I think she is, you know."

Hearing such comments from the Howe boys, I felt twinges of unease. For if what Mrs. Howe's loyal sons had told her about the manner in which each of them had dropped out of the FLSE program was true, then their mother had been exploiting their relationship to her to sell her views on sex education. Listening to her one could get the impression that her sons had begged her to take them out of the FLSE class and that she had—out of pure unadulterated mother love—not only removed them from the class but also gone on to fight the evils of sex education on behalf of all America's innocent young. And yet her own sons said that one of them had gotten himself out of the course without her help and that the other had dropped out at least partially because his mother, already a public critic of the program, had *asked* him to drop the course. I thought that the mere exposure of the Howes' conflicting versions of events would cruelly embarrass both the mother and her two sons. As I heard the two boys defending their mother, I was inwardly condemning the journalist's trade.

But Mrs. Howe had willingly courted publicity. And if her public stands were predicated upon what she declared to be a sense of outraged motherhood—a private and personal motivation—then her motherhood itself had taken on a public significance. She herself had made it into an issue, and hence her sons' experiences had become, in a sense, public property.

With lingering unease, I later questioned Mrs. Howe about the disparities between her own and her sons' versions of their withdrawals from the FLSE program. She insisted that her version was the correct one. Her sons, she said, "must have forgotten."

Whatever was the true history of the Howe family's disenchantment with the FLSE program, it was evident that Mrs. Howe had become totally committed to the nation-wide struggle against sex education. Her husband, Charles Howe, who came by the Celebrity Suite during my fragmented interview with her, said that the two of them had no time to relax by themselves. A retired Marine pilot, he was dressed in sports clothes, and he looked tanned and fit. Like so many of the former military men in Orange County, he had taken a job with one of the area's new industries. He worked at a Union Oil research laboratory, and in his free time, he played golf. An affable looking man, he seemed a little amused by his wife's and Mrs. Drake's fluttery anticipation of the Billy Graham contingent's visit. He really saw very little of his wife, he said, and then, with his eyes lit up mischievously, he added:

"I enjoy my golf game this way much better."

*   *   *

So the Anaheim Antis had among them passionate spokesmen for the holy trinity of the right wing: God, Family, and Country. They had Mr. Townsend championing America the beautiful against gun control legislation and the Commies in high government places. They had Mrs. Pippinger spreading The Word of Jesus across the land and worrying about schools in which "the colored" children dance with the white ones. They had Mrs. Burns and Mrs. Howe declaring their heartfelt anguish for their own innocent children for whose sakes they would read and expose every last description of coitus, necking, petting, masturbation, homosexual goings on, and even—Mrs. Burns had said— zoophilia (which means having sex with an animal, preferably a friendly one) that they could find in a sex education text book or a teacher reference book. They had, between them, the capacities for appealing to all the deepest fears of a father, mother, capitalist, monotheist, patriot, or any combination of these.

There was nothing new about what they were doing. The anti-evolutionists had made terrible prophesies to the godfearing decades before Mrs. Pippinger experienced her "call to Christ." The Methodist Association for Temperance, Prohibition, and Public Morals had as late as 1932 preached abstinence from nearly every pleasurable activity known to man. The Ku Klux Klan itself had enjoyed a period of dominance in southern California, its members winning elections in a rash of the smaller towns— Anaheim among them—and preaching patriotism and temperance to all its followers. For four years during the early twenties the pastor of Anaheim's Christian Church had sermonized against the "wets" and accused the town's Roman Catholics of plotting to bring the town (and eventually the nation) under papal domination.

During the thirties and forties a man named R. C. Hoiles had bought up a string of newspapers throughout the Southwest, which he had named "the Freedom Newspapers." This Mr. Hoiles had written editorials against unions, social security, and public education, and during the forties he had hired a columnist whose theory it was that an international Zionist conspiracy was plotting evil things with the Communists. Hoiles had bought the *Santa Ana Register* way back in 1935, and by 1968 that paper was sold all over Orange County. In Anaheim you could get *two* Hoiles papers by 1968 because six years before then Hoiles had also bought the *Anaheim Bulletin*. Hoiles did with his newspapers what the temperance leagues and the Klansmen and the antievolution people had done with their rallies. He and his columnists prophesied various doom states that would emerge, they said, if the "Jewish conspirators and other subversive enemies of the American nation" (the words of David Baxter, a columnist hired by Hoiles in 1950) were not exposed or controlled or at the very least recognized for what they were by right-thinking Americans. Baxter had even suggested that the right-thinking sorts buy up arms to prepare for the great confrontation (but that was before he came to work for Hoiles). Hoiles had said he was against things that he considered "un-Christian," and in line with that thinking he hired in 1966 a fundamentalist named Sam Campbell to run the *Anaheim Bulletin*. Campbell was the sort of Christian who liked to call the Old Testament "the Jewish Testament" to convey his singleminded devotion to the hero of the New Testament. Campbell had been a member of the John Birch Society until sometime in 1965—or so he said. Apparently the conservative political thinking of Robert Welch and company had fitted very neatly into Campbell's particular form of Christian metaphysics.

It was, above all, a metaphysics that the Anaheim Antis were preaching, a metaphysics older than the first Puritan settlements of New England. It was, after all, the thinking of those austere New Englanders that a life without sin, although no guarantee of salvation, could at least be looked upon as the outward and visible evidence of a man's inward and spiritual grace. And it did not take long for those early Puritans to forget the most troublesome part of their metaphysical system, its merciless determinism, and to start believing that perhaps Providence could be influenced in their favor by their own virtuous efforts here on earth. They came to think, or rather their progeny came to think, that a man could *earn* his way to Heaven through clean living and good works. It was a fine Yankee bourgeois theology based on sound economics, a theology by which men simply saved up their pleasures for the Hereafter.

And if the Anaheim Antis were anything, they were bourgeois. Mrs. Pippinger's husband alone was the only breadwinner in the lot who had not spent much of his life in the military working his way slowly up the ranks. The military had been, for many of the young men who fought in World War II, the best vehicle for social advancement. Orange County was full of those ex-military men who had risen up through the service ranks until they had reached a status from which they could choose good lower-middle-class civilian jobs. That slow process of advancement through the most rigidly organized bureaucracy in the country had to be called bourgeois.

The Anaheim Antis seemed to want the same slow process of advancement for their children. They complained, like so many parents reared in a poorer and less permissive age, that the liberals were producing children who no longer knew the value of their country. They wanted their own children, they said, to live by the character-building rules that had made America what she was. And included in their list of character-building rules were strict sexual codes. They said, when you asked them, that sex, any kind of sex, was a pleasure you were to indulge in only after marriage. You did not exactly have to earn your right to it in the value system they swore by, but you *were* expected to save yourself for it much as their spiritual predecessors saved themselves for heaven.

Hank Davis had said that he could not explain why the 80 per cent of the Anaheim Union High School District's parents had not stood up to the Antis, had not appeared, as the Antis had, at board meeting after board meeting to express their views. But perhaps that was because the notion that pleasure, especially sexual pleasure, should be deferred until by some magical process (usually the marriage ritual) the right to it had been conferred, had, not so long ago, been widely believed in America. It was still subtly present in the introduction to the Anaheim District's FLSE curriculum guide (and not so subtly present in an appendix on "The Physical Aspects of Necking and Petting" in the back of the guide). The Antis, with their superpiety for those indomitable cultural myths God, Family, and Country, were obviously aware of the lingering power of the puritan sexual ethic. Someone who stood up to them could be risking exposure to more than just the familiar epithets of the radical Right. He could risk being branded a libertine. And perhaps the parents of Orange County—whose own children styled themselves after the people who made a hit out of the song "Why Don't We Do It in the Road?"—just weren't ready to risk appearing sexually liberal.

The proponents of sex education *had* staged their own presentation for the board, it was true. They had gathered, as Davis told me, hundreds of supporters in a high school auditorium for that occasion. They had collected, for their presentation, a number of speakers with impressive credentials, a gynecologist, a pediatrician, an assistant professor of pediatrics from the University of Southern California Medical School, and several clergymen. Parents with children in the district schools had also spoken at that meeting. But, as Davis had said, "It was only that one time."

Month after month the Antis had gone back to the board meetings to reiterate their views. Except for the statements from irritated board members or from Paul Cook, the transcripts of the board meetings from August, 1968, through October, 1969, contained little praise for the program.

On one occasion, fairly early in the battle, one lonely soul had stood up to confront the Antis in the presence of the board. He was a student, and the transcript in which he is quoted does not contain his name. The boy had made his courageous defense of the FLSE program during the Antis' special session on October 17, 1968. Piecing together the meeting transcript with a *Los Angeles Times* account, I reconstructed the boy's exchange with the Antis. Dr. Melvin Anchell had been answering questions from the floor after his speech.

"I've taken these classes since eighth grade," the student had told Dr. Anchell, "and you say that the instructors are teaching the kids before they are ready to learn. And the fact is that our . . . these books are telling us what is right."

Before Anchell could respond to the boy's comments, a woman bellowed from the back of the room:

"Yeah, but are you a virgin?"

At that point, according to the *Los Angeles Times* account, the whole audience had started shouting, some trying to shush the woman, and some trying to silence the boy, who apparently looked as though he had more to say. When things had quieted down a bit, the youngster did manage one more comment above the din. He turned to the woman in the back and declared:

"Lady, that's *my* business, not *yours!*"

The *Los Angeles Times* had twice reported that incident, once buried in an article about the October 17th meeting, and a second time in the lead paragraphs of a general story about Anaheim's sex education controversy. Sally Williams later told me that the proponents of sex education were *Los Angeles Times* readers. If many of them had read about that incident, they could have developed some serious reservations about publicly defending the FLSE program. What other questions might such a hostile crowd fling at them, after all?

Family Living Can Be Fun

"Take care of business, Mr. Businessman.
Get down to business, Mr. Businessman—
If you can before it's too late. . . ."

The last chorus of the lyrical Dylanesque rock song faded away, and up in the front of the classroom the clean-cut, short-haired instructor lifted the arm of the phonograph off the record.

"Okay," he said, his firm brisk voice like the voice of a pep-talking coach, "any thoughts now? Does it say anything?"

The thirty-odd young nurses, Physical Education teachers, and Education students sat in uneasy silence.

"When I was listening to that," a girl hesitantly began, "I just couldn't help thinking that everything that he was saying, it's all very natural. . . ."

"Don't you wish you could just stay—" another girl brought out, her thought never completed.

"He's giving 'em everything," said the clean-cut young instructor, apparently thinking that the class had not gotten the song's basic message (*"Bigger cars, bigger houses, . . . Tuesday evenings with your harlot, . . . Placing value on the worthless, disregarding priceless value, . . . Where the smiles are all synthetic, Take care of business, Mr. Businessman. . . ."*)

"What he thinks are the good things," the first girl tried again, "are not. . . ."

"A lot of 'em hit me," said the young instructor, meaning, apparently, a lot of the song's phrases. "Let's be honest . . . husbands and wives, what are you doing here?"

"Could I ask you a question?" a large young man in the back of the room suddenly uttered.

"No!" the young instructor grinned.

"Is it a new problem?" the young man persisted, ignoring the instructor's playful response. "Right now we're faced with a problem of too much leisure time."

"I just don't buy that," said the instructor.

"That's because you're trying to get ahead," the young man quickly retorted.

The instructor then went into a rather confused defense of his views. People might not spend as much time at their actual jobs, he said. But their time was still taken up with the "work" of driving the rush-hour-cluttered freeway, for instance. "If that's what he [the Businessman] wants," the instructor declared, as if offering a summary, "then he ought to be honest about it."

He ought to be honest about his crummy values. But the song hadn't said he was especially dishonest—a little bit of a cheat, perhaps, with his harlot—but basically an honest striver. The song was about missing the point of life, and no one had caught the ironic pun in the phrase "get down to business," which meant, in the ghetto at least, both go to bed with your woman and get to the essence of things. That instructor did not seem to have understood the song. Or perhaps he had gotten rattled by the young man's, "That's because you're trying to get ahead," and, seeing himself suddenly as the grim striver, he had weakly said striving was all right if you were honest about it.

Such thoughts meandered through my mind as I sat among the students at Long Beach State College. The class was designed to teach teachers or Education students how to teach family life and sex education to junior and senior high school students. As I sat musing, I found myself forgetting to take notes. Already the discussion had ended, and the young instructor was passing out a "Sex Education Glossary." He told the class that he did not think it necessary for them to learn all the words listed, hence he would read off the ones he considered essential. I sat up. New sexual terms were always useful. Why, they could even be said to belong among the tools of my trade.

"Abortion," the instructor began, and he proceeded rapidly through the list. "Afterbirth, Aphrodisiac, Asexual, Autoerotism, Bastard, Bestiality, Birth control, Bisexual," all disappointingly familiar terms, I thought. "Breast, Carnal knowledge, Castration," the instructor read on. My disappointment increased. "Climacteric," he read. Ah, I didn't know that one. "The physical and psychological phenomena that characterize the termination of menstrual function in the woman and reduction in sex-steroid production in both sexes," was the glossary definition. Too clinical, I thought, hurrying to catch up with the instructor, who was not reading the definitions. As he continued, I found a few other words I didn't know, nearly all of them clinical and unexciting words such as,

"Dysmenorrhea" (def.: "painful menstruation"); "Ectopic" (def.: "a pregnancy outside the uterus"); and "Episiotomy" (def.: "incision in the perinium to facilitate the birth of a child"). Alas, there was only one new spicy word, but it was a good one, worth lingering over. It had a fine sound, which suggested its meaning ("Frottage: rubbing or massaging to stimulate sexual desires"), and I decided that it was a word one ought to know.

I had fallen behind again, but I soon learned that the students were also lagging. Two or three times a brave soul asked the instructor to slow down. But they were doing a good job of looking implacable, those students, and they took in the whole list with scarcely a murmur. Only once did they chuckle, and then it was with a kind of nervous amazement as the instructor read off the word, "Necrophilism," a term which, I proudly noted, I already understood.

At various points during his reading, the instructor would make gratuitous side comments, and he did this easily, as if he had quite lost the inhibitions of ordinary men. When he got to the word, "Menstruation," he looked up from his list to ask the students to *please* learn the correct pronunciation. Too often, he said, he had heard people pronounce it as, "Menestration." When he got to the word, "Rape," he hinted that he had his own private theory about that activity. (He later told me his theory was that rape was not merely accomplished by violence but occurred whenever a woman was taken against her will. It was possible, he thought, for a man to rape his wife. An interesting notion, no doubt, but not strictly semantically correct.) He stopped again by the word, "Tumescence," ("the condition of being tumid or swollen") to relate a little anecdote about a high school sex education class in which the teacher's learned vocabulary had confused her students. "One of the words that she used was 'turgid,'" he said, "I'm not sure how you spell it. [But after the class] many of the [the pupils] stampeded themselves getting to the library —to look up the word 'turgid.'"

"What *does* the word 'turgid' mean?" a young woman seated next to me whispered. I gave her a garbled definition and inwardly made an uncharitable observation to myself about the literacy level of California's young teachers.

Interpreting the lyrics of Youth Culture, offering the definitions for "climacteric" and "frottage," expounding your own private theories about the modern striver or the varieties of rape: of such fragments was the sex education class for future "Family Life" teachers molded together. Sex education was, as the instructor would later point out, a relatively new field of endeavor, new, at any rate, as a full-time profession. And judging from the polygynous nature of his class—which had on the same evening also included a spot quiz on the reading as well as a discussion centered on the reading material—judging from this intellectual hodgepodge, one would have to say that the field of sex education was as yet only vaguely defined. The sex educator had to borrow from the fields of medicine, psychology, sociology, and philosophy, and if he sounded a bit as though he were ad-libbing his way through his new profession, you had to at least give him credit for his innovative capacities. After all, what the SIECUS people would call "the sexual function" had been so long relegated to a separate or even a solitary confinement in the thinking of Western man that American sex educators must surely be confronted with a formidable task of intellectual integration. They must seek, as the young instructor was clearly seeking, to merge the study of sexuality with the study of every aspect of life to which it related. Hence, they could bring almost anything from the humanities, the social sciences, or the newspapers into the classroom. Not to mention rock records and other accoutrements of Aquarian Kultur.

*　　*　　*

Up in the instructor's office, he had taped a number of aphorisms above his desk. Some he had composed himself, and others he had collected from his reading materials. Under each he had typed the name of the source, and under his own he had typed his initials, "PBD." Thus, should he gaze at the wall during his studies, he could read:

"Facing the reality of *your own* life
Is easy to say——but difficult to do.
PBD"

"Almost anyone can become a parent
but
Few people can *be* a parent.
Unknown"

"If you don't stand for something,
you may f
a
l
l
for anything.
Unknown"

Inside the desk, below these aphorisms, the instructor had compiled voluminous files with headings like, "Love," "Marriage," "Necking and Petting." But stored away in a box beside the desk was the real guide for his research. It was a collection of students' questions saved over the four years when he had taught Family Life and Sex Education at the Anaheim High School. Written in childish handwriting or printed in block letters to disguise the author's identity, these unsigned questions were sometimes so crudely graphic that they had gone unanswered. The crudest ones, the instructor had assumed, were written with mischievous intent. But a good number of them were answered, and among the sort that got answers were the following:

"Most boys or men have masturbated at least once in their life. Is the feeling, the inner feeling, is it the same as intercourse?"

"I've read that love is emotional, spiritual and physical. Does this mean that without sex you cannot love your boyfriend?"

"Do most people pet before marriage?"

"Is discussing sex with your girlfriend the best way to gain an understanding and a control of both your feelings? I mean, is this a good way to keep your physical attractions controlled and thus keep out of trouble?"

"Why is the girl always blamed when she has sexual intercourse? Why must the girl keep her virginity when the boys can have intercourse whenever they want?"

"How can you tell you're really in love?"

"What should you do with an overprotective parent?"

Questions posed by the students in sex-segregated classes were even more probing. Some from the girls were:

"Why do people go to the extent of 69?"

"Is masturbation normal?"

"If a boy says he loves a girl and wants to marry her but wants premarital sex, does he really love her?"

"How far up is the hymen?"

"Is there any contact with anything besides the vagina wall when having intercourse? Say, clourtrous? [*sic*]"

Questions from an all-boy class were:

"When there are two or more ova, will the baby be deformed in any way?"

"Can you be pregnant and still have a period?"

"Where can a girl (who is over 18 years of age) go to find out if she is pregnant without her folks finding out about it?"

"Do birth control pills prevent menopause or do they just make it easier?"

"Why don't some women get a pleasure from sexual relationships?"

* * *

Paul Dearth, youthful-looking father of two, resident of the fancy Red Hill section of conservative Tustin, graduate student at UCLA, and self-directed philosopher, was the son of a mechanic who had never told his children anything about sex. Dearth had been trained as a health teacher, but when the Anaheim District administration asked for teacher volunteers to help plan the Family Life curriculum, he offered his services. He became the chairman of the faculty committee that planned the high school FLSE curriculum (Sally Williams headed the junior high school committee and later became the director of the entire program) and for four years taught and supervised the Family Life courses at Anaheim High School.

He was a man who quite literally beamed with good health, looking extraordinarily fit for a thirty-seven-year-old academic. His wife looked equally fit, for the two of them spent as much time as they could manage out of doors. Behind their house, they kept two spirited horses, which they trained and rode in their leisure hours.

The Dearths both said that their apparent affluence was hard earned, and that they were barely balancing their budget now that their breadwinner was back in school. But however tenuous their hold on the good life on the mountainside overlooking Tustin, they had the appearance of a status that was far above the tract-housing class of the Burns family and above the established lower-middle-class styles of the more cluttered Orange County neighborhoods where the Townsends and the Howes were living.

Paul Dearth himself exuded a confidence that seemed a little forced. He was so brisk, so cheerful, so nicely assertive, that he seemed just a touch too strident. His profession had been under attack for over a year at the time I met him, and perhaps because of this, he spoke occasionally with the edge of a defensive testiness in his voice. And he sometimes gave long circuitous answers when I asked him to comment upon some of the criticisms lodged against him or his work. Yet he also displayed a ready humor (to the question "How do you teach this course?" he replied swiftly, "Very carefully") as well as a strong and compassionate concern for the problems of adolescents, a concern which must have figured largely in his initial decision to become a sex education teacher.

Vacillating between expressions of appreciation for what he thought was the salvific effect of the course and expressions of resentment for the program's critics, Dearth sat talking on the soft carpeting of his living room floor one afternoon during my stay at Anaheim. He had asked for a lengthy interview when I first contacted him, and he was to prove capable of talking on about his field at great length. (The Anaheim controversy had obviously unloosed wellsprings of verbiage in others besides those Anti ladies.)

At the outset, I asked him how he had gotten his training to teach sex education.

"Okay, that's always a sensitive thing because I think you can read anything—I should say *all* things that you would read—about sex education [and learn that] the most important ingredient . . . in a sex education class is the teacher," he began in his circuitous way. "And don't take that egotistically, but you can have all the books and all the audio-visual things and all the good curriculum and the nice classroom and the backing from the administration and the community and everything else, but if the teacher doesn't do a good job, the class will fail. And it'll fail *miserably*, in fact, it not only will fail, but you could have, uh, great problems."

He said that he had taken courses in Psychology, Sociology, Marriage and Family, and Health, but that he didn't think "formal education" alone could produce a good sex education teacher.

"Now, I think the biggest qualification . . . is *really*: what kind of a person are you?" he went on. "And how can you relate to the kids in your class? Um, do you have good judgment? Do you have the kind of personality that would be acceptable in this kind of situation? Are you comfortable with the topic—or the topics—that come up? Can you communicate? Are you a good listener? Are you empathetic? Um, can you be realistic?

"Now, I think those are the kinds of things you learn in life. I don't think you learn 'em necessarily in a college situation," he summed it up.

How did the school decide, then, that such-and-such a person had just the right qualities for teaching sex education?

"You indicated you interest originally, if I remember correctly, you indicated your interest by going to those [curriculum planning] meetings," Dearth said. "In the state of California, like,

[with] a general secondary credential, you can teach *any* subject. So legally you're okay. But realistically speaking, the principal is the one who screened—and the district. In other words if anyone had any qualms about this person doing the job, they would not be allowed to switch from whatever subject they were teaching. . . ."

Dearth said that Paul Cook had tried to allow the various principals to select their own staffs, for sex education and for all other subjects ("The philosophy has always been in our district until . . . the recent problems . . . that the principal knew his school best"), but that Cook had "always been very strong in this program. He's the one who, I think, had the initial idea. I think he should be given the credit for it," Dearth continued, adding with a little ironic smile, "Of course, he's gotten the blame for it, too."

It was Cook's notion, Dearth explained, that the course should be taught in a "completely aboveboard" manner, that the sex education teachers should "not try to sneak anything in" that the community had not been informed about. Cook had argued strongly for putting "sex education" in the title of the course, even though much of it had been devoted to nonsexual topics. Otherwise, Cook had reasoned (according to Dearth), the community might think that the schools were trying to hide sex education behind an amorphous title. Dearth said that he himself had argued that the phrase "and Sex Education" ought to have been dropped from the title after the parents had been informed about the nature of the course. "It was never meant to be, like, 50 per cent is family life and fifty per cent is sex education," said Dearth, implying that he thought the current title gave too much prominence to the sex education aspects of the course.

Speaking of the course title steered Dearth into thinking about the Antis' claim that the course had actually contained "sex instruction," and beginning to sound a little indignant, he said:

"I tell the kids, 'We'll talk about anything that relates to sex education.' In other words, the knowledge of, the understanding of, the attitudes about, the feelings about, uh, *sex.*

"But when it comes to the point about instruction, which, I think, is basically how to *do* it, I think we draw the line. So that we could talk about contraception, but I'm not going to bring a condom in and show them how to put it on! . . . But to *not* talk about it, I think, is dishonest. I think it's hypocritical. And if we're gonna take an above the table, aboveboard approach and allow these kids to be aware of the whole spectrum," he said, never completing the sentence, but offering instead this little aside: "I think they're gonna get the spectrum whether we want them to or not. And typically they get the, if you will, the negative end of the spectrum before they get the positive end."

It was largely to illustrate the profundity of the youngsters' negative associations with sex that he had made use of the word "fuck," he later explained.

"I think one influence that people have had is that word f—u—c—k," he said, spelling it out. "And I think it should be brought out. I think it should be dealt with and then left alone, and [then] you go on to other things that are more important. But I think if you deal with it, then you've gotten it out of the way, and everyone has heard it. Many of the kids do not understand it, and I don't think that they're perceptive enough to know that it's had probably a negative influence on their attitude about sex."

Remembering Ralph Townsend's story at this point, I asked Dearth whether he had ever said to his students, "Can I be frank? I don't want you to squeal on me?" before writing "fuck" on the blackboard.

"No, no, I'd never do that!" he quickly responded. "I might say that in a completely kidding way, and I think even the most unaware student would know that I was kidding. I think the most ridiculous thing to do if you didn't want it to be taken home would be to tell them, 'Don't take it home.' Because then, you know, somebody is definitely going to."

Moments later, however, Dearth said, "I've told the kids in class, I've told them that every time I open my mouth my job is on the line. 'Cause you can blow the whole thing in one sentence. You can say the wrong thing to the wrong student at the wrong time, and you'd, you'd blow it."—Such a comment, I thought, could quite possibly have been interpreted by Ralph Townsend as a plea for discretion.

At another point Dearth said, "I think it's fair to say we don't teach morals, per se. Because I think it's fair to say, whose morals would you teach?" This was the same argument that Cook had used in his statement in defense of the program that had appeared in the *Anaheim Bulletin*. And, like Cook, Dearth went on to claim that a broad kind of moral concern had been woven into the course. "We do teach them to go into a direction," he said, "a positive moral direction, and we do give them reasons why we think it is good. And the best one I can think of in terms of being meaningful to kids . . . is that they'll lead a happier life, a more meaningful life, one with less trouble, they'll think better of themselves and other people will think better of them if they are moral."

"What do you mean by moral?"

"Being honest in their relationships with people, um, treating other people properly, not trying to take advantage of other people, not being destructive in what they do, uh, trying to love instead of hate, trying to respect instead of being disrespectful, caring about what you do, trying to be a productive person—you know. I don't think you can argue with things like that because I think they're good."

The Antis had not, of course, tried to argue with "things like that," with the broader moral positivisms in the philosophy upon which the FLSE course had been based. It was in actual practice, in the small, unmonitored classroom incidents that the Antis had seen—or thought they had seen—disturbing tendencies. They liked to say that the board members did not really know what went on during the class sessions, and they had brought stories of small outrages to board meetings to bolster this contention. The informal teaching style itself seemed to have frightened them; for it was just this sort of style that might permit the classroom discussion to stray into areas not mentioned in the curriculum guide.

When Dearth was asked about the anecdotes and criticisms circulated by the Antis, his tone shifted. His voice took on a slight edge, as if the effort to dissuade the Antis had begun to tell upon his patience. He also exaggerated the counterarguments, like a man who had been slowly drawn way from the strict empirical truth into the inflated verities of political debate.

He said, for instance, that the Antis' objections to the nondirective teaching methods and the circle seating were mainly derived from their fear that the class was actually a form of sensitivity training—and it was his view that it was *not* sensitivity training.

"This class . . . doesn't really deal with a subject; it deals with people," he said, "and I think that in itself is threatening to some parents."

There was no denying, of course, that some of the FLSE teaching techniques had been borrowed from sensitivity training, but Dearth seemed to wish to circle round that fact altogether, knowing as he did that the Antis considered sensitivity training a sinister brainwashing tool.

Dearth seemed, in fact, a little more interested in proving the logic of his own views than he did in quelling the fears of anxious parents. For when he discussed their objections to the relatively "value-free" atmosphere in the FLSE classes, he gave an example of a reply that he had used with Antis on that issue, and it was a reply that was less than reassuring. He said he had told such parents:

"You mean to tell me that a teacher can take your son or daughter and in an hour a day for four-and-a-half weeks once a year and can appreciably change them from what you have taught them to be, the values you've given them, and their outlook on life, and their attitudes and everything else? And if you've never told 'em anything about sex in the first, let's see, six plus five, eleven years of their life before they get to the seventh grade, I'd say it's a pretty good guess that you've probably done a pretty poor job up to that time."

Such a retort might be quite accurate, but it lacked the kind of diplomacy that might have stilled a few anxious Antis. Though one could not prove and really ought not to suggest that the Antis were unsuccessful parents, they had at least claimed to be the spokesmen for those parents who were most fearful that the FLSE classes might drive a "wedge" between them and their offspring. And if Dearth had really gone around telling those parents that it was a "pretty good guess" that they had "done a pretty poor job" if they hadn't told their children the facts of life, it seemed to me that he ought not to have been surprised at their injured and angry reactions.

From the reports I had gathered, it seemed clear that Dearth had sometimes also used less than diplomatic methods with the children of the Antis. He himself said that he had frequently posed the hypothetical question about handling a twelve-year-old child who is accidentally interrupted in midmasturbation. So I asked him what had happened to the child (whatever his true identity) who had been so embarrassed by the question.

"Well, I don't think he's permanently scarred by that, uh, particular incident," he said. "And I've really done that many times, and I've had lots of kids be really on the spot. But the point is, we've built a relationship in the class. . . . They're not the only ones that are momentarily uncomfortable. I don't even care if they're momentarily embarrassed. I think that's a good thing. I think we extract feelings and emotions out of education so much that it's become a bland mouthful of mush, and kids are bored with the whole stupid thing. So I think it's about time they realized that they *do* have feelings, that they *are* important, and we *do* get embarrassed, and we *do* have situations that we can't handle. And I think it helps them develop an appreciation for their parents and how difficult a thing it *is* to be a parent and raise kids, particularly nowadays."

Dearth viewed the embarrassment, then, as a kind of emotional exercise, a preview of the much more devastating embarrassment that might descend upon his students when they encountered a real child playing with himself. And that kind of exercise, however mild when compared to the grim "encounters" and role-playing gimmicks used by sensitivity trainers, was essentially a behaviorist technique. To the Anaheim Antis, behaviorist techniques looked frightening. They saw only the manipulativeness of such methods and did not look at the good intentions behind them. To the Antis the temporary discomfort of a child "on the spot" in a sex education class was proof positive that a darker purpose lurked beneath the high-sounding philosophy of the FLSE course.

The Antis tended to clutter up their arguments with their conspiracy theories and hence distracted themselves and their sympathizers from the more valid questions that they had raised. But one *did* have to take Dearth's reasoning on faith—even if one saw no trace of Communist determinism in his teachings. One had to suspend one's immediate sympathies for the embarrassed child and to take on faith the promise that such difficult moments now in the relative safety of a classroom would indeed yield good results later. For there was no body of science that supported Dearth's contention that the exercises he used in the classroom would protect his students when they faced real sexual problems in the future.

Fretting inwardly for the more inhibited students, I asked Dearth what happened to a youngster who found himself expressing a minority view in response to one of the more difficult questions.

"If that did happen, I think someone would stand up for them," he said. "If they didn't, as a last resort, I would stand up for them. But I don't want to do that because I think that tends to be . . . for the person that I would be helping, it makes them feel kind of funny that the teacher has to be on their side."

There was about Dearth the air of someone who is playing it by ear, someone who is groping along guided by his instincts and perceptions rather than any kind of certain knowledge. The contradictions and the qualifying little extras in his statements betrayed his lack of certitude. And it was that lack that seemed to have made him both flexibly responsive and rashly impulsive. You

could easily imagine, as you listened to him, how he had im-
pulsively decided to try one of the more difficult questions on one
of his inhibited students and then, having asked it, had felt obli-
gated to wait for the child's response, however painful the waiting
—because he had told himself that such discomfort in the classroom was somehow good practice for the child. If he had not, for
instance, pursued Rick Howe (assuming that Rick Howe told the
truth, of course) after the boy had refused to define the word
menstruation (or whatever related word had offended Rick), he
might have been able to keep Rick in that class.

*   *   *

On another occasion Paul Dearth assembled—for my convenience—four of his former students in his comfortable living
room. They were all students who displayed considerable fondness
for him, and, seeing him with them, shifting back and forth between the tones of a teacher and the raucously flippant tones of
someone who is just one of the guys, it was not difficult to understand why he had been entrusted with the difficult sex education
classes at Anaheim High School. Even the Townsend children had
told me that Dearth was an uncommonly popular teacher, and, as
his former students beamed and joked away at him in his living
room, that report did not seem at all exaggerated.

Jerry Stanley was perhaps the most thoughtful of the students
who appeared. He was a sensitive-looking, blond nineteen-year-
old, and he wore his hair about as long as the Howe boys had
worn theirs, nowhere long enough to approach a hippie style but
nowhere near the length of the older generation's bare-necked
styles. Jerry, like all of Dearth's students, lived in Anaheim proper,
and he had lived in the town for an unusually large portion of
his life, seventeen of his nineteen years. He said that he was born
in North Carolina. Both his parents worked near his home, his
father as a "houseman" at the Disneyland hotel, and his mother
as a cleaning woman.

When first questioned, Jerry had some difficulty remembering
just what he had liked about the FLSE course. Mrs. Howe or Mrs.
Pippinger might have ascribed Jerry's memory lapses to the
subtlety of the sex education teachers' brainwashing techniques,
but it seemed clear to me that the FLSE course had simply failed
to leave indelible imprints on Jerry's mind—in fact, he seemed at
first to remember so little of it that I was tempted to conclude
that the course had had no effect upon his life at all.

Anaheim High School had instituted the program only at the

tenth-grade level the first year (1965–66), and it was that year that Jerry had been in the tenth grade.

"That's when I wasn't too interested in, you know, school and stuff," he began, apologetic about his vague memory. "And that class was a—let's see, they told us we got, I think—you didn't get a grade for it, you know, so that was good. . . . 'Cause I didn't think in terms of getting a good grade. I just worried about getting bad ones.

"And let me see . . . oh, tenth grade. It was kinda the things about, well, you know, the sex things with, uh—"

"You don't have to tell me what was in it," I interrupted. "I know what was in it. But how did you like it?"

"Well, let's see, there were certain things. I mostly, I liked the class, but not from the standpoint of, uh, the sex education part. I liked the class when it was about, when we started talkine about roles, family roles. And, uh, you know, the person's part in the family, or why you're like what you are."

Jerry said he also remembered being impressed with the way "Mr. Dearth," as he called him, had talked about cheating. According to Jerry, Dearth had not argued against cheating on the grounds "that it's *wrong*" but had stressed instead the way that it robbed the cheater of a true feeling of accomplishment. Dearth, said Jerry, had told his students that they would be "happier" if they didn't cheat, "and that made more of an impression on me *not* to than anything else . . . [the argument] that I would be a *happier* person, you know, if I didn't."

Jerry also said that the factual material relating to sex had sometimes been helpful, especially material "that you need to learn about, you know, that you feel kinda dumb raisine your hand about if he didn't just tell you. . . .

"The sex part as far as what to watch for an', uh, just the informative stuff was good," he continued. "But . . . the part I liked the most was when we talked about, you know, the relationships of the individual as, you know, correlated *with* things to do with, you know, sex or with family life or with growine up and things like that."

With a little prompting from Dearth, Jerry soon recalled another topic, one which had been covered during the twelfth-grade session of the program. And this one seemed to have affected him quite deeply. The topic was one which must have interested a number of his classmates, too, for it was beginning to touch all their lives. It was: drugs.

Jerry said that he "used to be in the drug thing, gettine stoned and stuff, droppine acid" from some point during his tenth grade year until a few weeks before he started twelfth grade. He had already begun to feel disenchanted with the drug scene before the opening of school his twelfth-grade year, he said, but he seemed quite sure that he had been helped to swear off drugs by what he subsequently learned in the Family Life class—statistics on the possible chromosome damage caused by LSD as well as first hand accounts of the lives of former drug addicts and reformed hippies, who had been invited to the class.

"I might add that my senior year was the best year I could tell you about," Jerry said, seeming more confident of his powers of recall by now. "Because everything else was, you know, talkin' or passin' notes or, 'Let's put a good question in the answer box for Mr. Dearth.' *Really* embarrass him, you know," Jerry digressed a little, starting to chuckle over the memory of such pranks.

He said that before his senior year he had "always been a, just a C student," and although he did not state outright that Dearth's class had helped him to improve his grades, he seemed to be implying as much.

"A little thing that he used to say was, 'It's, you know, your world. I'll be thirty, forty years older an' I'll be in my wheelchair when everything has changed—' you see, 'cause it'll be *our* society an' *our* generation!" Jerry said, his brightening face showing how that thought excited him. "It related the future to us better . . . him makin' the statement about, you know, really, this is his now, but ours is the one that was coming, you know, an' [he would ask us], how do *you* want things to be? What do you think's right as far as moral law? . . . 'Cause our viewpoints and stuff are gonna come up into our society. 'Cause it would *be* ours."

I knew by this time that the supporters of the FLSE program in the district administration had often argued that the sex education classes provided the students with rare opportunities to express their own views, opportunities that were, such administrators claimed, sorely needed. So I asked Jerry whether he had ever been given the same kind of opportunity in other classes, whether any of his other teachers had seemed to respect his opinion.

"Maybe from my American Government teacher," he said. "That's when things, let's say, [when] we began to reap part of our harvest. The American student revolts were beginning, you know. Watts had begun in eleventh grade . . . Riots, student demonstrations . . . you could say the truth was comine out. That Senator, the one that was accused of embezzling money, you know. Unheard of. A Senator? [It was] finally coming out.

Just things—this was when the big change over began as far as America not bein' the big white father an' all so good. An' maybe we *are* kinda imperialist a little bit. And then what we've been taught all along just isn't *there*.

"An' my American Government teacher was feeling these things, too. An' he didn't just teach a straight text, you know. We could talk about things, current events. He'd try, he'd start out every day with the text, but we'd get him off on sumpin' that was goin' on. . . .

"So, I mean, he [the Government teacher] cared about us, but . . . I don't know if I could relate the two [courses] because that was on . . . the secular type of thing—how can I say it?—an' his [Dearth's class] was on a more personal, you know, the individual type thing."

(The Howe boys had praised this same Government teacher, but they had claimed that his course was far superior to the Family Life and Sex Education class, that it was, in fact, the only course in which they had learned anything new when they were seniors.)

Despite Jerry's high praise for the respect that Dearth had shown for his students' views, he unwittingly revealed how the course had stressed the virtues of certain views over others. This he did when talking about a film which had especially struck him, a film called *Phoebe*, which had been produced by the National Film Board of Canada and was being distributed in this country by McGraw-Hill.

The central character of *Phoebe* is a teenage girl who has discovered that she is pregnant, and most of the plot was a series of flashbacks depicting events leading up to her pregnancy.

Jerry said he thought that it was "the best film against, uh, you know, havin' an affair" that he had seen. "Or, at least, for the girl's point [of view] and what she's gotta go through, and the load she carries, you know. . . . 'Cause you don't, you don't really worry about these things until they happen. We're not that kind of a society. . . .

"The guy from the Left, from Harvard or Berkeley, who, he wrote a book," Jerry continued, the memory of *Phoebe* having stimulated a more elaborate thought, "uh, *Strawberry Fields.* [Jerry meant *The Strawberry Statement,* by James Kunen, a Columbia graduate.] He made a statement last year that was really a prophetic statement. He said that this generation—or the society—is a violent one, and it only listens to violence. And that's why, like they tried peaceful marches and peaceful this and that, and only, you know, they [the authorities] only listen to violence, and that's why violence has to be applied."

In his own laborious way, Jerry seemed to be drawing an analogy between the shock effectiveness of violent demonstrations and the dramatic impact of the film *Phoebe*—which included an unpleasant morning-sickness scene. It seemed clear that the possible negative consequences of premarital sex had been well impressed upon him through that film.

Yet at a later point, Jerry effectively said that he did not think the FLSE program had changed the students' behavior outside of class. He thought that "a double type standard thing" had operated, by which the students considered their more sober values while they were in the class but had seemed to "just let it slide after class."

The two most popular arguments of the Antis were that the class actually stimulated the students erotically and that it encouraged them to "go out and experiment" with sexual activities which they had either learned about in the class or which had, through the class discussions, lost their stigma. I asked Jerry what he thought of both these arguments.

Yes, the students were stimulated by some of the discussion, he said, but he added, "Sex has always been such a, a controversial subject . . . that just as soon as he [the teacher] begins [to talk] about no matter what it is, you've heard so little about it that even if it's [the topic] not even, you know, physically sexually exciting, it becomes exciting anyway, simply because you're talkin' about it."

"And do you think the class encouraged kids to go out and experiment?"

"I don't think," said Jerry, and then he paused and let out a sort of groan, as if saying *that* question really troubled him. He shifted uneasily. Pitying him, I said, "You can answer it any way you want."

But at this point Dearth interrupted to invite Jerry along on a drive—he was going to pick up another student, who was without a car. Jerry did not look terribly enthusiastic about accompanying Dearth, and he lingered in the living room as his former teacher went out to start the car. I posed the question again.

"Hmmmmmm," muttered Jerry. "That is a pretty hard one to answer. Uh, it could [encourage experimentation]. It would depend on the student." From the front of the house, Mrs. Dearth or one of the female students was calling to Jerry, telling him to hurry up.

"I can't go," said Jerry.

"What do you mean, you can't go?" came an indignant female voice; whose, I could not divine. Outside Dearth was vigorously honking his horn.

So Jerry roused himself and went out to Dearth. When he returned from the little trip, he qualified what he had previously said about the class being erotically stimulating.

"I didn't mean to say that what he [the teacher] says does, you know, stimulate it [erotic response] just like readin' a *Playboy* or hearin' a dirty joke . . . The stimulation is already there in you before, you know, he begins to talk about whatever he does. And, uh, what he says isn't the reaction or the stimulation. The excitement is already within you."

I asked him once again whether he thought the class had encouraged experimentation.

"Wow. I, I don't know," he said. "I don't know if it does or not. I don't think the class itself directly does. . . . 'Cause really it's kind of a downer. It's kind of a downer, you know. . . . You start talkin' to girls about what do boys really like in girls, you know. . . . And they like respectable girls."

"Let me brainwash a minute, okay?" Dearth, who had been listening attentively, broke in. "Give me just one minute, and I just wanta say something to you," he said, addressing me. "Okay, you ready?" Ready for what? I wondered, trying to appear outwardly cool and professional.

"Sex tends to be thought of in the narrow context of sexual intercourse, right? That tends to be the worry, right? And so we don't want the young kids to go out and have premarital sex, right?"

"Well, I don't think that's the only thing these parents are worried about," I said, still nervous about what Dearth had up his sleeve.

"But that's a pretty good one, isn't it? For openers, that's a good one, isn't it? So, many people say, 'Well, go out and tell 'em, don't do it.' Right? Or something like that, or be a little more subtle, you know, like, wait a few lines, and then tell 'em don't do it.

"If you were a boy—[this is] a little role-play—if you were a boy, and you were trying to hustle this girl and trying to physically get as intimate as you could, and, hopefully, maybe you could do the whole thing, what do you think, what do you think would be one of the things that would tend to dampen or deter you that she might do to keep you from getting this?"

"Throw water in my face," I said. Dearth did not seem to think my answer was funny.

"All right, let's turn it around the other way," he continued, quite serious. "All right, you kinda got the idea what I was saying about this guy, what he's doin'. Okay, now you're the female, and you're in this situation. You're at his house, or you're at your house, and your folks are gone. Or you're in the car . . . or something, but you're isolated. It's like you and he, you know, if you'll pardon the expression, one on one. Okay? All right, now, what do you think you're gonna do to, uh, keep from this gentleman succeeding in his goal?"

"Talk," I said, beginning to feel distinctly uneasy and quickly going over in my mind the actual clumsy tactics I had used on such occasions.

"You shouldn't have been there," said Jerry, which, I thought, was what I should have said.

"Talk," said Dearth, looking dissatisfied. I began to think I wouldn't have done very well in an FLSE class.

"Okay, you're gonna talk," said Dearth, his face brightening as if he'd just thought of another way to stump me. "And what did I tell you—and, I think, hopefully, you're convinced it's the truth—what did I tell you that probably the main thing we try to accomplish in the class is? What? Learning how to what?"

"To talk," I said, knowing that was the answer he wanted.

"To talk. To communicate, right. And so the more the person is aware of, let's say, the circumstances that tend to go with this kind of situation and the things that don't go with it. Don't you think, in a way, that's kind of a subtle way of saying, 'Don't have premarital sex?' "

"Um, yeah, I think it is," I said.

It was slightly more subtle than an outright admonition, I thought, but the message was still quite clear: Don't violate the conventional morality.

Dearth had just treated me, apparently, to his method of putting students "on the spot," and I had not found it enjoyable. There had been something condescending in his manner. He had seemed to consider me extremely dense and therefore only reachable by that laborious step-by-step questioning. And I did not like the gimmicky way he had quickly taken my answer, "Talk," and woven it into a point about the purpose of the FLSE class. It was true that he had said during his own lengthy interview that one of the primary purposes of the FLSE class had been the development of easier communication among the students—especially about sticky sexual questions. But that was one of the many purposes he had listed. And I thought that just now he had tried to tie it all up too neatly with that one word, "Talk." Again, he had shown his tendency to ad-lib. He had taken a momentary inspiration and drawn a lesson from it.

It also crossed my mind that he could have been using his method to unsettle me temporarily in unconscious retaliation for the audacious questions I had put to Jerry. It was also quite possible, however, that he had merely put me through the little exercise to show me how he taught sex education. And if the latter were true, then he had done me a great service, for he had roused in me a hint of sympathy for the Antis, something which was, at that point, quite difficult for me to do on my own.

It was also quite interesting that Dearth had felt it necessary to demonstrate how the course actually bolstered the conventional morality. For if the planners of the course had reasoned correctly —that a value-free classroom atmosphere would strengthen the student's *internal* value system by liberating him from the need to react against *externally* imposed values—then the teaching methods as Dearth had demonstrated them were not consistent with the basic premise of the course.

Dearth's apparent desire to stress the underlying respectability of the program could, of course, have been derived from his keen sensitivity to the political situation in the Anaheim District. The Antis, he must have realized, would love to hear that his students had been erotically stimulated by classroom talk of sex. They could seize upon that one admission of Jerry's and broadcast it throughout the district, never bothering to tell people that Jerry had also said he thought the class was "a downer" on premarital sex. Facing such enemies, Dearth must have felt that he, too, should be politically selective in what he said about the course.

And if Dearth, who would probably not return to high school teaching, was that sensitive to the critics of the Anaheim FLSE course, there could not have been a teacher remaining in the district who would dare to use a truly value-free approach in the FLSE course when it was resumed. The controversy could, in effect turn the classroom into a peculiar kind of political arena— indeed, it might already have done so, with those little girls acting as *agents provocateurs* to a teacher displaying the Dickenson models, with Rob Howe sensing tension in his teacher's manner toward him.

The Antis would later complain to me that their own children had been used as targets of the teachers' indirect retaliations against their parents. And in the transcripts of the past board meetings, similar complaints were detailed. Mr. Townsend had complained that one teacher remarked to his class, "He certainly is a rude man," about Townsend himself. There had also been complaints that the letters to the *Anaheim Bulletin* written by Antis were displayed on bulletin boards in some schools. Some of these complaints were probably groundless. But there had been enough of them to indicate that a few teachers must have allowed their feelings about the Antis to surface in their classrooms. Hence, students like Rob were cruelly (and perhaps unwittingly) wounded in the crossfire.

The Antis had begun the fight, of course, and they had seemed quite brazenly willing to parade their own children, in name or in the flesh, before the board and the press, no matter how much their children shrank from involvement in the battle. But once the struggle had begun, those precious Anti children seemed to have been getting it, in a sense, from adults on both sides.

*   *   *

To Dearth's former students, however, the greatest harm the controversy had accomplished was the indefinite suspension of the FLSE program. They had all enjoyed and benefited from that program immensely, they said. And they thought that the majority of the district students felt as they did. As they spoke, I began to think that the blunders with the more inhibited students had been rare exceptions and that Dearth himself had been an unusually effective teacher.

While he and Jerry fetched the fourth student (an eighteen-year-old boy named Ray Welch), I questioned the two girls, Lisa Harrison, age nineteen, and Thoraya Rade, age seventeen. Just as Dearth and Jerry returned with Ray, I was asking Lisa whether she thought the FLSE program had encouraged the students to experiment sexually outside of class.

"She's hung up on that question," Dearth said jovially.

"What can I say but, no? I don't think so," said Lisa, trying to ignore the laughter of Dearth and the two boys. She was a shy girl, and I was afraid she had said what she thought would please Dearth.

"You don't think so?" I tried again.

"No, no!" Lisa said with conviction.

"You didn't experiment any more than you were doing at the time," Dearth said to her, an impish expression on his face. He obviously liked to tease her with such bold allusions to her private behavior. For she was outwardly restrained, and she had earlier said that her own parents did not discuss sexual matters with her. Hence, Dearth's teasing seemed a gentle attempt to dispel her shyness.

"What if you weren't doin' any [experimenting]?" Thoraya asked Dearth in a playful tone. She was much bolder than Lisa, and she seemed to want to draw a few humorous jabs of her own.

"Then your level of experimentation will increase," he told her, breaking into laughter.

It was this kind of exchange that the students loved, and it went on all evening. But between the bouts of hilarity, the students managed a good deal of serious praise for the FLSE program. Thor, as Thoraya liked to be called, and Ray Welch had graduated from Anaheim High School in the spring of 1969. It was Ray who had been the student-body president at Anaheim High the previous year. Lisa, who was Jerry's girlfriend, had graduated with him in 1968. Both Ray and Thor were enrolled in a local state-run junior college (Fullerton Junior College). And Jerry, who had spent one year at a small southern college, said he was thinking of transferring to a school near Anaheim.

Ray and the two girls were more quick and glib with their answers than Jerry had been. Each of them gave a different reason for his or her remembered fondness for the FLSE program. Thor said she thought it had helped the students who could not discuss sex with their parents. Lisa said that she had liked "the freedom in there," but she did qualify her praise by suggesting that perhaps the teachers ought to have offered a little more overt moral advice. Thor firmly disagreed with this suggestion, saying she thought that the students already had their own value systems by the time they entered the course and would not be appreciably influenced by advice from the teachers. What was important, Thor maintained, was the fact that the class had allowed the students to discuss their own sexual values with an adult. She said that at the beginning of each session, Dearth would ask his students, "How many of you have a good relationship, you can sit there and talk to your parents, bring up any question you want?"

"And maybe two of us would raise up our hands," she said. (Of course, the Antis would say that Dearth had no business asking such a question.)

Thor had been so firmly convinced that the class was valuable that she had once defended it at an adult orientation session, which was liberally stocked with Antis. She said that the Antis had been telling the parents that the FLSE teachers would "brainwash" their children. Thor had countered with the observation that if their adolescent children hadn't developed their own values before they got to the class, then they had better "start worrying." Whereupon the Antis had accused her of being a "plant" and had demanded that she leave. As she walked out of the room, she said, she had heard them calling her a Communist.

Ray Welch, whose term as student-body president had brought him into contact with large numbers of students, said he had noticed a marked change in the twelfth-grade students after they had completed their FLSE session. "Alot of 'em opened up their communication lines between their fellow students to a degree where you could talk about things. Not, uh, not things ridiculous, but things [which] before it had been sissy [to discuss], like guys talkin' about family budget and realizing how much it costs to pay for a car and a house."

As Ray was still in contact with the younger students at Anaheim High School, I asked him whether they had been upset over the suspension of the FLSE program.

"There are kids who are disappointed," he said. "It's the only time that we have to sit down and have things hashed out that are on their minds, things that they can't talk about with their parents.

"You'd be surprised," he went on, "how many girls at the school can't talk to their mother[s] and let them know that they are in trouble, that they are pregnant. But they can talk to the school nurse. And people say, 'Oh, that's because you're far removed from the situation and everything else.' That's not true. Because, actually, the school nurse is very close to these kids.

"I talked to the school nurse about a problem I had at home—when I was a sophomore. Because she opened up a communication line.

"Yes . . . a large number of the kids that I've talked to are disappointed. But what can they do? . . . If they make a protest and do something irrational and ridiculous, it's gonna show the adults what the adults are looking for, that the kids are, they're not responsible, they're not old enough to handle it."

Ray Welch was no radical. That was obvious in the way he envisioned a student protest as an event that might lead to "irrational and ridiculous" behavior. He liked the kind of student protest that was orderly and respectable such as the politely worded list of suggestions and criticisms that he and the other Orange

Country student leaders had delivered to their school boards after the student conference in the Disneyland Hotel. Ray was a volunteer lieutenant at the Anaheim Police Post ("We work emergency situations such as last year's floods and lost child situations"), and he told me that he hoped to become a full-time police officer with the Juvenile Department. He wore his curly hair in a longish crew cut, and his clothes looked as though they had been chosen for their comfort rather than for any popular image. Outwardly he seemed the most "square" of the four former Anaheim students.

But if he appeared the least sympathetic to the styles and the political tactics of student radicals, Ray seemed more acutely aware than the others of the growing influence of the New Left culture heroes among the students of the Anaheim District. Already, he said, the students at Anaheim High School were forming their own political party. And if the dress code were to be reinstated, he thought that the more active among them would be able to organize quite a number of the high school students in the district.

Would they also protest against the removal of the FLSE program?

"Who knows?" he shrugged. "I can only tell you what's happening right now. . . . The students this year would be easier to set off on something like [the dress code]. And, uh, do silly things, you know, pull out of classrooms and say, 'Man, you can't do that. That's violating our civil rights,' and all this other stuff. Whereas last year, I'm not sure they would have done that. . . .

"This year it's a completely different attitude on campus."

What Ray was saying was borne out at least superficially by the motley dress styles visible at the cruising ground, the sticks of incense burning on the dashboards of youngsters' cars, and the Howe boys' reports that drugs were available "just *any*place you go" in the area. Even a high school football schedule in the window of the taco place across from my motel had been marred by some young politically minded sort. It bore a tiny drawing of a hand giving the peace Vee over which was written in small lettering, "PEACE" and "LOVE."

Whether they signified a wholehearted adoption of the Yippie political extravaganzas or of the sexual defiance of people like Linda LeClair, the Barnard girl who had publicly defended her right to shack up with her Columbia boyfriend, the signs of a new youth culture were everywhere in Anaheim. And they carried with them the appearance of a new self-consciousness, which had its political manifestation in the student conference in the Disney-land Hotel.

And against this background the cheery, clean-cut face and earnestly voiced educational theories of Paul Dearth appeared strikingly dated. He was, after all, a health teacher who had been trained in the fifties, and the FLSE course he had helped to develop was grounded in a morality that still had some practical application in the 1950's before the birth control pill was widely available. He seemed to have based his own teaching on the expectation that students would see the same hazards in premarital sex that had existed during his own youth.

After the interviews were completed, the four students, Dearth, his wife, and I gathered in the Dearth's ultramodern kitchen for doughnuts and milk. Two evenings before, the Dearths had generously invited me for dinner. They had sat there in the same glistening kitchen with her two blond boys and Mrs. Dearth's mother, all of them waiting in silence until Paul Dearth asked one of his sons to say grace. It was a scene that could have been the model for a thousand Norman Rockwell paintings. The pretty, well-groomed wife, the plump mother-in-law in a shapeless long-skirted dress, the closely shorn, clear-eyed father, and the two very blond, very healthy boys, all seated around their cheerful glass table, their heads bowed as one of the very blond boys lisps the words of a simple grace. Two evenings later there were not enough chairs for everyone, so Dearth offered his wife a seat on his lap. She balanced there a little self-consciously as if too well aware that the two of them were being eyed by five people who had known her husband primarily as a Family Life and Sex Education teacher. It looked a little like a lesson in how Family Living Can Be Fun, and yet, that was, after all, the essence of Paul Dearth's teaching. Family Living Can Be Fun, but It's More Fun If You Wait Till You're Married to Start It. And if that belief sounded a little old-fashioned to a journalist from the country of the effete snobs, Paul Dearth and his wife did look as though they had thrived on it. Still, I couldn't help wondering whether Jerry, Lisa, Thor, Ray, and their classmates would find that it also served them well.

The Victims

Communities and their school systems differ in size, sophistication, and readiness to accept new courses of study. There are regional differences and differences in the degree and kind of cooperation between a community and its school board. In a largely urban area, with its sprawling population and stratified school system, there is not likely to be strong or particularized community involvement in school policy. The impetus for initiating a family life and sex education program in an urban center would thus most often come from the school board, working with community leaders. In rural and suburban areas, where parents of school-age children are likely to be the community leaders, the involvement would have a more "grass roots" character.

But no matter where the impetus comes from, the school and community need to work together closely to implement a sex education program. If the leadership comes from the school, parents and interested civic groups must be invited to participate in getting the program started. Their views should be solicited, their doubts and concerns sympathetically listened to, their suggestions carefully considered—for their support is absolutely essential if the program is to be a success.—from chapter 2 on "Community Acceptance" in the book *Family Life and Sex Education: Curriculum & Instruction,* by Esther D. Schulz, Ph.D. and Sally R. Williams, R.N. (New York: Harcourt, Brace and World, 1968).

It was one of the many ironies of Sally Williams's career that she had written (with Esther Schulz) the above passage several months before its message was resoundingly brought home to her. It was another of the ironies of her career that her very expertise and reputation as a prominent sex educator invited special hostile attention from the Antis, attention that eventually brought about her removal from the Anaheim FLSE program. And the supreme irony of the entire Anaheim controversy was to be seen in the way that both Mrs. Williams and Paul Cook were victimized by the overzealous defenders of the value system the FLSE program ultimately upheld. The Antis had mistaken the mild sexual liberties that the FLSE curriculum condoned and the relatively free sexual discussions of the FLSE classes to be signs of the school administration's secret larger purpose: the repudiation of all conventional morality. But as I listened to Mrs. Williams and Paul Cook, I came to the conclusion that their motivation had always been quite the opposite. It was my impression that they had planned the FLSE course as a means of inducing students to work through their questions and doubts about a morality that Cook and Mrs. Williams thought they had learned almost by rote, in the expectation that this process would lead the students to see the practical derivation of the conventional morality. And when one studied the FLSE curriculum guide after listening to Cook and Williams, one was forced to observe that the liberties that the course had allowed—the freedom to question and argue the merits of the conventional morality—had been mild indeed. The curriculum guide contained an abundance of excerpts from the advice-to-teenagers books, *all* of which contained negative or extremely cautionary stances on premarital intercourse, and those materials were far more numerous than the materials included to guide classroom discussions about the validity of existing moral standards. In fact, except for the straight information sessions provided for in the guide, sessions dealing with physical changes during puberty, the facts of reproduction, and the basic biology of pregnancy and birth, almost the entire curriculum guide was devoted to lessons in problem solving *within* the context of the conventional morality. Even as the guide materials for student consumption informed them that masturbation was no longer considered to be physically harmful, the materials also contained the cautious admonition, "A boy or girl should carefully consider his other feelings and religious beliefs before practicing masturbation." The guide materials on drinking behavior informed students that "the self-respecting boy and girl in their teens should never have a single drink before or during a date. Alcohol does not make the sexual urge more insistent as people used to believe but it is extremely dangerous because of the way it inevitably acts to lower sex restraints and reduce self-control." (That's an excerpt from a book called *Sex and the Adolescent* by Maxine Davis.) And the guide even contained some material that could be interpreted as discouraging student militance, material like the little "Self-Evaluation Test of Social and Ethical Maturity" for ninth-graders, which asked students to rate, among other things, the degree to which they placed an "accent on the positive instead of the negative qualities in environment"; or the little essay from the book *Building a*

Successful Marriage by Judson T. Landis and Mary G. Landis that told students that the mature person "sees rebellion against social standards as an immature way of gaining attention."

(It should be emphasized that the curriculum appendix materials were intended for student consumption only at the discretion of the teacher. But the fact that these materials were so heavily weighted in favor of the conventional social code did give some indication of the philosophy behind the course—even if it was impossible to tell from a reading of the guide how those materials had been used in actual practice.)

If you read the entire curriculum guide, and then went back to the guide's introductory material, you could not have any doubts that a basically conformist philosophy had pervaded the course. For there in the introduction, it was stated in no uncertain terms:

The curriculum has been designed to prepare students to establish:
   A family with strong bonds of affection, loyalty, and cooperation.
   A family whose members are happy and enjoy living together.
   A family which contributes actively to the community.
   A family which can mature on stress and trouble and is rooted in spiritual values.
   A family which can permit expression of aggression and clashes of opinion, secure in its ability to live with them harmoniously.
   A family which works and plays together with mutual sharing of tasks and activities.
   A family which fosters the growth and development of its members, each to his full potential; a family in which individual personality is sacred, and democratic interaction is encouraged.

In short, the FLSE curriculum had been designed to prepare the Anaheim students for a family life that was like none you or I had ever seen. Oh, we had seen it, but only in the pages of our own elementary school health textbooks or in the glossy color pages of the *Ladies Home Journal* or *House and Garden*. It was a family without pettiness or passion or jealousies or any of the real anguish that has kept our divorce rate up so high that we might as well stop marrying each other to save ourselves the legal fees. What's more, the definitions of the "mature person" that Anaheim students had learned in the course would exclude just about every rebel, heretic, or revolutionary leader who shaped our culture, our religion, and our politics.

The overwhelming emphasis on socially acceptable—if idealized —codes of behavior in the FLSE curriculum guide should not have gone unrecognized by the Antis. Indeed, a reading of the guide could leave one deeply puzzled about the exact source of the Antis' concern. For the standards of behavior that they seemed to be defending were quite openly supported by the material in the guide. Those standards were *not* supported by the youthful culture heroes, but if *these* were the people who had really alarmed the Antis into their moral crusade, then Sally Williams and Paul Cook were the victims of a misdirected struggle.

The two of them had their own theories about the reasons that they and their program had been picked as the targets of what developed into a full-fledged right-wing attack. Both of them thought that the more conservative elements in Orange County had resented the kind of publicity that the program got and the attitude that the publicity created among educators. Mrs. Williams called this attitude the "If *Anaheim* can do it, anybody can do it" mode of thinking. And she thought that the Antis had thus seen the program as a kind of blight upon Orange County's reputation for conservatism. When I told her that Townsend had mentioned the way journalists had waxed incredulous over the juxtaposition of conservation politics and progressive sex education in Orange County, she said wryly, "Yeah, I knew that sticks in his craw."

The kind of thing that must have annoyed Townsend can be seen in this excerpt from an article that James Lincoln Collier wrote for *The Village Voice* in April, 1967:

The Anaheim Union School District, located in the country of John Birch and Mickey Mouse, is today giving its school children what is unquestionably the most intelligent, realistic, honest, and complete course in sex education anywhere in the United States, if not the entire world. (It is probably superior to the highly touted Swedish system which, so far as I have been able to find out, plumps heavily for virginity and spends a lot of time telling boys and girls not to take candy from strangers.) Since the path taken by Anaheim, with modifications, is almost certainly the way the American sex education boom is going to go, in April I flew out there to see what it was all about.

And Collier was not the only journalist to high tail it to Anaheim to see what was in 1967 considered to be *the* number one sex education program in the country. Nor was he the only person to conclude that the Anaheim course would be a model for other such courses. Writers from *Redbook*, *Time*, and a number of other mass-circulation magazines observed the Anaheim course in operation. Cook told me that people had come from "all over the world" to see the program. And he said that hundreds of school boards and school administrators had written to him asking for copies of the curriculum guide.

The notoriety of the Anaheim program inevitably made Sex Education Authorities out of Paul Cook and Sally Williams, the principal architect of the course. Cook either did not desire or could not spare the time for much more fame than magazine interviews could bring him. He did write one article for *Good Housekeeping* entitled, "What Your Child Really Wants to Know About Sex," which was published in April, 1968. But Sally Williams managed to get a good deal more exposure—and perhaps there was a greater demand for her views, since she had helped design the course and was supervising the thirty-odd people who taught it. (By the end of the 1969 spring term, there were thirty-six full-time FLSE teachers working in the district.) She spoke to countless professional groups; she became such a respected sex education authority that another one asked her to collaborate on a book. Her judgments were so highly thought of that Disney Enterprises paid for her advice on two new sex education films the outfit was producing. And finally, she was invited to join the board of the Sex Information and Education Council of the United States (SIECUS), which put her right up there with the elite of the professional elite.

It would later develop, of course, that the reputation of the Anaheim FLSE program, which brought Paul Cook fame and projected Sally Williams up into the world of the professional elite, was a serious liability for both of them. For it gave them each a status and an aura, which were most heartily resented by the people who eventually attacked sex education.

Sally Williams came in for the first outburst of concentrated hostility because she had joined the board of SIECUS. Mrs. Howe just couldn't get over the fact that Mrs. Williams was a member of the SIECUS board, and from the transcripts of board meetings during the winter of 1968–69, one could see that Mrs. Burns, too, had been struck with outraged motherhood every time she remembered in public that Sally Williams was connected with SIECUS. Mrs. Burns liked to ask at board meetings whether Sally Williams intended to resign from the SIECUS board and whether she intended to do it *soon*.

The California State Board of Education eventually proved of some assistance to the Anaheim Antis in their attacks on SIECUS—and hence also on Sally Williams. For in April of 1969, the state board passed a resolution (based on a set of recommendations from the enlightened State Superintendent,

Max Rafferty) that was a compilation of guidelines on the teaching of sex education. Included in that resolution was a clause banning the use of "SIECUS materials" in the public schools. What exactly was meant by the phrase "SIECUS materials" was not quite clear, SIECUS as an organization having produced no materials for actual classroom use. But maybe the state board was more interested in showing its sentiments about SIECUS than it was in attacking specific onerous texts written by individual SIECUS members. It must have been that sentiment that counted, for the California State Board had been getting a lot of pressure from the decency forces who called themselves California Families United. The Anaheim Antis naturally belonged to that group, and they had been in on it from the start, having helped Gordon Drake to organize its first meeting in early November of 1968. California Families United included the most conservative people in various parts of the state, and though Ronald Reagan did not like to admit it, some of them were the people who had worked long hours in his campaign headquarters. He must, then, have felt he owed them something when they started fulminating about sex education.

After the April school board election in the Anaheim District, the incumbent board members apparently began to re-examine some of their previous stands on the Family Life and Sex Education program, encouraged, no doubt, by the election results but perhaps also by the mood in Sacramento. By June they had decided to make some concessions to the demands of the Antis, and firing Sally Williams—or rather, transferring her back to her old position as school nurse—was one of them. (Passing a restrictive ruling on the screening of "controversial" outside speakers, who were often used in FLSE classes, was another one.)

Sally Williams should have realized that she was in a shaky position by the end of the 1969 school year. The Antis' hostile attitudes toward her were by then strikingly clear. She was also on rather tenuous professional ground, for she did not hold a teaching credential and had been technically hired to run the FLSE program under the salary title of "consultant." But apparently, the board gave her little warning of their increasing uneasiness about her. She said that she had gone up into the mountains for a workshop during the first week of June that year, quite unaware of what she would learn upon her return.

"We came down off the mountain, I think, Tuesday afternoon. And it was Wednesday morning that I was called in and told, um, that I was removed, or that I would be terminated as of

June 30th, when my contract for that year was through. And I
never knew any more about it," she told me.

I asked her whether there was any system of appeal for her.

"Well, yes, there'd be a system of appeal in that I had never
received any criticism. I had never been told that I had any areas
in which I needed to improve or, you know, had any evaluation
at *all*. Except to say what a good job you're doing kind of thing.

"But I was told through our professional organization," and
here she gave out a heavy sigh, "that, if I said anything, that they
would wash out the program."

"You mean that was the threat to you?"

"That was the threat," she said evenly.

"That was the threat via the professional association to you?
Or that was what the professional association thought [might
happen]?"

"No, it was, [it] came from Mr. Marten to the professional
organization to me."

(Mr. Marten later told me that the primary consideration in
the decision to remove Mrs. Williams had been her lack of a
teaching credential.)

Things had gotten so bad for Sally Williams during the height
of the Anaheim controversy that even at home she and her husband, a gentle, humorous insurance salesman who playfully described himself as "a gangster," had been plagued by hostile phone
calls. And once, Mrs. Williams had received a letter that was
addressed to "Comrade Williams, Anaheim, California," although
she lived in Garden Grove, and she had begun then to think
that even the postal workers were perversely interested in aiding in
her persecution.

It was hard to believe, as one listened to her telling of such
incidents, that she could have been the object of so much hostility.
For Sally Williams in the flesh was about as homespun as any of
the ladies who had sat through Mrs. Howe's showings of the
Pavlov's Children film. A large-boned and plumpish woman with
a plain face and short, rather simply styled hair, Mrs. Williams
did not look like anybody's version of an evil and sophisticated
corrupter of young minds. She did not even look like a member
of the professional elite. Nor did she sound like one. She frequently said "a course" instead of "of course," and she liked
rural expressions like "sticks in his craw" and "not a lick of difference." Her speech was noticeably free of the professional lingo
of the behavioral sciences with which she must have been thoroughly familiar. She dressed in some unflamboyant way, which I

failed to take note of at the time and which left so vague an impression on me that I could not later recall it. She was altogether unglamorous and unaffected and one felt immediately at ease with her—especially if one's basic sympathies were not with the Antis.

But if she did not carry herself with the subtle arrogance of someone who had rubbed shoulders with the professional elite, her living room was strewn with the signs of her status. A table near her adjoining kitchen bore stacks of unanswered letters, and her coffee table was covered with professional journals.

Her ranch-style home, located on a neat, suburban street in Garden Grove, was like thousands of other Orange County homes, with its short-clipped, crisp lawn, its split-level interior, and its large picture windows that let in the startling California sunlight. And on the living room mantelpiece, she had placed pictures of her children that could have appeared in any of her enemies' homes, pictures with a coloring that was too sweet, too full of cheerful pastels, to look real.

She said that she had grown up in Detroit and begun her professional work there. But she and her husband had migrated early to southern California, and she had worked for nine years as a school nurse in nearby East Santa Fe Springs before coming to the Anaheim District. For several more years she was simply a school nurse in the Anaheim District—until that priest walked into the school board meeting in 1962 and made the complaint that was to lead to the development of the FLSE program.

She and her husband would probably be considered "liberals," she said, because they believed in "guaranteed annual living" and "humane treatment of humans"—this last phrase was uttered with a tinge of irony.

Sally Williams possessed a wry and evenhanded humor that must have borne her easily through the most difficult moments in her sex education classes. Nearly everything she said about those classes corresponded to what Paul Dearth had said about them, and although she said that she, too, was quite disturbed that the classes had been halted, she rarely displayed the aggrieved testiness that I had seen in Dearth. She explained, as Dearth had, that "academic preparation" alone had not qualified a person to teach the course and that she had considered his ability to relate to the students and to empathize with their problems as important as the teacher's grasp of the factual material. She spoke more exhaustively than Dearth had done about the importance of the anxiety-dispelling function of the course, saying, for instance, that when homosexuality was discussed, the teachers could "see the kids relax and almost sigh with, 'Oh, *that's* what it was. . . . I'm not a bad kid.' Most boys *do* have a homosexual contact," she explained at this point, "and if their body responds the way it was designed to respond, then immediately they think they're a homosexual. And this is a *tremendous* burden of guilt— where only simple knowledge is going the take the anxiety burden off."

Because of the teachers' concern for relieving that anxiety, she further explained, they had not dealt with the topic of homosexuality in the course unit on "deviations." This, she said, had upset the Antis, who had taken it as a quiet condoning of homosexuality. The Antis, she added, with her dry humor, seemed to think that if "you ignore it [homosexuality], it'll go away."

It was, of course, a basic assumption of the Anaheim District Administration that sex loomed larger in children's minds when it was ignored by the adults who surrounded them. The FLSE teachers had gone to great lengths to demonstrate the desexualizing—or at least the de-obsessing—powers of their program. And Mrs. Williams seemed to share their faith in these powers, detailing, as Dearth had, the socially acceptable results she thought she had seen in the students who had been exposed to the course.

"Plenty of kids have come in and told the teacher that they had *thought* of having sexual relations," she said, "but after studying it in class, they felt that it was too risky."

What had she told the students who wanted contraceptive advice?

"Not to my knowledge have we ever had a case like that," she replied, frowning as if searching her memory. "Because they talk about family planning [in class].

"What will happen, or what *has* happened, I ought to say, is the couple come in, and they are considering sleeping together. And they've usually been a student in Anaheim and the other a student from some other district [The Anaheim girls, she had said at another point, tended to go out with older boys.]. And they've come in to see the teacher and ask about it. And a' course, you have a built-in handle right there [because] you know if they've come to ask about it that they have reservations. And so you explore all the issues with them.

"And as far as we know, . . . the ones that have reported back —not all do—have said they decided not to. It was too hazardous. [They said] that they thought too much of each other and they didn't want to spoil it.

"So, if you have them look at it intellectually before they get all emotional," she went on, talking now as she might to a new group of sex education teachers or perhaps to a group of anxious parents, "then they can begin to take the appropriate steps to see that they *don't* get involved emotionally when they didn't really want to. But again, by understanding basic physiology, they have a better idea of what they're toying with. And, look at that ninth-grade appendix on the physical aspects of necking and petting." (That appendix material had been taken from a book called *On Becoming a Woman*, by Mary McGee Williams, and Irene Kane [New York: Dell, 1958]. A long passage from the book was quoted in the FLSE guide's ninth-grade appendix; some excerpts from the passage, which was obviously addressed to girls, are:

Kissing and petting are physical contacts perfectly designed to arouse both a boy and a girl. They are the first steps in intercourse. And that's why they have to be kept under constant and firm control.

You may think you have everything under control. You're enjoying the pleasure of petting, and feeling very mature and womanly—when suddenly you realize again that in boy-and-girl relationships *two* people are involved, and it takes *two* to keep control. The boy you're petting with is aroused faster—and loses control faster. His need for physical release is stronger than his concern for you, or his own desire for self-control. You've petted too far and it takes all your strength to get things back on an even keel.

Don't underestimate your own capacity for passion. Once stirred, a woman has a physical urgency that rivals a man's in its single-minded drive toward completion. You're a big girl now, if you're petting, and you must know yourself. You're playing with fire if you're telling yourself, 'I can go so far—and no farther—any time, without trouble.'

For sooner or later, the girl who is aroused and excited by petting will be faced with a choice. She must make up her mind about an old-fashioned-sounding word that is as modern as today: chastity. . . .

Well, we've got news for *you*. The word may be dated, but the principle isn't.

Sooner or later if you date a boy steadily and frequently, and pet enthusiastically, one of the petters won't want to apply the brakes, and will demand the next stage—actual intercourse up to the point of climax but not actual union—either because the male sperm is ejected outside the body or because a physical device is used to prevent conception.

We could make a case for chastity right here by pointing out that despite the wonders of modern science, despite your own faith in your self-control and ability to stop at a given point, you are by no means "protected" from pregnancy by such methods of "controlling" intercourse. . . . Any *one* act of intercourse (even if it's your *first* mistake) can lead to the permanent mistake of an unplanned and unwanted pregnancy outside of marriage.

The birth control pill was, of course, not widely available to American women until two years after this book appeared.) "To the kids," Mrs. Williams was saying, "this is a, why, this is a *startling* revelation to them that you can reach a point in necking and petting where your good sense really is virtually turned off. And physiology is operating. And they need to understand that they all reach that point and that . . . they should set their *own* cut off point, their *own* guidelines.

"And, of course, this is what I told some of the Antis. . . . It's all done in a very objective manner, and it's not dwelt on. It's not purient [her pronunciation] interest."

Anyone who could have gotten his kicks from reading that passage from *On Becoming a Woman*, I thought, must not have read much English literature or even seen the covers of the more interesting magazines and tabloids available right in downtown Anaheim. But Mrs. Howe and her friends had in their possession some of the spiciest nudie magazines that I had ever seen. So they couldn't have felt exactly deprived of prurient reading matter. In fact, they ought to have developed a rather high titillation threshold by the fall of 1969. Indeed, the reasons for their objections to such writings as those in *On Becoming a Woman* were growing ever more obscure to me.

But perhaps the Antis were actually well aware of the amount of class time that had been spent on bolstering the morality that they themselves swore by. For when I asked Mrs. Williams what she thought had set them off in the first place—and I thought to myself that she would immediately answer: the discussions on premarital sex—she said without any hesitation, "Masturbation."

That wasn't going to get any daughters pregnant or infect any children of either sex with the dread "social diseases," I thought. But it had made Philip Roth into a best-selling author, thereby proving itself a topic, at least, of widespread concern. Perhaps masturbation was still troublesome enough to the parents (and the children) in the Anaheim District to have a more immediate and compelling shock value than premarital sex. Cecelia Townsend had said she thought it caused psychological problems, her brother had said he'd been taught it was "about as low as you can get"; and Mrs. Burns had spoken of it with more repulsed motherhood in her voice than she had mustered when speaking of any other horrors. So perhaps the Antis were not only leery of attacking the FLSE program in those areas where the course clearly supported the conventional morality, but they might also have been more tolerant of premarital gamboling than they were of masturbation. Premarital intercourse involved the violation of a social code, it was true, but the activity was also a manifestation of what they seemed to consider, as Mrs. Pippinger had frequently put it, normal sex.

"That [masturbation] started it [the controversy]," Mrs. Williams was saying. "That started it in 1962, and that started it again [in 1968] . . . .

"If you look at the subject of masturbation, you can't find anybody in this day and age that will say that it is physically harmful. And I've searched all the books—or a great deal, not all. And we carefully selected our wording for that appendix material and pointed out that there were, uh, religious points of view on this topic that did not feel that it was correct behavior." The appendix material—which the seventh-graders and older students were to read at the discretion of their teachers—said in its entirety:

Most students have some experience with this activity sometime before puberty, although many of them are unfamiliar with the word: masturbation. They hear it called "touching yourself," "playing with yourself," "self-abuse," or the slang term, "jacking off."

Authorities tell us that it is an almost universal practice among healthy boys and is also a common, though not so frequent, habit in girls. People learn it all by themselves or else from their youthful friends. Masturbation may begin at almost any age. It has been observed in children under three years old. It is usually started again in adolescent years and continues to a limited extent in adult life.

From the medical point of view it is necessary to emphasize that fact that [sic] the commonly quoted medical consequences of masturbation are almost entirely fictitious. Masturbation will not impair the mind. It will not interfere with the successful performance of the sexual function under normal conditions.

Any harm resulting from masturbation, according to the best medical authorities, is likely to be caused by worry or a sense of guilt or fear, and a boy or girl should carefully consider his other feelings and religious beliefs before practicing masturbation.)

Mrs. Williams said that "even as late as 1932, the medical books were still saying . . . that it was harmful." And she thought that there were probably a number of people "in the general population" who still believed that masturbation was harmful. "How many doctors are still practicing that had their training prior to

1932?" she asked with a so-look-what-we're-up-against kind of exasperation showing in her face.

"I think it's *criminal* to deny kids the information that [can]
make life easier for them!" she had said earlier. Here, obviously,
was the sharpest edge of the conflict, for what she—and a good
number of authoritative medical people as well as educators—
considered a salvific dispensation of knowledge, the Antis viewed
as a violation of their outdated moral and/or medical scruples.
Townsend and Mrs. Howe were Roman Catholics, and there
were still plenty of parish priests who taught their young pa-
rishoners that male masturbation was a sin because it involved—as
in intercourse with birth control—a waste of the Lord's bounty.

The Antis had frequently told me that they were not against
sex itself—they knew that many of the proponents of sex education had labeled them as "hung up," tortured by sexual anxieties.
Oh, no, they would say, we're not against sex. Sex is wonderful.
It's the most beautiful thing God gave us. But it's only for married people—in bed, facing each other with *both* their heads at the
same end of the bed.

Mrs. Williams didn't think they were being honest. And she
shared with the other sex education proponents a profoundly di-
agnostic view of the Antis.

"What we're facing in a large body of the opposition," she
told me, "is [the fact] that they have been brought up *all* their
lives [to feel] that sex is dirty, and there's no other way to look at
it. And [they think] that we are just doing the most vicious thing
by talking about this *dirty* subject with innocent, pure white children. An', no matter what the news media or television or any
of the magazines say, *they* believe it's dirty. And they believe
[that] in order to live effectively, you must believe it's dirty.

"And I feel sorry for them," she wearily concluded, "but there's
no way to change their minds."

*   *   *

Paul Cook, whose age (sixty) and impending resignation
seemed to have put him in a philosophical frame of mind, offered a broader analysis of the Antis' reactions than Mrs. Williams
had put forth. Speaking in his office adjoining the main district
administration building, he mused and speculated at length with
the air of a man whose battles had all been fought. There was
nothing left for him to do, he told me, save to wait until he
had worked out suitable retirement terms with the board. No
one was sending him directives. The board had ceased to deal

with him as the Chief Executive of the district and was working instead with the Deputy Superintendent, Kenneth Wines. So Cook had endless time to spend talking about his long career in Anaheim. And talk he did in a deep fatherly voice that ought by rights to have soothed the most hysterical of Anti women.

It was not his voice alone that reassured. There was about his whole person such an air of certitude that even his unfounded speculations seemed undeniable as he uttered them. He seemed a man who was utterly convinced of his own worth. He was like those doomed and yet invulnerable, literate old lawyers in Faulkner's novels, who were always too intelligent and too compassionate to accept the cruel conventions and the politics of the old Confederacy but who always seemed to view the world and themselves with an irony that would not allow them to fall morosely into self-pity.

Cook did not look like a Southerner, however. He looked like a professor from some eastern university or perhaps a lawyer in some notable eastern firm. He had a reasonably handsome face that was taking on a craggy, wizened look. With his still blondish hair and lively blue eyes, he appeared younger than his years and yet also older than the face I had imagined for him when reading about his bold new sex education program.

By the time I actually got in to see him, I had heard so much criticism of Paul Cook from the Antis that I had come to think of him as a cruelly victimized individual. The Antis were not at that time sure that he would be forced to resign, and they had been giving him the kind of attention that they had earlier bestowed upon Sally Williams. One of them had given me a two-page "Bill of Particulars for the Dismissal of Paul Cook as Superintendent of the Anaheim Union High School District" that was drawn up by the California Citizens Committee. Twenty-five "particulars" were listed, among which were:

He has introduced material into the curriculum of questionable educational merit.

He has verbally harassed and embarrassed parents who come before the board to present their grievances or even to obtain information.

He has made the community of Anaheim an object of national ridicule by promoting an educational theory that is preposterous on its face.

He has downgraded parents in the eyes of their children by declaring without submission of evidence that 99 per cent of parents are dishonest with their children on the subject of sex.

Both outside and inside the district he has fasely [sic] represented that opposition to the program is small, when, in fact, from the very beginning that opposition is [sic] great in number and intensive.

While hurling charges of near-universal dishonesty at parents, he himself has been less than frank on the connections of the district with the notorious Sex Information & Education Council of the United States.

At the end of this "Bill of Particulars" was a little paragraph entitled, "Summary," which read:

Mr. Cook has traveled too far too fast down the wrong road and fights any attempt at restraint. His uncompromising, negative, and often arrogant attitude leaves no recourse except his immediate removal.

Mrs. Pippinger had shown me a similar leaflet, which she proudly claimed to have printed up at her own expense. This was the leaflet she had recently placed atop teachers' cars.

The *Anaheim Bulletin* had long been troubling Cook, the paper's cleverest attack upon him having appeared in that April, 1969, edition that had contained his long defense of the FLSE program. Sam Campbell, the *Bulletin* editor, had printed, alongside Cook's statement, a list of sample questions from a sex knowledge test which had been administered once—unauthorized —in one of the district high schools. The questions had appeared under the heading, "TEST GIVEN," and a few of them were, "Is frigidity in women most often found to be caused by a physical condition?" "Will frequent self-gratification (masturbation) cause undesirable mental or physical consequences?" "Will having sex relations several times before marriage enable a couple to judge whether they are likely to be sexually well-mated?" and "Do persons who commit sex crimes generally have an unusually strong physical sex drive?"

All of the questions were directed at popular misconceptions about sexuality—and so could easily have been considered educational—but the district administration had judged the test inappropriate for classroom use and had asked the teachers who had used it not to do so again. In very small lettering under the sample questions, the *Bulletin* had informed its readers that the test had been administered in Loara High School during the fall of 1968, but there was no mention of the fact that the district administration had later issued instructions that the test was *not* to be used again.

(The remainder of that particular *Bulletin* section had been devoted to stories of sex education battles in other parts of the country, reprints of earlier *Bulletin* "exposés" of the Anaheim program and/or SIECUS, and an editorial opposing the FLSE program.)

It was this editorial treatment of Paul Cook's statement that later led Royal Marten, the board chairman, to favor a moratorium on public discussion of the sex education issue for all school employees. Or, at least, Marten implied as much to me.

Paul Cook himself seemed, after a reading of all this material, a man who had been truly persecuted. He invited, in fact, so much sympathy before one met him that his actual undefeated bearing came as a surprise.

Cook seemed, for one thing, to have separated himself from the issue—so that he was able to view the reaction against sex education as a large and general outrage *not* directed against himself.

"I believe that the John Birch Society and the Christian Crusade have gradually and then, you might say, almost suddenly realized that in our society, the so-called Western Civilization, where children are raised with slaps and frowns and sharp words to realize that parts of their body are unacceptable, uh, except under the most restricted circumstances, where little girls of four years old and three years old are taught to pull their dresses down. . . . that you could gain power and political influence by frightening people and by raising within their minds the old, age-old, shames, fears and embarrassments," Cook said right at the start of my session with him.

"And I feel from my own observation that these organizations and other local organizations of a more formal nature are *primarily* concerned with political influence and power," he went on. "However, I think they have gathered to them many individuals who do not see this [issue] as a [means for gaining] big political power but see it actually as a terribly dangerous thing, the infringement of the family, a lot of personal things where their own fears are exposed, where their lack of ability to deal with their own youngsters is exposed.

"In effect when the Birchers and the Christian Crusaders made their national pitch and wrote these wild pamphlets, they gathered to them all the bits and pieces of human flotsam and jetsam we have that are wild with fear, shame, embarrassment, hostilities. You name 'em; they got 'em.

"And I think the shocking part of it is that you have to think of a man in Germany fifty or forty years ago who proved beyond a shadow of a doubt that if you tell big enough lies and tell them frequent enough, there're a lot of fools in the world who will believe 'em. And we're seeing this every day. There are people right in this town who could go right down and look at our books and look at our films who won't do it. Even though we could demonstrate that the savage lies and falsehoods that are being told are utterly and completely false. And yet people won't bother to come and find out about it.

"And yet at the same time any parent who is at all rational [and] who has had a youngster in the program supports us tremendously."

This last remark led him, without any question from me, to speculating about the timidity and political apathy of the apparent majority of sex education supporters in the district.

"But here again, you have this fear," he mused. "Apparently parents don't like to get up and defend sex education. A few will, but not great masses of people. If, for instance, we cut off the busing, four or five buses, and 50 or 75 kids or 200 kids had to walk, man, you'll get the fightin'-est bunch of people in this board room you ever saw in your life! Screaming and just raisin' hell.

"And yet, to *our* knowledge, from the point of view of insight and mental health and making better human beings, a well-taught program in family life and sex education is a thousand times more important than busing."

Cook said he had no explanation for the sex education supporters' reluctance to show up at school board meetings. It was especially baffling to him, he said, because he had received numerous letters and phone calls from people who favored the program. And he said that the notable absence of militant supporters struck him as most odd after the beginning of the current fall term—when 80 per cent of the youngsters had come to school with parental permission to sign up for the FLSE classes.

Except when he considered such puzzling questions, Cook was not a man who needed much prodding to keep up his flow of thoughts. He seemed to enjoy expanding his points and challenging his own theories quite without the aid of his listener. And his speech was peppered with folksy expressions somewhat like the ones Sally Williams had used, expressions he would pronounce with relish, as if at base he considered the curious battle a source of rich and vastly entertaining material.

Cook had been reared on a farm, which could explain his particular style of speech. He told me that he and his sister had been orphans and that they had been adopted by a "very wonderful," poor couple who owned a farm in Imperial Valley, down near

the Mexican border. Cook said his adopted parents were fundamentalists, and although he thought they had made every effort to
educate their children, he said he remembered having had "a
furious argument with my mother and father" about Darwin's
theory of evolution when he was in high school. But he also said
that his mother had tried to give her two adopted children the
"elements" of sex education when they were quite young. He
said that she had spoken with them about the basic facts of life
and had later given them the children's literature on sex that was
available at that time.

However poverty-stricken his adopted parents had been—and
Cook implied that they had just been able to maintain their
small family—Cook got to Dartmouth College. Which meant
that he was able to land one of the few good jobs available in
Imperial Valley in 1934, soon after his graduation. It was the
Depression era, when thousands of Dust Bowl Okies were migrat-
ing to California. "It was a tragic and pathetic time," Cook
reminisced, "and I learned a lot about our society. I saw a lot of
rough problems." At a later point, when he was speaking of the
affluence of the families in the Anaheim District, he again recalled those days in Imperial Valley.

"When I was a youngster struggling through school, I mean, it
was a life and death business getting a job," he said. "I can never
forget [how], after struggling and just barely living a hand-to-
mouth existence, when I got a job as a teacher in the schools in
El Centro—when the kids chased a teacher out of the classroom,
and I got the job—man, that was like the Second Coming! I
still remember what an enormous feeling it was. I just have never
had a job since that even *began* to give me the thrills that that
job gave me!"

One of the mysteries of Cook's character resided in the fact
that despite the early poverty, despite his rural beginnings and
memories of the Depression, he seemed to hold no rancor for the
Anaheim young of 1969, a generation infinitely more fortunate
than his own. He was not only without rancor for them; he
seemed extremely fond of them. At the same time, he seemed to
sympathize with the parents who could not understand the
new stridency that affluence had created in their young.

"I think the fact of the matter is that kids are *so* much better
educated today," he would observe. "I think the kids are better
kids. They are subjected to more information. . . . They make
money rather readily—so much more readily than we ever did.
. . . So the kids are more independent than they have ever been

before. And, of course, they can tell the old man to flake off, forget it! And, of course, many of them *do*.

"And, of course, *these* are the problems that we are not facing up to. Because the kids today are as fine a group of kids or finer than I can ever remember. . . . If we as parents could learn to be honest with our kids right from their childhood, from the cradle, and just answer their questions and give them reasonable guidance—they're just great."

Coming from a man who had grown up on a small farm and with fundamentalist parents, such views were indeed startling. James Townsend, Sam Campbell, and John Steinbacher (the *Bulletin*'s anti–sex education columnist) also had rural backgrounds. All of them younger than Cook, they had grown up during the most miserable Depression years, and Campbell and Townsend had lived in "Bible Belt" areas of Oklahoma and Kentucky, where fundamentalism and residual populist bitterness against the banks and big landowners who were running poor folk off their farms ran deep. Steinbacher had been raised as a Roman Catholic, but he said that the little community of Drain, Oregon, where his immigrant parents had settled, was as straight-laced as any New England hamlet. Paul Cook's earliest environs had been quite similar to theirs. In fact, he said he had attended many a revival meeting during his childhood.

Yet it had been Paul Cook's peculiar destiny to end up as an uncompromising opponent of the rigid backwoods morality that he had learned even before Campbell, Townsend, and Steinbacher had been conceived. And whether or not they knew of his origins, they went after Cook with the sort of hunger for vengeance that one of their own preachers or political evangelists might have shown toward one of them if he were suddenly to renounce the Lord and join the Weathermen. It wasn't, of course, just the way Cook seemed to be repudiating all that they still clung to in their Old-Time Religions that had infuriated them. It was also the fact that he had real power and real prestige, so that however humble his origins, he had effected in their town and their school district much greater changes than they had been able to bring about with their ranting against the Communists, income taxes, unions, hippies, and the Anti-Christ. Cook had made it into a professional sphere of power that they would never enter. For however many right-wing readers might be doting upon the *Anaheim Bulletin* and however many Ronald Reagans Jim Townsend's committees might have helped to elect, none of them had ever been treated to anything like the national acclaim that Cook and his program had won. And if they boasted of their power in Anaheim, they knew very well that they had little or none in the hallways of, as Wallace pronounced it, "Aiche Eee Dubbayuh." They knew very well that the national press laughed at their quasi-religious politics, scorned their antiquated economics and implied—often not so subtly—that they were all mentally deranged.

They knew that Paul Cook—and Sally Williams—had earned a status among the professional elite, an elite whose books and speeches and consultant advice did more to influence the direction of American public education than they, the mere parents (and political minority—71 per cent of the American people favored sex education, George Gallup had announced in June of 1969) could ever hope to do with one measly board election or defeated bond issue. They were the followers of George Wallace, who had long passed himself off as a genuine populist and who, recognizing a good right-wing issue when he saw one, had put out a statement against sex education in one of his 1969 newsletters. They would also become, as the *Bulletin* letters to the editor were later to show, the followers of Spiro Agnew, who delighted them with criticisms of a broader-social intellectual elite whose influence had irritated them for some time. They sensed an inequity about our social and educational status system, the inequity that gave men like Arthur Schlesinger, Jr., and John Gardner a power far beyond the exercise of the franchise, and their political outrage was thus sometimes oddly similar to the outrage of the student leftists who, from the opposite critical polarity, had condemned the status system that amplified the voices of academics like Daniel Bell far above their own.

The Antis had mixed their populism with Goldwaterite paranoia, zesty fundamentalist puritanism, Wallacite anti-intellectualism and racial prejudice, and bourgeois conformist thinking, but at bottom it was populism that they preached. And they made Paul Cook and Sally Williams into symbols of the detested professional elite and went after them with the fury of the dispossessed.

Paul Cook and Sally Williams were probably right when they said that the Antis had drawn to them people with uncommon sexual fears and nameless anxieties of varied strains. But the real festering heart of their collective grievance was that after years of what they must have realized were profound defeats, after the Goldwater fiasco and the Wallace humiliation and the Supreme Court prayers decision and, worst of all, the apparent decline of moral values among the young, the last and final insult had been dealt out to them: They were effectively told that they were not "qualified" to carry the full responsibility for their children's moral and sexual training.

"He has downgraded the parents in the eyes of their children by declaring without submission of evidence, that 99 per cent of parents are dishonest with their children on the subject of sex," the California Citizens Committee had complained about Paul Cook. And though they had exaggerated the figure, they were in essence correct. Cook did not trust them to tell their own children the facts of life. "If you ask our students, you'll discover that less than ten per cent have any meaningful discussions with their parents about sex," he had told *Look* magazine. And to someone like James Townsend, that was an intolerable insult.

How far the Anaheim District's sex education teachers had actually intruded into what the Antis considered the sacred parental domain, the personal value systems of their students, was difficult to judge at a time when the offending course was not being taught. Sally Williams had told me that the teachers had been trained to gently divert a child who started to spill out too much about his personal life in class. But in the introduction to the course guide, there was a little item, which might have led some teachers to think (and some Antis to fear) that their tasks involved a great deal more than the simple imparting of knowledge. The item read:

"The program is further designed to supplement and support the home that is doing a good job and to make up for the shortcomings of the homes where parents have not accepted their responsibility."

Making up for any domestic vacuum was not, in Townsend's eyes, the responsibility of any teacher. And there was about that little statement a hint of just the sort of professional arrogance that must have evoked fresh Wallacisms in his mind as he read it.

To Paul Cook, however, the sex education program had never seemed a usurpation of parental functions. It would be "a *terrible* injustice" if sex education were "taught to make the kid scornful of his parents," he said. "It should bring the parents and the youngsters closer together, and the parents and the school should have more trust and more confidence [in each other]. And under ordinary circumstances, that's the way it worked." Many parents had called him, he said, to tell him that the course had made it possible for them to discuss sex with their children for the first time.

Thus, if Cook appeared arrogant to the California Citizens

Committee, it was because he truly believed that parents *needed* (and usually welcomed) help in imparting sexual knowledge to their youngsters. And the facts appeared to be on his side. Sally Williams had compiled statistics from some student evaluations written after the first term of the full program (fall, 1965). According to her figures, 60.5 per cent of the students had reported that "they would not get this information from another source." The percentages ranged from 68 per cent in the seventh grade to 49 per cent in the twelfth grade, and if those figures were representative, then a good portion of the district parents were abdicating their own sacred responsibility without any coercion from the school district.

Because Paul Cook believed so firmly that the FLSE program had served a function that the majority of the district parents had been quite willing to leave to the schools, he had exhibited little patience with the Antis after they had voiced their initial complaints to the district board. He had considered them to be representative of a minority, and he had let them know that in no uncertain terms. Several times the Antis told me of a particularly galling exchange he was supposed to have had with Mrs. Burns, and I later found one in the transcript of the October 24, 1968, board meeting which must have been the one they remembered.

The transcript indicates that Mrs. Burns spoke up spontaneously. The board let her make her point, although they had tried to establish a rule under which all citizens were to file their statements before the scheduled meetings and to speak only at specified points on the agenda. Nevertheless, Mrs. Burns had her say, complaining about the books that she had found at the junior high school where her daughter was then enrolled.

"I would appreciate it if it concerns you that you put it in writing for me and I would be most happy to look at the book and read the pages," the board chairman told her. She had mentioned one of her favorites, *He and She.*

Then began the exchange with Cook:

Mr. Cook: Do you realize that this program is voluntary?
Mrs. Burns: In a sense, but I also realize that—
Mr. Cook: Now, just don't say, "In a sense." This is specific. It is voluntary on your part as a parent and on the part of your daughter or your son—
Mrs. Burns: But you tell me what good does it do me—
[The transcript says "remarks" here, which means that the secretary couldn't unscramble the voices at that point on the tape.]

Mrs. Burns: Your children are put in first; you have to write a letter to keep your child out—

Mr. Cook: You can't understand English, Ma'am. If you don't have to have your child in it—do you?

Mrs. Burns: My child isn't in it. My neighbor's child isn't in it.

Mr. Cook: Is it right for you to come here and say, "Not only do I not want my child, but I don't want anybody else's child in it?"

Mrs. Burns: Yes, because who do you think my fourteen-year-old girl is going to date next year?

Cook seemed to have allowed his impatience to get the better of him as he uttered that phrase, "You don't understand English Ma'am." But he had obviously been provoked to it. And, in his office, he admitted that he had several times displayed sarcasm in the face of such provocation.

"When somebody gets up and makes some statements that are so palpably fraudulent, or when they attack people in a grossly obscene manner, I would have to say I tend to get a little bit irritated," he said. "I have been sarcastic . . . to every nut in the community. . . . Because I don't, I don't owe these people anything, and I, since I can retire now, I have never had to pull any punches."

He had spoken just then with some force, as if the memory of those encounters had reawakened his fighting spirit. But in a graver tone he added:

"On the other hand, I never started this argument, I don't think anybody would tell you that knew me over the last eighteen years that a person comes to my office or comes to a board meeting, and I'm immediately hostile and jump on them without any reason. I think that's not—I think that would be demonstrated not to be true."

Paul Cook's secretary, a white-haired woman with a ready motherly smile, had worked with him for something like eighteen years, and she thought he was magnificent. She told me as much as I stood waiting for some xeroxed material outside of Cook's office. In rapid succession she listed all his wonderful accomplishments, which I failed to record exactly. But I later recalled her saying something about his having obtained special state funds for special programs and having introduced flexible scheduling in the high schools so that students didn't have to attend the same classes at the same time every day. She also said that he had insisted all the needed schools be built before the permanent administration building was completed. (Part of the administrative structure looked permanent, but a number of odd makeshift sections had been added onto the back of it. One of them looked like part of a trailer. And Cook's own office, which was in a separate structure, looked almost as flimsy as a construction hut.)

Cook had been a truly innovative administrator, his secretary said, and it was her opinion that the board had been eyeing his progressive approach with uneasiness for quite a while. So, it wasn't just the sex education program that had figured in their decision to force him to retire, she said. (I later found a *Los Angeles Times* story that paralleled much of what she told me.)

Cook had himself spoken of his long-standing disagreements with the board. He said that the flexible scheduling had been especially disturbing to them. "A couple of years ago," he explained, the board had tried to ease him into retirement—after he had suffered a heart attack. "They wanted to give me a subsidiary position here, which I would not accept. . . . They wanted somebody that would call 'em up every day and check with 'em on all the decisions, and you can't run a big system like that. It makes no sense."

During the eighteen years that Cook had worked in the area, the school district had expanded, along with the population, at an extremely rapid rate. Cook had started in 1951 as superintendent of the Anaheim elementary schools—with 2,500 pupils to look after. In 1957 the high school board had asked him to take on the job as superintendent of their much larger district. And in the fall of 1969, Cook was presiding, in name, over a district that contained some 35,200 junior and senior high school students. Cook had devised a form of decentralization to cope with the increasing administrative burdens of his swelling district, and it was this decentralized rule that had apparently disturbed the board members more than any of his other innovations.

"I think our difference is this: They believe in rules and regulations, and I believe in people," he told me. "And, you know, this is a big district. It covers forty-six square miles, and I believe in a decentralized school—but where you keep in close touch with everybody. So I set up a program where I met with the principals, and we discussed our problems for half a day every week. And they still do that. . . . Everybody meets regularly and talks, and we have basic regulations. But each school is a little different than the other school because I feel that a person's personality can then flower better—if you have more freedom.

"The board, of course, many of them are people who've never

had any big positions in life, and they, this being on the school board was a big deal for them. And they wanted to get in and run the show."

(The old board included: a teacher from one of the state college campuses, an owner and an employee from a local construction-materials–manufacturing business, a lawyer, and an ex-policeman. In the April election the two men from the manufacturing business were defeated, and the two new board members were a former state narcotics officer and a systems analyst.)

The night before I met Cook, I had attended a board meeting at which there had been some debate over the merits of the previous board's ruling on the screening of "controversial" outside speakers, a ruling which they had voted through in the wake of the April election—but before the two new board members' terms had begun. I told Cook about the debate, which had resulted in no decision, and he was soon deploring the stultifying effects of the sex education controversy.

"No superintendent or no board is gonna think of very many ideas," he said. "But if you can create an atmosphere that's open . . . then you're gonna get some great people. . . . And that's what's happened here. And, man, we've just been goin' like gangbusters!

"But if you look at the rules and regulations that this board has put out. . . . They're just *slowly* squeezing things down. And in two years, a year, it's gonna be dead. There's gonna be no spontaneity left in this district."

* * *

A few weeks after he made that remark, Paul Cook resigned. He was to be kept on as a consultant to the school district until his contract ran out, but he was no longer, in name even, the Chief Executive of the district. The *Anaheim Bulletin* ran a front-page story announcing his resignation, and the story included the subtly critical disclosure of the salary he'd be getting as a consultant. In the January 1, 1970, issue of the *Bulletin*, the report of Cook's resignation was listed as one of the area's top stories for 1969. The editor of the *Bulletin* was, of course, proud of his paper's crusade against the FLSE program, Paul Cook, and Sally Williams.

Cook appeared not long after his resignation at a public meeting, where he debated John Steinbacher, the *Bulletin* columnist. The debate was duly reported in the *Bulletin*, and then Paul Cook disappeared from the news. Other sex education experts and school administrators read of his retirement in their newsletters and got new attacks of the shivers.

It was odd that Cook and Mrs. Williams had been picked as the targets of a moral outrage that appeared to be grounded in the very value system that their sex education program had upheld. But then, it was odd the first time a man was accused of denying the gods, defying the state, and corrupting the youth because he asked a few impertinent questions and had the wrong friends.

Steinbacher and Campbell: The Amazing Pair

In the dim recesses of history, prior to the 1950's, traditionalism was practiced in the printing trades, with few if any materials being presented without capital letters where capitals belonged. . . .
However, something strange happened. Maybe it was just part and parcel of music without melody and paintings without pictures, or could it have been on orders from somewhere that suddenly the capital letter died in many quarters from pole to pole. [sic]
Why mention such a thing? . . .
On page 98 of a little book called Prophetic Years—1947–53 *by Wing Anderson and published by the Cosmos Press, Los Angeles and London, we read what the author first wrote in 1945: "Take heed of the Russian influence in America. Watch the main streets of all the big cities in America for stores that use no capital letters in names and advertisements. It is a sign."*—JOHN STEINBACHER, *in his "School and Family" column, Friday, December 19, 1969.*

My conviction is that when you talk about sex instruction, you are talking about the family. When you are talking about the family, you are talking about the home. When you are talking about the home, you are talking about the country. When you are talking about the country, you are talking about survival. So the issue is a life-and-death matter.—SAM CAMPBELL, *editor,* Anaheim Bulletin, *in a letter addressed to Fred W. McPeake, Secretary-Treasurer, Scottish Rite, Knoxville, Tennessee.*

The writings of John Steinbacher and Sam Campbell alone did more to bring down the Anaheim Family Life and Sex Education program and banish Sally Williams and Paul Cook than did the utterances of any other individuals on the side of the Antis. Or so claimed the defenders of the program.

"Actually, the destruction of the program was carried out by a group of people that couldn't possibly have been more than twenty-five supported by the venomous, as venomous and distorted [a] series of attacks in a local newspaper as you could *ever* wish for," Paul Cook had told me.

"The local newspaper, the *Bulletin*, has always had, has always been known to be anti–public education, and they picked up this sex education thing and have made a thing—you just look back to their newspapers over the past few years, and I think you can take 'em back probably to almost the beginning of the program," Paul Dearth had said.

There was very little information to be gotten from Anaheim sources about Sam Campbell and John Steinbacher. The two of them had appeared in the town—Campbell first, Steinbacher later —with the customary vague pasts of southern Californians. And those who came to abhor them were hard put to dig up details from their former lives.

The two of them had met at a news conference not long after the assassination of Robert F. Kennedy. Campbell was already editor of the *Bulletin* (He had held that job since 1966), and Steinbacher was at the time working with Walter Winchell on some theories about the Kennedy assassination. As Steinbacher tells the story, he asked Campbell to hire him at or soon after that news conference. At any rate, Campbell soon hired him, and the two men seemed made for each other—and for the *Anaheim Bulletin*.

The *Bulletin*, an afternoon paper, which came out six days a week, had been purchased in 1962 by R. C. Hoiles, whose political viewpoint is best expressed in a letter he once wrote to the national director of the Anti-Defamation League in answer to a complaint that one of his columnists was smearing the ADL. In his letter, Hoiles denied the charge, adding that the only time he censored articles was when they advocated such programs as public education, social security, or the minimum wage. All of these, he felt, go counter to American principles "as outlined in the Declaration of Independence," and he told the ADL director that any copy praising them was thrown "in the wastebasket."

On other occasions Hoiles had stated that "the most harmful person in every community is the superintendent of compulsory education" and that "our government school system is Socialism or Communism."

The *Bulletin* was assiduously antilabor, but that somehow did not prevent Hoiles from hiring Sam Campbell, who claimed to have been a labor organizer for the Newspaper Guild during the time that he'd worked for a couple of Long Beach papers. If Hoiles had had any apprehensions about Campbell, he would have been wasting his concern, for Campbell turned out to be the most rigidly Hoilesian editorial writer that the old man could have desired. You just about had to say Hoilesian in describing Campbell's biases, for they fit into no ready-made right-wing mold. Some were conservative, and some were radical. Perhaps they could be approximately described as constituting a philosophy of right-wing anarchy.

Campbell's editorials were antiunion, anti–federal income taxes, anti–public schools, pro-Robert Welch, profundamentalist Christianity, pro–laissez faire economics, pro-Wallace, pro-Agnew, and pro-Lawrence Welk. But they were also anti–military conscription and antiwar. If you read them over a period of time, you would get the sense of a mind that had mixed the old populist hatred for Big Government and Big Business with the new conservative hatred for Welfare Statism. It was a confused populist mind, for it seemed to feel compelled to defend monopoly capitalism against the enemies of what it considered the American Way. And yet at the same time, it was a mind that was quite capable of viewing the draft as a form of "involuntary servitude." But it was also capable of criticizing Nixon's Vietnam war policy and Johnson's past Vietnam war policy on the hawkish grounds that "the U.S. can't win in Vietnam, and Hanoi can't lose."

The *Bulletin* consistently referred to the Anaheim FLSE program as "family-life instruction" to emphasize Campbell's contention that the course offered, in effect, instruction in sex techniques. Campbell did not exactly like to draw attention to those aspects of the program which were not controversial, and he was capable of grossly exaggerating district policy related to the program. His handling of the unauthorized sex knowledge test was a case in point. And when Cook finally decided to restrict parent visits to classrooms—allowing only those parents who actually had children enrolled in the course to sit in on class sessions, Campbell ran a story headed: "COOK BARS PARENTS FROM SEX CLASSES." (Davis, it should be recalled, had claimed that Campbell was bitterly disappointed when he failed to produce a story detailing the Communist plot behind sex education.)

The sex education controversy—and John Steinbacher—brought the *Anaheim Bulletin* a notoriety among right-wingers that was second only to that of the major Birch Society and Christian Crusade publications. (The Birch Society publishes a monthly bulletin and something called *American Opinion* magazine. The Christian Crusade also publishes a monthly bulletin plus a large number of pamphlets on various popular right-wing issues.) John

Steinbacher was a journalist of uncommon energy—and more than the usual propensity to make mistakes in favor of his biases—who had become known to right-wing publishers through his compositions for Fact Records (which you can purchase at: American United, P.O. Box 1122, Malibu, Calif.) and his book about Robert Kennedy entitled, *The Man, the Mysticism, and the Murder*. In that volume, he had put forward his incredible Illuminati conspiracy theory (Bobby was supposed to have been one of them—gone wrong), and, according to Davis, Sam Campbell had swallowed the theory hook, line, and sinker.

Campbell did not admit to such a belief in my presence, but he had obviously placed a great deal of trust in the churning gray matter of John Steinbacher, for he regularly gave the man the top local stories to cover, and he faithfully ran Steinbacher's weekday column, "School and Family."

Steinbacher had really made good—for himself and for the *Bulletin*—in December 1968, when he had produced a three-part series on a teachers' sex education conference held earlier that month in Anaheim's Charter House Hotel. Attributing his information to an anonymous source who had allegedly "registered as a delegate," Steinbacher implied that the conference had been organized in strictest secrecy. And the headline over the first part of his series read: "SCHOOL SEXOLOGY PLANS CHARTED AT HUSH-HUSH SESSION."

The three stories, which appeared in the December 18th, 19th, and 20th issues of the *Bulletin* centered upon the statements of Lester Kirkendall, the now retired Professor of Family Life from Oregon State University, who had been one of the featured speakers at the conference.

"Kirkendall admitted there was considerable resistance to the sex program, and gave the formula for getting around opposition," Steinbacher wrote in the first installment. " 'Just sneak it (the sex program) in as an experimental course and see how people react,' " he quoted Kirkendall in that first piece.

" 'Morals are relative and should consist only of exercising responsibility toward another person,' " was another of his Kirkendall quotes. And Steinbacher went on to report:

"Further expanding on the theme of 'sneaking' in the sex program, Kirkendall said, 'Don't say that you are going to start a sex education course. Always move forward. Say that you are going to enrich, expand, and make it better. The opposition can't stop something that you have already started.' "

Steinbacher's series—especially the "sneak it in" quote—spread like the Words of the Sweet Savior among those of the nation's sex education opponents who were organized enough or experienced enough in right-wing politics to know where to get the literature. Copies of the series were being sold—and handed out free of charge—at the Labor Day weekend convention of the Antis in Chicago. The series was also distributed in West Milford, New Jersey, a suburban township about an hour away from New York where during the spring and summer of 1969 local Antis were trying to obstruct the operations of a citizens advisory committee set up to develop a sex education program. A dedicated woman in Madison, Wisconsin, passed out copies of Steinbacher's stories to the Antis in that town during the fall of 1969. And in the files of various organizations that seem to thrive off of watching the right wing go ever deeper off the ends of reason, I saw reprints of Steinbacher's stories that had been produced all over the country.

Lester Kirkendall, who suffered a heart attack while he was becoming famous as the author of the great Sneak-It-In statement—a statement whose multiple connotations so beautifully merged the political and sexual fears of the right wing that I hated to think that it had been thought up by the proponents of sex education—later sent me a detailed rebuttal of the Steinbacher series.

Kirkendall wrote that he could not recall the "precise words" he had used during the workshop at which he was reported to have uttered "sneak it in," but that he was quite certain he had been "voicing, in just the same phraseology," a view he had expressed in an article for the HEW publication *Children*. Quoting his own article (which had appeared in the July–August, 1967, issue of *Children* and had been coauthored by Helen Cox), Kirkendall wrote that Steinbacher's anonymous source had probably heard him say:

The school "starting" a sex education program can "start" in a relative sense only. Sex education, broadly defined, occurs inevitably in both home and school. The student learns something about reproduction in biology class; about family life in social studies; and about love between the sexes in literature classes through poems, plays, and novels. Both at home and at school he sees men and women relating to each other with love or hostility. He notes that sex is treated openly, ignored, or evaded. Though much of his learning is nonverbal and attitudinal, it is learning. For this reason, any school, any community is fully warranted in saying that it is "expanding and improving" rather than "starting" a sex education program. In presenting the idea of formal sex education in the school to the public, school officials would do well to keep this in mind. The public is less afraid of expanding than of innovating and has more confidence in the judgment of school officials who have forged ahead than of those who, because of fear or indifference, have neglected an important aspect of education.

(Sally Williams also told me that she was sure Kirkendall had never used the phrase "sneak it in" during that Charter House session.)

As there was no exact record of the proceedings at that Charter House conference, it was impossible to determine which version was correct, but certainly Steinbacher had caught the sense of Kirkendall's statement—even if he had vulgarized it a bit. For you couldn't read Kirkendall's carefully constructed theory about the child's early and wide exposure to sexual teaching without observing that it *could* be used as a high-sounding rationale for a less than ingenuous method of starting a formal sex education program in a school—however valid the theory might be. Of course, Steinbacher had transmitted only part of it to his readers, nicely omitting Kirkendall's all-inclusive definition of sex education without which the quote, "The opposition can't stop something that you have already started," sounded much more dishonest—and to the Antis it could sound downright ominous.

Steinbacher's series had contained some additional details that Kirkendall considered inaccurate (Steinbacher had reported, for instance, that Kirkendall recommended *Dickens' Atlas of Sex Anatomy* and *The Dictionary of American Slang* as two books that were "especially useful in teaching about sex." And Kirkendall wrote that this report was "pure fabrication."), but it was the Sneak-It-In quote that really counted with Steinbacher's readers, for that quote fitted beautifully into their theories about scheming educators.

That little phrase made Steinbacher's series the sex education exposé *par excellence* among the right-wingers, who had, by early 1969, begun to tire of quoting the first Gordon Drake pamphlet. Even Robert Welch's material, which appeared in the Birch *Bulletin* for January, 1969, was largely a rehash of the tired old Birch line about nameless, faceless Communists trying to "destroy one whole generation of American youth." Except for a few titillating paragraphs, you could have substituted "fluoridation" or "Earl Warren" for "sex education" in Welch's January, 1969, essay, and it would have read like the things he had been putting out for the past five or so years.

Steinbacher had written something that sounded like an *inside line* on the Great Conspiracy. And it was to the right-wingers about as refreshing as the published letters of Harvard's Dean Franklin L. Ford had been to the anti-Establishment types on the Left. (Except the difference was that the Dean's letters about his efforts to get around the faculty's decision to oust ROTC were uncontestably real. As there was no exact record of the Charter House conference, posterity would never know whether the Sneak-It-In phrase had ever been uttered on that occasion.) Steinbacher's series was reproduced so many times that he was to tell me confidently of reports that "close to ten million" copies were in circulation by the fall of 1969. Whatever the figure, the reprints had brought him a rush of invitations to speak to the true believers in states as far apart as Oregon and Texas. And he said that so many letters poured into the *Bulletin* offices after the series appeared that Campbell suggested he start a special column for the sex education readership. Eventually, several other right-wing papers started publishing the Steinbacher column.

When I arrived in Anaheim, Steinbacher had just returned from a speaking tour. His columns during my stay there were full of chatty details about the little towns he had spoken his wisdom in plus encouraging bits of news about the Antis' struggles for school board seats and right-thinking parents' moves to set up private "Christian" schools in places where the political struggle wasn't going so well.

An enterprising editor in Astoria, Oregon, one of the stops on Steinbacher's tour, wrote to Paul Cook soon after Steinbacher returned to Anaheim. The editor of the *Daily Astorian*, Michael A. Forrester, told Cook (in a letter dated October 6, 1969):

Mr. John Steinbacher . . . delivered a talk here in Astoria last week on sex education and in the course of it said several provocative things. . . . Among them, he said that the [sex education] offerings had caused a "civil war" in Anaheim, resulting in the throwing out of an expensive sex education-family life curriculum and program. . . .

Some of the [additional] statements made by Steinbacher were:
—That the sex education-family life curriculum was "exposed" publicly in Anaheim after a youngster told his parents that his teacher had asked him in class what his parents would think if they caught him masturbating. . . .
—That the sex education–family life program in the district (I'm not sure whether he was including curriculum in Anaheim schools other than the union high school district) cost some $1.5 million. And he said that the school budget (for your district, I presume) was some $40 million.

—Your district sent out 10,000 curriculum guides on your sex education-family life program to 10,000 school districts in the country, resulting in your program being featured in many national magazines.

—That the superintendent (he named Paul Cook) is paid $40,000 a year.

We are interested in what Mr. Steinbacher said because the sex education issue has been raised here. . . .

Cook wrote back to Mr. Forrester, telling him that the FLSE program brought a "tremendous response from our students and their parents" until the attacks launched "by a small but extremely vociferous group of people representing the philosophy of the John Birch Society and/or the Christian Crusade. Our program was so successful," Cook's letter continued, "that they probably would not have made much impact [without] the *Anaheim Bulletin*. . . .

To my knowledge, this statement about the masturbation incident is completely and utterly false. . . .

Our sex education course, year in and year out, has cost on a per pupil basis about $8.00, going up slightly each year as our teachers' salaries are raised. The district's total budget for the present year, with 35,200 students in our junior and senior high schools, is $31,000,000.

The district has duplicated and sold between sixteen and seventeen hundred curriculum guides to schools that have requested them throughout the nation and in some cases from countries all over the world.

My salary at the present time is $30,000 a year.

On October 25, 1969, hardly a month after he had stated that Cook's salary amounted to $40,000, Steinbacher reported—on the front page of the *Anaheim Bulletin*—that Cook was to be retained as a consultant to the school district "with full salary of $30,000 per year until the end of the spring semester."

*   *   *

John Steinbacher was a man in such good standing with the right wing by the time I got to Anaheim that he had taken on a special stature in my mind. I had read his stories in nearly every file on the organized right wing that I had studied. I had heard his name spoken in awed tones by the upstanding mothers and grandmothers who had gathered for that convention over Labor Day weekend in Chicago. And when I first tried to reach him at the *Anaheim Bulletin*, I was told he was a hard man to get hold of. He was in demand everywhere.

John Steinbacher, of all the Anaheim Antis, could be expected to know that I was not exactly their sort of woman, I reasoned. It was in one of his columns that I had read of the convention planned for Chicago. And the lady who organized that thing must surely be in correspondence with the great John Steinbacher—I had unwisely told her I would be going to Anaheim. Surely she must have warned Steinbacher about me. And he, being (as I then imagined) a real and true right-wing paranoid, well, there was no telling what he might do to me. And if he was smart, he would simply refuse to talk to me.

As it turned out, the first time I met Steinbacher it was by accident, and I got a few hurried statements out of him along with the encouraging promise that he would save some time for me. I had run into him in the bedroom of the Celebrity Suite, where Mrs. Howe and Mrs. Drake were resting their feet in between their little lectures to the *Pavlov's Children* audiences. Steinbacher seemed in high spirits, for he had thought of the prank of inviting the California Marriage Counselors to come up and view the film. He asked one of the ladies to lend him a pen so he could copy down the Marriage Counselors' number, and Mrs. Howe told him he was the only reporter she knew who never had a pen. (Maybe that's why he was always mixing up his figures.) It was all in the spirit of good fun between friends, and there was such a general bustle in the room that Mrs. Drake, who was attempting to do a little homework on me—asking where I'd gone to school and where I'd been published—gave up after a few minutes. Steinbacher, whose paranoia seemed to have deserted him altogether, never even asked me if I'd undergone sensitivity training.

Steinbacher should have known better. But Steinbacher was neither the twenty-four-hour-a-day paranoid I had imagined him to be nor did he seem to be naturally unfriendly. He was possessed of a curious naïveté, the same kind of naïveté, apparently, which had allowed the Anti women to pour their garbled stories forth without once reflecting that the easily accessible facts would tell me different.

And Steinbacher was not only naïve; he was likeable. He had a cheerful boyish quality that could have been quite disarming to someone who had not read his incredible columns. He liked to tell a good story, and he had plenty of good stories to tell. They often came from anonymous sources and sounded suspiciously like the tales in Gordon Drake's pamphlet. But Steinbacher would tell them with his eyes lit up, his face all innocent with wonder. It was as if he really did not know when he was altering the facts or improving on them a bit (as he obviously had done with that apocryphal classroom question about masturbation) but had merely gotten carried away in the telling, inspired, you might even say, like a fine front-porch gossip.

He was a tall man who was starting to get plump around the middle, and he had one of those changeable faces that can one moment look nearly handsome and the next moment appear eerie, almost mad. This curious effect had something to do with his coloring, which was all whites and greys, and something to do with the swollen fleshiness of his face. His eyes appeared to be unusually small for they were set beneath little puffs of flesh like those in a boxer's face, and these had a faint grey hue toward the outer edges that in photographs made Steinbacher appear mildly decadent and ill nourished.

The brightest and most articulate of the Antis, he was putting out an average of three news stories a week in addition to his weekday columns. He spoke rapidly, almost hectically, as if under a compulsion to divest himself of the numerous facts, rumors, quotes, and anecdotes that he picked up in his dizzying work week. Cancer would get him long before the Communists did. He smoked constantly. Despite his rapid-fire monologues, he managed to affect the reporter's air of slightly cynical fatigue, dragging on his ever-present cigarette with the perfect City Room squint.

He was a participatory journalist in the extreme. Twice in my presence he spoke proudly of the part he'd played in initiating events he would later cover. One of these was a kind of decency rally, a "Yes-In" for youth held in Hollywood, and the other was the issuing of a publication called, "The Medical Case Against Sex Education," a thing put out by SIECOP, an anti–sex education doctors' group. Steinbacher later wrote a news story about the Yes-In and hailed the publication of the doctors' pamphlet in his "School and Family" column.

He seemed to be spending a good portion of his free time on speaking tours. And he told me that he charged a minimum of $100 for each speech—plus expenses. He said he had given about 100 speeches in Orange County and environs alone—although he claimed he charged no fee for local area presentations.

Steinbacher's basic speech is taken from a script that he wrote for a record called "The Child Seducers." This record was one of the many propaganda—and money-making—gimmicks developed by the Antis during 1969. It was narrated in Shakespearean tones by John Carradine, who plays excellent Hollywood villains and who often narrates Fact Records.

The front jacket itself is a masterpiece of right-wing politico-sexual imaginings. It shows a prepubescent blond girl clad in a modest white slip and tied to a chair beneath a dangling un-shaded light blub. Behind her in a murky half-light is a collage of posters and large photographs of Marx, Lenin, Hitler, Trotsky, and Castro. The words, "Ein Volk, ein Reich, ein Führer!" are distinctly visible on the Hitler poster. The little girl's face, half in shadow, has a tight-mouthed, suspicious expression, as if she is watching someone opposite her prepare for an unmentionable act.

"A Factual EXPOSÉ of America's Sexploitation Conspiracy," says a helpful little notice to the left of the girl. "Written and Researched by John Steinbacher, M.A., America's Leading Authority on the S.I.E.C.U.S. Sex Education Program in the Public Schools," appears in yellow lettering to her right.

On the backside of the jacket large yellow letters scream against a black background, "THE CHILD YOU SAVE MAY BE YOUR OWN!" Here there are no more scary pictures, just a list of fifty-four "alarmed parent organizations" with the familiar acronyms like, "PURE," "CREED," "CHIDE," and, "POPE." The back cover makes interesting reading, for it also bears ads for Fact Records with engaging little blurbs about their contents such as, " 'THE NEW MORALITY' RAPE, RIOT AND REVOLU-TION from SATAN WORSHIP to the MARQUE [*sic*] DE SADE," part of an ad for a record called "PORNOGRAPHY." There is also some biographical material about the author ("A graduate of Pacific University, he attended San Francisco Theological Seminary for three years, and was a student at Long Beach and Sacramento State Colleges, as well as UCLA. He was for ten years a teacher and has been a professional social worker") and Mr. Carradine. And when you get tired of reading about them, you can glance over to a sinister little story about General William F. Dean's alleged exchange with his captors as he was being released from a North Korean prison camp. (Evil North Koreans: "We are going to destroy the moral character of a generation of your young Americans.") The General Dean story is repeated in the narration of the record itself, but the jacket designer must not have listened to it attentively because his version of the story does not exactly match the one Carradine recites.

The narration on the record is a brilliant piece of right-wing propaganda. It covers all the horrors of the right-wing para-noid thinker: student unrest, pornography, progressive education, behavioral sciences, crime, race riots, drugs, sexual perversion, and, of course, Communist conspiracies. Over half of the first side of the album is devoted to a kind of state of the nation essay in which sex education is not once mentioned. Instead we hear the paranoid litany, the touchstones of right-wing fears, gravely reviewed in the richly resonant tones of the Hollywood villain.

"Today the average age for assault and rape is fifteen," is the opening shocker. "The crime rate in the United States has risen 99 per cent in the past year, and over 90 per cent of the teenagers arrested for sexual assault are found to be in the possession of pornography. It is a time of flagrant immorality. A time when the old standards have crumbled as if hit by history's greatest tidal wave of filth and perversion and sexual promiscuity undreamed of even five years ago."

And atop history's greatest tidal wave undreamed of even five years ago, Carradine is off into his solemn reading of Steinbacher's masterpiece. For it really is a masterpiece, and it is a pity that the 1,900-word introduction runs on too long to be quoted here in full. One can hardly do justice to Steinbacher's rhetorical skills without reproducing the thing line for line. Here, however, are a few selections:

Nothing is sacred. And the profane is sold in the open market places of our cities, while God is mocked and the churches themselves stage dances for sex perverts. . . .

Free love is an outmoded and old-fashioned sounding term in a day when trial marriages and permanent shack ups have become the rule among America's college students.

The children are encouraged, on every hand, by the mass media and by the educators to consider their parents as hopelessly outdated and stupid old fogies. You've heard the expression, "Don't trust anyone over thirty." . . .

The Communist change agents are among us.

Such a change agent was John Dewey, infecting the entire bloodstream of our educational system with his vicious philosophy of permissiveness. Such a change agent is Dr. Benjamin Spock, whose changed young minds are now following him down the path of hatred of country, of love for America's enemies, and of assaulting all the institutions in our society.

This kind of thing takes up, as I said, at least half of the first side of the album, and John Carradine lets it roll forth, garbled syntax and all, in a voice that could be Caesar's own. Until finally the listener's patience threatens to give out, and Steinbacher's script—masterfully composed—comes to a climactic summation:

"These change agents have now come to the fore," we hear

Carradine intone, "brazen in their calculated efforts to subvert the moral will of America's young. The name of their diabolical game is: sex education, an innocuous-sounding name that contains within it," and here Carradine makes a slight dramatic pause, "the germinal seeds for," another pause, "*America's final downfall!*"

The remainder of the album contains little anecdotes—or sex education atrocity stories, as I had dubbed them (They reminded me of the "daily atrocity" tales told by the student activists in Nicholas von Hoffman's novel about a university take-over, *Two, Three, Many More*)—some tidbits about the alleged Communist affiliations of SIECUS members, wild tales of Anaheim classroom incidents, and vaguely attributed stories about teacher sensitivity training sessions. Toward the end of the second side, listeners are urged to write to the *Anaheim Bulletin* for more information.

Everything following the introduction could have been written by any number of anti–sex education pamphleteers. But that introduction was a rare piece of rhetorical outrage against twentieth-century America. And Steinbacher seemed to know it. For he used whole passages of it during his speaking tours.

*   *   *

Not long after I encountered Steinbacher in the Celebrity Suite of the Grand Hotel, I overheard him telling a joke to one of his fellow reporters in the newsroom of the *Anaheim Bulletin*. That newsroom was a cramped place, and from where I was sitting—behind the partition separating Campbell's corner from the rest of the room—you could easily hear conversations in other parts of the room. Steinbacher's desk was not far from the partition behind which I sat waiting for Campbell, and Steinbacher's voice was unmistakable. It had a nasal, faintly Midwestern timbre, similar to but deeper and sharper than the timbre of Hubert Humphrey's voice.

Steinbacher was telling an off-color joke. It was not a very crude joke, and it was certainly not a very funny one. But nevertheless, the fact that John Steinbacher, right-wing moralist *par excellence,* was telling it gave it some zest. It was the joke about the old couple who married in their dotage, and I remembered having heard it in something like the sixth grade. The punchline is, "They spent the whole honeymoon trying to get out of their car," the point being that the couple was too feeble to move, much less consummate their marriage. Steinbacher seemed to think it was a pretty funny tale because he told it with his characteristic enthusiasm and chuckled after he'd delivered the punchline. His listener, someone with a younger voice, was not appreciative, and remarked sourly that people don't have enough respect for the old folks nowadays. In more subdued tones, Steinbacher said something like, "Oh, you're quite right. I agree with you."

With his disarming friendliness, Steinbacher offered a few days later to treat me to lunch at a place where you could get "the best chili in southern California." It was a little restaurant in an older section of Anaheim called "The Soup Toureen" or "The Soup Bowl," and its chili was indeed good. But its clientele—several of whom seemed to know Steinbacher—were ladies who wore American flag brooches.

In that restaurant Steinbacher talked extensively about himself and his works. He said he was the child of Catholic immigrants (his father German, and his mother Hungarian) and that he had spent most of his young life on a farm outside the little town of Drain, Oregon. He seemed to think that his early environs had provided him with a good sex education. "You just sort of absorbed it, like osmosis," he told me. "Kittens were being born, baby colts were being born."

It was curious that he would boast of having gotten his own earliest sex education by observing animals, for the Antis all over the country were criticizing the Time-Life textbook which contained the pictures of dogs and chickens copulating. Still, Steinbacher did not want to seem sexually ignorant or even overly prudish. He, too, was sensitive to the proponents' charge that the Antis were full of "hang-ups." In the Grand Hotel, Steinbacher had told me that he and the other Antis were "not squares. We're not the kind of people who get up tight about seeing a little sex in a movie, for instance," he had said, adding, "We didn't get too upset about the topless place in Melodyland last year." (Nevertheless, the town fathers had tried to get rid of those topless dancers.)

But if Steinbacher did not want to be considered "square" or hung-up, he also had to worry about maintaining his image as a defender of decency. So he told me that his family had not allowed him to view the farm animals begetting all those litters at too tender an age.

"I think my parents kept us away from that sort of thing until we probably were in our, getting pretty close to the teens," he said. "I can remember my sister becoming quite upset at one point because—I was in about, I'd say, probably a freshman in high school—and my father had the female horse, the mare. He brought over this stallion from some neighboring farm, and he was going to breed the two. And my sister became very upset when she found me outside near the horses, see, and she shooed me away and raised Cain with my dad for letting me be out there."

Of course, most American children were no longer raised on farms, but Steinbacher definitely thought they did not lack opportunities to learn about procreation outside their classrooms. He had on occasion said that they would "be better off learning in the gutter because they would learn in bits and pieces and the filth wouldn't come with the authority of the classroom." He had made that remark to an audience in San Marino in April of 1969. "A lot of what is going on in Anaheim," he had told that audience, "borders on voyeurism."

Like Townsend, Steinbacher possessed an unusual capacity for making imaginative leaps. He could set forth in quick succession observations and theories that were totally contradictory. During the course of the lunch, he indicated that he thought being knowledgable about sexual matters and being sexually corrupt were "perhaps part and parcel of the same thing." He cited Sodom and Gomorrah to buttress his contention, calling those cities "probably the most well-informed country in history." Yet he later stated that he saw "nothing wrong" in children's becoming sexually enlightened—as long as they got their information from each other.

"I have a lot of confidence in young people," he explained with a benign expression on his face. "I think they're able to sort these things out pretty darn well."

If he had so much confidence in the young, I brought out, then why was he against their learning about sex in a classroom?

"Because I don't have confidence in all these teachers, see. I think," he said gravely, "some of the teachers have some ulterior motives."

Anyone studying Steinbacher's career might conclude that he had some ulterior motives of his own for his involvement in the sex education controversy. He had held at least seven different jobs since 1951, the year he completed his undergraduate work at Pacific University in Oregon. He claimed to have spent at least ten years as a teacher. But the information I gathered accounted for only seven years of teaching. And his work as "a professional social worker," in the record jacket's language, turned out to have been—when I questioned him closely—two brief periods of employment with the Los Angeles County Welfare Department. (I later wrote the Los Angeles welfare department to check this but received no answer.) He had taught at four different schools in the space of nine years (between 1952 and 1961), although for two of those years there was no record of his employment that I could find. He told me that he spent one of them, 1957, trying to run a talent school for aspiring actors and actresses in Hollywood. He was rather vague about his occupations during the period between 1961 and 1968, the year he came to the *Anaheim Bulletin*. And he said nothing about having attended the San Francisco Theological Seminary.

However he kept himself alive during the early 1960's, he turned up in June of 1965 in Huntington Beach, a town not far from Anaheim, and he got involved in a local struggle there between the Chamber of Commerce directors and the John Birch Society. The fight was over the Birch Society's right to enter a float in the town's annual Fourth of July parade. The Chamber of Commerce had refused the Society permission to enter its float, and John Steinbacher complained—on behalf of the Birch Society— to a reporter from the *Los Angeles Times*. On June 26, 1965, the *Los Angeles Times* carried a story about the Huntington Beach float debate, and in it John Steinbacher was referred to as "float committee chairman of the society."

Steinbacher told me that he had never been an "actual card-carrying member" of the John Birch Society. "I work with them," he said. "In this county . . . you can't hardly walk across the street without rubbing elbows with somebody who's involved with the John Birch Society."

When I asked him what year he had gotten married, he said, "Well, I don't think I really want to go into that part of it. I—all I want to say at this point is that I have a twelve-year-old son. My wife is dead. Let's not go into the other part of it, okay?"

Okay. It would be cruel to press him, I thought. But it was nevertheless interesting that he was the second of the more active Anaheim Antis who had declined to divulge a marriage date. His son, he said, was in a boarding school "up north. It's a problem, but not one that will last forever, I hope."

Steinbacher's past employment had been neither glorious nor, from what I could gather, very secure. He had never had it as good as he did on the staff of the *Anaheim Bulletin*. And even after he landed that job, he might have remained an obscure right-winger if Sam Campbell had not put him on the sex education beat after Hank Davis failed to come up with evidence of the great Commie plot. In one swift year Steinbacher had been transformed into an expert on the evils of sex education, but he had also, during that year, become about as famous and successful as an extreme right-winger could be—nearly as famous and successful as Gordon V. Drake.

Toward the end of our lunch I asked him where he had gotten the evidence that had convinced him that sex education was harmful. He immediately brought up Sweden. He was told that Sweden didn't really suit as an example because that country had never had universal sex education of the sort that had been offered in Anaheim, that only about 50 per cent of the Swedish schools had offered anything remotely comparable, and that there had been periods of puritan reaction causing a fluctuation in the type and extent of sex education in Swedish schools during the years after it had first been introduced (1938).

Steinbacher looked crestfallen.

"Has there been any, uh, any research done to show whether or not those schools that have it—if the kids are more moral or—?" he asked haltingly. Steinbacher, I had heard, frequently cited Sweden as a horrible example of a country ravaged by sex education. Yet his question revealed that he knew nothing concrete about the possible adverse or positive effects of sex education in Sweden. (His own newspaper would later print a tiny item about Denmark, which stated that "from 1650 to about 1880 the number of Danish women who were pregnant when married remained unchanged at 48 to 50 per cent, according to church registers. Since World War II the rate has dropped to 27 to 30 per cent." Steinbacher liked to say that 50 per cent of all Swedish brides went to the altar pregnant. But if he had done his homework, he would have discovered that brides in all Scandinavian countries had gone the the altar pregnant for centuries. Their men had often deferred marriage until they could be sure their prospective brides were fertile.)

I had found no studies on the effects of sex education in Sweden, I told Steinbacher.

"There's no research in the United States; for instance, there's no research on the Anaheim program as to good or bad," he said, sounding for a moment like a companionable fellow journalist sharing a frustration common to the trade: The behavioral sciences lagged behind events and were never ready with the answers to the social questions in the news when we needed them.

"So all we're going on is conjecture," he added with a smile.

But in a flash he had dug out of his trick bag of logical catch-alls another rationale for his stand.

"I think, frankly," he said, "that if you wanta experiment for the next ten years on these kids, that's, you know, fine, but not in a mandated situation." (Apparently he considered the voluntary Anaheim program to have constituted "a mandated situation.")

Here we had another of those curious contradictory switches in his reasoning. For if he thought that sex education was, as he had written for *The Child Seducers,* a "calculated effort to subvert the moral will of America's young," then how could he also think that it was an experiment? A "calculated effort" is made with foreknowledge of results, is it not? But such questions never seemed to trouble the leaping mind of our Steinbacher.

He was asked, after he imprudently admitted that he knew of no studies which showed beyond any doubt that sex education was harmful, whether he was not, in fact, simply using the sex education issue to broadcast his political philosophies.

"Well, actually it's part and parcel of the same thing," he replied, using his favorite expression. "When you have a state-mandated situation, you can't separate this one issue from all the other issues. It's all part of the same—of all these other issues.

"If you say, Am I using it? Yes, I am," he went on. "Because it makes it easy to point out to people how in other areas the state has also, uh, made certain incursions into their lives and into the lives of their children. And they become *aware* that the state has made these incursions and is making them in these other areas. And so it takes this incursion as a visceral issue to focus their attention, to get their attention. It's like shocking [a man] with electricity to get his attention."

*   *   *

While John Steinbacher was out covering Yes-Ins and telling people in other states that Paul Cook made $40,000 a year, Sam Campbell sat in his cubbyhole behind that partition in the *Bulletin* newsroom, grinding out his editorials in defense of Lawrence Welk and Old-Time Religion.

His secretary sat near him in the cramped newsroom, and on her desk was a basket of letters to Campbell, waiting to be answered. The answering must have been going pretty slowly during the time I spent in Anaheim, for the same letter lay on top of that pile for several days. "Dear Sam," it said, "Thanks for, . . ." and I could never manage to read any further because someone would always walk past the desk or Campbell would reappear from somewhere. But I had been able to read the name of the person who wrote the letter. Gary Allen. Gary Allen was a regular contributor to the Birch Society's *American Opinion* magazine, and the Society had even put out a few of his pamphlets. Allen discovered the evils of sex education not long after the Christian Crusade people discovered that they could make friends and money deploring those same evils.

Campbell himself had been a member of the John Birch Society, he told me, but he claimed he had dropped out in "something like" 1965 because he felt "that coercion was not the way to solve national problems."

Campbell was a balding, roly-poly man with an odd singsong voice that over the telephone sounded like the voice of a radio preacher, oozing piety. He wore dark-rimmed glasses behind which his expression was continually fluctuating. His eyes were responsible for this fluctuation. They would crinkle up at the edges, looking warm and twinkly one moment; the next moment the lids would squeeze closer together into a hostile squint. Campbell's favorite facial expression seemed to be the twinkly one, but even this one lost its appeal after you noticed that he especially liked to use it when he was making a remark that had bigoted undertones. He would crinkle the edges of his eyes, for instance, as he used the expression "the Jewish Testament" for "the Old Testament," and it was impossible to tell whether the phrase gave him a secret pleasure that showed in his eyes or whether he was merely using his eyes to soften the effect of its subtly anti-Semitic tone.

His singsong voice had a drawl that was straight out of the Southwest, out of the Oklahoma wheat country where he had grown up. And his metaphysics seemed to have been forged somewhere in that same region of the country. Behind him in his tiny office, a huge Bible lay atop a stack of papers and books. Campbell needed it as most journalists need their dictionaries. For he liked to find scriptural justifications for almost all his views.

"I think the central question is whether this subject matter has a religious bearing," he told me straight off, "or whether it is inherently religious in character. And if you examine the different religions on this point . . . you find that virtually all of the major religions deal extensively on the subject of the, uh, man and woman relationship. If you take it from them, just strictly the scriptural point, you'll find a great deal turns on that verse in the first chapter of Genesis which states that God created man, 'Male and female created He them. In His own image created He them.'

"Now, one interpretation of that is that man and woman are separate beings, the male is separate from the female and [a] different individual. This is the Christian point on it. The other view, which is promulgated by many of the cults, is that what this means is that when God created man, he created him a little bit male and a little bit female in the same body. And this becomes a theological justification for bisexuality or what we would call homosexual, uh, practices."

"Who justifies it? I don't understand," I told Campbell. "Which group are you saying justifies it?"

"I'm talking about the, uh, sex cults generally, and this is easily—"

"Which sex cults?"

"Well, there's only one, uh, major sex cult, and that is called Babylonianism, or the Egyptian belief or the Hindu belief, all go for this in some degree or another. The sex aspect."

The sex aspect. Just what did Campbell mean by that? He did not explain, and soon he was moving on to his point about how sex education, or as he called it, "sex instruction," was a "religious subject." Campbell was capable of seeing religion in just about everything. He was really inspired.

"Did you attend the adult sessions when they had adult courses at Anaheim?" I asked him.

"No, I did not," he said.

"Why not?"

"My religion would prevent it because I do not feel that this is, uh, that genital sex is the proper subject for discussion in mixed groups."

"And that's dictated by your religion?"

"That's my religion," said Campbell, nodding.

"What is your religion?"

"I'm a Christian," he said, his face breaking into an odd smile.

"Are you any particular sort of Christian?"

"I'm a Christian," Campbell stubbornly repeated, his eyes now crinkled into that good-willed expression.

Although this line of questioning was obviously not going to yield the name of Campbell's church, it did lead to his disclosure that he believed the Bible—both parts included—was "the precise word of God . . . just as true now as it was" when first written. But the "Jewish scriptures," he said, had "special promises to the Jewish people that they do not have for me."

Yet Campbell, a fundamentalist, had minored in biology at the University of Oklahoma. He told me that by way of indicating the thoroughness of his own "sex instruction." For, like Steinbacher, he was eager to present himself as a person with adequate knowledge of sexual matters. He implied that he had first learned about reproduction quite naturally during his youth on his family's farm outside Enid, Oklahoma. And he said that during his adolescence he had assisted his father, who for several years held a job as a jailer. "I think in that kind of environment, you pretty well get the picture," said Campbell.

He said he had moved to California in 1951 and that he had earned a master's degree in journalism at UCLA. Then he had gone to work for the Long Beach newspapers. His present home was in Placentia. Thus his four children, the oldest of whom was thirteen, were not even enrolled in the Anaheim District schools.

Campbell claimed that he had first become alarmed about the Anaheim FLSE program when he read an article about it in *Time* magazine in the spring of 1967. The article had said that four-letter words were used in the FLSE classes, and Campbell claimed that it had shocked him into investigating the Anaheim program. According to Davis, however, Campbell had not started his crusade against the program until after a trip to Oklahoma during the summer of 1968.

Campbell claimed that he had never met Gordon Drake, that he had only spoken with him over the telephone and had corresponded with him. Drake later corroborated this claim. And indeed, Drake had written in his pamphlet "Is the Schoolhouse the Proper Place to Teach Raw Sex?" that a Mrs. Catherine Allen of Anaheim, California, was among the people who had first alerted him to the sex education issue. According to Mrs. Howe, Mrs. Allen had been trying to organize her MOMS (Mothers for Moral Stability) group since sometime in the spring of 1968. So perhaps it was Mrs. Allen who first prodded Campbell into action —but the fact remained that Campbell didn't really come down hard on the FLSE program until after Gordon Drake proved that titillation in the name of purity sells just as well as titillation for its own sake.

And if the letters to the *Bulletin* from numerous backwater towns could be considered evidence of the issue's wide appeal, then Campbell had chosen his crusade wisely.

He told me that he was in correspondence with organized Anti groups all over the country, groups in Chicago suburbs, Parsipanny, New Jersey, and Tulsa, Oklahoma. He claimed that he had no formal organizational ties to any of these groups; he was obviously aware of the criticism that spokesmen for the National Education Association and SIECUS had levelled at the Antis.

Those people had said that the national movement against sex education was a cynically orchestrated movement, designed to recruit new John Birchers and put more money in the coffers of the Christian Crusade. So it was not in keeping with Campbell's image of himself as a crusading "Christian" newspaper editor for him also to appear closely tied to the bigger right-wing organizations.

Whatever were Campbell's motives, the editorial page of the *Anaheim Bulletin* frequently contained letters from people who wanted anti–sex education materials. And John Steinbacher often would run little items about far-flung sex education opponents in his column, items such as this one from his column for October 9, 1969: "Joseph Krane, Box 50, La Verne, Calif., is looking for materials on sex education. He advises the 'problem' has cropped up in his school district." And Steinbacher also provided a good amount of free advertising for numerous anti–sex education pamphleteers. That same October 9th "School and Family" column included a plug for a new paperback published by the right-wing Catholic newspaper *The Wanderer*, a book entitled *Sex Education: The Basic Issues*.

Campbell's "Christian" newspaper had supported George Wallace in 1968. Well, Campbell didn't like to call it support. He said his paper had "commented" on all the Presidential candidates, "and I suppose we spoke more favorably of George Wallace than [of] any [of the rest] of them, but we weren't wholly in favor of him, either."

Wallace was the right candidate for a man like Campbell, for Campbell supported an education system that was based, as he put it, on "choice," the gentleman's word for segregation. Although in Campbell's thinking racial considerations probably emerged rather infrequently. The Anaheim District contained, according to Sally Williams, "about two" black students. And the district's Mexican-Americans, somewhere in the neighborhood of 18 per cent of the pupil population, were not the troublesome children of migrant laborers.

No, Campbell wasn't concerned about integration. He disliked the public schools because he saw them as an arm of a monolithic federal conspiracy to bring about a "controlled . . . planned society." The people who were trying to produce this society were men like "Lyndon Johnson [and] Richard Nixon," according to Campbell.

"So, the school curriculum system is designed directly by them to make the children more docile?" I asked him.

"The school system as we know it today originated out of the French Revolution as a way, method, of separating the child from the influence of religious, specifically Christian, training," said Campbell. "It was imported to this country by Thomas Jefferson, among others. And, uh, since has been used to the same end. Horace Mann was a tremendous proponent of the separation of sectarian training from the schools. He did not, however, advocate at that time the elimination of the Bible from school instruction, and this is the dilemma. That if we say the Bible should be in the tax-supported schools, we are saying that the state should proscribe morals, but if we say it's out, why, then we are saying that the state should proscribe no morals."

"Which do you feel should be done?"

"Why, I think this indicates that the state does not belong in the schooling at all," said Campbell, the edges of his eyes again crinkled.

"You don't think there should be public education?" I asked.

"Because the," he started, and then caught himself, "no, now that's not what I said, is it?"

"You said you do not feel that the state belongs in schooling at all."

"That's right," he grinned.

"So that's the same thing as saying there shouldn't be public education," I insisted.

Campbell, however, was not going to let anyone put words in his mouth, and he gave me a little lecture about how he distinguished between the words "schooling" and "education." He was, as it turned out, hedging. For he soon declared, "I'm not even asking the state to get out of the schools. I say it doesn't belong in schooling."

After a few more questions, designed, I hoped, to pin him down, Campbell said, "Well, my ideal would be this. Put it oan [his Southwestern pronunciation] a competitive basis. If parents send their children to private or parochial school, then they ought not to be charged for support of a tax-supported system, or the state school system. Put it oan that basis, and let the best system win," he summed it up, his eyes, once again, twinkling with good cheer.

It was the contention of Hank Davis and the other defenders of the FLSE program that Sam Campbell's opinion of the public education system had a lot to do with his opinion of the FLSE program. They were convinced that Campbell would have found fault with the Anaheim school system even if sex education had never been introduced there. They thought that the FLSE program had merely provided the springboard for an anti–public education crusade that Campbell had long been eager to launch.

*   *   *

After I left Anaheim, Campbell took up a new education issue. He opposed a proposed bond-issue and a tax override, both of which were to be decided upon in January, 1970, by the district voters. Despite Campbell's efforts, there was a large voter turnout (26 per cent), and both of the items received the necessary two-thirds majority voter approval. Apparently the school administration had learned its lesson from the results of the April school board election. For there was much grumbling from Townsend about the political involvement of district employees, grumbling which got heavy play in the *Bulletin*.

As for the sex education battle, well, Campbell tried to keep that up, mentioning the "family-life instruction" program whenever he could in stories about the bond-issue and the tax override. But in early December the district board had decided to reinstate the FLSE program—drastically altered, according to Davis —in February, 1970. By the time the board made this decision, Royal Marten, its chairman, had resigned, and a new man had been selected by the four remaining board members. (Marten had resigned shortly before a new state law went into effect, a law which required that a vacancy that would run for more than four months be filled by a public election.) Dr. Dean H. Pritchett, a Long Beach anesthesiologist, had been selected, and as Edward Hartnell, the most liberal of the trustees, had refused to participate in the decision, it was thought that Dr. Pritchett was the Antis' man— for, of the three board members who selected him, two were considered anti-sex education.

Nevertheless, in early December the board—including Dr. Pritchett—voted to reinstate the FLSE program, albeit an altered version. Also by that time Kenneth Wines had been appointed the new superintendent for the district. And Wines had argued before the board in favor of reinstating the FLSE program.

In a melancholy editorial, which appeared one week after the board voted to resurrect parts of the old program, Campbell commented on their decision. His editorial, carried in the December 16, 1969, edition of the *Bulletin*, must have made the Anaheim Antis sadly wonder whether their efforts against Paul Cook and Sally Williams had been misspent.

Did family-life instruction fail because of a defect in the administration or because of a defect in the program? [wrote Campbell] After reading 800 documents and upwards of 200 books on the subject, our conclusion [is] that the failure is ascribable to neither cause. We lay the blame on the essentially religious character of the subject matter. In other words, we believe the subject itself is inherently unsuited for classroom treatment. We do not, therefore, pass judgement on the capability of any administrator past or present. Time will render the ultimate decision.

But the ultimate decisions against Paul Cook and Sally Williams had already been rendered. Yet the Anaheim right wing that had so fiercely fought for control of the district administration—and the direction of education in the district schools—found that that control had once again eluded them. Funny things happened to people when they got elected by single interest groups; they started thinking about broadening their appeal. And although Davis would later tell me during a telephone conversation that the sex education controversy had done lasting damage to the public education system in Anaheim—for that rule about the screening of "controversial" outside speakers was still in effect—the return of the FLSE program, even in modified form, was a sign of the limitations of the power of the area's right-wing radicals. They had not wanted any sex education—ever again.

Even the national movement against sex education seemed to be faltering in early December. For Steinbacher wrote an urgent appeal to parents in his December 11th column, trying to frighten them into keeping up the fight:

Dr. Mary Calderone said, not long ago, that the present wave of anti–sex instruction controversies is the last gasp for religious fundamentalists.

Unfortunately, in some ways, she may be right. Many people who have become involved, for the first time in their lives, were not prepared for the kind of long-range strategy and warfare required in these kinds of situations. . . .

If, in fact, the resistance does begin to pale, then the parents have surrendered their children to an arm of the political state, and it might just be the most important step they have ever made. . . .

What battle, parents, are you prepared to lose next?

How about when they come to your house to take your children away to a state-run nursery?

There was something about Steinbacher's tone in that column that made me think he had noticed a waning enthusiasm in the ranks of the Antis. Perhaps he was getting fewer invitations to speak to concerned parents?

One thing was certain: If the resistance to sex education did not continue, he and Campbell had a lot to lose.

The Fools Are Not All Dead Yet

At the time of the sex education controversy, the Anaheim Union High School District was the largest school district in the state of California. Yet the district's board room was scarcely large enough to hold 100 people. And Anaheim's fire marshall considered the place unsafe whenever it was occupied by more than fifty people. He had shown up at a lively session in November, 1968, to tell everybody as much. The transcript of that meeting does not reveal the exact number of people who were then crowded into the little room, but the fire marshall called it an "overload," and he insisted that all but fifty of the interested citizens clear out. (Needless to say, he was not well received.)

Every other board meeting was held in that small room, a place no bigger than an ordinary classroom. Board meetings were held twice a month, and when they were not convened in that room, they were held in the auditoriums of the district's twenty-three junior and senior high schools on a rotating basis. The board room was located in a building that stood right behind the flimsy-looking superintendent's office building, and it looked as though it too had been constructed under Cook's austerity plan. Over the doorway of the little structure hung a loudspeaker, which had been set up to broadcast the proceedings to the unlucky latecomers who had to stand in the parking lot outside.

It was the Anaheim district school board, or Board of Trustees, as they were properly called, that had suffered through the most consistent, relentlessly sustained exposure to the outraged mothers and fathers of the district. Paul Cook, Sally Williams, and Hank Davis had insisted that those unhappy parents belonged to a small, politically motivated minority whose real interest had no more to do with the sex education of their children than a politician's baby kissing had to do with his real and private feelings about infants. Cook, Davis, and Mrs. Williams could point to the convincing statistics of student enrollment in the FLSE program to bolster their contention that the Antis belonged to a definite minority. They could argue also that the April, 1969, school board election had not constituted a real test of community support for the FLSE program, that it had demonstrated instead a tired old truth about political organization: that a factionalized majority can lose to a well-organized minority.

There had been sixteen candidates running for those three school board seats, and at least five of them had sought the support of the sex education proponents. Three of these candidates were incumbents, and two of them, William Almand and Irving Pickler, had suffered some disgrace when it was discovered that their own company had sold some building supplies to the school district. Both men had also lost favor among the teachers because they had opposed one of the teachers' organizations on several occasions. One of the teachers' organizations refused to endorse them, and individual members of this organization (the Anaheim Secondary Education Association) went to work for two other pro–sex education candidates. The third incumbent, a lawyer named John Barton, did receive solid support from the pro–sex education elements of the community and the Anaheim Secondary Education Association. He was re-elected.

There had been at least two other anti–sex education candidates on the April ballot, and when the returns came in, they trailed behind Almand and Pickler, who received, respectively, the fourth and fifth largest totals. Robert Bark, an employee of McDonnell Douglas industries and a former state narcotics officer, had received the largest number of votes. He was a sex education opponent, but a relatively mild one, and his main campaign issue had been the student drug problem. "I firmly believe the (FLSE) program should undergo modification and I will make such recommendations at the right time," Bark had told the *Los Angeles Times.* "One will be that all ties with SIECUS be severed."

John Barton had received the second largest number of votes, and the lucky winner of third place was James P. Bonnell, a senior systems analyst who had put in many appearances before the old board. Bonnell had frequently complained that the FLSE program was teaching children how to masturbate, and he was a firm opponent of the program. Bonnell had told the *Los Angeles Times* that the SIECUS issue was secondary. "The main issue here," he had said, "is that the district program in itself is all wrong."

Hank Davis had analyzed the votes after the election, and he had come to the unhappy conclusion that Pickler and Almand might still have lost even if they had received the votes that had gone to the two other pro–sex education candidates. But the more general conclusion that Davis (and with him Cook and Mrs. Williams) drew from the election results was that a greater turnout would have meant victory for the sex education proponents. (The January, 1970, bond-issue and tax override votes—in which the turnout was over twice that in the April election—seemed to prove the validity of Davis's contention.)

To the three remaining board members, that April election seemed to have had a significance way beyond its actual vote count. It was after the election that Sally Williams was transferred and that the ruling on the screening of "controversial" outside speakers was passed. And when, in July, the two new board members took their seats, a thorough review of the FLSE program was undertaken, a review that led to the removal of all but five sex education books and two films from the district schools and to the ordering of public silence on the FLSE issue for all district employees.

The three remaining board members, Royal Marten, John Barton, and Edward Hartnell, had all defended the FLSE program in January of 1969—when the first review of the program had been completed. At that January 30th meeting, Royal Marten had stated:

It is my opinion, and I find no reason to default it, that the majority are in favor of the program in this district, a large majority. However, there are some who have a concern regarding certain things in the program. This is normal, and this is right, and this should be brought out, and this should be explored. The students need someone to talk to. I think the sex education program, for one thing, should be highly supportive to parents. . . . We have to develop additional devices or means by which we involve the parents, because this must be a cooperative effort. We must have a feeling also that we have the support, confidence, and ability to refer to moral and religious institutions. We must make additional efforts to be sure that we are screening the best possible teachers for this program.

And with those conciliatory statements, Marten had cast his vote in favor of continuing the program.

John Barton, who also voted in favor of continuing the program, had delivered a very strong statement, full of jabs at the California Citizens Committee and at their reasoning.

If one argues that pre-knowledge of bodily functions is somehow the exclusive domain of God [Barton had stated], I wonder with all due respect why He gave me a brain that is able to comprehend my body and even order its functions more capably to His service.

If I believe that truth is sometimes harsh, I have also seen that ignorance can be terrifying and cruel. So I choose, therefore, to seek truth rather than the questionable bliss of ignorance.

Finally, Mr. Chairman, I firmly believe that those in our district who share the concern of the outside group known as the Citizens Committee of California are honestly concerned. . . . I simply don't know what their exact concern really is.

All five board members had voted in favor of retaining the program, but Edward Hartnell had qualified his support. He alone had suggested some specific changes. He had urged that "intimate physiological discussions relative to development of the human body be carried on in separate classes in the seventh, eighth, and ninth grades"; that "the specific topics relative to marriage, child rearing, and husband and wife relationships be limited to the twelfth grade"; that "the topic of family planning by artificial birth control methods be confined to those students in the twelfth grade who have prior consent of their parents or guardians"; and that "the topic of sex perversion be confined to the twelfth grade and include a complete perusal of those sections of the California Penal Code that relate to this topic."

Hartnell had opened his statement with some sweeping generalizations about "the rising tide of pornography and immodesty," in the face of which he thought the FLSE program could provide a "healthy and wholesome attitude toward the procreative processes. Sounding suspiciously like a man who had bought one of the right-wing theories about the menace of moral decay, Hartnell had declared, "History reveals that the rate of the rise and fall of nations and cultures past can be correlated to the establishment and deterioration of the moral fiber of those nations and cultures." (Needless to say, Hartnell received the largest amount of space in the *Bulletin* the next day.)

When I arrived in Anaheim everyone I interviewed told me that something had happened to the three experienced board members. Ed Hartnell, said the Antis, was utterly changed. Royal Marten and John Barton, said the Pros, could no longer be relied upon for support of the FLSE program. Some of the local pundits thought that Hartnell had merely stood by his original views, while Marten and Barton had moved to the right, bending under the relentless pressure from the Antis.

But whatever course these three men had followed after that April election, all of the local analysts agreed that they had changed quite radically by the following October. And almost everyone said that Hartnell had been left high and dry by his two former allies, a lone and persecuted defender of the FLSE program. Marten and Barton had yielded to the demands of the two new board members, going along with their proposal for a second review of the program. Hartnell had fought the proposal, and, finding himself ever more frequently the target of the Antis' hostility, he had become embittered. And although he described himself as a liberal Republican, he had won so many liberal—and probably Democratic—supporters among the teachers and PTA chairmen that he was beginning to sound like a Kennedy Democrat. During a board meeting I attended, Hartnell took a liberal position on nearly every item that came up, and I got the distinct impression that he had undergone a painful shift to the left in the preceding months. Marten said that he recalled Hartnell casting his vote in support of the ruling on restrictions for outside speakers, for example, and Hartnell obviously was no longer in favor of that ruling by October of 1969.

Hartnell and Marten were the only two board members who submitted to interviews for this volume, and if Marten had had his way, he alone would have been my source for an administration version of the history of the Anaheim controversy. Marten had served for nearly fourteen years on the Anaheim district board, and he seemed to have acquired a patriarchal and proprietary attitude toward the affairs of the district. Since July of 1963 he had served as the board chairman, and he ran the board meetings in a style all his own. He sat in the middle of the row of tables that separated board members from their interested constituents, and he dealt out smiles and frowns to his colleagues and to speakers from the floor with a self-conscious and condescending pomposity that was most entertaining. If there was a large number of people in the audience who wished to speak, Marten often made room for them on the agenda. And if there was a great deal of business to be accomplished, he could speed it along, asking for quick votes from his colleagues and often persuading the hesitant ones to cast their votes with him in the interest of expediting the proceedings.

One year younger than Paul Cook, Royal Marten had himself taught in the Anaheim Union High School District for five years just before World War II. During that time James Townsend had been one of his students. Since 1947, Marten had worked at Santa Ana State College (a junior college), first as its head counselor and later as a member of the Sociology department.

He had also helped to set up a combined junior college district for the northern section of Orange County, and he had served for a time as president of the interim board for that district.

Marten had a variety of expressions and manners, which he could employ quite deftly in or out of board meetings. He bore a remarkable physical resemblance to former Secretary of State Dean Rusk, but his style was more like that of an aging judge. He could look reasonably fierce when he screwed up his eyes and spoke sternly. But he could also look like the personification of benevolent concern when he allowed the hint of a smile to creep into his eyes. And when he seemed to be uttering something he thought deserved special attention, he could peer over the top of his glasses and turn down the edges of his mouth like the most solemn of judges.

When I went to see him at the Santa Ana campus, a place where signs tell students to wear shoes and "acceptable dress," Marten scrutinized me through his screwed-up eyes and would not at first say anything for the record. He wanted to know what I thought of the Anaheim controversy and who my sources had been. I named a few of the ones that were not on the school payroll and then muttered something bland about how perhaps both sides had exaggerated their claims. Marten seemed to think that was a pretty sensible view, and, telling me to leave my tape recorder behind, he ushered me into a cafeteria where he bought me a cup of coffee and proceeded to dictate a statement for my notebook. (Later, he asked me to type up the entire statement and give him a copy of it.)

"One of the real problems that has caused a distorted image, a distorted picture of these classes," he said, peering intently at me as I copied down his words, " has been the tendency of reporters and news media, both magazine and newspaper, to seek out and magnify any matter that is sensational—neglecting to include what they consider the boring and prudent realities." As he brought out the last two words, he broke into a smile and then added an aside, something to the effect of, "That's good, isn't it? Prudent realities." He was, I realized, quite a vain man and that should have annoyed me, coming, as it did, along with his pomposity and his assumption that it was quite within his authority to forbid certain sources to talk with me. But Marten's vanity was not annoying; it made him somehow more appealing. He reminded me of one of those tyrannical fathers in a Henry Fielding novel, the sort of man whom everyone humored and liked in spite of their resentment for his arbitrary household rule.

"You can say that the board chairman felt that the election basically represented to a number of moderate voters a concern for a look at the program to assure themselves that it did not and would not involve salacious or overly frank discussions," Marten dictated for my notebook. "They were confused by the charges. . . . [And] the men who were elected did not run on the basis of complete removal of the program.

"I think the attack occurred—on the FLSE program in the schools—because many reasonable school-supportive parents became concerned over an overwhelming flood of pornography in the motion pictures, in magazines, plays, the whole bit, and felt that it could overflow into the schools. And this was where they [could] make a last ditch stand. This was also the point at which parents could express their concerns. . . .

"What I see on one side is a minimal group that sees a panacea for all our ills through some intimate form of group therapy, and on the other side, individuals who see in such a course the final destruction or our republic, of all morality basic to our republic. As a sociologist, I cannot accept either polarization. I believe that most parents are concerned with a full and good educational program for their children and [are] not desirous of taking extreme positions and embroiling their schools in useless conflict that would only interrupt the educational program for the youngster.

"If the program fails to be continued in some areas, it will probably not be because of the lack of its value, which I feel is well established, but because people tire of conflict and say, 'A pox on both your houses.' "

Marten seemed to think of himself as a kind of mediator, and he picked his words slowly and carefully. Despite the fact that he knew his statements would not be published for many months, he was not taking any chances with me. I could quote him to someone in the district, and he did not want his statements to stir up more wrath on either side than had already been generated. Throughout the interview I sensed that he was withholding his true judgments; he was using the kind of bland phrasing—calling the Antis "moderate voters," for instance—that a man running for office might use if he needed support from both factions.

Adding to my impression that Marten was holding back his true feelings about the controversy was the way that he spoke of the board meeting transcripts. He was the man who had to authorize their release for me, and he took great delight in telling me that I would find them interesting reading. It was as if he were saying, "When you see those things, you'll know what I really think."

It may have been wild speculation on my part, and it was certainly not fair to Marten, but I could not help imagining that behind his pompous façade, he was laughing heartily at the comic politics of Anaheim. The next time I saw him, he was presiding over the October 9th board meeting, using his variable manner to its full capacity. And he played the benevolent patriarch so skillfully that I could not decide, watching him, whether he was, as the students might say, for real, or whether he was simply giving a masterful performance.

Edward Hartnell did not find Marten particularly entertaining, however. For Edward Hartnell thought that Marten had retreated in the face of pressure from the Antis. Hartnell thought that John Barton had joined Marten's retreat. And Ed Hartnell, as he was known to everyone who attended board meetings, was one unhappy man when I met him.

He was a dark-haired man of medium height who had to tell you he was of Mexican-American descent before you noticed that his long aquiline nose resembled the noses of El Greco's saints. Hartnell's ancestors had occupied the land in Orange County long before those hardy Prussians bought a piece of it, and Hartnell told me that one of them, a William E. P. Hartnell, got honorable mention in some of the literature out at Knott's Berry Farm. William E. P. Hartnell had been an official translator at the transactions for the formulation of the Republic of California. But William E. P. Hartnell had lots of descendants, and Edward Hartnell's family was not among the more fortunate ones.

Edward Hartnell had grown up in neighborhoods where it didn't help to have fancy ancestry. He said that he had seen his father once, "for forty-five minutes," and he had gone to work selling newspapers and magazines at a tender age. When he was fifteen, he left home (which was then Oakland) and made his way down to Anaheim, where some of his other relatives lived. And if he didn't know by then, he was soon to have it impressed upon him that Mexican-Americans in twentieth-century America had to know their place.

He went to a public swimming pool where one of his relatives worked. He was told to come back on another day. "Mexicans and Negroes had to swim on Monday because they cleaned the pool on Tuesdays," he told me with a kind of grimace. And that was one of his earliest memories of Anaheim.

But America was very democratic when it came to accepting people like Ed Hartnell in the armed forces. So he managed to get into the air force underage, and when he came back, he had the G.I. Bill to help him through college. He went to Fullerton Junior College and then to Berkeley, coming away from the latter in 1957 with an M.A. in Art.

He had lived in Berkeley when the first Beats were there, and he dressed like a mild version of an old-fashioned Bohemian, with a turtle neck jersey under his white shirt. He owned an art shop in the middle of Anaheim, but he spent little time there while I was in Anaheim—or at least, he was seldom there when I called the place. His health had been bad for some time—he said he had had "a seizure" during the summer—and he attributed his malaise to the pressures of the sex education controversy.

Everyone had a theory about Ed Hartnell. The Antis' latest one was that he had been "conditioned" by a course in sensitivity training. (Hartnell had disclosed at a recent board meeting that he had been required to take a term of sensitivity training while he had served on the Anaheim Police Force.)

Hartnell's face looked strained, and he had great dark circles under his eyes. I had heard that he had grown quite irritable in recent weeks and that he sometimes walked out of board meetings in fits of exasperation. (Later Hartnell was to walk out of the session at which Marten's successor was selected.) When I first called him to ask for an interview, he insisted upon knowing my views about sex education, my politics, and who else I had talked to. When he asked where he could reach me and heard the name of my motel, he said, "Oh, my last investigation was out there." And he said it in a tone that seemed to carry a faint threat, almost as if he were telling me I had better watch my step. Later, after I read over the school board transcripts and saw one of the meetings live, I began to understand why Ed Hartnell was such a jumpy man.

For one thing, Ed Hartnell had not always been the enemy of the Antis. "I ran for the board of trustees when I was a police officer," he told me. "The connotation in this area is that a police officer must be conservative. These people probably thought that I was more right-wing than them. And what they did was they backed me." By "they" he meant the people who were associated with Townsend, the California Citizens Committee members, and the Telephone Taxpayers' Committee that Townsend had organized to combat the "socialistic" Anaheim city government. (Townsend didn't think that the city ought to be competing with "private enterprise" through its utilities holdings and its tourist facilities.) And Hartnell attended the same Catholic church that the Townsends and Howes attended. (Although he claimed that he never saw Mr. Townsend there.)

Hartnell had won his school board seat in 1967, and he told me that the Antis had invited him to their meetings when they first began to organize their decency crusade. They had obviously assumed that Hartnell would support them, and they must have been especially angry when he publicly defended the FLSE program. And although he did not say so, it must have pained him to invite the antagonism of the people who had supported him during his campaign.

For nearly twelve months Hartnell, Marten, and Barton had listened to the repeated complaints of the Antis from the floor of that little board room and from the floors of auditoriums all over the district. Mrs. Burns had told them about that tenth-grade girl who was alleged to have started masturbating after exposure to the FLSE program. Other mothers had submitted or read aloud sections of books that they found offensive, books allegedly used in the FLSE program. And a mimeographed pack of questions, allegedly swiped from one of those classroom question boxes, was passed around the district. The questions were crude and full of misspellings. A few of them were, "What happens when a man's penis won't fit in the vigina?" "Do you think frenching is the proper way of making out?" "What's six inches long and has 2 nuts?" "What happens to a girl who gets PG by a donkey? How does it happen? Does she have a baby or what?" "Are blow jobs sanitary?" At the top of each page which bore these and similar questions was typed: "SAMPLES FROM ANAHEIM HIGH SCHOOL SEX EDUCATION QUESTION BOX (They were not taught to spell but some of them can teach sex diviations [*sic*] to decent adults.)" And at the bottom of each page was the question, "How can people keep their minds on education if excited and mated by so called sex education?"

(Sally Williams had told me that the mimeographed questions were not typical but could possibly have appeared in an FLSE, question box. If so, some of them were obviously the joke questions that Dearth and Mrs. Williams had claimed went unanswered.)

The board had had to answer to the people who printed and distributed such material for almost a year.

But on July 1, 1969, the pressures on Marten, Barton, and Hartnell were compounded by the entrance of the two Anti representative into their own ranks. After that date, the arguments that had previously taken place between board members and speakers from the floor were carried on among the board members themselves. The arguments slowed down the regular business and wore out Ed Hartnell's patience.

The transcript for the August 21st board meeting contains a good sampling of the kind of exchange that Hartnell bitterly called "a return to the nineteenth century." On that date, Hartnell was getting some help from Barton. Much of the transcript is devoted to a discussion among the board members about whether or not the FLSE program was, in fact, a form of sensitivity training.

Bark and Bonnell had dug out some records and correspondence that indicated that a Dr. Iverson had run some workshops on group interaction for some of the Anaheim district's faculty and administrative staff. Bark was convinced that Dr. Iverson wanted to turn the whole FLSE program into an experiment in group therapy or "reality therapy." Bonnell was pressing for "a moratorium" on the whole FLSE program (which he later obtained). Dr. Iverson was involved with something the board members referred to as the "GIGI program." (GIGI was not explained in the transcript, but the acronym obviously stood for "Group Interaction something or other.")

To read the transcript with a full appreciation for its earth-shattering significance, you had to remember that sensitivity training was considered by the Antis to be a form of Communist-inspired brainwashing almost as bad as sex education itself.

During the discussion on August 21st, Hartnell, apparently unaware of the fact that he was serving as a Communist pawn, tried to explain to Bonnell and Bark what sensitivity training was designed to do. As the transcript shows, Hartnell did not have an easy time of it.

He said:

My experience with sensitivity training is that I have one semester. . . . I had one semester of it at Long Beach State College as a police officer. The primary purpose of that particular course was to allow individuals to improve their ability to communicate with each other, which seems to be one of the problems that has plagued the world since its beginning. . . . Now, I have found that by taking this course my ability to communicate with people and to sense what they meant by what they said was improved. Now, as far as the GIGI program [is concerned], I, as a board member, participated in the gathering of the principals two years ago. . . . All the principals, myself, the administrators, and Mr. Marten [were] there, I think, a day and a half. No-where did I experience a change of personality, nor did I experience a change, in the semester I took at Long Beach. . . . Our concern was that since there seems to be a communication gap that is widening among students and parents and teachers for reasons of probably lack of understanding . . . [we wanted] to improve the ability for the students and the teachers in class to communicate. That's what we did up there.

Hartnell went on to say that he still stood by his recommendations for changes in the FLSE program, the recommendations that he had made during the January 30th meeting. But he added, "I do not believe that this program warrants a moratorium nor do I believe—and I know—it's not being used as a vehicle for sensitivity training."

Then Bark and Bonnell had at him, as the transcript shows:

MR. BARK: Ed, you stated that there was no attempt or there was nothing in the GIGI program to change personality, however, I have the report here from Dr. Iverson that says, "Our goals in education must be to develop personalities who can live more comfortably with change than with static rigidity," and it's signed by Dr. Iverson.

MR. HARTNELL: May I answer that, please? So what? What does that mean?—to develop personalities that are already there so they can deal with change. . . . Are you modifying a personality by telling what happened in history? It certainly gives them a basis by which to make decisions in the future. . . .

MR. BARK: Without getting into a debate on the subject, I do feel that any attempt to modify or alter personalities so that the acceptance of change comes about automatically [means] there is an alteration of a personality, and I think that some people's personality is best presented with static rigidity. And why should we make everybody conform to change?

MR. BONNELL: Ed, I'd also like to say something to you here—

MR. HARTNELL: I'd like to end first, then I can answer you, okay?

MR. BONNELL: All right, go ahead.

MR. HARTNELL: It's a pretty obvious fact that none of us are the same by our contact with individuals daily. . . . You change, our personalities change without us wanting [them] to. It just does. It might change tonight.

MR. BONNELL: [who is obviously thumbing through some document] Well, I have the . . . my GIGI program is funded under ESEA Title I funds, and the major objective code list was to change attitudes of the participants . . . wait a minute until I find it . . . the major objective of the Title I in-service component [etc.] . . . Now, if this is not akin to sensitivity training, then I cut diamonds for a living.

Mr. Hartnell: Now, you talk about the change of attitudes. Every one of us knows that the formation of an attitude [in] engaging in any course of study, the job that you have—you have to have an attitude that reflects your ability, that will improve your efficiency in that job. It's all a matter of attitude and change. . . . We bring it about by ourselves sometimes. . . . You're saying sensitivity training like it's a bad word. If this is sensitivity training, attitude . . . change—I don't understand. What's the big deal?

Mr. Bonnell: Ed, I have five children, and I want their outlook on life to be that which is taught at home. I want the teachers to be supportive to that which I am teaching because I am legally responsible for the child. Now, if my child goes to school and his personality characteristics, his basic personality characteristics, his attitude, by whatever name you want to call them, are changed against my will or against a patron's will by someone who has instituted a course to make my children less than that which I want them to be, then I as a patron have the right to object.

Mr. Hartnell: Have you had the experience?

Mr. Bonnell: Yes, I most certainly have. That is what brought me into looking at Family Life and Sex Education as a parent, and that is what has brought many of these people into looking at it. . . . It is not the sex education part but the family life part, and there is a conflict between that technique being used in schools and that being used in most of the homes today. At least there is in my home.

Mr. Hartnell: All right. You have five. I have one, two, three, four—

Mr. Bonnell: Bob [Bark] has six.

Mr. Hartnell: I have seven, which is okay. Now—

Mr. Bonnell: You can see this board is not against sex education; sex per se, excuse me, sexuality.

Mr. Hartnell: Apparently your kids, you say your children's basic personalities have been changed by the program.

Mr. Bonnell: Let's put it this way. My children, my children's friends, have come home confused with the attitudes they have learned at school versus that which they have been taught at home and in their church. . . . Now, I have found the vehicle which has done it, whether you agree with me or not, and that is GIGI.

Mr. Hartnell: Absolutely, I disagree with you. My children, I have one entering junior high and one through high school and one just through high school. Now, their basic personalities have not been changed by this particular program. . . .

Mr. Bonnell: You see, Ed, you missed the point. Because the morality process as they describe it here is that of getting people to make a value judgement. . . . Every time . . . you have to concern yourself with values, you must make a student make a choice in behavior. No teacher will teach my child to make a choice in behavior.

That's my responsibility. I want to go back to the four R's, reading, 'riting, 'rithmetic and respect.

[This kind of thing went on for pages. And finally even Barton— who was later to go along with Bark's suggestion that all SIECUS materials be banned from the district—tried his own reasoning on Bonnel:]

Mr. Barton: I'm concerned with the possibility that this board may compound a nearly horrible mistake I once made—or almost made —as a father. I became quite concerned with my children's lack of appreciation of material things. Things came so much more easily for my kids than they did for my father's kids. But at one time I decided to impress my children with the feeling of less affluence. I would create a Depression in my own home. And you know what happened? It was quite foolish. In no time at all—the kids, of course, had to accept it because I'm bigger than they are—in no time at all the reaction from their own peer group was pretty bad. Not just from their peer group— "What kind of kooky father do you have?"—but the children them- selves were bewildered because the environment was confined to their own home. In my time and years, it was confined to the entire world.

Mr. Bonnell: That's exactly what I'm talking about. That this program is taking the child away from the parents, putting them in another world. And it's counter-opposed to that which most parents are teaching their children in high school, in the Anaheim High School District today. And I don't believe you can disagree with that.

Mr. Barton: I certainly will not. That's part of my point and my question now is this: no matter how valiant an effort we perform here to remove such an exposure, if we're so inclined, how, Jim, are we going to combat the influences we find in every visible and audible media there is: magazines, newspapers, television and radio? Again, the majority, the peer group, how can we shield them from it? In fact, is it not better, rather than to shield them, to hope that the strength of the moral training we give them at home will sustain them against what they are exposed to outside of home and, as a matter of fact, prove or give us as parents a chance to prove the validity of our own moral premises?

Mr. Bonnell: But the moral premises that you teach at home—in a sensitivity training class, [they] are teaching that there are no moral premises. . . .

Mr. Barton: . . . Jim, I don't know what your moral teachings are, and perhaps I am lulled myself into complacency on the premise you and I heard a long time ago. I think this was ascribed to a Jesuit priest centuries ago that said, give me a child until he's twelve, and you can't change him. I suspect, if not believe, that your child, ex- posed to a semester or a term of teachers who accidentally or delib- erately negate or contradict your teachings, [they] cannot be as [in- fluential] as you have been, having those children for years and show- ing them by practice and precept.

MR. BONNELL: I would have to agree with you but I would also ask you to read or look back at what you've told me previously about your children and whether or not their father is a kook. It is the peer group who judged them and not the teacher, and if the peer group judgment comes from the teaching profession, then it's second hand to your children. Do you understand what I'm saying here?

MR. BARTON: I'm afraid I understand you to say, Jim, that despite the intensity of your training as a father at home, it cannot withstand the rigors of the community outside your home. Is that correct?

MR. BONNELL: No.

And Bonnell could have gone on forever, it seemed. But Bark, finally losing patience with the discussion, moved to take up the next item, the matter of SIECUS materials. Bonnell was for banning all books by SIECUS members because "they have the same feelings when they wrote it as they have now." But when pressed by Hartnell, Bonnell said he didn't "know the facts." Marten suggested banning all books "which either bear the blessing of SIECUS or have been written by members of the board of directors at the time of their membership or thereafter." Hartnell wanted to know "how in the world" they were going to determine what books bear "the blessing of SIECUS." Marten then amended "blessing" to "endorsement." And in the end Hartnell cast his vote with the majority.

* * *

Things had been going from bad to worse for the FLSE program—and Ed Hartnell—since that August 21st meeting. The day I arrived in Anaheim, September 28th, the *Santa Ana Register* reported that the board had adopted, by a 4 to 1 vote, the "interim report," which forbade public discussion of the FLSE program by district employees until the program was revised and reinstituted. The report, prepared by Bark and Barton and handed to me by a gleeful Mrs. Pippinger, who referred to it as "our report," in effect, ordered the FLSE teachers to revise the whole curriculum of their program so that it involved the use of only the five textbooks and two films. (The five "acceptable" textbooks were: *Building Your Life*, by Landis and Landis; *Human Growth*, by Lester F. Beck; *Love and the Facts of Life*, by Evelyn Duvall; *Personal Adjustment—Marriage and Family*, by Landis & Landis; and *When You Marry*, by Evelyn Duvall. The first two books were to be used with seventh- and eighth-graders, the third with ninth-graders, the fourth with tenth-graders, and the fifth with eleventh- and twelfth-graders. The two "acceptable" films were

Girl to Woman and *Boy to Man,* both of which had been criticized by Anti groups in other parts of the country.) The "interim
report" had also stipulated that the revised FLSE program be
limited, at the appropriate grade levels, of course, to seven topics:
"boy-girl relationships, dating, etc.; necking and petting; onset of
menses and menstruation; bodily functions; body changes during
adolescence; marriage counseling (future family orientation);
[and] venereal diseases." Gone were the troublesome "deviations"
that Mrs. Pippinger and Mrs. Burns had with horror read about
in all their "borrowed" books.

Hartnell's vote was the lone holdout against this "interim report." He had called it "no more than a series of delays in getting
the program back into the curriculum." He told me that he had
interpreted the 80 per cent registration of students for the FLSE
program that fall as "a mandate" in favor of the program. And he
thought that his colleagues on the board were catering to the
whims of a minority of the district parents.

"Thus far they have had the teachers rewrite the program, the
course of study, four times!" Hartnell had exclaimed during the
interview for this volume. "Since last April. This is the *fourth*
time they're working on right now.

"This is making me mad, just telling you about this!" he had
burst out. And he had sounded as though he meant it.

*   *   *

Gathered in that undersized board room just two weeks after
the vote that had so exasperated Hartnell were some of the un-
swerving protagonists of the Anaheim controversy, among them,
Mrs. Howe, Mrs. Pippinger, and Mr. Townsend. They sat in the
front row, beaming up at the board that had recently done their
bidding. There appeared to be little purpose for their appearance
beyond the exercising of a habit. But perhaps they had also come
just to show themselves, gleefully, the current victors in the life-
and-death struggle for the preservation of Christendom. Mrs.
Pippinger was there with a new grievance; she thought that God
and Billy Graham had been unfairly slighted. For she had been
trying unsuccessfully to put up posters advertising the Graham
crusade in the district schools. So perhaps Townsend and Mrs.
Howe had put in an appearance to give her moral support. In
any case, Townsend's time wasn't wasted. Luckily for him, a
young social studies teacher provided an object lesson in just the
sort of liberal lobbying that Townsend was ever on the lookout

against, and Townsend was inspired by that young teacher into giving a spontaneous little speech on "academic freedom."

Gathered also in the board room, behind the Antis and along one wall, were a number of district teachers, come to support their Federation of Teachers.chapter president, Harold Rice, and their colleague, Frank Petrick, who had come to read a statement in opposition to the board's ruling on "controversial" outside speakers.

There were also some one-issue petitioners, like the parent who had come to put a plug in for a Band and Drill Team trip. But much of the audience for the October 9th board meeting appeared to belong to one of the two political poles in the Anaheim District, and the Antis appeared to be outnumbered, an unusual ratio for board meetings, I was given to understand.

Up front, behind the row of tables, sat four of the five board members (Barton arrived later) along with the chief administrators of the district, each with his own name plaque and special microphone. Hank Davis was there, wearing a suit and looking very proper. Beside him sat Paul Cook's loyal secretary. But Paul Cook was notably absent, and in his place sat Kenneth Wines, a large, dour-faced man who handled hostile board members' questions about expenditures with admirable restraint.

You could not tell by looking at the two "freshman" board members that they were not of the same mind as their colleagues. Bark, who appeared to be putting on weight, wore his hair quite short, but then so did Hartnell. Bonnell had a round, pale face that might have given some hint of the intensity of his political visions, and he wore thick, black-rimmed glasses that, once you heard him speak, seemed to suit a man with rigid tastes. But Barton, when he appeared, did not look like any wild sort, either. He was tall and long-limbed, thin almost to the point of gauntness, and he sat way off at the end of the row of tables, as if he needed extra space to think in.

The meeting was already underway when I arrived, which meant that I had missed the Pledge of Allegiance, a ritual I would like to have seen Townsend perform. But barring that, there was little of interest that had occurred. The board members had approved the minutes of the last meeting and given their reports, so the agenda told me. And just as I sat down, they were taking up the first item of business, their "revised policy for recognition of employee organizations." Harold Rice had something to say about that policy, representing as he did, the relatively new

Anaheim Federation of Teachers. Bonnell then displayed a little concern, which led me to believe he wasn't sympathetic to unions. But no sparks flew, and the board soon took up the next item on the agenda: "Lee Baxter, industrial arts chairman, Western High School, has asked permission to take five eleventh or twelfth grade students to UCLA to participate in a research project. . . ."

This was, I feared, going to be like any school board meeting anywhere. A boring series of trivial decisions. After two weeks in Anaheim, I had hoped for a better performance, a heated argument, a fresh display of titillating materials in the name of decency, George Wallace's statements thinly disguised and rephrased by James Townsend, an impassioned outburst against "this poor white trash" from Hank Davis. Surely, the board room was the one place in the district's forty-six square miles where one could expect to see the vital and dramatic heart of the curious sex education controversy. Surely, one could count on the Antis to perform their best here. So I reasoned, and as the board methodically ticked off its mundane and tedious business, I became more and more discouraged.

But eventually, the anticipated clash occurred. It was milder and subtler than the sort of clash I had hoped to see, but it contained all the dramatic elements of the controversy I had been reading and hearing about from the protagonists offstage. It came after Petrick read his statement in opposition to the outside speakers rule. The teachers applauded him; Bonnell and Bark questioned him sternly; Townsend jumped up to question his motives; Hartnell came to his defense. And Royal Marten treated him to a pompous put-down, which revealed just how sensitive to the judgments of the right wing Royal Marten had become.

You could not fully appreciate the meaning of that clash, I was later to realize, without first understanding that the tiny board room was inhabited by more than the sixty-odd corporeal beings sitting there, visible to the naked eye. It was inhabited also by ghosts. It was inhabited by the spirit of Max Rafferty, the state superintendent of public instruction, who had in April of that year told his state board that "the SIECUS program is not appropriate for California schools." Rafferty had let the Antis know how he personally felt about sex education, too. When they wrote to him, he sent them copies of an old article he'd written (although he didn't say where it had appeared) called, "Who Needs More Sex Education?" The piece was allegedly written in December, 1964, which, some might say, made Rafferty a kind of prophet. The reasoning he used in it was similar to that used in the Antis' propaganda, only they usually compared sex education to driver education rather than lessons in safe-cracking:

People are not discouraged from becoming safe-crackers by learning how to manipulate tumblers in the dark [Rafferty had written]. They avoid a life of crime because they are taught from infancy that crime is evil.

Similarly, I don't think we are going to crack the sex delinquency puzzle by seeing that all the kids understand the mechanics of sex. The only way society has ever found to discourage misconduct is to label it clearly as either a crime or a sin, or both, and then punish it accordingly. Until we as a people recognize openly the ancient truth that illicit and premarital sex is an offense against both God and man, if only because of its chilling selfishness and complete disregard for others, we will not see the current situation improve.

Mr. Rafferty had doubtless observed how effectively our society had discouraged drinking by labeling it first a sin and then a crime. But then, Rafferty was the kind of man who took things like sin and public morality seriously, or at least he had made a good show of doing so. He had not only recommended sex education guidelines for the California schools but he had asked one of his assistants to prepare a set of moral guidelines as well. (As of this writing, Rafferty's moral guidelines had not been adopted by the state board, and they were considering a revised version that had been prepared by a Protestant minister, a version the true believers criticized as being too "pluralistic.") Rafferty told *Harper's* reporter Marshall Frady that "the trouble is relativism—this teaching that there are no moral absolutes. This breaks down all lasting values. This is what many think is responsible for the breakdown of our moral heritage, the trouble on the campuses."

There was in addition the ubiquitous spirit of Ronald Reagan, the darling of the Orange County magnates of moral absolutism, hovering in the air of that board room. Reagan had brought his own bright flesh and blood face to Anaheim to be photographed with Billy Graham at the opening of his Anaheim crusade. Everybody knew where Ronnie stood, of course, but he still liked the people to *see* him standing with the legions of Jesus. Ronnie was the kind of man who liked to ask his audiences, "Where were we when God was expelled from the classroom?" Ronnie thought that the movies were being ruined with all those sex scenes. And he had been urging his state legislature to pass antipornography laws that were unconstitutional, just to keep the theater owners and topless dancers tied up in the courts.

·There was also the spirit of State Senator John Schmitz, whose corporeal self had appeared before the Anaheim board almost exactly one year before, when the Antis had presented their case in a packed high school auditorium. Senator Schmitz, who was an avowed Bircher, represented the 34th Senatorial District—which included the two-thirds of Orange County where Anaheim lay— in Sacramento, and he had made it clear that he represented particularly the more decent of his constituents. He had told the Antis during the famous October 17th meeting that he was going to introduce legislation to make sex education voluntary, and he had carried out his promise. Thanks to Schmitz, California teachers could lose their credentials if they took any child into a sex education class who did not have written permission from his parents to be there or if they used any materials in such a class that had not been first displayed in a well-advertised and convenient place for parents' perusal. Schmitz had told the Anaheim Antis that he thought they could "make a real excellent case that the whole movement for sex education is part of this general humanistic movement in this country and in this state." They might be able to fight it in the courts on the separation of church and state issue, he had implied.

Rafferty, Reagan, and Schmitz had what one might call top billing on the list of visiting spirits from the right wing. There were whisps and traces of countless others hanging in the air, traces of every religious or political fundamentalist from George Wallace to the incredible Mrs. Margaret Scott, mother of thirteen from San Mateo County, where sex education was creeping into the schools. She, too, had spoken at the Antis' extravaganza the year before, declaring then that the "little people who have the children and who pay the taxes and love our God and our children and our country" would "fight to the death to defeat this program." (Mrs. Scott and her husband were later jailed for keeping several of their children out of school.)

But there were also some phantoms from the Left along with some of the vague, ineffable *Zeitgeists* of the young. There was, for one, the image of Angela Davis, a young instructor from UCLA, who had for nearly two weeks been in the news. Angela Davis was a very beautiful black woman who had gotten the Regents all in a flap by proudly flaunting the fact that she was a bona fide Communist. The newscasters never showed us her Party card, but they showed us a lot of her Afro-coifed head, a head that the Regents wanted and that the UCLA faculty and administration would not yield up.

So there was photogenic Angela Davis, the latest living insult and outrage to the local anti-Communists. And surrounding her in the hazy allegorical visions drifting through that small room were all the young heroes of the campus revolts, of the Chicago and People's Park battles, and of the whole spectrum of black movements and eruptions. There were, most potently, the spirits of the Black Panthers with their gleaming guns and proud posture. There was, worst of all, that defiant exile who had made a best seller out of righteous wrath, that terrifying Cleaver who could impudently herald the Twist and the Beatles for having accomplished just what the right-wingers were afraid they had accomplished. "The Twist," Cleaver had written, "succeeded, as politics, religion, and law could never do, in writing into the heart and soul what the Supreme Court could only write on the books. . . . It was Chubby Checker's mission, bearing the Twist as *good news,* to teach the whites, whom history had taught to forget, how to shake their asses again." And the Beatles, Cleaver wrote, had "highjacked" the Twist from the blacks and made a music that was "soul by proxy. . . . A long way from Pat Boone's White Shoes. A way station on a slow route traveled with all deliberate speed." If the Anaheim Antis had not read Cleaver, they got his message from Congressman Utt and others like him who thought that the new music, soul or otherwise, was eating away at the moral fibres of America's young. Cleaver was to them perhaps the most terrifying of youth's heroes, but there were ample more. There were the Beatles, themselves, whose message could be understood without a reading of *Soul On Ice,* the Beatles, who had sung "Why Don't We Do It In The Road?" to millions of innocent young. And there was Abbie Hoffman, whose sexual and political defiance was best expressed in his favorite line, "We don't want any Mothers. We want Motherfuckers!"

In the nimble minds of the Anaheim Antis it was a small jump from Angela Davis, who spoke in a gentle voice and didn't swear on camera, to the angrier or wilder heroes of the young.

But there were other youthful spirits, closer to the walls of that board room, and these had been lately threatening to enter the board room in a more solid form. These were the spirits of the Anaheim students themselves, a group that dressed and smoked in manners that were close enough to the styles of the eastern ragamuffins to worry the likes of Townsend. Whether they had also picked up much of the political philosophy of the eastern crew was still undetermined, but Ray Welch and two other students had sent the district board a politely worded letter in June of 1969 which could have given the more panicky among them grounds for worry. The letter had said in part:

We would like the establishment of a student advisory board, formally recognized by the A.H.U.S.D. Board of Trustees, for the purpose of a "communication channel" between the Board of Education and a group of students *so the board may, if they desire, seek the students' opinion on an issue or proposal!* [their emphasis] . . . We do not feel it is necessary for students to sit at each Board meeting. However, if there is something that should be shared by the students or the Board, time should be allowed so the student[s] might be placed on the agenda. This direct channel of communication could resolve many issues with promptness which under the present circumstances act as lingering problems.

The letter was signed with a courteous "Respectfully submitted," which was light years away from the "nonnegotiable demands" style of the college radicals. But it had been written "on behalf of the Associated Student Bodies" of the whole 35,200-student district. That smacked dangerously of an emerging group consciousness.

That all-day student conference in the Disneyland Hotel had also smacked dangerously of an emerging group consciousness. And if you read the "recommendations and suggestions" to come out of it, you could begin to think quite seriously that more than marijuana and crazy costumes had wafted into Anaheim from Yippiedom. According to a list drawn up by Ray Welch, some of the suggestions were:

—Get student participation in school regulations, curriculum and administration.
—When twenty or so students want a particular study subject taught, such as philosophy or ethnic studies, give them this opportunity.
—Have students evaluate the faculty and counselors.
—Teachers guilty of racism and discrimination should be fired.
—In teaching, facts should be given, but a student should be allowed to develop his own opinion and express it.
—The school newspaper should be the voice of the students.
—Abolish dress regulations and concentrate more on interesting and exciting learning experiences.
—Plan a meaningful sex or family life education program aimed at students in a particular community. We might have been able to avoid a lot of "guesswork" in regards to the F. L. & S. E. program if students could have voiced [their views on the original curriculum].

The students had already been granted their liberalized dress code, but they apparently wanted a lot more. (And the board members were later to set up a liaison with a student advisory board—perhaps out of the fear that those mild-mannered students would otherwise begin making their suggestions a little more forcefully.)

So balance in your mind the statements of Max Rafferty; a picture of Reagan smiling beside Billy Graham; the fundamental-ism-saturated reasoning of Senator John Schmitz; the head of a gentle-voiced and photogenic lady Marxist; Cleaver's guns and allegorical (because mostly in jail or dead) black army; Chicago, 1968; Woodstock, 1969; wild-haired Abbie Hoffman; and the respectfully submitted demands—sorry—suggestions of the Ana-heim District's students. Because they were all there in that flimsy board room as young Frank Petrick rose to speak.

Petrick was a tall and earnest-looking man who appeared to be in his early thirties. He was dressed in a style that gave no clue of his civil-libertarian concern. He rose from the ranks of the teachers in one of the back rows, and talking quietly but in the rushed phrases of tension, he told the board that he had two documents to read. "Oh, get this," Mrs. Pippinger whispered to me, meaning that I ought to turn on my tape recorder. Petrick be-gan to read:

"Teachers who wish to make use of outside speakers are required to have said speakers, if deemed controversial or possibly controversial, approved by the Board of Trustees. It is the considered opinion of the Anaheim Federation of Teachers that this policy will not serve the best interests of students, parents or educators and will seriously curtail the effective utilization of community resources by the schools.

"A closer examination of the Board's decision immediately brings to mind a number of crucial questions. *What* is and *who* is con-troversial? Everyone would agree that we live in an age characterized by great social change and upheaval. Youth, our students in particular, are as never before seriously questioning and examining their own and society's values. In the context of our age, who is not controversial? The policeman? The churchman? The legislator? The businessman? The revolutionary? The teacher?

"The above question leads naturally to the next. By what criteria will the board judge who may or may not speak? Students, teachers, parents, board members, each individual has a commitment to his own particular view of the world. It would be most unfortunate if a hole were torn in the pluralistic fabric of our American society by a prevailing exclusiveness of a point of view of any one group or in-dividual.

"A clarification of the criteria of judgement to be used notwithstanding, the present policy still appears unwise in view of two other considerations.

"What will be the practical consequences of such a policy? One may comfortably assume that those approached to volunteer their services to the schools would be articulate, involved individuals to whom time is a very valuable commodity. How many will be made unavailable because of the successive, time-consuming scrutinization that they must agree to . . . undergo?

"Finally, and perhaps most important, what effect, whether intended or not, would this policy have on teacher morale? And further, again whether intended or not, how does this policy reflect on the capabilities, character and discretionary powers of teachers?

"Teachers themselves are members of the larger community of which the school is a part. They are certainly aware of that community's standards of taste and propriety. At the same time, they have a commitment and a responsibility as educators to examine with their students the points of view, values and objects available to them in a free society. Much lip service in educational philosophy is paid to the idea that a good teacher is challenging, provocative and objective. And common sense tells us that that which is provocative, challenging and objective must be construed as controversial.

"In view of the above arguments, the Anaheim Federation of Teachers requests that the board of trustees rescind its directive governing the use of outside speakers by the teachers of the District."

Flipping through his papers, Petrick told the board, "The second document I have here relates to the, what I believe are the practical consequences of this program. It's a letter addressed to myself at Western High School. . . .

"Dear Mr. Petrick," he read, "Pursuant to our conversation concerning a prospective talk by me on the Soviet invasion of Czechoslovakia, scheduled for some time in November, I now wish to inform you that I must reconsider your invitation. When you recently informed me of the decision of your school board to screen guest speakers, I was deeply amazed by that decision. It strikes me as highly unusual policy for a school board to execute. Since I have never been exposed to a similar procedure in my previous speaking engagements before crowded groups and professional audiences as well as several schools, I am stunned by the necessity which now seems to have [been] imposed on me to be officially cleared or accepted.

"Can you please tell me of the exercise of this kind of policy in any other neighboring school district?

"In discussing this matter with colleagues and friends, who unanimously react with disbelief to what is now the policy of your school, I find that I am the butt of ridicule. One of the most frequent questions thrown at me is, 'Bill, when did you last get a security clearance?' Speaking candidly, I must confess that it is unavoidable to consider that what I am supposed to do in order to speak to your students is exactly what free men in Czechoslovakia are now compelled, under penalty of the most vile punishment,. to do also by the Soviet masters who recently invaded that tragic land. They must be screened and possibly censored before they speak. That was one of the unmistakable issues that helped the Soviets intervene in Czechoslovakia. Is this what is intended in my case?

"As you can clearly gather from this letter, I am extremely displeased by your news. I suspect that this is not of your making. I understand that you yourself are compelled to comply with it. May I share an opinion with you? It is simply that I react to your Board's new policy as dangerous and an obnoxious precedent that is, to put it mildly, unhealthy, unnecessary and undemocratic. Why does your Board apparently distrust and fear the judgment and discretion of the teachers?

"I regret very much that, under the present circumstances, I must refuse the invitation to speak to your students."

Petrick read the name of the letter writer (but it was inaudible) and his title, Doctor of History.

Bark was the first to respond. He wanted to know whether Petrick would invite a speaker "who appeared at three previous schools, and each of their appearances ended in riot."

"Well, I believe that someone who is going to speak, if there is clear-cut evidence that this individual might necessarily attack one of the students or, uh, become physical, I certainly wouldn't do that. But I think that teachers have enough discretion to see through these kinds of things," Petrick answered quietly.

"What grade do you teach?" asked Marten in his finest stern tone.

"Eleventh and twelfth."

"Do you feel that your reference also covers the seventh, eighth and ninth—with equal strength?" Marten asked.

"It's a question of trusting *teachers*," said Petrick, his voice beginning to sound impatient. "Teachers who teach seventh and eighth and ninth grade *know* what kinds of speakers they can handle in their grades. . . .

"And I might say, some of the most engaging teaching days, the most enjoyable teaching days, the most exciting teaching days, the most effective teaching days I ever *had* have been when guest speakers have come. And guest speakers, by the way, who in some respects challenge the value systems of our students because—I invite any of you gentlemen to walk into a classroom someday, uh, and try to sell a point of view.

"Our students today are *aware* of what's happening," he went on, speaking more rapidly as his excitement grew. "They're *concerned* with what's happening. And I think we ought to *prepare* them for what's happening—by exposing them to all kinds of points of view in a controlled situation, where we have follow-up, where they *know* what's coming, where they have an opportunity to question people, to clear their own minds, to arise [*sic*] questions in their own minds. After all, this is what education is all about."

In the back of the room the teachers broke into applause.

"One more question, and then I will leave it at that," said Bark. "I think in the Anaheim High School District I share with you the, the integrity and responsibility of our teachers. But are you saying that *all* teachers are infallible?"

"We *certainly* aren't infallible," said Petrick, "but I think it's a *very dangerous thing* to institute preventative legislation. . . . The very foundation of this country and our jurisprudence system is that a man is innocent until he's proven guilty." Petrick's voice now expressed real exasperation. "And if we want to close all channels and stop people, not give them the opportunity to even make a mistake, I think what we'll *lose*, what we'll lose will be much greater than what we will have gained if someone *does* make a mistake."

"Are you aware of any speakers that this board has not approved?" asked Bark.

"As the policy came down," Petrick started, and then, catching himself, said, "that is not the question. The question is that— from a practical sense and from a, the reflection on the integrity of teachers, I don't think that the board *needs* to do this. It's time-consuming and in a sense—how does the—what policy? What criteria will the board use?"

"I think there's an issue you keep missing, if I may interrupt this just a second," Marten broke in. And looking ever so professorial, he lectured:

"The function of a public school is more than to provide a forum on public issues. I mean, there must be some other purposes for which citizens have established public education."

"I'm certainly aware of that sir, and—" Petrick tried to cut in.

"And I think you are making a judgment," Marten went on, "that the total position of this board or the total effectiveness of the educational program of this district would be seriously *impaired* if there is, shall we say as you're inferring it, some restriction on making the school a public forum, you know, for discussing public issues.

"Now, I think there's a difference between education and a forum. And I point out to you, sir, that, if you're worried about what happens in Czechoslovakia, you didn't need to worry. The television is working night and day on programs that give them a full aquaintanceship [*sic*] to public problems. And I think nearly everywhere young people turn, they have this. And, of course, you have a point. If speakers can come in and enlighten them and give them an understanding of these things, this is good. But what you are talking for is complete freedom, is it not? So that, in a sense, the teacher could, if he wants to, make his class into a forum rather than—"

"You're missing the point, Mr. Marten," Hartnell spoke up. (Marten, it dawned on me, was the only board member whom no one addressed by his first name.)

"No, I don't think I do!" Marten exclaimed. Hartnell muttered something. Bark or Bonnell stood up for Marten. Hartnell went on muttering. "No! No, just a second," Marten said, turning to Hartnell, "you can have speakers, that's *one* thing. But a public forum is a different thing."

"I'd like to address myself to your question, if I may," Petrick politely drew their attention back to him.

"Go ahead," said Marten.

"Nowhere—implying that, uh, teachers would make it a public forum, again, I think, is a reflection on, on, again, our character and our discretionary powers.

"You suggested that education is something else. Education *is* to make students aware, as I said, become aware of what's happening. And they can't always *do* this, by the way, in the public media. They can't always do this effectively. I might refer to, uh, Brinkley from Huntley and Brinkley, and someone once said that most people in America get their news from his program. And he said, 'They'—excuse me—'They get damn little news.' And, I'll have to agree with him."

At this point, Bonnell roused himself. He started saying something about how there were "two sides to the question," the first part of which I missed because Mrs. Pippinger was grumbling next to me.

"What was the statement you made? I don't have my glasses on [and he didn't]," Bonnell was saying to Petrick.

"In reference to what?" Petrick asked.

"In reference to, uh, uh, the board usurping, not having faith in the teachers. What was your terminology on that again, please?"

"Well, I'll read it," Petrick shuffled through his papers.

"You don't need to read it. I think you recognize, I think you recognize by the same token, can't we turn around and say that you're doing the same thing to us, Mr. Petrick? [Bonnell had obviously remembered Petrick's point, for he hadn't waited for Petrick to repeat it.] That you have no faith in the ability of the board? And, finally, the last question is, regardless of, of what decision is made, who has the final accountability for that which happens?"

"I would imagine the teacher has a great deal of accountability," said Petrick.

"I imagine that the board has the entire accountability," Bonnell said flatly. Hartnell started to groan.

"Well, again, I'm thinking of the practical consequences of this kind of program," Petrick tried once more. "I realize that you are accountable, but I can't help saying that it goes back to the issue of having faith in your teachers."

"Yeah, then, why don't we have television in every—tape recorders and tape every single class so that we make sure that we're *responsible* to all the citizens and we know *exactly* what's going on—" Hartnell broke in, his voice sharp with sarcasm. Marten tried to cut him off by uttering "Ed, Ed," like a conciliatory parent, but, in the end, what·stopped him was the applause from the teachers in the back of the room.

"Ed, you're making a bad mis—" Marten started after the applause died down.

"Well, I think it's—" Hartnell interrupted.

"*You are putting this board in a bad light!*" Marten interrupted him. "You are—"

"I don't, I'm not heading to that, Mr. Chairman. I was thinking that the particular discussion bordered on the ridiculous at some times," Hartnell said shaking his head.

"You're purposely misinterpreting. And I don't think it's even the responsibility of this present board. I think that's [a rule passed] by the previous board—" Marten brought out, his own exasperation making him stumble over his words.

"We have an accounting—" Hartnell tried to inject more sarcasm.

"It was *made* on the previous board of which *you* and I, also, were members! And I'm not sure you didn't vote for it!" Marten declared with a chuckle.

"Yeah, I'm sure I, I wouldn't now!" Hartnell retorted, shaking his head again.

"No, he's had sensitivity training since then," Mrs. Pippinger said to me, almost loudly enough for Hartnell to hear. Actually, Hartnell's sensitivity training had occurred before the ruling was passed, but maybe Mrs. Pippinger thought that sensitivity training produced a delayed reaction.

Hartnell lapsed into silence and Marten told Petrick that the board would not make any decision on the ruling that night. Petrick asked for a clarification of the ruling. Then Marten, who was apparently still worried about Hartnell's comments, turned to him and said:

"Ed, it was also agreed, Ed, that the board would not actually check the speakers, but where the deputy superintendent did not feel he would take the responsibility, it would be referred to the board."

"May I ask a question of the board, sir?" Petrick, who was still standing, politely asked.

"Yes!" said Marten, all cheerful benevolence.

"You mean [to say] now, of course, you wouldn't screen every teacher. [He had obviously meant to say "speaker," but the slip expressed his fear.] What criteria would you use in determining which speakers you would decide to—?"

"I would presume that when you ask us our criteria, we could equally well ask you yours," Marten said, sounding less benevolent. "And I think if you have faith in your criteria, perhaps you can have faith in ours."

Petrick persisted in his polite tone, asking how the teachers were to work with the ruling as it stood. It left teachers "up in the air," he said, because they didn't know what kinds of speakers would be regarded as controversial by the district powers. Bark helpfully explained that he had heard that some speaker had caused trouble the previous year, "destruction of school property" and the like. Kenneth Wines, the deputy superintendent, said his office did the screening, anyway.

"For teachers this is a very difficult thing, the question of who is controversial, who can cause trouble and who cannot cause trouble," Petrick explained, and, using cunning diplomacy, he asked for the board's help. "If the board has some insight into this above and beyond that of the teachers," he said, "or if they would like to work with teachers, perhaps social studies teachers in particular, I'm sure we'd be happy . . ."

"The door is open," said one of the board members (I think it was Bonnell).

"What are you doing tomorrow?" asked Petrick. And even the Antis laughed as the board members looked momentarily uncomfortable. Reaching board members outside of the meetings, it seemed, was a universal problem, shared by the decent and the indecent alike.

Meanwhile, Townsend had become inspired. And he asked for the floor. Marten urged him to be brief.

"I asked for a time to speak after Mr. Rice and after Mr. Petrick," he began. "One, I'd like to call this board's attention to the fact that as the elected representatives, you are here, as you know very well, to govern the district and to represent the people.

"In a free society, we have long since discovered that if we are to remain free that we as people must always stand behind those public officials that represent us. And this goes into the very subject that came up here tonight regardin' controversial speakers, for example.

"In the twenties to the forties, it was the other fellow, it's two sides to the question, you should always hear it. And then a little later it was academic freedom. And then it was a Communist under every bed, until now when somebody mentions Communism, 'Oh, you see 'em under bed.' And now, it's become a question of, 'Well, what do you mean? What is controversial?' And questioning every law that we ever established by the liberal element of the teachers' profession. So that they cast a shadow of a doubt as to whether we have a right to do something or whether we don't.

"Here we have something that the public has suddenly recognized that falls in the realm of common sense. And no longer are we going to tolerate this cry of 'academic freedom' as a license for the teaching profession to do anything that they desire.

"Now, I'd like to ask this board, and I'm sure this board will do so without my even bothering to ask, to govern what goes on in this school district, and that's certainly a part of the controversial speakers."

And that, if you could follow it, was what Townsend had to say about Mr. Petrick's concerns. Of course, Townsend was all for supporting his elected officials that week because they had been doing things the way he wanted them to.

He had more to say on another point. Well, it wasn't really a point. It was the establishment—for the record—of his hostility toward the newly formed Anaheim Federation of Teachers.

"And while we're on the subject," he concluded—"the subject" apparently being teachers—"I think it would also be well if we considered some dress codes for some of these teachers, including haircuts, clothes and such." That got a laugh from the teachers at the back of the room.

Townsend made a few more remarks about "the guise of academic freedom" and then sat down. He had given the cue, apparently, for two other people rose from the Anti ranks to say their pieces. One man read from a *Bulletin* article about some professor of education who had told (according to the *Bulletin*) a chapter of the California Association of Student Councils to "break the rules" and "develop political activity." The speech had allegedly been delivered at one of the high schools in the district.

"If you allow so-called professors of education to advocate breaking the rules, teacher evaluation, and political activity," Townsend's friend told the board, "you'll have a Berkeley on your hands before you have a chance to understand what is going on!"

Then Townsend's second friend rose to say he had hoped the new board would "have totally removed" the sex education program forever. "The name of the course by itself is such a flagrant deviation from the public [something] that on its face the course cannot possibly be incorporated into what might be defined as the concern of the public. I think the board has evaded the principle of, lacks the definition of what is the realm of public education. And I think their abdication of the principle, that is, to hide it is what they've done. I think the majority has a legitimacy when it argues a point between a good, a better or a best proposition. But to assume that the sex education program falls in that category is a contradiction. The only time that a majority is *illegitimate* is when it decides something is good when it is absolutely bad. The Family Life program is, in fact, bad."

This speaker, who later would refuse to give me his name, was rather difficult to follow. But his awkwardly stated message was that the board had compromised when it adopted the "interim report" on the FLSE program.

"You're trying to hide," he concluded, "by the vagueness, the nameless, and the shameless vote of the majority something that should be brought to the surface and determined: What was wrong with it [the program]? And if in fact this portion is good, *why* is it good?

"I'd like to tie this into the bond issue," he went on, as I began wondering just what it was he was trying to say. "There're a couple of types of murder that I know of," he said. "One is where another person assails you and you—become dead. The other one is known as suicide. In the one, or in both instances, the thing that causes them is a lack of self-defense. Actually, not a lack of self-defense; it's more or less an abdication of it.

"This program is, in my opinion, a form of moral suicide. It always has been. Now, then, for you to come along and kill a portion of it and not complain or prosecute or determine or discipline any of those people that brought it in is an abdication of responsibility.

"Now then, for me to support a bond issue to continue along in a process which was, in fact, immoral to start with, or evil to start with, is a form of moral suicide for me because I hate it. Thank you."

Mrs. Pippinger then rose to put in a good word for the Billy Graham posters. "If Billy Graham can't even be announced, how many tears are you going shed over the SDS not being allowed to talk?" She got a little applause from her friends for that gem. And, really, I thought, she had a point. Because Billy Graham's religion and her strange politics were so closely linked in her mind that she must have felt as though her political freedom were being violated as she had been turned away from the schools clutching her Graham posters.

Marten then called a recess. And when it was over, he sped the business along, rushing to complete the agenda before the evening drew on too long. The Antis had not returned after the recess. They had had their say.

The next afternoon the *Bulletin* carried a frontpage story about Mrs. Pippinger's little speech. The headline said something like "Billy Graham Too Controversial For Schools." There was nothing in the *Bulletin* story about Mr. Petrick's statement or the discussion that followed it. Sam Campbell knew what his readers' interests were.

*   *   *

The day before the bond election was held I called Hank Davis. "I'm probably gonna get fired day after tomorrow," he told me. He had been working too conspicuously with the committee that had been set up to canvass voters and push for passage of the bond issue and the tax override. "I don't think we're gonna win both issues," he said. "There are too many people blaming us for Angela Davis."

But they did win both issues, and about ten days later Hank Davis was fired. The Antis tried to get the Orange County District Attorney to look into what they called "irregularities" in the balloting. The County Board of Supervisors and the County Clerk certified the ballots nevertheless, and they told the Antis that their own board would have to deal with any possible irregularities. And, no doubt, the Anaheim board did hear from the disgruntled losers.

Nearly two months later (March, 1970) Davis sent me a press release announcing the formation of a new political organization in Orange County, an outfit called People for Educational Progress, which had its own catchy acronym: PEP. Claiming a "charter membership" of more than 400 people, the president of the new group had told newsmen that "it was the students who really prodded us parents into standing up for positive programs in education. I am one of many parents involved in PEP because my daughter was so distressed at the destruction of the Family Life and Sex Education program in the Anaheim Union High School District. We think it was a very important program to many young people." In the press release, Edward Hartnell and a number of elementary school district board members were listed as members of the new organization.

After a good year and a half of right-wing dominance in the odd scenes of the Anaheim sex education controversy, the reluctant liberals seemed to be mobilizing themselves. Davis was of the opinion that it would take them at least two board elections (or until 1973) to gain firm control of the district board, but he thought it could be done. That January, 1970, bond- and tax-vote was the largest in the district's history, he wrote. And that meant that if they could just get the voters to the polls next time around, the liberals would have nothing to worry about.

Meanwhile, however, the board was still effectively dominated by the Antis. "Teacher morale is low and declining," wrote Davis. "The present FLI [Family Life Instruction—he unconsciously used the *Bulletin's* acronym for the course] is an emasculated mess. Few students are attending."

And meanwhile, you could count on the Antis to go on practicing their politics of last-ditch outrage. They could never win—or not for long. They could not salvage those poor old myths that they had learned back in Enid, Oklahoma, Drain, Oregon, and rural Kentucky any more than they could legislate against the Beatles. Though they might rant and rave against all the strange and terrible invasions of a godfearing man's universe, though they and their friends might pursuade Max Rafferty to take a stand against a nonexistent atheistic Commie blueprint for mass seduction of the young, they were, in the end, outnumbered and alone.

One of their own children had confessed to me that he had stopped going to church on Sunday, and all his friends had, too. He didn't want his parents to find out, so he asked me not to refer to him by name. Every Sunday he dutifully left the house and went off to eat breakfast at some restaurant to keep up the charade. But sooner or later his parents would find out that heresy was slouching toward the most decent of Anaheim homes.

And, really, the Antis seemed to know this already. They seemed, in fact, to feel themselves virtually surrounded by heretics. Like their anonymous spokesman, who had declared, "The only time a majority is *illegitimate* is when it decides something is good when it is absolutely bad," they would rage courageously against the tide, trying to do battle with the majority and the enlightenment that had so cruelly dwarfed their certitudes. They spoke with the passion and the fury and the meanness of the dispossessed, and it was only natural that they should develop elaborate visions of their doom. For they had been besieged by a world that no longer lived by the rigid transcendentalism that had kept them going all those years when they were struggling out of rural America. And they were not only surrounded now by the indifferent, tepid believers and nonbelievers in the adult population. They had of late suffered the outright blaspheming of all that they held dear—not merely Jesus but also the toil and trouble and hard climb out of Drain, Oregon, or wherever—in the pages of the national magazines where the supple and irreverent young were grinning out at them topless and bottomless and everythingless.

It was not for nothing that Mrs. Howe took *Life's* special issue on the Woodstock Music Festival with her wherever she went to speak against sex education. She knew how it would infuriate those tired and pent-up or, perhaps, just wasted flag-waving ladies to see the young throwing away whole lifetimes of ascetic and purely private agony before their eyes. It was as if the young were taking all their coins, as if they were breaking into every secret hiding place, the brick, the board, the mattress, and tossing

all those coins to the wind or, worse still, giving them to the first
beggar to come along unwashed and without one trace of the bitterness that comes from the long and pointless agony of restraint.

If the Antis liked Wallace, it was not merely because he was a
racist or even, as some saw him, a populist. It was also because
Wallace, too, was a loser. Wallace was a last-ditch regionalist
every bit as doomed as was their last-ditch regionalism of the
mind. And they were ranting against a Reconstruction even more
devastating than his, for theirs was metaphysical and without
borders.

Still, they had had their impact. They had exercised an influence over the district board that far exceeded the power of
their numbers. They had purged the Anaheim District of three
administrators and they had pretty much banned all talk of non-
coital sex and premarital sex from Anaheim's classrooms. If you
read back through the *Los Angeles Times* file on the controversy,
you could see that they had also scared a couple of boards in
neighboring districts away from sex education. If you read the
right-wing literature or the newspaper clippings from countless
other cities, you could see that they had become symbols of hope
to just about every mother and father who feared the awakening
in their children's loins. They had also become symbols of dreaded
community reaction to countless school superintendents and
school boards, and the movement they had helped to spawn was
keeping a man at the National Education Association busy doing
full-time muckraking on the right wing. For that brief period
during the fall of 1969 when they had seemed to control the
Anaheim district board's every move, Sally Williams and Paul
Cook had not regarded them as the pitiable keepers of a waning
creed.

"I think it [the Anaheim controversy] will hinder districts who
were going to follow our plan," Sally Williams had said during
that period. "Because no superintendent wants to get into this
Donnybrook that we have been in. And rightfully so. There's a
lot of other things going on in the school district. And Mr. Cook
has had to devote his full time to this controversy instead of taking care of other matters in the district. And the other staff are
getting very unhappy about this and are not too understanding.

"So there is a lot that a superintendent might risk—even
though he were in favor of this kind of education. He's risking his
whole district operation."

Paul Cook saw it all as part of a larger and ominous resurgence
of the right wing.

"I think there are many rather influential people in this country who are discounting the influence of the Christian Crusade and the John Birch Society . . . and other similar groups," he said, several weeks before Spiro Agnew was to make his "effete snobs" speech.

"But the people in the, what you might say, where they make news and where they make opinion, New York, Los Angeles, Hollywood, and so forth, they tend to deprecate all the [right-wing groups]—'The Birchers are old-fashioned,' or, 'They're out of it.' They're *not* out of it by any means! They are today making more of an impact on our society than I believe they've ever made. . . . Because we're now in a conservative political swing. They add to this, and I think we're gonna find their influence is gonna rise in this country, and it's gonna be, to my mind, it's very, extremely negative."

Cook was, of course, speaking before the bond-issue victory. But if he could be faulted for possessing a certain myopia of political vision at that time, his words at least expressed the pessimism he was then feeling for the Anaheim District.

And yet, what, in the end, did the Anaheim District lose? Not nearly as much as the Antis had hoped to destroy. The schools had lost a program that was merely a reasonably subtle preparation for middle-class living in the very middle-class monogamy that all those righteous mothers and fathers revered. They had lost an imaginative superintendent and (except for the one school that got her) a school nurse with a fine dry wit and a manner that invited the trust of students with difficult adolescent problems. And they had lost a public relations man who had considerable political skills and pluck enough to stand up for his principles.

Temporarily, at least, the teachers had also lost some of the freedoms that they had enjoyed before that April board election. Their board of trustees—dominated by three conservatives—had not withdrawn that ruling on "controversial" speakers. And Davis wrote that the board members were beginning in early 1970 to cater to the Antis in their policies on "censorship and social studies." (While I was in Anaheim some of the decent ladies had told me that they wanted to get rid of certain shocking English texts and all traces of un-Americanism in the social studies courses.)

But in the long run, the Antis would probably lose out. Because they had succeeded in rousing the lethargic liberal voters of the district. Their valiant attempts to transcend their initial weaknesses (being a minority; enjoying little respect among the professionals) with shock materials and spokesmen from the medical right-wing were beginning to backfire on them. They had obviously alienated more adults than they had succeeded in winning to their cause.

Just before the new liberal organization emerged into the news, however, Sam Campbell was named as one of the recipients of the God and Country Awards that are given out each year in June by Congregation Mishkan Yicheskel, Tujunga, in Los Angeles. Lawrence Welk was to be getting a God and Country Award along with him. Campbell had been picked "for his defense of decency and the rights of the producing individual." So, at least, the Antis got *something* for their trouble.

When I asked the wise old soul who probably knew more about the history of Anaheim than anyone else in the town, who had seen in his youth the fiery evangelists and Klansmen rave against the wets as James Townsend raved against the sex education proponents and the culture of the young alike, when I asked this "long-time interested citizen" of Anaheim what those Prussian draft-dodgers would have thought of the Antis' curious crusade, he replied:

"I think their opinion would have been:
    'The fools are not all dead yet.' "

three

•

Beyond Anaheim

"It didn't matter what sex education could do because the argument was not about facts, it was about beliefs."

Two Missionaries Contend

Sex in the Old Testament is clearly regarded as a precious gift from God, not only for bringing children into the world but also for the satisfaction of one of mankind's deepest needs and for sheer enjoyment. The one basic restriction placed on the satisfaction of sexual desire is that it should occur only within the framework of God's holy institution of marriage.

God speaks out plainly and repeatedly against all adultery, fornication, prostitution, and such perversions as homosexuality.

The attitude toward sex expressed in the New Testament reinforces Old Testament conclusions. . . .

Like all other blessings, it is to be received with thanksgiving and sanctified by the Word of God and prayer.—from "Is the School House the Proper Place to Teach Raw Sex?" by Dr. GORDON V. DRAKE (Tulsa, Okla.: Christian Crusade Publications, 1968).

This is the message that we need to get to our young: that sex is not a problem to be controlled but a great force to be utilized; not a relationship to be played at by children, but an intense and vital human excursion, admission to which must be earned by some degree of maturity.—DR. CALDERONE, in SIECUS reprint No. 12 entitled, "Sex and Social Responsibility," which appeared in the *Journal of Home Economics* in September, 1965, adapted from her speech at the American Home Economics Association Annual Meeting in Atlantic City, New Jersey, June 22, 1965.

In March of 1964 an obscure little college professor with troublesome patriotic instincts had a run-in with the local Establishment that was to shape his destiny. It could be argued, of course, that his destiny had already been shaped, that he had long since entered upon an irreversible course toward the outer limits of the American Right. For he was the son of a cost accountant, and he was reared in Wauwatosa, Wisconsin, where conservative Republicanism was writ upon men's genes. It even could be argued that the polio that struck him motionless and speechless in his prime gave the final and irrevocable shape to his destiny. He had made a stubborn struggle back to mobility, the kind of struggle that might have inured any man to a fiercely individualist world view of the sort that he was later to express. He had hobbled his way through graduate school in Arizona and then earned a doctorate in Education at the University of Denver, and, with his legs still too weak to hold him for very long, he had gone back to his home state to teach at a college in Oshkosh. His legs were never to regain their former strength, but his speaking powers returned to normal, and along the way he acquired a passion for using them that was to prove itself a liability in Oshkosh. Well, it was not strictly the use of his speaking powers that got him into trouble but merely his compulsion to be heard. For that compulsion led him to write an article for a local newspaper, the *Appleton Post-Crescent*, an article in which he imprudently displayed his overdeveloped patriotism, "an article," as the university president would later remark with a clear effort for understatement, "which we thought at the time did not reflect good scholarship."

The piece appeared on the editorial page of the *Post-Crescent*'s March 15, 1964, edition under the headline, "Teacher Lambasts History Education." It's author was therein described as "a full professor of education at Wisconsin State College—Oshkosh [now Wisconsin State University—Oshkosh]," as an "associate dean of instruction and director of institutional research" at the aforementioned institution, as director of something called "the Wisconsin Foundation for Educational Research," and as a former Democratic candidate for Congress in the state's sixth congressional district. The professor's impolitic article began:

What some senior college students in teacher education don't know about the U.S. Constitution is amazing . . . amazing because in a short time these students will have the responsibility for the education of our youth.

Their knowledge of our Constitution reflects the pattern in many of today's public schools that stresses the world history–U.N. concept at the expense of American history.

You could get the gist of the article right there, but if you read further you learned that the people behind the "world history–U.N. concept" were those questionable power brokers in the National Education Association and the offices of UNESCO. Especially dangerous, you learned, was the UNESCO pamphlet series, *Toward World Understanding*, which, the professor was convinced, made readers think that "it is wrong for parents to teach their children to be patriotic." (It should be recalled that the same UNESCO pamphlet series was banned by the foresighted Anaheim school board during the early fifties.)

"We don't wish to revive the colonial school where 'fire and brimstone' were so eloquently taught," the professor continued. "We certainly don't advocate a system in which the civil and church governments are one, but there must be a way to recognize God in the schools, and to eloquently teach about the religious experiences which gave strength and purpose to so many of our patriots who founded and *built* our nation."

The professor was bothered by a few things outside the schools as well, for he went on to say that there was in the general population too little respect for the local police force, that TV programs sometimes discouraged respect for the law, and that politicians cared little for morals and ethics. He deplored:

"Above all, a watering down of virile patriotism. It has reached a point where red, white and blue poles, mail boxes, soft drink signs, and gas stations are very nearly the only reminders of the symbol of America, 'The Stars and Stripes.' "

But before you gave up in total despair over our waning national spirit, he offered you one hope—the Wisconsin Foundation for Educational Research (which had, incidentally, been incorporated the previous week). This organization would be reexamining teacher education with a view toward discovering the antipatriotic influences in the field of education. For, as the professor put it:

"We can no longer afford to have our future citizens conditioned to accept a socialistic panacea for all problems of government and society."

The day after his article was published, its author, Dr. Gordon V. Drake, was summoned to a meeting with the president of the university, Dr. R. E. Guiles, and several administrators. According to his own account of that meeting, they told him that any articles he might write in the future "should be submitted to the administrative officers for their guidance, counsel, and approval." And one week later they told him that his administrative titles and duties were being withdrawn.

President Guiles was later to tell me that Dr. Drake had given the newspaper two false titles for himself. Dr. Drake was a full professor at the time, said Guiles, but he was neither an associate dean nor a director of institutional research. According to Guiles, Drake's administrative duties had instead involved "work in the Guidance Center" and the responsibilities of "As-

sociate Director of Registration." Nevertheless, Drake stoutly
maintained that he *had* used the proper titles and that the university administration had simply denied that those titles ever
existed after the article appeared in print. It was Drake's belief
that the administration merely used the quarrel over the titles as
an excuse to censure him because they did not like his views.

It is, of course, Drake's word against theirs, but Guiles did tell
me that the article was not considered evidence of "good scholarship" by the university powers. And certainly the administration
must have regarded Drake with uneasiness ever since he had arranged for Wallace to appear on campus (another of Drake's
impolitic shows of patriotism). Drake could not be fired, because
he had earned his tenure. But a godfearing, patriotic sort like him
could be made to feel uncomfortable on a campus where his
critical powers were not appreciated. He could get to feel downright discriminated against—especially after being told to let the
administrative officers advise him on how to exercise his right to
freedom of expression.

If you look at the pattern of Drake's career after that administrative reprimand, you can easily conclude that it was what the
student militants would call a radicalizing influence. For Gordon
Drake went from the Oshkosh campus to a superfundamentalist
college in Cape May, New Jersey, where its founder, the Reverend Carl McIntire was busy cranking out right-wing attacks on
the National Council of Churches and broadcasting his rabid
anti-Communism over his Century Reformation Hour, a program
carried by hundreds of radio stations.

Drake went to Shelton College in the fall of 1964, having
landed the position of Dean there. And from that time forward,
Drake was a darling of the far Right. His writings were read over
the radio outlets of the Manion Forum, another Commie-haters'
program produced by a man named Clarence Manion, who in
1967 was known as a member of the National Council of the
John Birch Society. In 1966 Drake began writing fairly regularly
for the Birch Society's *American Opinion* magazine, and he was
listed in the program for the Birch Society's annual Fourth of
July God, Family, and Country rally, in 1967.

Drake was a born pamphleteer, so once he had cast his lot with
the radical Right, he had no difficulty becoming one of their stars.
He was considered such a fine propagandist in those circles by
1967 that McIntire's biggest rival approached him with a tempt-
ing job offer. Billie James Hargis, the founder of the Tulsa-
based Christian Crusade was the man who made the offer.
Drake should have considered it flattering, for Hargis was trying

to usurp McIntire's role as the Biggest Bible Thumper of them all. He must have considered Drake as one of McIntire's prize possessions. (Drake had a bona fide Ph.D., after all, and those were rare documents in right-wing circles.) Hargis offered Drake the job of planning and staffing the college, that he, Hargis, said he would be building in Tulsa.

In early 1968 Drake deserted McIntire and moved to Tulsa. Thinking that he was helping to raise funds for the new college, he went out on the road with Hargis, armed with speeches about the creeping socialism in the schools and the Communist plotters behind the National Education Association. Drake was ultimately to resign from the Crusade, bitterly claiming that the money he had raised was being used to pay off the organization's old debts. (A spokesman for the Christian Crusade later claimed that Drake had never helped to raise funds for the new college and that all monies raised for that purpose had been put into a special account. Those funds, said the spokesman, were *not* being used to pay debts unrelated to the proposed college.) But for nearly two years, Drake traveled the country with Hargis, speaking at his revival meetings, writing up radio scripts for the Crusade's many radio programs, or putting together pamphlets about the terrible things your schools had been doing to your children.

Drake resigned from the Christian Crusade in mid-November, 1969, after he and Hargis had a falling out over a suit that Drake and a group of parents had started against the Tulsa school board. (The suit was an attempt to get sex education out of the Tulsa schools.) Hargis had repeatedly asked Drake to drop the suit because he did not want to antagonize the local powers. But Drake stubbornly refused to drop it. In late November, 1969, Drake decided to move back to Wisconsin to try starting his own college there.

Drake's short career with the Christian Crusade made him about as big a right-wing celebrity as it is possible to become—without campaigning for the Presidency. And if he slips back into obscurity up in Wisconsin, his speeches and writings will be remembered by school boards, superintendents, and anxious parents for years to come. For Drake had, in less than two years, invented a new right-wing movement. It was a movement that had been incubating in the minds of the antipornography pamphleteers and the minds of the more vocal segregationists for a long time. But Drake gave the movement its direction; he gave it ammunition and targets; and at times he gave it tactics. And he started it all with one little pamphlet that might never have been published had the Oshkosh administration not tried to exercise a mild form of censorship over his statements.

* * *

Dr. Mary Calderone, Executive Director of the Sex Information and Education Council of the United States (SIECUS), has a burning mission: To alert and convert the youth of America to a new sexuality. She pursues children and youth for her cause as ardently as the missionary of old pursued souls.

"I have a covenant with the young people of these times," Dr. Calderone confides, "a personal covenant by which I will settle for nothing less than total honesty with them." The "honesty" she refers to is in telling young people about their right to enjoy premarital intercourse—if they so desire. As she jets across America from school to community hall to college campus, she preaches her revolutionary gospel.

For example, speaking to 320 boys at Blair Academy in New Jersey, Dr. Calderone declared, "What is sex for? It's for fun . . . for wonderful sensation. . . . Sex is not something you turn off like a faucet. If you do, it's unhealthy."

She continued: "We need new values to establish when and how we should have sexual experiences. Nobody's standing on a platform giving answers. You are moving beyond your parents. But you can't just move economically or educationally. You must move sexually, as well."

When a Blair student asked her, "What is your opinion of premarital sex relations among teen-agers?" she snapped back, "What's yours? Nobody from up on high (referring to God) determines this. You determine it. . . . I don't believe the old 'Thou shalt nots' apply anymore."

This is a remarkable admission coming from a person who claims to be a religious person, a Quaker with "concerns." Dr. Calderone's concern—after tossing God aside—is to teach American youth a new sex morality independent of church and state.

That is how Gordon Drake's pamphlet, "Is the School House the Proper Place to Teach Raw Sex?" begins. The Dr. Calderone quotes are for the most part butchered versions of quotes taken from a 1966 *Look* article called "Education Comes of Age."*

* In the *Look* article, Dr. Calderone was quoted as telling the Blair Academy boys:

> What is sex for? It's for fun, that I know, for wonderful sensation. It's also for reproduction, sedation, reward, punishment. It's a status symbol, a commercial come-on, proof of independence, a form of emotional blackmail. Many of these are negative ways of using sex. What we are trying to feel our way toward are the positive ways. Sex is not something you turn off like a faucet. If you do, it's unhealthy. We are sexual beings, legitimately so, at every age. Don't think that sex stops at the age of 50. It doesn't.

Although Drake could not be credited with the discovery of the subversive and evil plot behind the establishment of the Sex Information and Education Council of the United States (*Herald of Freedom*–publisher Frank Capell had made that discovery), he was clever enough to know that the agency was an ideal target for his anti–sex education campaign. If the audacity of the organization's name was not enough to set his readers against it right from the start, he could always try for a little political outrage by naming all the liberals on the SIECUS board, people like that terrible Reverend William Genné, who had been associated with the National Council of Churches for years, or that blasphemer Dr. Albert Ellis who wrote essays like the one titled "The Case Against Religion," or the most depraved of them all, Dr. William H. Masters himself. All Drake's readers needed to know about Dr. Masters was that he had studied the sexual responses of 382 females and 312 males as they performed *in his laboratory* to develop a profound hatred for the man.

The people who belonged to the SIECUS board came from the highest levels of the university or church hierarchies, and there were a few random bigwigs among them, people like Earl Ubell, the science editor for CBS, and Vivian Cadden, a senior editor at *McCall's* magazine. These were the kinds of people whom Billie James Hargis's followers had long resented with quite the same passionate sense of disenfranchisement that fed the

---

We need new values to establish when and how we should have sexual experiences.

Drake simply cut out great parts of that quote. He did an even better job on the quote in answer to the Blair student's question about premarital sex among teenagers. He performed a kind of transplant, making the first part of his version of Dr. Calderone's reply just as it had appeared in *Look:* "What's yours? Nobody from up on high determines this." But the *Look* article gave no indication that Dr. Calderone had been alluding to any divinity with her phrase, "Nobody from on high." And the second part of Drake's version of the reply was actually part of a remark Dr. Calderone had made during a speech to the National Congress of Parents and Teachers, *not* to the Blair Academy boys. The complete version of it was: "I'm a religious person, but I don't believe the old 'thou-shalt-nots' apply anymore."

If Drake had really been attempting to present Dr. Calderone's views accurately, he could have added another quote from that *Look* article, one which had been included among Dr. Calderone's remarks to the Blair student who had asked her opinion on premarital sex. "Where I personally stand on all this," the remark went, "is unquestionably in favor of a monogamy that precedes as well as follows the marriage ceremony." Although that statement did make Dr. Calderone sound somewhat virtuous—for being in favor of monogamy—the quote would still have shocked Drake's readers. After all, they weren't in favor of *any* premarital sex, monogamous or no.

Anaheim Antis' resentment against Paul Cook. Hargis had encouraged his flock's sour feelings with conspiracy theories every bit as wide-sweeping as those spouted by James Townsend. And Hargis had thrown in some racism to warm the hearts of the southern Bible Belters.·

"There is a master conspiracy loose in the world today headed by Satan himself," Hargis liked to say. "In the field of religion, the satanic conspiracy uses the National Council of Churches. . . . In the field of education, the satanic conspiracy uses the National Education Association. . . . In the field of politics, the satanic conspiracy uses the Americans for Democratic Action. . . . In the field of race relations, the satanic conspiracy uses the National Association for the Advancement of Colored People. . . ."

Although Drake was later to tell me that he did not believe in "this monstrous conspiracy thing," he was bound to write material that would please the followers of the Christian Crusade while he remained in Hargis's employ. The list of SIECUS board members read like a membership registry for the satanic conspiracy, and it was just too convenient a thing to leave out of propaganda against sex education. Drake liked to list the names of the worst offenders in his writings, accompanied by a few relevant facts about their liberal backgrounds and/or academic writings on sexuality. He really didn't have to come right out and say that they were *members* of the conspiracy. His readers, trained by Hargis, could put two and two together.

And so it turned out that SIECUS was a brilliant choice for a new target of the Right. The agency was to receive a volume of criticism—as a result of Drake's writings and speeches—that was quite out of proportion to its actual effectiveness.

It was not even the primary purpose of the organization to promote or design sex education programs for the public schools. SIECUS staff members and board members spoke to any and all groups who wanted to hear expert opinions on any and all aspects of human sexuality. They ended up spending a good deal of their time talking about sex education because there was a high demand for advice on that topic.

If Drake had wanted to find out what SIECUS had really been organized to do, he could have looked inside any of the little teacher guides that the outfit published. There, right inside the cover of each, was a summary of "The SIECUS purpose," which read:

To establish man's sexuality as a health entity: to identify the special

characteristics that distinguish it from, yet relate it to, human reproduction; to dignify it by openness of approach, study, and scientific
research designed to lead toward its understanding and its freedom
from exploitation; to give leadership to professionals and to society,
to the end that human beings may be aided toward responsible use of
the sexual faculty and toward assimilation of sex into their individual
life patterns as a creative and re-creative force.

Now, how Drake could have perceived anything about sex education in that amorphous little statement was an interesting puzzle in itself. How he could have read *anything* ominous into such
phrases as "responsible use of the sexual faculty" was beyond me.
I couldn't even understand phrases like that, let alone perceive a
darker purpose behind them. They smacked to me of stuffy college deans and people with faintly anglicized speech who would
positively *search* for expressions like "sexual faculty" to keep between you and them the safe, chill barrier of their erudition.

And yet it would not be fair to Drake to say that all of SIECUS
was directed toward that vague but high-sounding goal, the "responsible use of the sexual faculty." No, SIECUS board members
and staff members *had* performed some practical, down-to-earth
services for the forces of sex education. The director of SIECUS
estimated that, by the fall of 1969, the organization had helped
at least thirty community groups establish some kind of sex education program. This had come about because of the aforementioned demand for such help, combined with the fact that
many SIECUS board and staff members were considered to be the
top people in the field of sex education.

By rights, then, Drake should have attacked the school boards
and the PTA's and the liberal parents in every community that
sought the advice of the SIECUS members. But that wouldn't
have been as convenient. Besides, those SIECUS people were
the holders of valuable pedigrees or professional privileges and
powers that had made them the enemies of the right wing even
before Drake discovered their shocking organization.

And none of them was more highly pedigreed or more pro-
fessionally elevated than the founder and executive director of
SIECUS, Mary Steichen Calderone, M.D., M.P.H.

*   *   *

Dr. Calderone and Gordon Drake were natural enemies. They
were, you could almost say, doomed to a mutual antipathy that
had as much to do with their places of origin as it had to do
with their attitudes about sex. For in this great land of the free,

they were by birthright as separately and unequally endowed as were the Virginia gentlemen and Georgia criminals who settled here before them. And although Dr. Calderone's early environs were in some ways as cruelly constricting as the home of a cost accountant in Wauwatosa, Wisconsin could be, they gave her access to an education and a society that no follower of Billie James Hargis—except for a few odd millionaires—would ever see.

Mary Steichen Calderone, nee Steichen, was born in New York City into the family of Edward Steichen, the famous photographer, a.id Carl Sandburg, the even more famous poet. Edward Steichen was her father; Carl Sandburg, her uncle. That was the kind of lineage that expected its little girls to be not only beautiful but also clever. They were sent to the fine private schools in Manhattan and Boston, where, surrounded by other well-born little girls, they were to pick up both education and social grace. Mary Steichen was sent to the Brearley School in Manhattan, but not until she had spent enough time in France to learn that country's language more thoroughly than the tongue of her native land. Growing up, as she did, in the early part of this century, she was also subjected to the Victorian strictures that now seem incredible to us. Her father once told her she had lost her innocence (at the ripe age of six or seven) after he learned that she'd been watching an unaggressive exhibitionist who'd been hired as the Steichen gardener.

Her family brought her back to New York at a still tender age, and, innocent or not, she was enrolled in the Brearley School, where, according to one of her old friends, she was soon getting on famously. Introducing her to some Vassar alumnae many years later, the friend said:

"When I was about ten years old, my class at the Brearley School was jolted out of its stodginess by a new little girl, Mary Steichen." This new little girl, whom her classmates were soon calling "Steich," was, according to her friend, "a brilliant and well-organized student," who had time to act in the school plays in spite of her formidable academic performance. On the same occasion, Dr. Calderone described herself as "this little maverick who came in [to the class] speaking mostly French."

The little maverick mastered her English well enough, however, for she went on to Vassar College, the University of Rochester Medical School, and the Columbia University School of Public Health, chalking up a B.A., and M.D. and then a Masters in Public Health.

As she was married and became a mother soon after her graduation from Vassar (1925), she did not complete her medical school training until 1939. Her first marriage had ended in divorce after seven years, and she was later to marry Dr. Frank Calderone, an eminent physician who was to serve as the Chief Administrative officer of the World Health Organization. She had two more children by him, and thus it was not until the early fifties—when she was turning fifty herself—that she began her public career.

Dr. Calderone had served for several years as physician to the public schools of Great Neck, Long Island, as her children were growing up, but it was in 1953 that she began her major public health work. That year she took on the job of Medical Director of the Planned Parenthood Federation of America. And she stayed with Planned Parenthood until 1964, when, at the age of sixty, she helped to found SIECUS. She served as the executive director of SIECUS for over five years and as of this writing, she is still an active member of the SIECUS staff—at age sixty-five.

She has received, in her seventeen years of what is referred to by physicians as "voluntary health work," more honors and citations than it is possible to remember. Many of these were awarded to her after the founding of SIECUS, among them:

The Fourth Annual Award for Distinguished Service to Humanity, from the Women's Auxiliary at the Albert Einstein Medical Center in Philadelphia in 1966;
an Honorary Doctorate of Medical Science from the Women's Medical College of Pennsylvania in 1967;
the Woman of Conscience Award from the National Council of Women in 1969;
and the Woman of Achievement Award from the Greater New York Chapter of the Women's Division of Albert Einstein College of Medicine of Yeshiva University in 1969.

It took me a little over three months to obtain an interview with Dr. Calderone. The first time I called her to ask for an interview, she told me that I could get everything I needed from the official SIECUS biography of her and the SIECUS reprints of her articles. She was, for the time being, only granting interviews for immediate publication, she said. She was a *very* busy woman. She traveled thousands of miles a year. Why didn't I call back in a few weeks? I did. And a similar conversation occurred. Finally, she agreed to see me on October 15th, after my trip to Anaheim. When I returned to New York, there was a message for me at *The*

Village Voice. Dr. Calderone could not see me on the 15th. So sorry. I called again. We made another appointment, this time through the secretary. Two or three days later, the secretary called back. Dr. Calderone has to cancel. At which point I began to sound angry. I *had* been trying to see her for nearly three months, I remarked. The secretary apparently took pity on me. She set up another appointment—and this time it was not canceled. It was set for a day during the last week of October. The first phone call had been made in mid-July.

The SIECUS offices are located in a modern glass-and-steel building on Broadway, just north of Columbus Circle (1855 Broadway, to be exact). They are located on the second floor of the building, and they are always locked. There is a discreet white buzzer beside the main door, and as you press it to signal your arrival, you are reminded of visits to your doctor. The receptionist explains that the buzzer system has been installed because people are always stealing things from the office. But right behind the receptionist is a huge set of files. And on the drawer containing the "C" files, you can easily read the word, "CRANKS." The door, you suspect, is locked against them.

On the day of my appointment I arrived several minutes early, armed with my tape recorder and my morning paper. I had just settled down with the paper when Dr. Calderone walked around the corner looking fresh and cheerful. She was wearing the soft leather shoes with thick soles that are popular with people who have foot trouble and ample funds. They were really thick-soled sandals with two wide leather bands that held them to the front parts of her feet. She walked in them with an easy, long-limbed stride that made her seem quite unaffected, not at all the Very Important Person who had no time for young writers.

She led me into her office, where her degrees and awards decked the walls. I put my tape recorder on her desk and began to thread the new tape into its works.

"You should have done that before you came in here," said Dr. Calderone.

Gordon Drake, on the other hand, agreed to see me immediately. He, too, was a busy person. He had just returned to Tulsa after a two- or three-week tour of the sex education hot spots. I called him the day I arrived in Tulsa. He agreed to see me the next day. Tulsa is a town that covers an amount of territory that is quite out of proportion to its population. In all that flatland, the city's growth simply seeped out over wider and wider reaches of the plains. Thus when you must travel around Tulsa, you have to be prepared to travel for miles. My visit there coincided with one of the worst rainstorms of the year. The radio announcers were giving the day's rainfall rates in whole inches. So Gordon Drake called me on the day I was to visit him to ask if he might not save me the trouble of securing a cab in that terrible weather. He had a car, he said. He could just as easily come to see me. And that is what he did.

Gordon Drake was at some points less than candid with me. He was a man who saw no harm in bending the truth or even altering it for his special purposes. He had not even minded lending his name to an organization that was dedicated to a politics with which he was not totally in agreement. He had started a movement with which I could feel precious little sympathy.

But I liked Gordon Drake himself. Dr. Calderone, whose courage and relatively enlightened sexual attitudes I admired, had disappointed me. And although I thought that my vision of these two individuals might be colored by their treatment of me, I also considered the contrast between their respective behavior toward me a valid illustration of the qualities that had made them enemies. Drake's ready friendliness seemed partly derived from his almost childlike eagerness to be interviewed, to increase his fame. Dr. Calderone's standoffishness seemed to indicate, similarly, her profound self-assurance, a self-assurance that needed no sustenance from a flattering press. Their disparate attitudes toward publicity alone, I thought, made them uniquely suitable antagonists.

You could not hear the two of them speak without wanting to side with Drake. Dr. Calderone made a great deal more sense, and she had the most learned theological, educational, and medical opinions in her favor. Drake uttered many absurdities, and he had every antediluvian thinker who could afford a mimeograph machine on his side. But Drake was a little man with twinkly eyes and a merry laugh who could joke easily about himself. Although he did have a Ph.D., he spoke in a folksy style that anybody could understand. He was totally lacking in arrogance. Dr. Calderone, on the other hand, spoke literally with her chin in the air. She had a fine stage voice with a faintly nasal quality, and although she, too, used fairly simple language, she could make it sound fancy with the special modulations of her voice.

There was about her tone and the tilt of her head an inborn arrogance. She seemed to speak not with the voice of a person but with the voice of a class, a voice that had been bred in generations of parlor and salon gatherings, the kind of voice that Henry James's wise older ladies must have used when they uttered their forever ambiguous conclusion, "So there you are." She looked and spoke like the personification of *Noblesse Oblige*.

And when I asked her why she had not attacked Gordon Drake's statements as often as he had attacked hers, she said: "I just won't stoop to an interchange. I will *not* go on a talk program, call-in program; I will not go on the same platform as any of these people. Because this *dignifies* them. I don't recognize them. They're liars. I don't go on platforms with liars, deliberate liars. I'm a Quaker. My conscience is too, too strong for that."

Unwittingly she had put forth an image of herself as being elevated, being *above* the tactics of a man like Gordon Drake. "I won't stoop," she had said, and "this *dignifies* them," as if the very encounter with the likes of her would lift him out of the depths of mediocrity, as if debating her on equal terms was in itself a rare privilege granted only to those who knew and respected the proper rules.

Yet for all her apparent arrogance, there was something naïve about Dr. Calderone. She seemed to think that her irrational critics would lose their effectiveness if she did not enter the fray with them. People like Paul Cook knew better. He had seen the right-wingers intimidate a school board, and he knew about Steinbacher's outrageous claims in far-flung towns. He had received letters from newspaper editors and school administrators after Steinbacher's visits, and he knew how those people hungered for material with which to expose his inaccuracies. Cook had seen the effectiveness of such inaccuracies himself. That was why he had said of the right-wingers, "They're *not* out of it by any means! . . . These people are developing techniques and learning as they go along."

The right wing had been effective enough in Dr. Calderone's case to pretty much guarantee that, by October of 1969, she would be picketed everywhere she went to give a speech. And she became such a well-known right-wing target by the end of the year that in early 1970 she stepped down from her position as executive director of SIECUS.

Yet it wasn't until October of 1969 that Dr. Calderone published a real rebuttal of the right-wing attacks. And that was published in the relatively obscure *Vassar Alumnae Magazine*. SIECUS had earlier put out some rather general materials in defense of itself, materials that explained that the organization produced no program for the public schools, that its former board member Isadore Rubin had never been "officially charged with being a member of the Communist Party," and that the attacks on SIECUS and sex education were being promoted by the large right-wing organizations.

In her article for the *Vassar Alumnae Magazine* ("Attack on Education"), Dr. Calderone boldly called the right-wing allegations "lies." She credited Drake with having triggered the attacks, and she pointed out that he and his followers repeatedly referred to a SIECUS "program" that was "nonexistent as such." She accused the Christian Crusade of "controverting the Ninth Commandment" by spreading "hate, lies, and suspicion." And she strongly implied that the Christian Crusade's enthusiasm for the campaign against sex education was directly related to the financial success of Drake's pamphlet. Dr. Calderone continued:

Early in 1969, the bandwagon was joined by a second kind of group: chronic aspirants to power, led by the John Birch Society, one by one picked up the Drake materials almost verbatim and spread the words of hate and falsehood. In the spreading the lies naturally grew: a police chief named Fish publicly and baldly stated . . . "that Dr. Mary Calderone, executive director of SIECUS, 'has been with Communists,' and has been labeled a Communist by the House Committee on Un-American Activities." . . .

In the month of April, 1969, SIECUS received about 4,000 attacking clippings from smaller publications across the country. . . . Agreement [among observers of the right wing] appeared to be that extremist right groups, using Christian Crusade materials, radical extremist techniques, and SIECUS as whipping boy, were sowing seeds of distrust toward educators in their own local communities, with the objective of gaining control of Boards of Education at election time. This has already happened in some communities, and where it has, it is not merely the desire of the majority of citizens for sound sex education programs that may be thwarted, but there may be vitiation of programs in social studies, psychological and guidance counseling, programs on the United Nations or world problems and other "Communist" plots.

That was a fairly strong critical analysis of the movement against sex education, and it probably brought SIECUS some new sympathizers among Vassar alumnae. But the vast majority of people who bought Drake's pamphlet weren't Vassar alumnae. They were not very often college graduates. They were middle-aged women who seemed to believe every piece of literature that contained footnotes and reverent comments about the flag and the divinity. It was quite possible that those women would not believe any rebuttal of Drake's pamphlet, but, in any case, SIECUS did not make much of an attempt to reach them.

Drake's pamphlet was full of amply footnoted inaccuracies and misleading statements about the SIECUS board members, alleged classroom incidents, and Swedish society. And if the SIECUS staff had really wanted to worry those Anti mothers, they could have made a systematic list of every false or misleading statement in the pamphlet. Right-wingers *were* impressed with a show of scholarship—as all those footnotes indicated—and they just might have found a publication or an article that compared Drake's material to the relevant texts of his source materials interesting reading. Drake was capable of writing, for example, that one "super-realistic classroom demonstration is the application of a condrum [*sic*] on a life size plastic phallus," and giving as his reference an article by John Kobler in the June 29, 1968, issue of the *Saturday Evening Post*. Actually the information came from a *McCall's* article by Marjorie Iseman, and Miss Iseman had clearly indicated that the classroom demonstration had occurred once in a private school. Drake wrote of it in a context that made the reader think that such demonstrations were common in the public schools.

And even when Drake stuck fairly close to the facts, as he had in a paragraph on the San Diego, California, sex education program, he used them selectively.*

* On page 21 of his pamphlet, Drake had written:

In San Diego, California, traveling sexologists carry their wares in large canvas bags from school to school. They display their formerly taboo materials in unemotional succession to the sex-liberated students. Masturbation, homosexuality, abortion, and premarital intercourse in films such as *The Game* (which depicts a boy's feelings after coitus with a virgin) are but a sampling of what students are exposed to. *The Game* purports to warn 13- and 14-year-old girls of *the game of love* and its many traps. They also learn about sex, deviation, illegitimacy and venereal diseases.

Drake's footnote here indicates that his reference was the John Kobler article in the *Saturday Evening Post*, and, indeed, this time it was. But Drake cleverly left out those details that Kobler had given which might have detracted from his general theme—that sex education was evil. Kobler had written:

In San Diego, Calif., they are called "social-health teacher counselors." Five of them—two men, three women—circulate among the city's thirty-one secondary schools, trying to promote "wholesome attitudes toward boy-girl relationships and respect for family life," in the words of Dr. G. Gage Wetherhill, director of health services, who initiated the effort. The counselors carry from school to school big canvas bags containing classroom materials which, not so very long ago, would have scandalized the community and even invited prosecution. The materials include literature, charts, models, tapes and films dealing in explicit terms with such formerly taboo subjects as sexual anatomy, masturbation, homosexuality and pre-

Despite Drake's attacks on SIECUS—or perhaps because of them—there were few rebuttals written by SIECUS members that contained any kind of detail. The press did a good deal more investigating of Drake's claims (and of a number of rich sex-education atrocity stories of untraceable origin) than did most of the sex education proponents. And *Playboy* magazine had kept up a running debate with and among its readers since the spring of 1969. The *Playboy* Forum columns carried extensive and detailed editorial replies to Antis' letters. It was in the November Playboy Forum that the detailed analysis of Drake's doctoring of Mary Calderone's quotes had appeared.*

---

marital intercourse. The counselors, however, shock hardly anybody. They go their rounds with the majority approval not only of the school administrators but also of local physicians, clergymen, civic leaders and the PTA.

Kobler then quoted at length from a classroom discussion about the film *The Game,* and it is clear from the quotes he used that the film was not exactly encouraging to youngsters who were thinking of experimenting with premarital sex. The quotes that Kobler used also showed that the counselor who showed the film was rather unsubtly underscoring its lesson.

" 'Now consider the cultural influences on Peter and Nancy [the pair in the film],' " Kobler quoted her. " 'The rock-'n'-roll music at the beach. Dancing in their swimsuits. The car—a car can be a mobile bed, you know. Weren't they both losers? The guilt, the shame? Why is Peter so dejected?' "

Kobler also stated that the San Diego program was twenty-six years old, and that the ninth-graders studied "the psychological dangers of promiscuity . . . social attitudes toward sex . . . selecting a mate, courtship . . . and marriage and family responsibilities"—in addition to the more shocking topics that Drake later listed.

As the point of Drake's pamphlet was that sex education was erotically stimulating and designed by permissive adults, it was not to his advantage to include details that might show the conventional moral lessons threaded through much of sex education. It was also not to his advantage to state that *any* sex education program was twenty-six years old—for he was trying to present sex education as a symptom of a recent national conspiracy.

* *Playboy* had also published a rebuttal of the Antis' arguments about the evil effects of sex education in Sweden, arguments that had first appeared in Drake's pamphlet. Drake had written: "After 10 years of mandatory public school sex education in Sweden the results can now be measured:

The VD picture *is what some Swedes describe as a 'catastrophic' increase in venereal disease among youngsters, especially since* 1959. . . . *Physicians say that gonorrhea and syphilis are more widespread in Sweden today than in any other civilized country in the world* [his emphasis]. . . . Reported rapes went up 55 per cent in the two-year period [Exactly which two-year period Drake meant was not indicated].

Drug-taking among Swedish school children has "risen wildly over the past few years" [taken from *U.S. News and World Report*] and students operate as narcotic agents in the schools. Swedish pornography is flourish-

It should be mentioned that Dr. Calderone herself urged me to read the Playboy Forum columns and that Gerald Sanctuary, the British marriage counselor who later inherited her position, gave me some statistics on Sweden and told me where I could find more. But in general, the National Education Association and two shoe-string muckrakers in Washington (Charles Baker of the Institute for American Democracy and Wesley McCune of Group Research, Inc.), proved the best sources of material that contradicted the Antis' claims. And they, in turn, often got their material from the press.

---

ing, clubs for homosexuals advertise for new members in newspapers and magazines, and movies frequently display a couple having intercourse.

In his speeches, Drake liked to say that "50 per cent of brides who present themselves at the altar are pregnant in Sweden." John Steinbacher also liked to use that figure. And Steinbacher also tried to blame sex education for Sweden's celebrated suicide rate.

The October, 1969, *Playboy* Forum contained an extensive, well-documented denial of these claims—most of which had been expressed in a letter from a reader. One of the Antis' favorite sources for their allegations about Sweden was a book by Birgitta Linner called *Sex and Society in Sweden*. *Playboy* pointed out that Dr. Linner had written that only about 50 or 60 per cent of Swedish students were offered a thorough sex education in the schools.

"Dr. Linner makes it clear that, since 1938, sex education has been alternately moving forward and backward in Sweden," wrote the editors of *Playboy*, "in reaction to various pressures from conservative and liberal groups. . . . Thus, insofar as there is a causal relationship, Swedish sexual behavior can't be considered exclusively the result of modern sex education and liberal laws but, rather, the product of a continuing conflict between forces of freedom and repression.

"It is true that 30 to 35 per cent of all Swedish brides are pregnant at the time of marriage and that there is a rather high rate of premarital sex. This must be understood within the framework of the Swedish attitude toward sexuality—which is not the product of modernism but part of the tradition of the country, as Ewald Bohm points out in *The Encyclopedia of Sexual Behavior*:

In general, then, ancient tradition gave social sanction to premarital sexual relationships. The legal responsibilities of marriage, however, began with the promise to marry. Such forms of "trial marriage" have persisted in some rural regions of Sweden from the ancient past . . . [and] also in some regions of Finland, the Baltic Sea provinces and other parts of the European continent, especially Austria and Bavaria.

"As for premarital pregnancies, the Swedish rate is no more astonishing than the American rate: Dr. Alfred A. Messer has estimated that, in one large city, one third of the brides were pregnant at the time of marriage, and Dr. Alfred Auerback states that 50 per cent of all our teenage brides are pregnant on their wedding day. The difference is that in Sweden, the marriages are not *caused* by the pregnancies but by a real desire to marry, since there are no stigmata on illegitimacy there. . . .

It struck me as altogether strange that SIECUS proved such a poor source of "dirt" about the Antis and their atrocity stories. For I had learned in my brief time as a journalist that the best source of "dirt" about a public figure is someone who is in competition with him, such as a political rival or a professional antagonist.

But as I discovered, Dr. Calderone did not want to "dignify" Drake or others like him by answering his charges in detail.

* * *

Gordon Drake, on the other hand, was willing to dig up and exploit any and every piece of dirt about Dr. Calderone and sex education in general that he could find. He and his imitators amassed such a volume of anti–sex education and anti-Calderone tidbits that one could not fault the poor small SIECUS staff for

---

"As for venereal disease, Dr. Linner . . . points out:

Sweden's VD problem is by no means a unique one—countries all over the world are facing similar difficulties. At an international VD conference in Lisbon, Portugal, in 1965, delegates were reminded that the gonorrhea incidence is rising in most countries. The syphilis picture is about the same, with an upward trend in about 75 per cent of the countries investigated.

"As for rape . . . for 1965 and 1966 (the latest years for which records are complete), the arrest figures were, respectively, 87 and 78—a decline of 10 per cent, not a rise of 55 per cent. In a population of 7,847,395, this works out to approximately 1.1 per 100,000 in 1965 and 1 per 100,000 in 1966, one of the lowest rates in the world. (The United States, by comparison, had 10,734 rape arrests in 1965, or 5.36 per 100,000, and increased 8 per cent to 11,609 in 1966, or 5.8 per 100,000.)

"Turning to drug taking, this refers chiefly to marijuana, which is increasing among youth everywhere. . . . As for freedom in publishing (including pornography), its existence has apparently had no adverse effect on Swedish life. . . . Where censorship does exist in Sweden, it is primarily concerned with violence.

"The Swedish divorce rate is one of the highest in the world (but not nearly as high as that of the United States—one out of six Swedish marriages ends in divorce, compared with one in four here).

"As for the oft-repeated allegation that Sweden has the highest suicide rate in the world—this was true 17 years ago but not since. Among European countries, Austria, Czechoslovakia, Finland, Denmark, and Hungary all have higher suicide rates than Sweden, which has now dropped to ninth in the world."

Abigail Van Buren, who received many letters from Antis after she wrote a column in defense of sex education and SIECUS, also published some statistics on Sweden. Hers were gathered from the World Health Organization, and they matched the *Playboy* figures. Miss Van Buren was obviously aware of the demography of the sex education controversies, for she added an extra little fact: "In 1968 there were more suicides per 100,000 population in the state of California than in Sweden."

letting *some* of these items go unchallenged. But as you examined the nature of the Antis' "evidence," you could begin to think that it was not its volume alone that had discouraged SIECUS and Mary Calderone from trying to refute a good portion of it.

The volume factor was formidable, however. And Drake did get around. He would appear in Nashville and claim that children in a California classroom had been shown "a vagina the size of a blackboard." During a tour of Mississippi he would use his inaccurate statistics on Sweden. After Steinbacher's Charter House series appeared, he was apt to mention Lester Kirkendall's mythical Sneak-It-In speech. Keeping up with Drake could have proved arduous, and he was, from what I could gather, one of the more scrupulous story tellers, preferring to skim along the truth rather than depart entirely from it.

There were other pamphleteers and free-lance right-wingers who printed sex education atrocity stories without bothering to check them out. One of these was Lee Dodson, the former carpenter who went to work as an organizer for the Liberty Lobby and then in 1967 branched off with his own outfit, the American Education Lobby. Dodson printed a story that became a favorite with the Antis. It had to do with a teacher in Flint, Michigan, who was supposed to have stripped in front of her class. What Dodson didn't tell the readers of his anti–sex education literature was that the teacher (a female) had been demonstrating various effects of clothing styles to an all-girl Home Economics class and that she had never appeared before the girls without her underwear.

Another story that was told and retold with relish among the decent sorts had to do with a twelve-year-old boy who was alleged to have attempted to test out his school sex education lessons on his four-year-old sister. This tale first appeared in a letter allegedly written by the boy's mother to the *Phoenix American* in November, 1968. Her son was supposed to have been enrolled in the Phoenix schools before his family moved to Laurel, Montana, from whence the letter was sent. I called Laurel, Montana, Information and was told (in early 1970) that no family by the name of the letter writer (Mrs. Erwin Handel) was listed in the directory. Perhaps they had moved—or perhaps they didn't have a phone.

At any rate, stories like these were everywhere believed by the anxious parents who attended anti–sex education rallies. Such tales, coupled with the faulty statistics on Sweden and Anaheim VD, accumulated into something like what the *New Yorker's* Washington reporter Richard Rovere had termed, in one of his columns about Joseph McCarthy, the "multiple untruth." Writing about McCarthy's skillful use of mind-boggling mendacity, Rovere had explained that the "multiple untruth . . . can be repeated over and over again with impunity because no one will remember which statements have been disproved and which haven't." That was doubtless the advantage Drake had over his enemies.

But it was Drake's capacity to fight dirty that must have really protected him. He liked to mention, for instance, how many times a SIECUS board member had been divorced. And he promoted an inquisitional zeal in his audiences, urging a group in a Chicago suburb to do something about the fact that Henk Newenhouse, a prominent distributor of sex education films, lived in their neighborhood.

His best piece of mud was an item about Dr. Calderone's past. And it was perhaps the true measure of both her naïveté and her courage that she had handed it to Drake by revealing it publicly herself. Drake liked to use it, as he had in the middle of a speech in Nashville, as follows:

"SIECUS is headed by Dr. Mary Calderone. She is an interesting woman. She admitted on television that she went to the altar pregnant, and, as I say, perhaps brought about this program trying to justify the mistake she made."

Thinking that the story was an incredible lie, I later asked Dr. Calderone about it. In a weary tone, she said:

"Well, I don't know where it was, but in one speech I remember talking about the dangers of premarital sex. And I remember saying, 'In my first marriage'—and that was in the twenties—' in my first marriage, I *did* get premaritally pregnant, and it *was* a forced marriage, and it was a very poor marriage followed by a divorce, so that everybody suffered.' Now, that was approximately what I said."

There was a moment of silence after her answer. It had surprised me.

"Uh, well, that's a very brave thing to say," I offered wanly after some reflection. "You understand the way they [the Antis] interpret that kind of thing?" I asked.

"Of course!" Dr. Calderone uttered. "But they do this deliberately. For instance, they never quote in the *Look* article where I say, 'Where I personally stand is in favor of a monogamy that precedes as well as follows the marriage ceremony.' [A moment before she had been urging me to get all my refutations of Anti claims from the Institute for American Democracy. But the boldness of that story about her first marriage seemed to have irked her, and, for a little while, she remained irked enough to do a little refuting herself.] That is the *same* Look *article!* And they never quote that. And in *Christianity Today*, which is an evangelical journal—see, all of this major stuff has come from this fundamentalist group, Christian Crusade—and *Christianity Today is* an evangelical journal. And they very *definitely* state that Mary Calderone is *not* for premarital sex. She has *said* so. *This* has been thoroughly misinterpreted. So that even within the ranks they're beginning to recognize what the truth is.

"And I just won't stoop to an interchange," she went on, making here the remark about how she did not wish to *"dignify"* the Antis.

*   *   *

Neither Drake nor Dr. Calderone *liked* to reveal unpleasant facts about themselves, of course. And as Drake had the less glorious career behind him, it was a good deal more difficult to wring autobiographical material from him than it was to get such material from Dr. Calderone. (In an extended interview with *Playboy* magazine, which appeared in the April, 1970, issue, Dr. Calderone revealed so *much* about herself that her enemies would doubtless be mining that issue for months after it had gone off the stands.)

There was precious little to learn about Drake from other sources. His opponents had even gotten a couple of details confused in the little Drake biographies they composed for worried school administrators. For a time during the summer of 1969, Wesley McCune and Charles Baker were reporting that Drake had been fired by the Oshkosh administration ("I could have sued them for that!" Drake would chuckle as he thought of the error) and that he had spent a year in Hong Kong before taking the job at Shelton College.

But Drake himself made that Hong Kong item even more confusing by telling me that he had been offered a job by the American Lutheran Church's Division of World Ministries there, a job which would have put him in charge of "all the Lutheran schools in Hong Kong and the university." In fact, he said, he had accepted the position, but "unfortunately, about two weeks before we were going to leave, I found out that I would only be a figurehead and that the Lutheran Church no longer was running it's schools, but the local Chinese and the Communists were really doing a job."

The Lutheran Church people had quite a different version of this story, however. Lester A. Dahlen, the man who served as a liaison between the Hong Kong Lutherans and the Minneapolis headquarters of the church's Division of World Missions during the time Drake was considering the job, informed me that "the Lutheran Church in Hong Kong does not conduct a university or college," and that Drake was originally asked to serve as educational administrator of the church's primary and secondary schools in Hong Kong. In a scrupulous attempt to be fair to Drake, Dahlen explained that the Lutheran schools had not been run under a central administration up to the time of the job offer, and that the plans for centralizing fell through as Drake was considering the job. Thus Drake was offered a "revised job" that would have kept him in "full-time educational work . . . but . . . with only a section of the [Lutheran] schools" in Hong Kong. "The reference to the Communists running the schools is unfortunate and is not based on any known facts," Dahlen quietly maintained.

Furthermore, when Drake finally turned down the job he had given "his responsibility to his widowed mother" as his reason, Dahlen said.

Dr. Calderone's disclosures of autobiographical material never departed startlingly from others' versions of that same material. But there was one little factor that she did not volunteer on her own and about which she would not comment when I brought it up. Her enemies made much of it because they thought it illustrated her inconsistency.

This was the fact that her husband owned a few movie theaters on Long Island in which, as Steinbacher liked to put it "the Hollywood product" was shown. Although only two of them were operated directly by him at the time when the sex education controversy erupted, the Antis had obtained a photograph of one called the Calderone (not one of the two he operated), and they displayed it prominently in the revised edition of the "Pavlov's Children" pamphlet under the heading "SIECUS Exec. Profits from Pornography."

Steinbacher also discovered that a burlesque production called *Life Begins at Minsky's* had been staged at one of the theaters that Frank Calderone still operated directly. From somewhere Steinbacher had gotten the report that the Nassau County District Attorney had threatened to "close down" the theater if Dr. Calderone (Frank) did not "clean up" the burlesque show. Thus the "Pavlov's Children" pamphlet also contained this item:

"In his two theaters on Long Island in New York, Mrs. Calderone's husband, Dr. Frank Calderone, helps titilate [*sic*] the public with girlie shows. In 1967 at Calderone's Nassau County theatre, Minsky's Burlesque Follies ran for five weeks. The district attorney had received numerous complaints that the show was lewd and pornographic. After a preview, the D.A. insisted that the show be toned down."

It wasn't "Minsky's Burlesque Follies," of course, and the show ran for three, not five, weeks, but the Antis always seemed happier when they could expand a little on the truth.

A spokesman for the Nassau County District Attorney told me that Frank Calderone and the D.A. had watched a preview of the show together and that *together* they had decided that one or two of the routines were a little too erotic. The spokesman indicated that Frank Calderone had himself suggested that the offensive parts be eliminated without any threats from the D.A.'s office.

At any rate, Mary Calderone liked to argue that sex education served as "a balancing force" upon the minds of the young—who were being bombarded with sexual material in the media.

"I'm personally deeply concerned about what happens to the young at critical and sensitive stages in their evolution when, let's say, they see these trailers [movie previews]," she had told me. "They may be seeing a family picture, but they'll see trailers with some of the hot spots in, well, De Sade or you name it. What does this do to them? Or what does this do when they pick up *Playboy*—as they do—in November? [The November, 1969, issue of the magazine contained some spicy shots from new movies.] . . . We now find ourselves in a key role of helping the helping professions—particularly in teaching and medicine and in the churches—to *balance* this explicitness for the young people."

The Antis thought Mary Calderone's own husband ought not to be making money, even indirectly, off the "explicitness" she deplored and used as a partial justification for sex education.

When I asked her about her husband's theaters, she said she would not talk about them but would give me a statement, which he had prepared in response to such inquiries. The statement turned out to be a little history of the Calderone family theaters ("My family and I have built and own a small number of theaters in Nassau County, Long Island, for the past half century") including some tedious detail about various transactions with the two legitimate theaters he owned, and, attached to the history was a list of plays that had been produced (including the Minsky's production) at one of the legitimate theaters between February, 1967, and November, 1968. The list was arranged to show which productions had brought a profit. The *Life Begins at Minsky's* production had, according to Calderone's list, failed to pay for itself.

Frank Calderone's statement explained little beyond the fact that you couldn't make money off a burlesque show these days. And although I did not share Mary Calderone's worries about the possible harmful effects of explicit sex in the media, I thought that the Antis could well call her inconsistent for deploring the products of the industry from which her husband was indirectly profiting.

Yet if there were some easy method for measuring integrity, for weighing it up in concrete units, Mary Calderone's endowment of this quality would weigh several times over the meager endowment possessed by some of the opposition. The irony was that the very integrity Mary Calderone wanted to maintain with the young was a political handicap with the adults. If she could have carried on her work locked in some lecture hall with young people who still needed the kind of sexual enlightenment she was offering, if she could have done that with the guarantee that never a word would leak out, she would probably have got on famously. But she was not talking to the young exclusively. She was talking much more frequently to adults, and she was doing it in full view of the media. She was attempting a kind of public relations for what she called "sexual sanity." And in the area of public relations, as any good press secretary will tell you, integrity will not take you very far.

It struck me as a sign of her considerable integrity that Dr. Calderone had publicly disclosed the unhappy circumstances of her first marriage. But that disclosure seemed also a sign of her profound political naïveté—it was not good public relations, if you will, for her cause. A story like that, however potent its lesson, would make her immediately suspect in the eyes of the people who—by her own standards—were most in need of her teaching. As Drake's comments revealed, they would consider her work an attempt to justify her own lamented act, never realizing that she had used that lamented act to illustrate the ill effects of precipitous sexual behavior. Drake's followers would merely consider her a bad example for the young. And they would see in her story a subtle attempt to gain sympathy.

*　　*　　*

Although Gordon Drake did not say that there was a great Commie conspiracy behind the efforts of SIECUS and the numerous respectable organizations that favored sex education* in so many words, his allies did. And he implied as much. In his original pamphlet, he stated:

What the sex educators have in mind is simply this: Sex should be as easily discussed as any other subject in the curriculum, and any inhibitions or moral and religious taboos should be eliminated. This obviously drives a wedge between the family, church, and school— bolstering the authority of the school while casting cynical doubts on the traditional moral teachings of the home and church. If this is accomplished, and the new morality is affirmed, our children will become easy targets for Marxism and other amoral, nihilistic philosophies —as well as V.D.!

When Robert Welch decided to launch a Birch society campaign against sex education, he wrote much more confidently of the conspiratorial design behind such teaching:

This [sex education] is a final assault upon the family as a fundamental block in the structure of our civilization. The program is designated to destroy one whole generation of American youth (with similar programs doing the same thing in other countries). . . . A vital part of the Communist strategy for subjugation of the American people is the breaking down of their will to resist. Many forms of pressure have been planned, and are being utilized, to contribute to that total attitude of defeatism, despair, and resignation. Most important among them is simply the erosion of American character

* The National Education Association and SIECUS drew up lists of national organizations that had passed resolutions or issued statements in support of sex education before or during the first year of the controversy. These were: the American Association for Health, Physical Education, and Recreation; the American College of Obstetricians and Gynecologists (Committee on Maternal Health); the American Public Health Association; the National Congress of Parents and Teachers; the American Academy of Pediatrics; the American Medical Association; the American School Health Association; the National Council of Churches; the National Education Association and American Medical Association's Joint Committee on Health Problems in Education; the National School Boards Association and the American Association of School Administrators (through their Joint Committee); the National Student Assembly, YMCA & YWCA; the Sixth White House Conference on Children & Youth; the Synagogue Council of America; the United Nations Educational, Scientific and Cultural Organization (UNESCO); and the United States Catholic Conference. SIECUS and the NEA also liked to point out that in 1966 the U.S. Commissioner of Education, Harold Howe, had issued a statement saying that "the U.S. Office of Education will support family life education and sex education as an integral part of the curriculum from preschool to college and adult levels."

through the total effect of abrasive influences and activities. . . . And certainly among the most important of all the sinister schemes for achieving this result is the program for converting the present young generation into debilitated, directionless, unprincipled wastrels of their whole cultural inheritance. . . . Among the most important of these purposes, is to help all of the other forces at work to destroy completely the very concept of morality. For once man can be brought to believe that nothing is really either intrinsically good or evil, then he soon comes to feel that nothing else really matters, except to feed his appetites by any means that he can, and to avoid pain—by torture or otherwise—to the best of his ability.—from the *Birch Society Bulletin*, January, 1970.

There were countless other right-wing pamphleteers who picked up the Commie conspiracy theory, but Welch and Drake had pretty well summed up their reasoning. The idea was that the Commies would first arouse the child's erotic feelings, and then, as the child suffered with the conflict between the restrictive teachings of his parents and the urgings of his own desire, the Commies would side with his desire, encouraging him to throw off the values of his parents—thereby weaning him from their influence.

This argument might sound absurd to a liberal who did not fear the sexual awakening of his child, but when one recalled that Robert Welch was a fundamentalist, that the Christian Crusade was a fundamentalist outfit, and that the conservative Catholics who admired both Welch and the Christian Crusade also exhibited a fundamentalist mentality, one could begin to sympathize with the Antis' fears. Their sexual teachings were quite rigid. They feared masturbation like the plague, and they were unflinchingly opposed to premarital intercourse. They were, the historians and social scientists who had studied them told us, in the minority. Hence, their children were not only afflicted with the tension created by the conflicting demands of their parents' rigid mores and their own physical needs, but they were also exposed to alternate value systems among their peers. One had only to recall Gary Pippinger's remark to his mother upon his seeing the scantily clad girls at the beach ("Mother, I don't know where to look") to perceive the isolation of the fundamentalist adolescent. Such youngsters must be, I imagined, something like the proverbial minister's son, the kind of children who are especially ripe for rebellion and who, when they make the break from home, do it wildly.

Then, too, the Antis' tendency to read political implications into sexual attitudes was not unique. Herbert Marcuse had made a similar analysis of our sexual codes in his book *Eros and Civilization*. But Marcuse, unlike the Antis, thought sexual repression made people more malleable and obedient to the demands of the political state, not less so.

Marcuse's view was shared by A. S. Neill, the man who founded and wrote about the British school for disturbed children. Neill thought that restrictive parents feared their children's awakening sexuality because they knew it could involve them in attachments outside the home. In his book *Summerhill*, Neill expresses his theory this way:

If sex were allowed to go over the garden wall to the boy or girl next door, the authority of the home would be in danger; the tie to father and mother would loosen and the child would automatically leave the family emotionally. It sounds absurd but those ties are a very necessary pillar of support to the authoritative state—just as prostitution was a necessary safeguard for the morality of nice girls from nice homes. Abolish sex repression and youth will be lost to authority.

The Antis were, I thought, correct in viewing sex education as a *potential* threat to their authority over their own children. Whether sex education would, in fact, free their children of their dominance, no one could as yet predict. But the differences between the kinds of sexual behavior the Antis and the proponents of sex education considered acceptable were real and considerable. And those differences could conceivably create conflicts for children who were acutely aware of them. The differences were strikingly clear in the transcripts of the Anaheim board meetings. In the Anti literature they were clear to the extreme. And the Christian Crusade had started selling two records of the advice of a man named Dr. Earl A. Goldsmith, which defined the radically curtailed version of sex education the Antis considered acceptable. The records, entitled unimaginatively, *Dr. Earl A. Goldsmith Tells Your Daughter About Sex,* and *Dr. Earl A. Goldsmith Tells Your Son About Sex,* each had a side addressed to parents and a side addressed to their children.

The parents' side was rather liberal in one respect, for several times in the course of it, Dr. Goldsmith urged his listeners to answer all their children's questions about sex and childbirth without flinching. But the material on the children's sides was, to put it mildly, outdated. The basic reproductive physiology of both males and females was described on each. But the sex act itself was never explained. The narrator merely stated that children were conceived by a method called "mating," something that the

narrator said went on between married people who were expressing their love for each other. And on the boys' record, there was a
strong admonition to keep one's hands off the girls. The girls'
record urged young listeners to "use our bodies as God intended"
and to play "the game of life and love" by the proper rules.

"If you stuff yourself with food, any kind of food," the girls
were told, "you will get sick. If you eat only one kind of food, you
will not get all the vitamins of a well-balanced diet.

"Do you see what I am driving at? There are rules for *everything* we do.

"When I feed my mind only with thoughts about sex, then my
life becomes unbalanced. If you are more interested in sex than a
girl your age ought to be, you may become mentally, and sometimes physically sick."

That kind of message was simply unacceptable to the proponents of sex education. You couldn't get one of them to say that
there was any conceivable way of discovering how much a person
ought to think about sex at a given age. They would not even
state that there was a maximum level of sexual activity beyond
which ill effects could set in. (Some of the sex education literature
for teachers did state that an overactive masturbator could be
compensating for a certain loneliness or tension in his life, and
the literature also stated that "compulsive promiscuity" could be
a symptom of insecurity. But none of the sex education experts
recommended attacking such behavior directly.)

But in a broad sense, the Antis shared the values of the sex
education proponents. For the proponents were also interested in
controlling the sexual behavior of the young. In fact, they frequently cited the rising venereal disease rates and illegitimacy
rates as evidence of the need for sex education—implying thereby
that sex education would serve as a deterrent against premarital
sex. In fact, there were very few sex education proponents who
argued that knowledge about sexuality was valuable in and of itself without also mentioning veneral disease and illegitimacy. And
if you examined the history of the development of SIECUS, you
could become convinced that this organization and its professional
allies were every bit as interested in preserving the conventional
morality as were the Antis. In that history, you could also see the
complicity of interest groups, which Robert Welch chose to call
a conspiracy.

* * *

Mary Calderone had told me that the notion of an organization like SIECUS had come out of a conference held in 1961 in Green Bay, Wisconsin. She had urged me to get a copy of a book called *Foundations for Christian Family Policy*, which contained a record of the proceedings at that conference. There, she said, I would find the "whole point of where SIECUS really started— even though we didn't become aware of this for at least four years."

The conference, called "the North American Conference on Church and Family," was organized by Evelyn Millis Duvall and her husband, the Reverend Sylvanus Milne Duvall. Evelyn Duvall was the woman whose books appeared to have drawn the least amount of criticism from the Antis, and I thought I had learned why when I saw an excerpt from one of them in Nicholas von Hoffman's column in *The Washington Post*. Mrs. Duvall's book *Love and the Facts of Life* was being used in the Montgomery County, Maryland, public schools (that county was the scene of a considerable sex education controversy), and von Hoffman had quoted the following passage from it:

Stopping love-making that is already advancing at a rapid rate is not easy. But it can be done. Cora was snuggling close to her boy friend in the car late one night. They were relaxed and happy. They were very fond of each other. He began to kiss her, and she responded eagerly. Then something new came into their love-making as his hand slipped down between her breasts and his kiss took on an intensity that was frightening. Cora struggled free of his embrace, shook her curls with a jerky laugh, saying, 'OOoo, please, you are too much for me.' . . . If two lovers are swept off their feet it is the girl that is blamed. She is held responsible. She should have known better.

I had next encountered Mrs. Duvall's wisdom in the Anaheim curriculum guide. There an excerpt from her book *The Art of Dating* was given the title "Erasing A Mistake," and the message was that if you make the "mistake" of sleeping with your boyfriend or girlfriend, and it leaks out to your friends or your teachers, you will have to behave like a model citizen to live it down.

"Andy is a case in point." Mrs. Duvall had written, continuing:

When he was a sophomore in high school, his girl became pregnant, dropped out of school, and left the community. He was allowed to stay in school but he was forbidden all extracurricular privileges. . . . He talked his unpleasant position over with his principal and his religious adviser, and they suggested that if he applied himself wholeheartedly to his work, his situation might improve in time. During his junior year, by dint of hard work and extra hours in the library, he made the best grades he ever had. He stayed out of mischief, got over his rebellious attitude toward his teachers, and began treating them with respect. He slowly regained the acceptance of both the adults and young people in his school. . . . It was a long hard pull, but Andy made it. He feels it was worth the effort now to be able to walk down Main Street and feel he belongs and is accepted.

Mrs. Duvall's advice to youngsters was so deeply rooted in the puritan traditions and popular misconceptions about the lack of sexual urgency in females that it hardly qualified as sex education in my mind. For Mrs. Duvall was not informing the young with her parables; she was indoctrinating them. She wrote not a word (in those passages) about the possible cruelty of the institutions and customs that demanded that Cora halt the love-making process before her boyfriend did and that Andy suffer a loss of school privileges as punishment for an action that had nothing to do with his academic abilities. It was as if Mrs. Duvall was saying to the young: You are human, and you will find it difficult to live by the rules of your society, so I want to give you a few helpful hints about the mastery of your reckless desires.

It seemed to me that Mrs. Duvall's approach was only stylistically different from that of the Antis. Where the Antis threatened the youngsters with damnation and mental illness, Mrs. Duvall threatened them with social censure, a social censure that was becoming as fictional as eternal damnation. And Mrs. Duvall was not telling the whole truth. She said nothing about contraception or abortion. I thought she did not discuss those prophylactic techniques because she wanted the youngsters to think that the wages of sin were indeed high.

The conference that the Duvalls helped to organize was held at the American Baptist Assembly, and to it came representatives of the National Council of Churches, the Canadian Council of Churches, the Disciples of Christ, the Methodist Church, the Episcopal Church, the United Presbyterian Church, and the American Baptist Convention. It was an assembly of enlightened Christians who prayed to a reasonable and forgiving god, a god who respected the low-keyed devotions of the graduates of Union Theological Seminary, a god who had in recent years seemed to forget about private transgressions of his children, concentrating instead upon their public and political sins. It was an assembly of all the modern Christians, the ones upon whom Billie James Hargis and Carl McIntire would call down all their old fiery wrath and desperately rage against from their pulpits in the Evangelical hinterland.

"Our efforts," Mrs. Duvall told the conference participants on the first day, "will be to search for what seems best for human well-being—of both the individuals involved and of society as a whole—as a basis for Christian family policy." And that is what they did. For five days they listened to the people whom the Antis called "sexperts," people like Lester Kirkendall, Wardell Pomeroy, and Alan Guttmacher (then chairman of the national medical advisory committee of the Planned Parenthood Federation), tell them that premarital sex was on the increase among teenagers, that masturbation was "the most important single source of outlet in terms of frequency" for young adolescent males (Pomeroy), and that the country's abortion laws needed reform.

The purpose of the conference was not to radicalize the churches through the use of these experts, but to encourage their members and leaders to develop new church policies in light of the most recent scientific research in the field of sexuality.

It was, apparently, an exciting conference, for at the end of it, Evelyn Duvall gave a glowing little summary of its "highlights."

"By Thursday [the fourth day] you began to realize that those research specialists were evangelists who spoke your language and shared your concerns," she told the delegates. "You heard Dr. Alan Guttmacher use the phrase, 'our Christian churches,' and one of your groups decided that he is one reason why we shouldn't try to convert the Jews.

"By Thursday you were really communicating as you'd never really talked before. Your discussion was animated, you stopped talking about *them*, and saw yourselves in many of the problems. You shared your experiences, your dilemmas, and your definitions with an unusual openness. When Mrs. Guttmacher asked what you meant by redemptive, you told her, 'That's what your husband was this morning.'"

Another of the "redemptive" specialists was Dr. Mary Calderone. She had told the gathering, "The churches should accept the responsibility for long-term, continuing, realistic, and idealistic sex education programs. Young people themselves should act as consultants in planning its curriculum for their younger brothers and sisters. Here let me say that if ever again another conference is held like this, we should not talk *about* the young people. We should have at least one workshop *for* our young people with no adults present. They have a lot to tell us."

That had been the main point of Dr. Calderone's talk, but she had said several additional things, which—when one considers her later work in SIECUS—shed much light upon her thinking. She emphasized above all the capacity for *controlling* sexual behavior that she thought sex education offered. She was primarily concerned, it should be made clear, with controlling the population explosion. But she did also show some element of concern for the moral questions.

"Those of us who have managed to learn how to combine, in our thinking and hearts and spirits and actions, all of the functions and meanings of sex, can have absolutely no concept of what it is to be a young person, ruthless and rootless, to whom sex is purely a driving urge," she had said.

"If we are not to be destroyed by this unleashed energy, we must learn to use it constructively, and learning implies education. Who is to do that educating? Again let us face the fact that parents can't—they don't know how and they are emotionably unable to. The schools won't. The reasons for this are many but the facts are there; they won't. Just think of the Los Angeles Public Schools where in the senior high school's biology textbook the chapter on human reproduction has been deliberately left out!"

What Dr. Calderone was saying at that time and to that audience made a good deal of sense. If the roundup stories on the new sex education that later appeared in mass circulation magazines were to be believed, the majority of the American public schools were offering little more than a one-shot lesson on menstruation (for the sixth- or seventh-grade girls) as sex education in 1961. If Dr. Calderone could enlist the support of the powerful Protestant churches, she might have reasoned, then one of the mythical barriers to public school sex education would be removed. (The sex education literature frequently stated that school superintendents had avoided sex education on the mistaken assumption that the parents and churches would oppose it. Actually, in many communities, the organized parent groups were to show more enthusiasm for sex education programs than would the school administrators, or so the literature informed me.)

But Dr. Calderone's phrases, "a young person, ruthless and rootless," made me wonder just what kind of sex education she favored. They betrayed a negative view of youthful sexuality, which made me suspect that she wanted to do more than educate the young, that she wanted to create better mechanisms for controlling their sexuality. "Even more important," she had said at another point in her speech, "is the concept of bringing together in the minds of the young the close relationship between religion and the proper use of sex," adding that "marriage is a sacred undertaking." Phrases like "the proper use of sex" and "a sacred undertaking" were borrowed from the language of the moralist and the theologian, and they left me with an uneasy sense that Dr. Calderone had merged her professional public health specialist's concern about the population explosion with her private morality. What she appeared to be arguing for was not merely population control but also a more sophisticated sexual conscience, one that recognized the sex drive as a natural force and gave it latitude within the boundaries of that vague area that she called "proper."

One of her listeners had found her dual message somewhat confusing. She had said at one point that sex is a privilege of emotional maturity (a statement not included in the text of the proceedings, but one which Dr. Calderone was later to repeat). She was asked to reconcile that view with another remark she had made about sex being a "driving force . . . that makes you feel as if you will explode if you don't release it."

"Yes, that's so," she said, apparently meaning, yes, I did say both of those things. "The first definition I gave was to a group of young people, and later on I gave the second definition, which they heartily accepted. I got applause from them for that one, too."

She had not explained the contradiction. And although implicit in her argument for "the proper use of sex" was the assumption that this meant avoiding the creation of unwanted children, she told another questioner that she was "*not* suggesting" the distribution of contraceptives or contraceptive information to teenagers.

By piecing together her various statements, you could begin to perceive what she meant by "the proper use of sex." She meant using it without guilt and without ruthlessness but only *after* you were emotionally mature—whatever that meant. (She did make one off-the-cuff remark concerning the old myths about the harmful effects of masturbation, a remark that led me to believe that she wanted the young to stick diligently to their masturbation until they had passed over that intangible border into emotional maturity.)

*   *   *

Three years after that conference was held SIECUS was formally incorporated. By that time the Anaheim district administration was already developing its sex education curriculum. The birth-control pill had been widely available for four years. The

Twist was already being replaced by the Watusi at teenage parties—black and white. College students were planning a mass invasion of rural Mississippi. And Gordon Drake was getting ready to move to Cape May, New Jersey.

SIECUS was incorporated in May of 1964, and its first office was, fittingly, Mary Calderone's bedroom. As she liked to tell it, she started her first work for the organization with a typewriter set on top of an orange crate. Incorporated as a nonprofit, voluntary health organization, SIECUS received about half of its approximately $500,000 annual budget from numerous foundations, and, until the controversy scared a number of foundations away from contributing money to the organization, it employed eight professional people. (In January, 1970, Dr. Calderone referred to herself as "50 per cent of the professional staff," so acutely was the controversy to affect the organization's budget.)

In the five years before the controversy made itself felt in the SIECUS treasury, the outfit published ten study guides "intended primarily for discussion leaders and for individuals interested in intensive, self-motivated study," put a collection of writings on sex education and sexuality together into a book paid for by a grant from HEW (Called *The Individual, Sex, and Society*, it was intended as a teacher guide), lobbied among professional organizations for expanded community and school sex education, and sent its representatives out into approximately thirty communities that had asked for help in setting up sex education programs.

The fifty SIECUS board members served for three-year terms, and they represented a wide spectrum of opinion and expertise, coming as they did from a variety of "helping professions" and behavioral science fields. Mary Calderone was their official spokesman, however, and thus her many articles and statements were considered by both the organization's friends and its foes as expressions of the SIECUS philosophy.

Over the years, SIECUS collected a whole series of reprints of Dr. Calderone's articles, speeches, and recorded interviews. When you read through these reprints, you could see the same confusing duality of concern she had exhibited at the North American Conference on Church and Family. For she was in favor of open discussion and relatively permissive sexual behavior; she thought no child's question about sex should go unanswered; she thought that categorizing sexual activities under the labels "normal and abnormal" was propagating a "myth"; she deplored the miseducation of women—prior to Masters and Johnson—about the nature of their orgasms (for the record, Kinsey's studies contradicted the

psychoanalysts' myth about the kinds of female orgasm years
before Masters and Johnson published their report); she argued
for providing contraceptives to unmarried "young people" who
were already sleeping together and not willing to give it up. Yet
she was also in favor of stressing to young people the possible
unpleasant consequences of premarital sex. And although she
deplored the exploitation of women inherent in the double
standard, she seemed to subscribe to the almost Victorian notion
that the male sex drive was generally more easily unleashed and
more difficult to control than was the female's.

She had told a freshman class at Vassar:

> If you put the questions to older people who have had a stable mar-
> riage, most of them will answer that it was all worth it—waiting lonely
> years for it, investing a total life in it, the angers, the difficulties, the
> self-disciplining—all made worth it by the golden moments of true
> communication, both sexual and nonsexual. . . . Only time can as-
> sure this—plenty of time, first, to grow up into the woman you were
> meant to be; then time to seek, to identify, and to get to know the
> person you want to relate to; and at long last, time to commune with
> that person within the permanence of a marriage relationship that was
> entered into by yourself consciously and as a whole person, not as one
> who has been nibbled at by bits and pieces given away prematurely.—
> (from a speech delivered in September, 1963, printed in the February,
> 1964, issue of *Redbook*, and reprinted by SIECUS.)

The language in that speech clearly betrayed a deeply Calvinist
view of sex. Dr. Calderone really did appear to think, as the first
New Englanders had, that heterosexual happiness—"the golden
moments"—was something you earned by chalking up years of
good behavior, of restraint. Only she didn't call it good behavior;
she called it, in effect, a worthwhile investment. What was disturbing to me was the way that she had also evoked a predatory
male image and implied that female sexual responsiveness could,
like property, diminish in value with usage through her phrase,
"not as one who has been nibbled at by bits and pieces given
away prematurely."

Most disturbing, however, was the fact that she was contradict-
ing the findings of the sociologists who had studied the staying
power of marital happiness, findings that her own organization
would later publish. Read along with these findings, her speech to
the Vassar girls seemed to contain false promises.

"In a longitudinal study, P. C. Pineo has shown that after
twenty years of marriage most couples reported being less satisfied
with every aspect of it, including the sexual," Carlfred B. Broderick

stated in chapter two of *The Individual, Sex, and Society*. And
he added that "Cuber and Harroff found that only about one-
sixth of their sample of stable upper middle-class marriages could
be rated as 'vital,' and that about half were dominated by a feeling
of mutual antagonism, either passively or actively expressed."
(Broderick was referring to Pineo's address to the Annual Meeting
of the National Council of Family Relations, entitled "Sexual
Communication and the New Morality," delivered in August,
1967, in San Francisco; and to J. F. Cuber and P. B. Harroff's
book, *The Significant Americans: A Study of Sexual Behavior
among the Affluent*; Appleton-Century, 1965.)

Dr. Calderone had delivered that speech long before the
studies that Broderick cited had been published. But it was a
speech that apparently still had the blessing of SIECUS in early
1970, for that was when I bought a copy of it. Even if the text had
seemed accurate when she read it to those Vassar freshmen, it
seemed, in the light of those studies, truly a falsification of the
virtues of marriage. I thought that it was just the kind of speech
that built up cruelly unrealistic expectations about the pleasures
of married life—unrealistic expectations whose ill effects were quite
possibly reflected in the American divorce rate. And it was, in
essence, an argument for chastity. For along with her picture of
the "golden moments" after "lonely years," Dr. Calderone had
given the girls such gems as:

Meaningful sex between a man and a woman probably does not remain meaningful for any appreciable length of time outside of the
marriage relationship; and in using the term 'marriage relationship' I
am not talking only of the legal ceremony itself but of the intent
behind it.

And:

For herein lies the key: marriage is not something *imposed* by society
and religion—far from it. Marriage is a state freely and consciously
and joyfully *sought* by men and women. It is an elective state.

Again, Broderick contradicted her:

Like every other society, ours has the problem of maneuvering its
young people into marriage. It is interesting to note that we are very
successful in doing so. About 94 per cent of our population is married
by the age of forty. This is all the more remarkable because, with its
emphasis on freedom of choice, our society depends upon the voluntary efforts of individuals to achieve this goal. As has been noted,

beginning in infancy, a series of pressures are applied calculated to motivate children to get married some day. . . . Boys are under considerable pressure to find female companions for various social events and girls are under similar pressure to accept and even to encourage such invitations. . . . Lining up a different girl for each occasion takes energy, and there is strong motivation for regularizing successful relationships through steady dating or some other similar arrangement. But even beyond these considerations, the boy has been taught to press for whatever degree of physical intimacy the girl will allow, and the girl has been taught to press for whatever emotional and social commitment she can obtain from the boy.

Broderick certainly did not make the whole process sound as though it was "not something *imposed* by society and religion."

He was too much of a sociologist to consider any socially acceptable behavior totally voluntary.

What bothered me about Dr. Calderone's statements was the way she seemed to be failing to admit her own private moral investment in a presentation that could be read as the observations of an experienced medical expert. She did not have to go around arguing against marriage or in favor of promiscuity—for, as the sociologists had also observed, not enough was known about alternatives to marriage—but I thought she ought to be accurate.

Her later writings and speeches contained the same mixture of expert opinion and private concern evident in her speech to the Vassar girls. She wrote and spoke convincingly of the need for formal sex education from the child's earliest schooling through his high school years. The child was getting sex education from his parents in indirect ways, in any event, she would explain. And she did not think that sex education would seduce the child out of what she considered a mythical innocence. "We have been very busy pretending that the sexuality of children does not exist when in actuality it is our relegation of it to nonexistence that is the cause of distortions and difficulties in later sexuality," she wrote in a chapter of the volume of collected analyses of the Masters and Johnson study (called, *An Analysis of Human Sexual Response*, the book was edited by Ruth and Edward Brecher and published in 1966 by Signet).

Yet in other writings she would state that sex "is a vital human excursion, admission to which must be *earned* by some degree of maturity," again, I thought, allowing her values to interfere with her scientific integrity. How could she say that admission to sex "must be *earned* by some degree of maturity" when she herself believed that sexuality was a constant phenomenon, present from infancy? Apparently, she really meant to say that heterosexual gratification should be earned, for she had made the latter statement to an audience of high school Home Economics teachers. She could criticize the society for denying childhood sexuality, then, but she could not look at the society's taboo against heterosexual gratification in adolescence with the same scientific disdain.

During her presentation at the North American Conference on the Church and Family policy, she had stated that fear of unhappy consequences was probably ineffective as a deterrent against premarital intercourse. Yet in another SIECUS reprint, she seemed to be arguing just the opposite view. (Entitled "Counseling Teen-agers Who Go 'All The Way,'" this reprint had first appeared in the November 25, 1968, issue of *Medical Economics*. It was the text of an interview with Dr. Calderone.) Explaining what she would tell teenagers who asked her why they shouldn't engage in premarital intercourse, she stated here:

We should show them all the fine print at the bottom of the page. Tell them, for example, not only the statistics on teenage pregnancies and divorces, but about the young brides who dash about taking care of a home and three little kids with soiled diapers and then sob into the pediatrician's phone, "I can't stand it anymore!" Tell them that more and more teenagers are leaving school, living in one room, battling parents and each other, and then breaking up their marriages and their own and their children's lives. Getting this sort of information across early might eventually swing the pendulum back toward somewhat less passion and somewhat more wisdom and restraint.

During the same interview, Dr. Calderone did advocate supplying contraceptives to young unmarried couples who admitted they were sleeping together. But it was interesting to note that since she disapproved of early marriage (and the divorce rates are much higher for teenage marriages, especially for those that begin with a pregnant bride), she was quite willing to emphasize the negative aspects of such marriages and to leave out any mention of "golden moments" when discussing them.

In her article called "Sex and Social Responsibility" (which appeared in the September, 1965, issue of the *Journal of Home Economics*), she again expressed some faith in the deterrent power of fear:

We have an obligation to place real-life source material before adolescents—because this is one of the best ways for them to learn what sex is all about—and to help them interpret it. *Teen-Agers and Venereal Disease* by Deschin, Vincent's *Unmarried Mothers*, and

Kirkendall's study of *Premarital Intercourse and Interpersonal Relationships* are studies with direct quotes from young people who have prematurely or distortedly experienced sex. These studies are certainly worth a thousand sermons from adults.

Again, she showed a willingness to present the truth selectively to youngsters. Instead of a propaganda by polemics, she was in favor of filtering material to them that supported her views on morality, and she gave herself away by equating her recommended selection of "real-life source material" with "a thousand sermons from adults."

Though Lester Kirkendall had been writing about the new value system of the young—their increasing tendency to value affection over chastity—I thought that Mary Calderone was still trying to help youngsters adjust to the value systems of their parents. She was a much milder version of Evelyn Duvall, for she did not insist upon chastity before marriage, but rather before "mature" commitment. And, like Evelyn Duvall, she advocated a sex education that was basically a form of moral indoctrination. Also like Mrs. Duvall, she tended to fall back upon the old-fashioned images of the two sexes, exaggerating the male urgency and the female passivity in an age when both were disappearing. Nowhere did she sound more like Mrs. Duvall than in that interview with *Medical Economics*, where she had said:

Well, there may be a shock or two built into giving sound and full sex information. But I'd rather see it transmitted a little too early than too late. For example, my 17-year-old daughter said to me one day about my 14-year-old: "Mother, you've done a very poor job with Maria. She has no idea what a boy suffers when she behaves in a certain way." This was perfectly true. You never do as well with your own as with other people's children, and I'm no exception. Many girls of 14, 15, and 16 don't know that a boy responds instantly with an erection to almost anything: perfumes, actions, words—and miniskirts. We haven't explained to our girls what their role is in avoiding this mutually embarrassing and often dangerous situation.*

*   *   *

* Dr. Calderone herself showed a capacity for lucid insight into her duality of concern during her interview with *Playboy* (April, 1970). She stated it this way:

I'm an individual caught in a moment of tremendous human evolution, an evolution that encompasses many aspects, including the sexual. Obviously, I can't—and don't want to—think or behave like a teenager any longer, even though I communicate with young people on many levels. This means I become caught in some of my own convictions—for example, my really profound belief that sex belongs primarily in marriage. As a

Dr. Calderone was cruelly misjudged by the Antis. Their ears perked up at words like "erection," and they missed the whole point of her messages surrounding such words. She was a woman who spoke out of a profoundly moral concern, and her work was, in essence, an attempt to bolster conventional morality by rendering it more tolerable.

The churches had listened to her, and they had responded. Many of the Protestant—and some of the Evangelical—churches had issued statements in support of public school sex education, and frequently during my travels, I heard complaints from the Antis that such-and-such a local church had started sex education classes for its youngsters. Additional conferences on church and family policy were convened. And by 1969, even the Catholic Church had started a program of sex education in its schools.

Apparently the public schools had responded, too. For by late 1969, journalists estimated that over half the country's public schools had instituted sex education programs. (The NEA people were more cautious in their estimates. They said that school administrators called anything from a lecture on menstruation to a comprehensive kindergarten-through-twelfth-grade program sex education.)

How much of the sex education that came into the schools after SIECUS was founded did so as a result of SIECUS' work and how much of it came as a result of the general relaxation of American strictures against explicit sex in conversation, journalism, art, and advertising during the second half of the sixties was impossible to determine. Dr. Calderone said that SIECUS was originally planned as a "resource" agency to fill a vacuum she had perceived toward the end of her time with Planned Parenthood.

"During my last two or three years as medical director of the Planned Parenthood Federation was when I first became con-

---

scientist and an observer, I know my belief runs counter to the current trend. So what am I to do? I can't stop society from evolving and I can't force other people to adhere to my personal beliefs. No single individual can, not even Gandhi. Not even Jesus—we're still struggling to interpret and live up to the ideals he propagated. Thus, my own life is a paradox in a very real sense. Many of the things I'm open-minded about as a scientist are closed subjects to me personally. But I think this makes me bend over backward to behave with integrity as a scientist. I still struggle to reshape my personal views, though, and I'm constantly learning, growing and changing.

Nevertheless, I did not think she bent over backwards far enough in the direction of science.

vinced that there was—a mission here to be accomplished," Dr. Calderone reminisced during her interview with me. "See, Quakers get concerns, and they worry at them—not worry with them, but worry at them—until they move into an area of *action*. This is *exactly* what happened to me."

She had started to feel that she had accomplished her goals at Planned Parenthood, she said. After she had edited "the first and *still* the only textbook, medical professional textbook, in the field of contraception" (*Manual of Contraceptive Practice*), helped to produce the American Public Health Association's 1959 statement on the importance of family planning, and helped to prod the medical schools and the AMA into paying more attention to family planning problems, she began thinking about a new project —or, rather, "mission."

"I was concerned that something was missing in the family planning program, the Planned Parenthood program. . . . You have to behave sexually before you reproduce. At least *one* of the couple has to. And [I felt] that this wasn't being taken account of at all.

"And I felt strongly that responsible parenthood, *vital* as it is, was really only a segment of something *much* bigger which I thought of as responsible sexuality—which, in turn, is also a segment of something bigger: responsible human relations."

Dr. Calderone was, at 65, what one would call a handsome woman. Her photographs did not do her justice, for she had deep-set blue eyes with great dark circles under them (acquired, I later gathered, from sleepless nights with an "acute back") which could look too cavernous and shadowy in pictures. But in the flesh they were fine, penetrating blue eyes that shone and flashed expressively as she talked. I saw her on three occasions altogether, and each time she was wearing something blue, which drew attention to her extraordinary eyes. And she frequently held her chin aloft when speaking, a mannerism that accentuated the handsome bone structure of her face.

She held her chin high as she spoke of the germination of her current "mission." I would later see her hold her head in the same way at a gathering in the Vassar Club. And on that occasion, I thought I finally understood her curious mixture of medical and moral purposes.

The Vassar Club was filled with white-haired ladies who had come to hear Dr. Calderone make an appeal for funds. By that time—January, 1970—SIECUS was in bad financial straits. The foundations, shaken by the House Banking and Currency Committee's attempt to kill them all off after a forty-year life, were in no mood to fund controversial outfits. Dr. Calderone, who was having back problems, was about to step down from her position as chief executive of SIECUS due either to her health or to the right-wing smears or perhaps both. She had that day gotten out of bed after four supine weeks with her "acute back."

Several of the women in the room were her old schoolmates, and one of these stood up to introduce her. The friend told the little story about young Mary Steichen jolting her class at Brearley "out of its stodginess," praised Dr. Calderone's academic performance, listed her degrees, and gave a brief summary of her career. Then the friend tried to read the complete title of Dr. Calderone's current job. It gave the woman some difficulty, and she haltingly read out, "The Educational and Informational—" and then gave up, looking miserable.

Dr. Calderone, who sat in a chair near her, majestically raised her chin, and, turning to her friend, said in her most dignified tone, "Say, 'Sex.' "

The audience chuckled appreciatively. There, I thought, was her mission. Helping shy old ladies and stodgy institutions to "say 'Sex,' " to recognize it as a legitimate area for discussion and study. Oh, she was performing a kind of service for the young, getting rid of a lot of dead wood between them and the truth, but she was performing a much greater service for adults. The women of her generation, Kinsey had told us, made the great behavioral break with the strictures and codes of the nineteenth century. It was in the twenties that the virginity rates of young unmarried women plummeted down, taking with them the old Freudian diseases like hysteria and the odd, periodic depressions that sent gentlewomen into lassitude for days. Incredibly, the virginity rates had remained nearly the same from the twenties to the late sixties. (Nineteen sixty-seven was the latest year that a study on these rates had been published.) The only change in all those years, so the sociologists told us, was a shift in values. "Although the same percentage of females have coitus, more of them accept this as proper behavior," explained Ira Reiss.* "The highly permissive behavior of the 1920's was probably accompanied by a great deal more guilt and self-recrimination than is now the case. Young people today have the benefit of the therapeutic effects of open

* From his chapter on "Premarital Sexual Standards" in *The Individual, Sex, and Society.* (Baltimore: Johns Hopkins Press, 1969.)

discussion, and they have two generations of permissive behavior behind them."

The women of Dr. Calderone's generation and the women of their daughters' generation had had to live with a cruel disparity between their values and their behavior. To them Dr. Calderone's attempts to eliminate that disparity must have seemed redemptive indeed. But to the young—at least to the vocal and strident young —her mission would appear to have already outlived its purpose. The granddaughters of those Vassar women would view that story of her first, unhappy marriage not as an argument against pre-marital sex but as compelling evidence of the need for repeal of the abortion laws.* Even as Dr. Calderone spoke to her peers, the women of their granddaughters' generation were arguing a pro-cedural point in their case challenging the constitutionality of New York State's then 142-year-old abortion law.

But if she had told her story to those women in the Vassar Club, they would probably have responded with a weary gratitude, thinking to themselves: "Oh, you, too. . . ."

*   *   *

As for the little man who so misunderstood Dr. Calderone's purposes that he made a politics out of opposing them, he had his mission, too. He might have doctored the truth somewhat in carrying it out, but he seemed to believe his own cause despite its sometimes tenuous ties to reality. He came to believe in it so much by November of 1969 that he sacrificed his fine job with that rising Bible Belter to remain true to it. Hargis had let him know in no uncertain terms that he wanted Drake to drop that case against the Tulsa school board.

"As far as I'm concerned, this is sheer hypocrisy," Drake told me not long after he resigned from the Christian Crusade. "How can he [Hargis] lead the fight against sex education all over the country and then here in Tulsa, where they have as bad an in-tegrated program of sex education [meaning integrated into the curriculum] as anywhere in the country, he won't fight it?"

Drake had resigned November 10th. He said that he would be moving to Milwaukee in the spring. He and some of his old friends up there were planning to start something that would be called the American College. And it would be a four-year college, not

* In her *Playboy* interview, Dr. Calderone said she favored abortion laws that would leave the decision to the woman and her doctor. Usually she avoided the subject of abortion.

one of those two-year Bible schools like the one Hargis was building.

Gordon Drake told me he really did think that sex education could damage children. In his pamphlet, he had written:

The embarrassing frankness of many sex education programs force the sensitive child to suppress his normal, emotion-charged feelings in listening to class discussion. This may develop into serious anxieties. On the other hand, he may either become coarsely uninhibited in his involvement in sex or develop a premature secret obsession with sex. The kindergartener and primary grade child may very well resort to sex play and involved experimentation.

When I asked him where he had gotten that theory, he said that it was his own, derived from his years of work as a guidance counselor.

It sounded, however, suspiciously like a theory voiced by one of the authorities quoted in the Kobler article in the *Saturday Evening Post*, an article from which Drake had drawn a good deal of his shock material in the pamphlet. This authority, a psychologist named Rhoda Lorand, had been quoted by Kobler as saying:

"How far is this folly [sex education] going to go? They're repeating the same mistake the Freudians made years ago. The rationale then was that since repressions may cause neuroses, get rid of all repressions. So parents made a point of calling their children's attention to sexual matters, and they condoned primitive sexual behavior. Yet children so reared often developed severe anxieties. When psychoanalyzed, they revealed the damage this system caused. We know now that the sublimation of sexual curiosity and behavior is necessary if children are to acquire intellectual training. Otherwise they might play sex games all day long. Sublimation, in fact, is the price we must pay to live in a civilized society. Cramming sex knowledge down kids' throats does not promote healthy growth. The likely effect is more anxiety, not less."

The Antis were proud of having Rhoda Lorand on their side because she was a bona fide child analyst—and she called herself a doctor, but that was because she had a Ph.D. in education.

I obtained a copy of a letter that Rhoda Lorand had written to one of the original California Antis, a Mrs. Alice Wiener from San Luis Obispo. She had written:

"Child analysts have, during the past 25 years, accumulated incontrovertible evidence demonstrating that it is a mistake to interfere with the latency period (6 to 10), when the major portion of sexual energy and curiosity is normally redirected into learning academic subjects and physical skills."

I subsequently wrote to Dr. Lorand, asking her for an interview. She replied that she could not, in any case, see me for two months, and that she would only agree to it if I gave her the right to edit what I wrote about her. In my letter to her, I had said that I wanted to ask her about her latency theory. And in her reply, she had said that it was not *her* latency theory, it was Sigmund Freud's. Perhaps she had never read Freud's open letter on "The Sexual Enlightenment of Children," in which he stated:

What can be the aim of withholding from children, or let us say from young people, this information about the sexual life of human beings? Is it a fear of arousing interest in such matters prematurely, before it spontaneously stirs in them? Is it a hope of retarding by concealment of this kind the development of the sexual instinct in general, until such time as it can find its way into the only channels open to it in the civilized social order? Is it supposed that children would show no interest or understanding for the facts and riddles of sexual life if they were not prompted to do so by outside influence? Is it regarded as possible that the knowledge withheld from them will not reach them in other ways? Or is it genuinely and seriously contended that later on they should consider everything connected with sex as something despicable and abhorrent, from which their parents and teachers wish to keep them apart as long as possible?

I am really at a loss to say which of these can be the motive for the customary concealment from children of everything connected with sex. I only know that these arguments are one and all equally foolish, and that I find it difficult to pay them the compliment of serious refutation.*

In the same piece, Freud stated that "children should never get the idea that one wants to make more of a secret of the facts of sexual life than of any other matter not suited to their understanding. . . . Above all, schools should not evade the task of mentioning sexual matters."

In any event, Gordon Drake was convinced that his sexual theory was all his own and was not derivative from Rhoda Lorand's interesting interpretation of Freud. Drake didn't like to give anyone else credit for his brilliance. He told me he consulted no one, that he was "a leader, not a follower." And during my session with him in Tulsa, he kept repeating variations on that theme.

He cared quite a lot for his independence—even though he appeared to be quite dependent upon the right wing's good graces.

* First published in *Soziale Medizin und Hygiene*, II, 1907, as an "open letter" to the editor, Dr. M. Fürst; E. B. M. Herford translation. (New York: Crowell-Collier, 1963.)

One of my sources told me that he had dared to antagonize the audience at the Birchers' God, Family, and Country rally in July of 1969, urging them to go a little easy on their foes, to stop calling them up in the middle of the night and the like.

His quarrel with the sex education proponents seemed at least partially motivated by his confirmed hatred for large power groups. He told me that he believed in "local control" of the schools and that he hoped the sex education battles would motivate more parents to take an active interest in school affairs. Perhaps that was a disguised form of segregationist polemics—the southerners used the phrase "local control" as a euphemism for segregation. But I thought that Drake was more frightened of big government and big professional lobbies like the NEA than he was of the blacks. Despite his absurdities, his Commie smears, and his exaggerated sex education atrocity stories, his populism had its appeal. For he *was* the son of a cost accountant from Wauwatosa, Wisconsin, and he would never be invited to the Yale Club.

And after he left the Christian Crusade, he made a remark that revealed just what a proud little loner he was:

"After all these years in the profession workin' for somebody," he said, "I don't work for anybody. . . . There's no point in trying to mold myself [to suit a boss]."

Still, proud little Gordon Drake, father of six children ("They say I'm hung up on sex, and I say: prove it!"), ace pamphleteer, spiritual heir to Joseph McCarthy and William Jennings Bryan, had made a terrible mistake. He, like Townsend, had gone after the wrong target.

Saving It for the Back Seat

Those crying loudest for sex education, they're disassociating the sex act from interpersonal relations. . . . Mary Calderone has been praising masturbation as a solution to all problems. Aquinas said that masturbation was worse than fornication because it was antisocial. . . . There is narcissism involved. You can't have a relationship with yourself.—DR. HERBERT RATNER, editor of *Child and Family* magazine, speaking to the delegates at the National Convention on the Crisis in Education, Chicago, August 31, 1969.

You have to love yourself before you can love anyone else; I believe this holds true on the physical level as well as the philosophical. My advice to the uptight is: Go fuck yourselves, you'll feel better.—VAL, in her column entitled "Ego Trip," volume 4, number 3 of the Chicago underground newspaper *Seed*.

Understandably, the maximum physiologic intensity of orgasmic response subjectively reported or objectively recorded has been achieved by self-regulated mechanical or automanipulative technique. The next highest level of erotic intensity has resulted from partner manipulation, again with established or self-regulated methods, and the lowest intensity of target-organ response was achieved during coition.—In MASTERS and JOHNSON, *Human Sexual Response* (Boston: Little, Brown, 1966.)

It started with a prayer for the Lord's help in the fight against "the humanistic godless effort to destroy the sanctity of the home and the well-being of the children of America." And following that there was the pledge of allegiance, and following that the national anthem. Then the chairman stepped up to the podium to announce that something special was coming. She asked the TV people to turn down their lights. The TV people didn't respond appreciatively, and in the back of the room, a woman snapped, "Who the hell wants the news media, anyway?" The chairman reacted more graciously. She sighed and got on with the business of ushering in the special treat.

Up at the podium appeared now a little blond-haired girl wear-

246

ing a party dress. She must have stood on a chair because she was visible from the waist up, standing immobile and expressionless. From somewhere behind the podium came a harsh female voice with a pronounced Southern accent. "Ah am a child," said the voice. "In me lies the hope of the future. . . . Protect me, for Jesus said, 'Let the little children come unto me.' " The voice went on to say something about protecting parents and teachers, too, and then closed with a reverent, "Thank you, God, for the beauty and wonder of our children." It was high and shrill and so very Southern that the sound of it alone without the face or body or history of the person it issued from told of a bitter and resentful politics.

Eventually a large woman dressed in pink and looking pinch-faced emerged from behind the podium and led her impassive little hope of the future away.

Thus began the opening rally of the National Convention on the Crisis in Education, a gathering of delegates from parents' groups in twenty-two states that had vowed to combat sex education in the public and parochial schools and, while they were at it, to prevent school integration through busing, to forbid psychological testing of students, to halt teacher sensitivity training sessions, and to get prayer back into all the nation's classrooms.

They were gathered that Friday evening, August 29, 1969, in the Willifred Room up on the third floor of the Conrad Hilton. There were, the Chicago papers later estimated, about 350 people at the opening rally, a number of them conservative Catholics from the Chicago area.

If Mrs. Albert Westerfield, the Chicago housewife who planned the convention, was at all aware of the peculiar irony in the timing and location of this affair, she didn't say. But it was just one year and one day after the Democratic party had wrought its own doom outside this huge hotel, and here they were, a collection of Richard Nixon's and George Wallace's most forgotten Americans, moved into Chicago for their very own convention. It was a convention that had been planned as far back as the previous May, for that was when Steinbacher had given it some free advertising in his column. Some of the delegates might have read about it there. But if you asked them how they heard about it, they would tell you they got the news "along the grapevine," which must have been a pretty big grapevine, for some of them had come all the way from Hawaii.

They came into the huge, expensive hotel where every inch of floor space is covered with spongy carpeting, and they greeted each other in the lobby near the hallway called Main Street, which didn't look like anybody's version of Main Street but rather like the hallway in some great luxury liner, with its little glittering display windows and shops. They looked out of place there in the hotel, these people from the real Main Streets of places like Bettendorf, Iowa, and Orlando, Florida. They looked as though they had long ago been taught the consequences of sin and hence could be expected to avoid exposure to the places where it was carried out.

But perhaps the Hilton represented to Mrs. Westerfield the real big time, the place where her husband's bosses (he held two jobs) might go to confer with one another. And indeed the Comprehensive Medical Society had held a conference for sex educators in the Hilton just two weeks before her convention. She said she had picked the place because it was "centrally located," it was a good $6 taxi ride from the airport where most of the national delegates had arrived.

In any case, there was little time for the delegates to be tempted by the fancy restaurants and jewelled watches on the main floor. And if any of them sneaked downstairs, it wasn't noticed, because those who cared about what they had come there to do were continually listening to speeches—there were thirty-four of these —or voting on resolutions from the time they arrived Friday evening until about one o'clock Monday morning. Unless, of course, somebody did a little sinning in the time allotted for church attendance Sunday morning.

"These people are hearty," Mrs. Norma Morrison, a Chicago suburbanite who did research on the right wing, had told me before I arrived at the Hilton. That proved to be an understatement. There wasn't even time, during that whole weekend of decency, for any of the delegates to sneak off to Grant Park to reconfirm their hatred of the enemy firsthand. The Chicago longhairs were all at a concert there Saturday afternoon, celebrating the anniversary of the massacre, but we only caught a few tantalizing glimpses of their bare feet and braless lasses in between the spirited speeches upstairs.

Even the bedside reading was more than a zealot could consume in one weekend. Mrs. Westerfield had prepared some handsome loose-leaf notebooks for every delegate, notebooks packed full of shocking quotes from behavioral scientists and sex educators, newspaper reprints about sex education classes and sensitivity training sessions, random sets of atrocity stories, and helpful texts of letters to the editor and the Attorney General with appropriate blanks to be filled in with the name of your own home town and school district. Mrs. Westerfield had really done her homework, for she actually quoted Lester Kirkendall correctly, and she did not push the Communist conspiracy theme, only going so far as to suggest that Mary Calderone had been influenced by a man named G. Brock Chisholm who had helped to found the World Health Organization. Chisholm had been so shaken by the rabid nationalism that led to World War II that he had written compellingly of the need to eliminate both nationalism and rigid moral strictures, both of which, he was convinced, helped to create sick societies.

In addition to the notebooks, there were three long tables out in the hallway on the third floor covered with piles of pamphlets and leaflets that the delegates had brought along to sell to each other. Some of these materials contained bold assertions of the Antis' conspiracy theories.

Each delegate who gave Mrs. Westerfield $27.50 was given a notebook and a little name card with the title of his organization typed next to a small, crudely drawn map of his state. Room costs, which were specially reduced for the delegates (down to $14 from the usual $22.50 Hilton minimum), were not included in the registration fee, but one lunch and one dinner were, along with voting rights and the abovementioned goodies.

In case you didn't get to read all those name tags, someone from each delegation gave a speech Friday evening. Lucky Kansas was allowed to provide two speakers, and there was even a man from Calgary, Alberta, Canada's Bible Belt province. So that first evening session accounted for twenty-four of the thirty-four speeches. It was a long evening.

There was a lady from a parents' and taxpayers' group in California who quoted the Reverend Billy Graham on pornography. There was the woman from Citizens for Moral Education in Orlando, Florida, who said, "We know our enemy is promoting revolution in this country by every means possible: sex education, drugs, music." There was the man from the Georgia Basic Education Council who drew hearty applause when he said, "Greetings from Maddox country." There was the woman from Concerned Citizens of Hawaii who brought orchids for everyone and in a choked voice related a story in graphic detail of the day her daughter, age nine, came home from school and broke her heart by remarking, "Mom, some of the older kids in school told me that in order to have a baby a man must rub his penis against a woman's vagina." She, the mother, blamed the sex educators for this incident (A sex education series called *The Time of Your Life* had been shown over educational television in Hawaii—the same series that Antis objected to in San Mateo County, California), and she warned her audience that if sex education came to their schools, "You'll be robbed as I was of the privilege of telling your child in your own way of the beauty of creation." There was a Mrs. Flemming who had led a fight two years past in the Chicago area against the use of a parochial school textbook that presented the Reverend Martin Luther King, Jr., in a favorable light. Mrs. Flemming received a standing ovation from the crowd in the Willifred Room after she urged Chicago's Catholic Archbishop to "stick to the business of saving souls" instead of using "our money for supporting the Poor People's Campaign . . . and the very questionable Cesar Chavez."

The vocal woman in the back of the room shouted, "Communist!" at the mention of Chavez's name.

There was the man from Bettendorf, Iowa, who kept straying from his points about the evils of sex education to make remarks about the generation gap and the "abnormal ideas about authority and respect" that he said his children were absorbing in school. There was the mother from Michigan who should have won a prize for delivering the spiciest talk of the evening. She drew a connection, toward the end of her speech, between the recent series of murders around Ann Arbor and an article in *Sexology* magazine (to which prominent sex educators contribute) on sex and cruelty. There was even a man from Long Island, a Catholic named James McKenna, who had a way of pulling in his chin and scowling out at his listeners in a manner reminiscent of Joe McCarthy. He didn't say much, but during the next two days he was to make himself known to almost every delegate, pushing for a national organization.

The oratory went on until well after midnight, and although the crowd had thinned out some by the end, the twenty-four nonstop speeches were laced with gripping sex education atrocity stories to hold our attention. These tales fell into two general categories: those that were personal and usually began with a child's indiscreet remark, and those that were of uncertain source. The latter group rated much higher in interest value, for they contained action. Some of the speakers considered this second group of tales so interesting that they did not at all mind repeating them, often with slight embellishments and editorial comments.

Three of the favorites were:

The gym class in which students go into a closet in pairs to explore each other's anatomy.

The seven-year-old girl who is found lying on top of a girlfriend after she's been told (apparently not too clearly) how babies are conceived.

The little boy and girl who come out of a sex education class, go into a building, and conduct a "scientific experiment" on one another.

The SIECUS staff and board members were frequently quoted during that first evening and throughout the next two days. And the speakers were not as careful as Mrs. Westerfield had been; they used both the Kirkendall Sneak-It-In quote from Steinbacher's column and the doctored Calderone quotes from Drake's pamphlets. They also gave slide showings of some antiseptic line drawings of adult nudes that had been put out by the 3M company (they were prepared by the School Health Education Study group in Washington, D.C., an outfit that had been studying health curriculae for over ten years). One of these slides—an "optional one" the 3M people later told me—contained a side view of a man with an erection, which could have been exciting if the artist who drew the graphic profile had only given the man an enthusiastic facial expression. Nevertheless, the Antis thought this slide was just about the living end, and I was later to see it reproduced on some Anti leaflets in Madison, Wisconsin, and included in Mrs. Howe's magazine and poster display. The all-time favorite visual shocker seemed to be the two illustrations from the Time-Life book *How Babies Are Made,* those cartoon pictures of the dogs and chickens mounted atop one another.

Just about everything that they had been able to dig up that a sex educator had said (or was reported to have said) or that was contained in a sex education curriculum seemed to bother the delegates. And any speaker was absolutely *guaranteed* shocked gasps and murmurs from the audience whenever he said that some sex educator someplace had written or said: Masturbation is normal, heavy petting is not sinful, premarital intercourse is becoming acceptable, or homosexuality should be regarded with compassion.

Mrs. Flemming really stirred them when she quoted a Dr. Finch (who, she said, denied the statement) as saying, "I would rather have a boy masturbate for eight or ten times a day than run around with wild women."

"*Both,*" said Mrs. Flemming, "are morally wrong."

Those people had come a long way to be among their own kind, and they didn't seem at all disturbed by the repetitiveness of their speeches. What mattered was that they were speaking to and being heard by *each other*. For too long, speakers would frequently say, they had been fighting the PTA or the school board or even the *churches* back home, and they were tired of being treated like a dispossessed kook fringe. One wondered, listening to them that first night, how often they had been in one room with 350 people who actually agreed with them. Oh, the southerners had probably not suffered from too much isolation. And those people from the potato states and big midwestern cities could probably draw quite a few fundamentalists 'and like-minded folk to their rallies. But that refrain against the local PTA's was voiced too frequently for anyone hearing it to believe that they had massive support back home. No, they were too eager to be together, too eager to hear and to give the same speech over the over again. They needed each other badly.

So when a minister from Kimball, Nebraska, read some questions from that sex knowledge test that Sam Campbell had printed in the *Anaheim Bulletin,* the audience didn't seem to mind— even though a number of them must have read the questions already. For Campbell had sent the whole section of his paper in which that test appeared to various scattered Antis. And when Edith Winter, a severe-looking woman from New Jersey, told them, "Behavioral scientists, they don't know what people are like," they applauded her warmly. They were as enthusiastic about the wisdom of Mrs. Dorothy Faber, a woman from Missouri who put out a paper called *Christian Challenge.* Mrs. Faber told them all about Brock Chisholm and the World Health Organization even though most of them probably knew all about him and that terrible Commie-controlled, atheistic, one-world organization he had helped to found. According to the behavioral scientists like Chisholm, said Mrs. Faber, "you and I are in a bad state of mental health."

Mrs. Faber was really quite moving. She said that recently a priest had come to her in despair and asked her:

"What would you do, Dottie, if a high school senior came into your office and said, 'Father, I have given up the pill for Lent?' "

And, of course, Mrs. Faber and Mrs. Winter were right. The behavioral scientists didn't know much about people like them and would probably classify them as unhealthy. That's because the behavioral scientists didn't believe in God and Country anymore, and what's more they thought they were of such superior intelligence that they could just about take over child rearing or at least tell the schools how to take it over. The very first night, the woman from Hawaii had told everybody how the Hawaii Board of Education was planning to take children away from their parents at a very tender age. She had proof because she had gotten a hold of a copy of the state's new master plan, which, she said, mentioned day-care centers for two-year-old children. Not only that, but those Hawaii master planners had the audacity to suggest that advances in biochemistry might make it possible in the near future to give children *drugs* that would help them learn more readily. (Mrs. Westerfield had put excerpts of that Hawaii master plan into the delegates' notebooks along with sections of an article entitled "Forecast for the 70's" by Harold G. Shane of Indiana University, which contained similar predictions about the use of drugs. Shane's article had appeared in the January, 1969, issue of *Today's Education,* a magazine put out by the NEA.)

The hatred of behavioral scientists was not new to the group. Some of them had been incensed years back when the schools started giving their children psychological tests that included questions about their family's economic status and general harmony. Now the behavioral scientists were not just telling them that they couldn't educate their own children in the facts of life, but they were also hinting that the good old morality was a crippling, devastating thing for a normal child.

And the PTA, the NEA, HEW, the "so-called intellectuals," and UNESCO all seemed to be linked together in the minds of the delegates. Those were the havens of the behavioral scientists; and the hated professional-intellectual elite were in cahoots with them. An interlocking directorate of, well, almost effete snobs who looked down their noses at women who could still so innocently say that sex education was like "an ugly snake."

"It's like fighting the Establishment," one lady from Texas remarked well into the second day. She was speaking to a young sociology student who was there to gather material for his paper about the reaction against sensitivity training. He was a gentle student, and he listened to the delegates respectfully. So the Texas lady had started telling him her troubles. But she obviously thought he was a radical.

"Boy, if you think you all are fighting the Establishment, you oughtta try fighting the NEA!" she had told him.

She, too, was, in essence, right. The NEA was a very powerful lobby. Just that spring the NEA had helped to organize a coalition of all the education lobbyists in Washington, which later in conjunction with powerful labor groups, had managed to twist a good deal of money out of Congress, despite the fact that the official 1969–70 appropriation bill for HEW had been held up in committee. Edith Green, a conservative Democrat from Oregon, was to call the education lobby the new "educational-industrial complex" later in the year. And if John Herbers of *The New York Times* could be believed, the NEA and its allies constituted by late 1969 "one of the most effective lobbies on Capitol Hill."*

What could a poor Texas parent do against a group like that? What's more, the NEA wasn't the only powerful group that supported sex education. Why, even the AMA had decided it was a good thing, and you couldn't get deeper into the Establishment than *that*.

But there was much more than a hatred of the Educational Establishment being voiced and voiced and voiced again at that convention. There was the segregationist ranting of the southerners. There was the wacky psychology of the right-wing doctors. There was the frequent lament for the good old days when children still respected their parents. And through it all there was an odd kind of verbal exhibitionism, an overabundance of sexual words and readings of descriptions of intercourse from sex education textbooks. It was as if the delegates felt that obscenity in defense of decency was required in their speeches. Quite frequently, they used the words they considered obscene "penis," "vagina," "clitoris," as well as words describing acts they considered obscene or evil: "sodomy," "bestiality," "numerality," "oral-genital acts."

Kent Courtney, the one avowed Bircher who was there, commented about their spicy language to me during the second day. "The people here are desensitizing themselves by talking about the things they don't want their children to talk about," he said. And he must have made the same remark to the Reverend David Webber of Oklahoma City's Southwest Radio Church of the Air, for on Sunday, the Reverend told the group:

"We are somewhat desensitized, sex-hardened. . . . Is that what you want for your children?"

Courtney and the Reverend covered two of the favorite themes between them. Courtney, who hadn't been made to feel welcome because the Westerfields were nervous about being associated with the Birchers, showed *Pavlov's Children* to a small audience up in his own private meeting room on Saturday night. And afterwards he gave a little talk about how they all should fight together to get

* In the November 3, 1969, issue of *The New York Times*.

the federal money out of the schools. He was a large, red-faced man who had displayed some humor about himself. Earlier he had, with a mirthful look, told me about the "underground newspaper" for the right wing that he'd started in New Orleans after he heard that I wrote for *The Village Voice*. Sharing shop talk with an easy friendliness, he had said that he put a young man in charge of it who was very good. "I'd say, 'Go after the Black Panthers, give me 1,500 words, and give me a footnote in every paragraph,'" he had said, his eyes alight with what appeared to be a touch of self-mockery—for he was rattling off the formula for a right-wing article.

Courtney was dressed in white from head to toe—well, his shoes were black and white—and he looked the very picture of a small town southern judge. After our little conversation, he would give me an impish wink whenever he caught my eye. That struck me as a nice friendly gesture and a welcome one among all those grim-faced women who regarded me with the edge of suspicion in their faces. Like Royal Marten, he seemed to be laughing at the politics of those overwrought parents.

But Courtney's mirthfulness lost its appeal after I heard him give that little speech at his *Pavlov's Children* showing. He was basically trying to plug his wife's new paperback, *The Sex Education Racket*, but he got in a few remarks that his political hero, George Wallace, would have been proud of. It seemed pretty clear when he began to talk about getting the federal funds out of public schools that he was advocating the southern version of "local control," and after he told a little joke about Martin Luther King, there was no doubt about it. He said that King had called him up "the other night" to tell him:

"You know, I got to the top of the mountain—and I fell off into hell."

To their credit, the people in Courtney's small audience did not laugh at the jest, and so Courtney lamely added, "Well, if Bishop Pike can talk to his son. . . ."

But most of the people hadn't come up to Courtney's private showing to hear segregationist polemics, and they soon got him back on their favorite subjects. One old man stood up to say he had been fighting rent control for years. "We started this Communist conspiracy thing in 1932–33 when Roosevelt recognized Russia."

Another, younger, man rose to say, "I work in the Michigan State Legislature. . . . People ask me [to help them].

"A couple of girls from our community went down to Kalamazoo Teachers College and in one year they were completely changed. What do they *do* to our girls?"

In distraught tones, the Michigan legislator asked where there was a "safe school." People in the audience suggested Bob Jones University and Shelton College—both fundamentalist schools.

What the schools might do or already had done to their girls and boys—but girls especially—was the real heart of the non-southern delegates' concern. And though they passed resolutions against school busing and "forced integration," though they ranted against psychological tests and deplored the Supreme Court's school prayers decision, they always seemed to come back to this fear: that their children would turn on them, or, worse still, abandon them and all traces of their teachings.

"I'm not so concerned about society's orphaned children," the Reverend Webber, who obviously knew their fears, said during his Sunday speech, "as I am about the parents that are being orphaned."

The Reverend Webber also got in a few lines about the Woodstock festival, the "so-called protest music festival," he called it, to show where he stood on children who abandoned the ways of their parents (even though it could not be proved that the Woodstock crowd had done so in more than superficial ways). He described them with "their unshaven faces and their tumbling blankets," and then went on to say:

"You would never find in the annals of medical history a bunch of better sexually educated kids. They are numerality students."

Strictly speaking, that was not true. The college-age youngsters in the Woodstock crowd had not gotten much sex education, or *formal* sex education. But that wasn't the point. They *seemed* to have gotten it. And in that crowd in the Hilton, it was the appearance that mattered.

The medical speakers provided the added assurance that sex education would not only produce evil behavior, but would actually damage the youngsters. A Dr. James Parsons told the assembly that children who were allowed to masturbate would grow up with weak characters. And a Dr. Herbert Ratner told them that the activity was "antisocial." One would be hard put to rate the wisdom of one of these medics above that of the other, but Ratner did seem to be a little more interested in general family problems. Parsons, on the other hand, spent a good deal of time talking about Swedish perverts.

Some of Ratner's gems were:

There's something about the, ah, sex drive that if it gets out of hand prudence disappears. . . .

The more education you get, the greater your chances of losing your common sense. . . .

The problem today is not education but *de*-education. We need to get back to nature. . . .

Man functions logically. Woman is like an angel. . . . She sees the conclusion immediately. This is the way a woman functions. . . . Woman has a telekinesthetic sense. . . . But the woman has to permit the man to make decisions. It's more than that, really. She isn't capable of making decisions.

I remember once . . . there were two cats copulating in the back yard. And my daughter said, "Daddy, they're getting married." And I said to myself, if my daughter grows up realizing that copulation belongs in marriage, then I have nothing to worry about.

Dr. Ratner was a harmless looking grey-haired man. Toward the end of his talk, he urged the delegates to abstain from "name-calling" and guard against "self-righteousness." He appeared to be getting mellow.

Not so Dr. Parsons, who worked as a consultant psychiatrist for Patrick Air Force Base and Pan American Airways in Orlando, Florida. Parson's appeared to know all about the various Communist plots in education and just about everywhere else, and his writings appealed to Congressman John Rarick so much that that patriotic southerner had inserted some of them into the Congressional Record.

Dr. Parsons wore the psychiatrist's dark-rimmed glasses on his southern preacher's baby-face, and he used the language of both professions. He called sex education "programed perversion" and told the delegates to "make no mistake" about it. It was, he said, "a continuing stimulation of school children beginning long before [such stimulation has taken place by] natural maturing and continuing long after their natural curiousity has been satisfied." But that was not all. Dr. Parsons even went on to imagine the shocking conversations that could be expected among children who had been exposed to such education.

"For a little red-headed girl with freckles to be told, 'I bet you have freckles on your vagina,' " he conjectured, "can do lasting damage."

That remark was, one had to admit, something to think about. And Dr. Parsons was evidently fond of it, for he had included a slightly altered version of it (in which the girl did not have red hair) in one of the articles that Rarick had inserted into the Congressional Record. There it was set down for all posterity to see (under the heading "The Gathering Storm: Sex Education Versus the 'No-No' Moralists") along with two gory case histories of the good doctor's patients, who masturbated into women's underwear —one, according to Parsons, because of a permissive mother; the other, because of early public school sex education.

According to a poll conducted by the University of Chicago— the results of which had been published ten days before Parsons delivered this speech (without the interesting case histories), 83.7 per cent of a large sample of the country's psychiatrists and psychologists thought that people who were exposed to pornography were no more likely to commit "antisocial" sexual acts than the unlucky ones who never saw the stuff. What's more, 86.1 per cent of the sample group thought that people who fought strenuously to stamp out pornography were often afflicted with unresolved sexual problems of their own.

Still, Parsons wasn't your ordinary psychiatrist, and that's why he had been invited to speak at the Chicago convention. He really belonged to a category all his own, as a little conversation he had with the anti-Establishment Texas woman revealed:

TEXAS WOMAN: The president of our PTA is a marvellous Christian woman, and she's convinced that sex education is going to solve the problems of illegitimacy. How do you convince people like her?

PARSONS: You know what the next thing will be? What happened in Orlando. They produce hypnosis by music. They play records that hypnotize the children and then inject certain messages. Or they just produce hypnosis and then the teacher can say anything to them.

TEXAS WOMAN: They want me to give a positive alternative.

PARSONS: I think Christ had a [good answer] when he said, "The poor will always be with us."

TEXAS WOMAN: But that's kind of a ho-hum answer.

Dr. Parsons broke off there, and it was too bad because he had neglected to tell her about the precious bodily fluids. As it was, the Texas lady went away dissatisfied.

She was seriously concerned, as a good number of the delegates seemed to be, about what she thought was the school's interference with sacred parental rights. Her trouble was that she didn't know how to convince the folks back home, and speakers like Parsons didn't provide her with the arguments she needed. For if she wasn't to be accused of having unresolved sexual tensions of her own, if she wasn't to be diagnosed into embarrassed silence by a professional establishment and by the more sophisticated parents, she had to keep clear of those wacky theories emanating from her more extreme allies. She seemed to sense this, and she sadly went back to the gentle young sociology student, almost ready to appeal to him for useful arguments. She was really afraid this sex education business would lead to other things and that eventually children would be taken from their parents altogether to be reared by "professional parents," she told him.

It was difficult to estimate just how many of the delegates were, like the Texas woman, among the more moderate right-wingers. The convention had, of course, been announced in the less than moderate columns of John Steinbacher. And a sizeable selection of chronic pamphleteers showed up, people with children long grown, and some with grandchildren. But Mrs. Westerfield *had* made her anti–Birch Society feelings known well enough in advance to incur the wrath of Birchers as far away as California. Townsend later handed me a xeroxed copy of a newspaper clipping in which an unidentified MOTOREDE committee chairman was quoted as saying, "When Mrs. Westerfield's motives are made clear, and she is exposed as a one woman committee, I doubt that other groups will bother to send delegates." The clipping had no date on it, and although it was credited to the Associated Press, it ended with an editorial comment that was quite uncharacteristic of any wireservice style. Mrs. Westerfield's friends (or someone—Townsend suggested Mrs. Westerfield herself) subsequently printed up a leaflet branding the story a "phony paste-up" designed to plant "doubts as to the integrity of a great leader. . . . There is sufficient reason," the text continued, "to believe a certain group in Orange County, after attempting to control CHIDE's [Mrs. Westerfield's organization] National Convention and failing, set forces in motion that resulted in the phony story on the integrity of Mrs. Westerfield and CHIDE." *That* leaflet was put out by something called the Parents Protective League of 1412 Ivar Street, Sacramento, California, and Townsend gave me a copy of it on which he had written, "This organization is not at this address, and this, too, is a phony story."

Mrs. Westerfield's attempts to keep the Birchers away from her convention seemed to have backfired on her—either that or she had grievously overestimated the legions of local Antis. For she had arranged to hold the first night's rally in the Auditorium Theater two blocks from the Hilton. At the last minute, the delegates who did show up were turned away from the theater—a place which holds several hundred more than the 350 who appeared—and sent up to the much smaller Willifred room of the

Hilton. (The Hilton management had thrown that room in free of charge because Mrs. Westerfield had brought them over 100 guests for the weekend.)

Throughout the convention there were little underlying tensions between the faction that had apparently believed the Birchers and those who supported Mrs. Westerfield. Nevertheless, a National Committee on the Crisis in Education did emerge intact from the last long-winded session, and Mrs. Westerfield was elected as one of the committee's national coordinators. Late in the evening of that last session, a woman from Wisconsin stood up and angrily called for a "rump convention."

Throughout the weekend, Mrs. Westerfield had been telling me that the Birchers were out to get her, and as the bitterness of the delegates who were opposed to any national organization headed by *her* showed itself that last evening, she became weepy. She circulated around the room looking flustered, her *lei* from the Hawaiian faction all askew, and, watching her discomfort, I began inwardly rooting for her.

Early in the convention she had explained to me that the delegates were just plain folk with no connections to the large right-wing organizations. She said they were people like herself who just wanted to be left alone—without the school busing she'd been fighting against for years, without the blacks, who were moving into her Southside neighborhood, without the hippies who wrote "motherfucker" on park walls in her area.

Just plain housewife Mrs. Westerfield (she voted for Wallace) had been founding organizations for two years. The National Committee on the Crisis in Education was her third. Before that it was CHIDE (Committee to Halt Indoctrination and Demoralization in Education), and before that it was the Illinois Council for Essential Education (ICEE). Or perhaps CHIDE came first. I had lost track. At any rate, she was well equipped for her activism. She had a ditto machine in her own home. And she sent out letters to her friends on stationery that was decked out with a picture of the American flag up in the left-hand corner, a quote from Thomas Paine in the margin, and this slogan at the bottom of the page:

> The ONLY Flag To Which We Pay Allegiance
> Either National or International.

She had sent me two letters after the convention, one of them on that stationery. She had chided me—justifiably—for writing (in my *Village Voice* article) that her notebook material had contained

Communist plot theories, and in her second letter she expressed concern about my portrayal of her "attitude toward blacks." (She *had* told me that her neighborhood was becoming black, adding, "I'm afraid," and that she had voted for Wallace.)

If true brotherhood is to come to mankind [she wrote], it will not come to those who preach and rant—and run, not *because* of them. It will only come through those of us who *live* it. And, while your peace-loving drop-outs from humanity, and militant civil-rightists, picket or riot, or turn out reams of love-thy-neighbor propaganda, at their age I was (very quietly) spending my summers working full-time as a volunteer at an all-Negro nursery-School on King Drive. Which do you think will *really* accomplish more for mankind?

Mrs. Westerfield was a woman of curious contradictions. She seemed to have the most complex character of all the Antis I met. She used a minimum amount of the standard right-wing language, and she made what appeared to be a sincere effort to communicate with me at that convention. She had a friendly, palsy-walsy manner with everyone, and she was quite unaffected, uttering at one point near the end of the conference this too loudly whispered remark to a man who was at the microphone urging delegates to contribute to CHIDE:

"With a little luck, we might have a couple hundred left over, but don't ask these poor suckers; they've already given enough."

Her whispered comment was picked up by the microphone, and several delegates heard it. "Don't ask *what?!*" a shocked old woman from Kansas said to her husband, not believing her ears.

But Pat Westerfield was like that. She went around in worn-looking sweaters and longish skirts with her late 1940's hairdo always a little mussed. She hugged the other ladies, and called them "dear" and told them all to please call her "Pat." And she used expressions like "dig" and "suckers." She seemed, in fact, so utterly ingenuous that she was both likeable and frightening. For despite her disclaimers, she had thrown her lot in with a movement that was full of segregationists and superpatriots. In one of the packets of anti–sex education material that she had sent out to an individual in the Chicago suburbs, she had included a copy of an incendiary black nationalist parody of the national anthem, a piece of writing allegedly found in the hallway of Chicago's Washington High School. What that poem—even if it *was* found in a local high school—had to do with sex education, only the Antis would know.

Well past 1:00 A.M. on the morning after the last speech had been made, the last resolution passed, Mrs. Westerfield, her husband, and a few remaining delegates gathered in a small sitting room in the Hilton. They were all exhausted, and Mrs. Westerfield claimed that she hadn't slept for three days. But she seemed keyed up and full of talk. I took advantage of her mood, and began asking her about herself.

She was, it developed, the child of rather domineering Jewish parents. At age fourteen, she had started "going steady" with a sixteen-year-old who wasn't Jewish, and her parents hadn't approved. "They broke it up," she told me. In her early twenties she married another man, and she bore him two children. But she wasn't happy, so she divorced him to marry her high school sweetheart, Albert Westerfield. "I did it," she said wanly, "my parents' way the first time."

She got her own sex education, she said, in the library, "and I also dug boys very, very much. And you find out a lot of things that way. And I didn't get knocked up. And I didn't go around screwin' everybody."

Her objections to formal sex education were, interestingly enough, more frequently aesthetic than moral.

"Why do little girls have to discuss [getting] rid of kotex in front of the boys?" she asked with some spirit. "If they [sex educators] don't think their parents know how to tell them how to throw away a Kotex pad—" she brought out with an exasperated look that completed the sentence.

"And sometimes it's fun to find out in the back seat of the car, although I get killed for making that remark," she added.

The sex educators talk about "the clitoris, and how many strokes in an average intercourse, and how frequently should boys masturbate. They're dissecting it," she continued, apparently lumping marriage manual material and sex education textbooks together in her mind.

"It can be beautiful, even after you get to be an old fogy," she summed up with a grin.

As she had said her own daughter was nearly fourteen, I asked her why she was not worried about becoming as overbearing with her own child as her parents had been with her. How could she be so concerned about the preservation of the family when she herself knew what restrictive families could do to children?

"I may do the same thing with my kids," she said. "My fourteen-year-old [She sometimes said her daughter was fourteen, sometimes thirteen] thinks I'm too protective of her, and maybe I am. She has a woman's body and a child's mind.

"I try not to [get too disturbed] when I think she hates me. Even if you hate each other's guts at the moment, there is still some feeling that you belong somewhere."

But as she pondered her own motherhood, she seemed to conclude that she was making an effort to be less imposing with her own child.

"If I tell her to do the dishes, she does them. But I don't stand over her and give instructions, because that's the way *I* learned," she explained.

Like Mrs. Howe, the Westerfields had made their own family a kind of issue in the local struggle. Mr. Westerfield had called up a radio talk-show on Chicago's WIND just two weeks before the convention to tell the listeners what he thought of sex education. A local marriage counselor and family-life consultant named Jesse Potter was being interviewed by a station commentator at the time, and Westerfield had a little conversation with her. During the course of it, he said that he had gotten his sex education in the gutter and *he'd* done all right. After he hung up, Mrs. Potter said that she was more interested in hearing from the wives of men who had learned in the gutter than from the men themselves. "I am suspect of any man that says, 'I did rather well,' under any circumstances," Mrs. Potter later remarked. Not long after the date of that broadcast, Mrs. Potter received a letter from Pat Westerfield, which said that indeed her husband *had* done all right.

The Westerfields were, with a familiar irony, caught up in a struggle against a sex education program that was, according to Mrs. Potter, the result of "a mass pooling of ignorance." According to that 1968 *Saturday Evening Post* article by John Kobler, which had provided so much of the original Antis' shock material, the new Chicago sex education program "excludes the subject of contraception altogether," this despite the fact that pill peddlers hung around the city's high schools with tablets to sell to youngsters along with "the promise that one swallowed before intercourse guarantees protection." Kobler had also stated that an Evanston (a Chicago suburb) junior high school teacher "responds to the frequent question, 'Why is premarital sex wrong?' by handing around a list of horrifying statistics on venereal disease, illegitimacy, abortion, and divorce." And Kobler quoted the former physical education director of Evanston's Nichols Junior High as saying, "The main thing I did [when the topic of birth control pills came up] was to stress their unreliability."

"Gynecologists insist, however," Kobler had observed, "that the

Pill, when correctly used, has proved to be just about 100 per cent effective."

Yet the Westerfields—with the Antis' characteristic tendency for overreaction—chose to view the Chicago program as dangerous and possibly seductive. They continued their efforts against it long after that convention, and in the months to come, unhappy school administrators from the more conservative Chicago suburbs would call upon Mrs. Morrison for advice about methods of combating the right wing. Even the Reverend Paul Lindstrom, the fundamentalist gadfly who had headed the Remember the Pueblo Committee, got into the action, holding his own anti–sex education rallies and, at one point, threatening to sue a local school board. MOTOREDE committees, some of which had been formed the previous spring, started bothering local school boards in the Chicago area. And one MOTOREDE chairman told his local suburban board that Jesse Potter was a "security risk."

In early 1970, during a special Illinois legislative session that had been called to deal with another unrelated matter, something called the Sex Education Study Commission was set up. Headed by State Senator Arthur Swanson and State Representative Otis Collins, men who had introduced legislation to restrict or ban sex education the previous year, the new commission worried superintendents all over the state. During its second meeting the commission viewed films and materials from the Chicago sex education program, and educators began to wonder whether other elements of their curricula would in the future be subjected to the same kind of scrutiny. As of this writing (early 1970), the commission's ultimate purpose is not known. But one Illinois superintendent said that state legislators had told him that the pressure they were getting from the Antis was absolutely unprecedented—more intense even than the pressure against gun control legislation.

Mrs. Morrison, who had been following the controversies in "half a dozen" suburban school districts, told me that the MOTOREDE committees had begun, early in the year, to give indications that they would concentrate their efforts for the next several months on the impending school board elections. In the suburban Deerfield district, the local MOTOREDE committee—whose affiliation with the Birch Society was well known—unashamedly drew up its own list of candidates for the board seats.

Mrs. Westerfield continued on as a thorn in the side of Chicago educators undaunted by the fact that two weeks after her convention was held, the local conspirators had all ganged up on her and issued a statement in support of sex education in the public schools, the conspirators being the area's major social service agencies among which were the Illinois Medical Society and the United Charities of Chicago. She went on struggling against the odds, and on last report she was making her views known to that state sex education commission in no uncertain terms.

*   *   *

Sources in the Department of Health, Education, and Welfare —which was funding teacher training programs and some of the actual public school programs in sex education—claimed that the mail from the Antis had fallen off considerably after the end of the 1968–69 school year. And Father James McHugh, head of the Catholic Conference's Committee on Family Life said in February, 1970, that he thought the controversies were losing heat. But that same month a Chicago physician who had been working with the AMA and NEA Joint Committee on Health Problems in Education and had followed the controversies since the summer of 1969 said she thought the battles were "spotty" but still quite intense in many areas of the country.

Robert Welch apparently thought that sex education would remain a top-priority grievance in the minds of his followers for some time to come—either that, or he had decided Mrs. Westerfield's national approach was a good one. For in January, 1970, he announced, via the *Birch Bulletin*, the formation of a new National MOTOREDE committee. The fifty-nine-member committee included a number of the people from the inner sanctums of the Birch Society (members of the Birch Council) as well as several contributors to *American Opinion* magazine and that notable sex education expert Governor Lester Maddox of Georgia. (Apparently Wallace, who had appeared at Christian Crusade rallies, was Hargis's Dixiecrat.)

Exactly how Welch planned to use this new committee was a matter of some concern to nervous educators as well as pundits of right-wing politics. For until the appearance of that *Bulletin* issue, sex education proponents had hoped that the organized right wing would take up another cause in 1970. (Much as I would like to have been the one to discover Welch's plans, I was unable to convince the man to waste more than about two minutes of his time on me. Reaching him by telephone, I asked him first how the sex education battles were going. This brought an angry response, for, as he explained, he was very busy at the moment and could not take the time to answer such a broad question. Would he have more time another day? Could he just quickly explain why he had set up that national MOTOREDE committee? *No*, he would *never* have time, and anybody who wanted to know about the committee could just send for the January *Bulletin*. But he couldn't spare another moment, he said, so he was just going to hang up. And he did. Fighting Communism must keep him pretty busy.)

Whatever he planned for that committee, he seemed to have decided his right-wing rivals had done well with their nation-wide anti–sex education crusades. (One possible indication of the success of the Christian Crusade's anti–sex education rallies was the fact that Hargis claimed the Crusade's income had "dropped by 50 per cent" one month after Gordon Drake resigned.) And perhaps Welch decided he could not let little Gordon Drake or rotund Billie James Hargis *or* a mere Chicago housewife with a ditto machine usurp his position as the Eminence Grise of reactionaries.

*   *   *

There had long been an overabundance of leaders on the Right. But the national movement against sex education was positively glutted with them. It was manned not only with pamphleteers, the people who, as Courtney had said, put "a footnote in every paragraph," but also with scores of distressed parents who seemed to have aquired a taste for leadership the first time they saw their names in the papers. All you had to do to become a leader in the movement was to speak out against sex education with some passion. It helped a little if you could throw in a few false statistics from Sweden or a shocking story from some distant school district, but if you hadn't learned that litany by heart, you could always fall back on heart-rending stories about your own children or your children's children or even your neighbor's children. And if you invited John Steinbacher to speak in your town, he might well write about you later. His columns frequently contained touching little stories about humble parents who were fighting the good fight back in places like Grand Forks, North Dakota, and Wenatchee, Washington.

Just which organization or pamphleteer won the loyalty of Mrs. Westerfield's conventioneers, I could not determine. But national unity didn't seem to matter much in their campaign, for in every state where a battle raged loudly enough to attract the local press, there appeared to be a thriving—if often small—organization. Around suburban Chicago, MOTOREDE had obviously done well. In Idaho, the righteous belonged to something called Idaho

Families United, and in that state, the Antis seemed to be positively flourishing. Steinbacher had appeared at the Idaho Families United convention in Boise early in the fall of 1969 where he had made a hit by announcing his new nationwide drive "to have Congress review the NEA charter." In early 1970, the Idaho group helpfully suggested a new law to the state legislature, which read in part:

No instruction in sex education shall be taught in the elementary school system except in an approved course in health education and physiology in which the reproductive systems of male and female anatomy might be discussed. Specifically, no visual media may be used that portrays both male and female reproductive systems or parts thereof at the same time, and there shall be no instruction regarding the union of reproductive organs. Any instruction in sex education in elementary schools in which the reproductive systems are discussed shall be given separately to boys and girls and not coeducationally.

In the state of Washington, where both MOTOREDE and a group called Parents for Responsible Education were active, the state legislature passed a resolution calling for guidelines on sex education and on the use of questionnaires in November, 1969. In early December, Washington's State Board of Education produced the required guidelines, which included the following point:

"The program should focus upon helping youth acquire a background of ideals, standards, and attitudes which will be of value to him now and later when he chooses a mate and establishes his own family."

Stipulating that a parent or guardian be allowed to remove his child from sex education classes, the Washington board also ruled that:

"No written or oral test, questionnaire, survey, or examination shall be used to elicit the personal beliefs or practices of a student or his parents as to sex or religion except with the written consent or parent or guardian."

That last point was one that had appeared in various forms in the anti–sex education legislation introduced in several other states. Idaho Families United had tacked it onto their suggested legislation. A restrictive measure that had died in committee in the Wisconsin State Senate had contained a similar section. And in early 1970 the Orange County State Senator, John Schmitz, introduced a brief new bill spelling out the same kinds of restrictions for testing in California schools.

Steinbacher had hailed the appearance of the Washington state guidelines in his column, and he seemed to think that they might serve as a model for other state boards. He had, of course, gone on speaking tours in the state of Washington.

But delegates from both Idaho and Washington had appeared at Mrs. Westerfield's convention. In fact, nearly every state represented at that convention got honorable mention in Steinbacher's column, which meant he had been covering the controversies in just about every midwestern and northwestern state, save Montana and South Dakota. Not to mention California and the southwestern states. (He also covered events in New Jersey and New York, both of which were represented at the convention, and Connecticut and Massachusetts, which were not represented there.)

And in nearly every state that had sent delegates to Mrs. Westerfield's gathering, anti–sex education legislation was introduced. Most of the legislation would have restricted rather than prohibited the teaching of sex education, but a good deal of it was quietly allowed to die in committee by lawmakers who were reluctant to speak out against such measures but were privately willing to block their passage. In some states, such as Illinois, legislative committees were set up to "investigate" local sex education programs. This tactic was used in New Jersey, and the local Antis there used the hearings to vent much pent-up right-wing spleen. At one of the New Jersey sessions—they were held in August and September of 1969—a representative of the National States' Rights Party used his time before the legislators to give voice to blatantly anti-Semitic propaganda, calling sex education a "satanic" plot inspired by writings in the Talmud.

In Louisiana, a legislative committee held sex education hearings in various parishes during 1969, and the State Board of Education ruled in May of that year that only materials adopted by its members could be used in the public schools. The State Board approved only the regular health and science texts, deeming it wise to institute no new sex education programs until the legislative commission had completed its work. The Louisiana board also decided to ban all mention of the facts of life in classes below the ninth-grade level.

In Tennessee a piece of legislation was passed, which was quite ineffectual, but it obviously meant something to the local Antis. The measure required that any sex education course be approved by the local and state boards. As all courses of study for the public schools must legally be approved by the State Board in Tennessee, the new measure (also passed in 1969) was an exercise in redundancy apparently designed only to appease the Antis. And in actual practice some local districts had been able to avoid the bothersome scrutiny of the State Board by introducing sex education "units" into parts of other courses. But there was a touch of the old Tennessee spirit in that law nevertheless, for the legislators had made violation of the thing a misdemeanor.

In Billie James Hargis's home state, a measure so extreme that it would have required a rewrite of all Oklahoma's biology textbooks was passed by the house but allowed to die in the state senate. The same fate befell a Wisconsin bill whose authors should have been awarded a special plaque for overreaction beyond the call of duty. Their measure would have banned any instruction in the "methods and techniques of human sexual intercourse and methods and techniques of contraception" in all grades "except for the traditional teaching of physiology, biology, or physical hygiene" in grades eight to twelve. Wisconsin educators found that section amusing because, as one of them remarked, "We're not going to talk about that [techniques of intercourse], anyway." And Wisconsin already had a state law prohibiting the dissemination of birth control information to unmarried people. Nevertheless, the local educators breathed more easily after the 1969 legislative session ended with the bill languishing in a senate committee, for it had also contained the familiar section banning questions about the "personal beliefs or practices in sex, family life, morality and religion" of the students or their families, a section that could have been so broadly interpreted as to pretty well eliminate school counseling services.

By the end of 1969, at least nineteen state legislatures had considered or passed legislation or resolutions having to do with sex education. And two congressmen had introduced bills to prohibit or restrict the use of federal funds for sex education programs. In addition, Congressman John Rarick had introduced a resolution calling for an investigation of SIECUS.

None of these federal lawmakers voiced strong hopes that their measures would receive much support on Capitol Hill. But out among the anxious mothers and fathers of America, those three congressmen were regular heroes, and frequently the Anti literature urged parents to write to their own representatives calling for the swift passage of one or the other of the two bills or plugging that proposed investigation of SIECUS.

* * *

It could be said that those three congressmen represented the three strains of belief that fed into the national reaction against sex education. Schadeburg was a minister, and he seemed to think that the nation's sex education programs lacked a crucial "spiritual element." Cunningham was a seasoned champion of right-wing causes, having not so long ago fought against the use of federal funds for water fluoridation projects. Rarick was a firm supporter of George Wallace and all that he espoused.

In their brief remarks for this volume, all three of them exhibited a knowledge of the field of sex education that was notably limited. Perhaps if they had each had more time in which to explain their views, they would have displayed a more impressive command of the facts. As it was, they seemed to know less about sex education than did, well, your average school board member.

Henry C. Schadeburg is one of the three ordained ministers in the House of Representatives—so says his official biography. He still "manages to preach as guest minister in his district [the First Congressional District of Wisconsin] and at military posts around the country," the helpful biography states.

His district includes the town of Racine, a place where the local Antis managed to scare the school board into delaying its proposed sex education program indefinitely. It was a group of women from Racine that first alerted Schadeburg to the evils of sex education. They pressed their cause so winningly that, in March of 1969, their Congressman submitted H.R. 8976 to the House Education and Labor Committee. The bill, which quickly made Schadeburg a darling of the nation's Antis, would prohibit the use of federal funds for any elementary or secondary school sex education programs, for teacher training in sex education, or for "research into methods of teaching sex education." Such legislation would, according to experts in the field, seriously hamper the nation's sex education programs, for it would send education students into other fields—wherever fellowships were available. As sex education is a relatively new field, there is a scarcity of teachers who have any expertise in the area.

Nevertheless, Schadeburg told me he did not think the measure would pass.

"My purpose in introducing the bill was simply to get this open for discussion," he explained. "My own personal opinion is that if it's that important for the community to have it [sex education], they should raise the money for it. . . . This is a matter for the local school district to decide. I just am not as trustful of big government as some people are."

He was trustful enough to approve of federal funding for other school programs, however, for he went on to say that he thought school districts that needed federal subsidies should apply for those funds "in some other area."

An innocuous looking man of medium height, Schadeburg bore a faint resemblance to Gordon Drake. And like Drake, he smiled frequently as he talked and seemed so much an ordinary fellow that it was difficult, listening to him, to remember that he was, in fact, a member of the U.S. Congress.

He said that he did not seriously consider sex education to be an element of a subversive plot but that he *was* worried about the manner in which it was handled in some school districts.

"You can't separate this matter of sex from the spiritual nature of man," he said. The school prayers decision had obviously disturbed him, for he briefly touched on it, adding, "They remove any moral atmosphere from our schools and at the same time these people want to take sex out of the Judaeo-Christian setting.

"The problem is different points of view. There are some people that do believe in a more permissive society. Somebody wants, quote, freedom, but it really is license. And I don't want them to teach my children to be more permissive—because I'm a Christian."

The Wisconsin Republican also said that he thought sex education programs were being taught "in the same way in every area of the country. Sex education, for instance, in the ghetto is not the program I'd want in my area," he continued. "The same program that might very well raise the level of the ghetto would depreciate the rural area."

Toward the end of the brief interview, Schadeburg showed himself to be a conservative of the good old-fashioned Calvinist variety. He criticized the Congress for accepting what he thought was the "economic man of Marxism" and said that in his view "all the government handouts" thwarted the "spiritual" part of man, a part which he thought could only be fulfilled through man's own self-help efforts.

Representative Glenn Cunningham, an austere-looking Republican from Nebraska's Second Congressional District, had introduced a milder bill than the one proposed by Schadeburg. Yet, listening to him, you could come to think that he should have written the stronger measure. He was one of some 175 Congressmen to introduce anti–pornography legislation in the last year, and he seemed to consider sex education about equal to pornography. His sex education bill, introduced in mid-October of 1969, was identical to Schadeburg's except for one added point: Cunningham's bill would allow the use of federal funds in those communities where the local school board "approved" any federal sex education grants. Like Schadeburg, Cunningham voiced doubts about the success of his bill, but expressed the hope that it would stimulate legislative hearings.

Sitting in an alcove just outside the House chamber, the elderly, gaunt Nebraska Congressman hurriedly gave vent to his fierce disapproval of public school sex education.

"I was brought up to live a clean moral life," he said. "My parents took me aside and told me certain things that occur as you reach a certain age. I say shame on the parents of today who want this taught in the schools. They don't have the time, the guts, or the courage to carry out their parental responsibilities."

Again, it was a group of women who had stirred him into action on the issue, a group whose title he claimed he could not recall. Whoever they were, they had apparently convinced him that some of the films used in sex education classes were the sort you might find at a stag party. He said that some teachers were even showing "actual films of intercourse," which immediately sparked my interest. But then he disappointed me by refusing to tell me precisely where I might find the films. "I'm positive that the films are the same type that the pornographers have been showing for years," he went on, adding in grave tones, "Pornography firms are moving into the field of sex education."

Cunningham appeared to be the kind of man who really swallowed right-wing propaganda whole, for toward the end of the interview, he launched into a little lecture about how there was "absolutely no proof whatsoever that fluoridated water doesn't have adverse effects on the older people." And after a few final comments about the irresponsible parents who wanted to "shift" the job of sex education to someone else, he went back to the business of making our nation's laws.

He and Schadeburg were both favorites with the Antis. But their popularity couldn't come near that of the baby-faced congressman from Louisiana. John Rarick enjoyed something close to adulation among the most committed of the right-wingers. The only Democratic congressman to openly support Wallace in 1968, Rarick was censured by the House Democrats and later stripped of his seniority for his disloyalty. In early 1969 he publicly associated himself with John Acord, the former national chairman of Youth for Wallace, founding with him a new organization called the National Youth Alliance (NYA). The Institute for American Democracy discovered that the NYA's phone number was the same as that for the American–Southern Africa Council, another project of John Acord's, which was devoted to the promotion of tourism in Rhodesia and South Africa. (The American-Southern Africa Council later moved into the same office occupied by Lee Dodson and the American Education Lobby people at 20 E Street, North West, Washington, D.C. Dodson's criticism of sex education was that "it's not American. It's not the American way as far as I was raised. America," he would explain, "is to me supposed to be a Christian nation, and the Bible teaches us that we don't do those things." "Those things" being the unspeakable acts he was sure were discussed in sex education classes.)

Rarick really deserved the credit for having first brought sex education to the attention of the right wing. Although a few distressed mothers in California may have convinced Gordon Drake to start writing and speaking about it, Drake got his Commie smear material on SIECUS from a *Herald of Freedom* article that Rarick had inserted into the June 25, 1968, Congressional Record. (Mrs. Westerfield claimed that she first learned of the evils of sex education from that day's section of the Congressional Record.)

On at least eight separate occasions during 1969 Rarick inserted additional articles on sex education into the pages of the Congressional Record. He did put in some material from the Washington papers, but most of his selections were taken from the standard right-wing publications such as the Birch Society's *American Opinion* magazine and the *Herald of Freedom*. He was apparently the sole publisher of Dr. James Parsons' piece, "The Gathering Storm," for he gave no indication in the Record that it had appeared in any other publication. He liked it so well that he included the piece in one of his reprints for constituents—along with an article by the Sarasota physician who had started the Let Freedom Ring telephone propaganda network, Dr. William Campbell Douglass.

Sometimes Rarick would make a few remarks to the Speaker of the House before submitting his articles, and these often made better reading than the articles themselves, most of which repeated the same basic arguments put forth by Gordon Drake and Robert Welch.

On April 16, 1969, for instance, Rarick had introduced a *Washington Star* article about a black doctor's talk (to an audience of members of the American Association of Sex Educators and Counselors) on the relationship between racial and sexual attitudes this way:

Mr. Speaker, the mothers and dads of schoolchildren can expect a further innovation in sex education. Apparently their children are to be educated not to discriminate sexually because of race, creed, or national origin.

According to the reported discussions at the recent American Association of Sex Educators and Counselors annual conference, we are to believe that many teenaged white female patients expressed interest in interracial sex to show their concern and atone for white guilt. [The *Washington Star* had reported that one member of the audience put forth such a theory after the doctor's talk.] Our poor brainwashed children.

What next will the antimorality crowd come up with? Perhaps a "civil rights" amendment to prevent legal marriage of any two people of the same race, religion, creed, or national origin. Sound impossible? Nothing is beyond the challenge from education these days.

On an earlier date, Rarick had inserted an Associated Press story entitled "Sex Education Teachers Take Sensitivity Course" into the Record. Including a description of the "cathartic" effects of marathon sensitivity training sessions for future sex education teachers at New York University, the AP piece dealt with several aspects of teacher training in the NYU program. But the sensitivity training was grippingly portrayed, and it obviously stood out in Rarick's mind. He submitted the piece for the Record along with these remarks:

Mr. Speaker, according to New York University reports, sex education instructors must qualify by undergoing sensitivity training, perhaps to become desensitized to morality to escape their guilt in using little children as guinea pigs for the new sex revolution.

I not only do not want any of these zombies teaching my children— I will even refuse to let my children associate with their victimized pupils.

Strange that none suggest sex education classes for the mommies and dads who, in turn, could be encouraged to give a healthy explanation of sex to their own children. Or would this restore the American tradition of parental authority and supervision—the real target.

If it were not that this training is being financed by the taxpayers, under the auspices of a large university, the entire matter could be dismissed as a sick, sordid cult.

Are the American people expected to discard the teaching of morality in favor of the teaching of perversion?

When you entered the office of the wise author of these remarks, you could be made to feel that you had with one easy step crossed the Mason-Dixon Line. His secretaries spoke with charming Louisiana drawls, and one of them looked underfed and mournful, as though she thought too much of bygone days. She even wore her skirts quite unstylishly long, like a woman who had just one day stopped living in the present and never bought a new dress since.

The first time I entered that small piece of the old Confederacy, the Congressman was not available. And while I waited in vain to see him, an old woman wearing white gloves and nervously clutching a few small religious pamphlets came through the door. She babbled to one of the secretaries about how Rarick was a godly man or something to that effect, and when she got through praising him, she started working on the secretary's soul, telling her the good news and handing her one of the pamphlets. She eventually got in to see the Congressman, and I was left to amuse myself with his police magazines and Congressional Record reprints. When the old woman came out, I pretended not to see her. Out of the corner of my eye, I thought I perceived her trying to size me up. If she caught my eye, I thought, she would be thrusting her pamphlets in my face the next moment, and she was not someone you could insult in that office. She must have sized me up fairly accurately though, for she passed me by without so much as a halleluia. And soon she was replaced by a whole family from Rarick's district, people who had brought their little girls in to see the Congressman at work. The little girls had those oddly unhealthy looking faces so common to white children of the deep South, but they were immaculately groomed, and they charmed the secretaries with their already ladylike manners.

Like the people who came to see him, Rarick himself could have been taken straight from the pages of Faulkner's Snopes trilogy. He would have been one of the lesser Snopeses, for he did not show the hardness of a character like Flem. But Rarick had smalltown written all over him, and he seemed just the sort of person who would envy the sons of the judges and the grandsons of the real Civil War heroes in his territory. He had a fundamentalist preacher's grin—he really looked remarkably like a thinned-down version of Billie James Hargis—and from what I could gather, he was at his best with the Bible-thumping sorts.

He was serving his second term in Congress when the sex education controversy became big business for the right wing. He had served as a judge in Louisiana's 20th Judicial District for five years before he ran for office, and it was that experience that first aroused his interest in sex education. This he told me when I finally got in to see him, in late October of 1969.

"Let's just say this, that it became very obvious that the youth that came before me as a judge were having their curiosity aroused subnormally by pornographic material that was creeping into the drugstores and railroad stations," he drawled, grinning all the while and seeming quite blissfully unaware of his malapropism. "Suddenly sex was becoming profitable. Sex exploitation was becoming profitable," he went on, "and it became obvious that there was some guiding hand."

When he got to Congress, he said, he had "access to more material," and he implied it was something in that material which had revealed to him "the guiding hand" behind the new sex exploitation.

He said he was not opposed to "some method of educating youth." But he thought that "what is being hoodwinked on educators of today is not sex education. It's pornography and it's filth and it's trying to be pawned off as education. If you were to see some of the material that comes in here [that is] called artistic or educational—and it's sickening! Much of it is being used to try to make lots of money.

"In many instances, of course, [the material would be] referred to me by the school principal. Little Johnny would show little Mary a picture of a girl with no britches on," he said, seeming to lapse back into memories of his days on the bench.

"And children who do not participate," he went on, now speaking of current sex education programs, "are still gonna be exposed to the same thing." Outside of class, he said, the nonparticipating child might be told by a friend, "Gosh, you should have seen the picture show we saw today! Let's go on out to the hay mow and try it." And with that remark Rarick amused himself so well that he laughed outright. Waxing serious a moment later, he said:

"The time is gonna come when they'll destroy sex. [With] no mystery, nothing, left in sex, you've destroyed it, haven't you?"

Rarick said that Gordon Drake had "come by the office one time," and that he and the Louisiana state legislator who introduced a bill to prohibit sex education below the ninth grade had both spoken at Christian Crusade gatherings. On his desk was a reprint of an article from the conservative *Manchester* (N.H.) *Union* and a copy of an essay called "The Pied Pipers of Sex," which had been reprinted by the National Defense Committee of the Society of the Daughters of the American Revolution.

*   *   *

Rarick was so obviously serving as a kind of mouthpiece for the organized right wing of the Christian Crusade white supremacist variety that any reasonably objective observer would have to con-

clude that his efforts on behalf of decency were not entirely motivated by his outraged sense of propriety. Those efforts were too
politically profitable for a freshman congressman with fundamentalist constituents and an eye on the national backlash vote
to be considered totally sincere. And the articles Rarick was forever inserting into the Congressional Record were so full of propaganda and so devoid of facts that they did not speak well of his
alleged concern for the children of America.

In all those reams of material, he had managed to make only one
valid point, it seemed to me, and he had quite possibly made that
one facetiously. It was the point he had made in the course of his
remarks about the article on the NYU teacher-training program.
"Strange," he had said, "that none suggest sex education classes
for the mommies and dads who, in turn, could be encouraged to
give a healthy explanation of sex to their own children." However
ironically he had meant that, it seemed to me quite a justifiable
challenge to the sex education proponents. For if the parents were
to be given all the up-to-date information on sex, they could very
well educate their own children. And that way no one would have
any worries about his children being exposed to alternative value
systems.

Thanks to a man named the Reverend Stanley Andrews (a
speaker at the Chicago convention who had proudly quoted
phrases from a *Washington Post* editorial criticizing him) and to
the efforts of the Reverend John Dekker, Montgomery County,
Maryland, was the scene of one of the nation's most intense sex
education battles during the spring and fall of 1969. The county,
which is the home of many lawmakers and high level federal bureaucrats, is one of the wealthiest in the country, and hence it
contains some of the nation's most progressive public schools. But
there are also pockets of tried and true fundamentalism in the
county, and these predictably erupted when those fine progressive
educators began introducing sex education into the local elementary school curriculum. The county educators had acted in
compliance with a state mandate, issued in 1967, requiring all
school districts to institute "a comprehensive program of family
life and sex education" in all grade levels. It was not until the
spring of 1969 that serious community reaction developed, and by
that time ten of the county's elementary schools had sex education programs which included some mention of human reproduction in the teacher guides for the first and second grades. In
June of that year 700 people appeared at an Anti rally to hear the
Reverend Dekker proclaim that "God gave us this issue to face."

God softened the issue somewhat over the summer via the Maryland State Board, which in August issued guidelines barring the facts of life from family life and sex education classes for youngsters under the age of ten. In response to parent demands the State Board also ordered every county to start conducting adult sex education classes at night.

The Montgomery County educators decided to offer no sex education classes to children (other than the standard hygiene sessions which had been offered before 1967) during the 1969–70 school year, because they were designing a new curriculum in compliance with the state guidelines. But they did institute the adult sessions in early 1970.

Six people attended the first evening class. Five attended the second one. Two hearty souls, an Anti couple, appeared for the third session. Richard Cohen, a young *Washington Post* reporter who regularly covered the sex education battles and had frequently heard the local opposition call for such courses, wrote a story about the sparse attendance at those adult sex education classes. It was carried on the front page of the paper's city news section, and after the Antis read it, they quickly called the county school administrators to protest. They said they hadn't realized such classes were being offered, and they would certainly show up the next time, etc., etc. According to one county administrator, the attendance was increased to the startling figure of twenty-five at the next session. In the same high school, Cohen had reported, an adult sewing class drew twenty-nine women.

So Rarick's wisdom had apparently fallen on deaf ears. His followers had quietly demonstrated their reluctance to inform themselves in the sacred area of knowledge their spokesmen had claimed only they should impart to their children.

They were indeed a strange lot. Seven hundred of them would show up at a rally to hear spicy denunciations of public school sex education programs. Another 150 of them would travel a good distance to tell each other the disgusting words that were being spoken in classrooms. Yet they could not bring themselves to sit through a class on human sexuality. Even in Anaheim, where the opposition parents tried to get their hands on every piece of literature that went into the FLSE classes, adult attendance at evening sessions was, Paul Dearth had said, woefully small.

Perhaps their arguments for adult courses were merely part of their tactical rhetoric, arguments designed to show that they were not enemies of enlightenment. Perhaps they did not show much enthusiasm for real adult sex education courses because they thought they were already well informed. That was an easy assumption to make if you had learned the basic facts of reproduction and kept abreast of the latest research by reading the mass circulation magazines. Or perhaps they feared that an appearance at an adult sex education class would be interpreted as an admission of sexual inadequacy.

One could speculate endlessly about the Antis' curious failure to demonstrate publicly their willingness to become well informed about sex. But some remarks Mrs. Westerfield had made expressed an attitude that appeared to be common to them all, an attitude that could have kept them away from the sex education classes.

"Sometimes it's fun to find out in the back seat of a car," she had said, and "It can be beautiful, even after you get to be an old fogy," and "They're [the sex educators are] dissecting it."

They had their own puritan aesthetics, their own peculiar romanticism, which they apparently thought they could preserve in a cocoon of ignorance. "[With] no mystery, nothing, left in sex, you've destroyed it, haven't you?" was the way Rarick had put it. Whether it was mystery they revered or merely the furtive passions that such mystery produced, they clearly feared that something at the very heart of their aesthetics might die in the sober pages of a sex education text book.

The Worship of Normalcy

The Sheraton Park Hotel looms out across a hillside in the northwest section of Washington, D.C., like some gigantic hospital. It consists of two huge building complexes connected by a kind of arcade, a long window-lined hall that suggests a tunnel. The floors of the place are carpeted in thick-woven stuff that is already drab with much wear.

In contrast to the Chicago Hilton, this Washington home for transients contains not the faintest promise of sin. There are no gleaming jewelry stores, the lights are harsh and bright, the staff looks harried and spent.

In the main thoroughfare, the lobby of the place, there is, if business is good, the atmosphere of an airline terminal during the weekend delays. And, like a terminal, the lobby branches off into hallways and landings in cavernous architectural confusion. It is easy to lose your way among the halls and numerous ballrooms of the first split-level floor of the main building.

Whoever put together the Sheraton Park Hotel must have been thinking of the huge national convention trade. There is nothing in the place to please the eye or soothe the spirit. It is all barren vastness, gaping out every which way in anticipation of the hordes. If people sin there, they must surely do it only after a night out on the town, after a dinner in one of Washington's myriad little restaurants where conversation is soft and lighting is so poor that it flatters the plainest of women. You would have to venture out from the great hotel to even work up a mood for wickedness. For within it, all is bustle and utilitarian strain. Even the Sheraton's bar looks as though it was designed to discourage lingering. Its chairs are made of a flimsy-looking plastic with thin metal spines for legs and whoever selected them must have decided from the start that the Sheraton would never cater to the leisure class.

It was here in this vast sterile hotel that the National Council

280

on Family Relations held its annual Convention in late October of 1969. The council, which was founded in 1938 "to bring together in one organization the leaders in research, teaching, and professional service in the field of marriage and the family," had since then grown to such vast proportions that only a place as large as the Sheraton could accommodate all its delegates. To the 1969 convention came some 500 people from forty-five states, Puerto Rico, and Canada. They were people engaged in all manner of professions related to the general problems of the society. They were sociologists, ministers, nurses, "family life" teachers, writers, physicians, psychiatrists, marriage counselors, social workers, high school superintendents, and high level bureaucrats from the Department of Health, Education, and Welfare. At least 100 of them had a substantial investment in the problems or the practices of the American family, for at least 100 of them were professors of child and family development (or variations on that theme), marriage counselors, family life educators, or the like. There was also a good number of clergymen among the participants, most of these from the Protestant and Catholic churches, but a few from the Mormon and Baptist faiths as well. In addition, there were editors and sales representatives from the publishing companies that put out home economics (and now also sex education) materials, companies like McGraw-Hill, Ginn, and Follett. And there were even some people from the Merrill-Palmer Institute. In fact, John Steinbacher, who liked to run long lists of his enemies' names in his columns, would have gone well-nigh batty trying to absorb the breadth and scope of Commie disguises evident in the list of convention participants.

You got a copy of the list along with a slick, shiny twenty-eight-page program of events when you finally shouldered your way through the crowds to the registration table—which was conveniently located just opposite a room full of the newest books on all manner of family and sexual problems. If you read down that list of participants and titles—it ran to twelve full pages—you could really begin to think you ought to send it to Steinbacher. For there it was, the master list of the Great Conspiracy itself. But reading the thing was something a sensible person would do only under compulsion, for as you reached the end of about page three, you could not easily avoid the depressing realization that a vast profession is sustained by America's unhappy spouses and their unfortunate offspring.

And if you had been free to skip the list, depression would not have escaped you as you read the twenty-eight-page glossy program of events. That could give you a veritable sinking of the heart. The mere social-sciencese in the titles of papers to be delivered and discussion topics to be covered discouraged the imagination and suggested dull, unfeeling professors. And the titles that seemed derivative from what Marcuse called the Power of Positive Thinking psychological school were about as inviting as the titles of Sunday school lessons. They smacked of goody-goodies, of cheerful rationalists, or of the new sensitivity training experts who had made a lot of money by discovering that misery loves company.

So you read that your choice that first afternoon, Wednesday, October 22nd, was the talk on "Group Marriage Counseling: An Experimental Project Focusing on Positive Interaction and Communication," or the one on "Family Counseling and Its Implications for Marriage Counseling," the latter being given by two people, one of whom at least had an interesting name: James Croake. Simultaneously, in another room, there was to be a discussion about "An Experiment with Closed Circuit TV Teaching in Large Family Life Classes" as well as a panel discussion, in still another room, on "Some Needed Areas of Research on Families with Implications for Social Policy." All these fascinating presentations and more were to be completed by 4:00 P.M. at which time you could, if you were still up to it, go to hear the lady from the (Massachusetts) Governor's Advisory Council on Home and Family explain something called "Collaborative Endeavor with Related Interest Programs."

As I was writing a book on sex education controversies, I dutifully wandered into the room where that talk on the closed circuit TV for Family Life classes was going on. A pale man wearing dark-rimmed spectacles stood at the front of the room making what appeared to be a concerted attempt to put his small audience to sleep. I got the impression that the real purpose of his talk had been thought up in the sales department of some educational film company. But apparently the company hadn't watched this gentleman do his stuff. Or perhaps I had wandered into the wrong room altogether. It was easy to mistake your way in among all the conference rooms that lined the halls. And there were two other talks on "the Media" and "Family Life" scheduled for that first afternoon. At any rate, I soon gave up on the Media and Family Life altogether and drifted out to the registration table. From there I could see into the publishers' display room. The place was bustling. The sight of it was cheering, and I quickly decided that the display room was the place to pick up the sense of the huge amorphous group of people that called themselves the

National Council on Family Relations. I walked in there, note-book in hand.

The first thing that struck your eye as you entered the room was the large blue and gold poster over on the far wall which read, "Glenn Educational Films, Inc.,/Health Guidance in/Fam-ily Living/and/Sex Education." Under the poster stood two inof-fensive looking women of indeterminate age. Next to their poster was a much drabber tan one advertising Henk Newenhouse's company, and under that one stood two inoffensive-looking, closely shorn young men. Henk Newenhouse, I knew, was one of the major distributors of sex education films, and Mrs. Morrison had told me that the Antis in suburban Chicago had been making life difficult for him for some months.

So I immediately tried to strike up a conversation with the in-offensive-looking young men. How was business going? Weren't those Antis crazy? Oh, yes, said one of them; Mr. Newenhouse "has been the recipient of most of the attacks. Sales have been hard hit. [They have gone] way down." But you should ask Mr. Newenhouse himself. (Mr. Newenhouse himself, I am later to dis-cover, does not like telling the public how badly his business is suffering. A witty but cautious man, he tells me during a phone conversation that he has had his "share" of difficulty, but "to give you an honest, well-documented set of statistics, that's impossible." He does name two films that cause him no trouble, both of them straightforward biology, both not radically different from the ver-sions of them that appeared over twenty years ago. These are, *Human Growth*, put out by an organization in Portland, Oregon, called the E. C. Brown Trust Foundation, and *Human Reproduc-tion*, produced by McGraw-Hill. And he names the two most con-troversial films: *Phoebe*, and *The Game*, both of which were produced by the National Film Board of Canada. In *The Game* an adolescent boy's doubts and conflicts about premarital sex are explored. In *Phoebe*, it will be recalled, one is given a strong dose of a pregnant teenager's regrets. But, alas, Mr. Newenhouse does not wish to dwell upon unpleasant matters. He keeps making jokes about the Antis, about how the birch tree is the national symbol in Russia. Yet still another source in the industry tells me that Henk Newenhouse was deeply troubled by the controversy's effect upon his business in the late spring of 1969. Newenhouse himself keeps a stiff upper lip, saying finally, "I [will] keep it all for the autobiography of the rise and fall of a small business-man.")

Over at the Glenn Educational Films, Inc. table the ladies were all smiles. They were handing out cheerful little leaflets that told you all about their *Health Guidance in Family Living* film strip series complete with sound "for grades two through ten." "From the producer of the highly acclaimed *The Miracle of Nature*," said their leaflet, over which was a picture of a couple smiling gloriously down at their baby. Dad had his hand placed unobtrusively on Mom's shoulder. Dad had very short hair; Mom had very sprayed hair.

Never having heard of the "highly acclaimed" *Miracle of Nature*, I nevertheless asked the two sales ladies for smiling Glenn how their company was doing. Oh, just fine, they said. We don't have any trouble from the opposition at all. "Our films are approved by all the faiths." I believed them.

In a back room off of this display chamber there were continual showings of films. Health films, lovey-dovey family films, sex education films. The twenty-eight-page glossy program had a list of them:

WEDNESDAY:

1:00	Nursery School Child Mother Interaction
1:45	Mr. Grey
2:00	Where Mrs. Whalley Lives
2:35	Hear Us O Lord!
3:30	Steve & Kathy: Going Steady
3:45	George & Betty: Career Versus Marriage
4:00	Tom & Ann: Making Out
4:15	Marriage: What Kind for You
4:45	Friendly Games
5:00	Your First Six Years
5:15	Never A Bride
5:40	Lonnie's Day

THURSDAY:

8:30	A Teenage Pregnancy
8:50	Encounter
9:05	Your First Six Years
9:20	Invention of the Adolescent
9:55	Nursery School Child Mother Interaction
10:40	Human Heredity
11:05	Walk in Their Shoes
11:35	Awareness
12:05	There Is No Time for Romance

—and so on throughout Thursday and Friday.

How anyone was expected to fit this scintillating entertainment into his panel-packed days at that convention was not quite clear.

But obviously the film producers' hearts had leaped at the thought of those 500-odd human relations types all gathered together in one place for three days, and it had been too much for them. They just had to send their wares.

And from the riches laid out in the display room, one had to conclude that the publishers had reacted similarly. Oh, what a wealth of problem-solving prose was laid out on those broad tables, and tables, and tables! The Johns Hopkins Press had sent *The Individual, Sex, and Society*. Monona Publications of Madison, Wisconsin, had sent three goodies: *Sex Guidance For Your Child: A Parent Handbook* the authors of which were several and included a couple named Dr. and Mrs. E. A. Cockefair; *The Story of You* by the aforementioned couple; and *Love and the Facts of Life*, by my favorite, Evelyn M. Duvall. Philadelphia's Fortress Press had sent two books by a Dr. Karl Wrage, one of them invitingly advertised in the program as containing "illustrations and diagrams." This volume, called *"Man and Woman, the Basics of Sex and Marriage*, sold for the meager sum of $8.75. The other, a book on family planning called *Children: Choice or Chance*, was more reasonable at $2.95. But then the first one sounded more interesting.

There was enough literature in that room to make you quite despair of ever mastering the human relations field. Wanly I studied it, trying to determine from the titles just where all this superconsciousness of *relationships* was leading us, and getting distracted by titles like *Beyond Success and Failure*, by Willard and Marguerite Beecher (New York: Julian Press, $5.95) which I thought might stand for something cheerful. Somewhere between a reading of the smiling Glenn leaflet and a wishful glance at *Beyond Success and Failure*, I was approached by a greyhaired man with an Edwardian jawline beard. He had heard me telling the Newenhouse people that I was writing a book on the sex education controversies, he said. Well, it just so happened that he was a writer, too, and what's more, he had written a book called *Dating and Marriage*.

It developed that his name was George Riemer. He wrote it down for me. And he gave me his address in Brooklyn Heights. Plus his phone number. Maybe he could help me, he said.

The conversation turned to George Riemer. George Riemer had just discovered *communication*, real *interaction*, and the importance of *dialogue*. Expounded in monologue. The thing was, we really didn't *communicate* with each other, Mr. Riemer wanted me to know. And he said it quite a few times in several different ways. As if he thought that repeating the intent would accomplish the act. I reflected to myself that he resembled the poverty program enthusiasts who had lectured to my Vista training group. They were, most of them, the social work types who believed that *communication*, reaching out, as some of them called it, was the magical panacea for the slums. And remembering that lesson, we Vistas, along with our friends, "the disadvantaged," had communicated quite a lot to judges and landlords and city officials. We told them mostly that the houses in East Harlem weren't fit to live in. And they got our message. There was no trouble making them understand. They understood and did nothing.

So as I listened to Mr. Riemer's monologue on the saving powers of dialogue, I reflected uncharitably to myself that I could give the man a three-hour lecture on the limitations of his philosophy. He had obviously caught ·on to the fact that the "group interaction" worshippers were very much in vogue, and a writer in the human relations field could, I reflected, survive well by following such styles. The Antis, of course, would say that Riemer had been brainwashed because that's what they thought the group interaction people did to others to gain their support. But Mr. Riemer had only been brainwashed by the fashions of his time. He was a camp-follower. And I didn't want any child of mine taking a camp-follower's advice on dating and marriage—or anything else.

Giving some excuse, some comment about how I had to "circulate" among the conferees, I backed away from Mr. Riemer and made my way to the door of the display room. Just before reaching the door, I overheard a short, bespectacled, scholarly looking man saying gravely to another, "We call our kind of family a *conjugal* family."

Circulating among the conferees was, of course, impossible to manage in any systematic fashion. There were 500 of them, and they were mingling in among the delegates of another convention that the gaping Sheraton had swallowed up that same day. The program told me that there were at least twenty different experts on sex education, sex education controversies, training for sex education, parent attitudes about sex education, you name it, there was someone there to talk about it. And during the next two days, they would all be holding their panels, discussion groups, or special luncheon table sessions simultaneously. At most I could manage to attend about six of these myriad sessions. Which would those be? Patricia Schiller's "section meeting" on "Group Centered Approach to Sex Education?" Roger Libby's talk on "Demographic Correlates of Parental Attitudes toward High

School Sex Education?" Bert Y. Glassberg's "theme section" on "Dealing with Opponents of Sex Education?" or Gerald Sanctuary's (of SIECUS) "theme section" on "Sex in the Mass Media?" —those were but the first morning's selection. And they all sounded equally dull—except perhaps for that one about dealing with the opponents.

Cursing my fate, I found a seat, one of the few in the lobby, and started devising a system by which I would tap all the assembled wisdom at the convention. I would make a list of every sex education expert, and call them all up. If one was presenting a paper, I would ask for a copy of it. If another was conducting a discussion, I would probe his mind for a while to determine its breadth and then, by process of elimination, pick the most interesting sessions. With this plan, I approached the house phone. Hello, operator, I'd like to leave a few messages. *How many?* Well, really, about twenty. No, I don't have their room numbers, but can't you look them up? Alas, she could not. The poor overworked—and black; we were, after all, in Washington, D.C., home of much surplus black labor—operator was going batty helping all those newly arrived family relations people to do their communicating. Therefore would I mind writing twenty messages out myself? When she had time she would put them in the proper boxes.

So I diligently wrote out twenty little notes to twenty strangers. It took quite a while. And it was to bring about a 20 per cent response. But I would not mind a bit. I would discover in the next two days that I neither liked nor respected most of the members of the Great Conspiracy.

The program said that Elizabeth D. Koontz would be giving a speech that evening at the "first plenary session." Elizabeth Koontz was, according to the Antis, an arch-conspirator and demoralizer of American youth. The former president of the National Council on Family Relations, she was listed on the program as Director of the Women's Bureau at the U.S. Department of Labor. She was scheduled to talk about, "Making Society Fit for Families." I decided that Mrs. Koontz would not be in my book. I was getting out of there.

*   *   *

Perhaps I should blame it all on George Riemer or the man who said so gravely to his colleague by the door of the publications display room, "We call our kind of family a *conjugal* family." Perhaps it was the utter drabness of the Sheraton. Whatever the cause, that first afternoon at the National Council on Family

Relations Convention marked a turning point in my whole outlook on sex education. For three months I had been listening to the wild arguments of the Antis. I had heard their liars and their religious fanatics, and I had thought them absurd. Everything they had said and done had increased my sympathies for the supporters of sex education. Everything they stood for was the antithesis of what I revered. They had played upon crude fears and used cheap McCarthyite tactics. They had frequently revealed their liking for the politics of George Wallace and had even more frequently called for bloody victory in Vietnam. At one of their rallies I had purchased a button which bore a picture of a bomber under the words, "DROP IT." That button, which didn't tell you where or why they wanted the bomb dropped, had come to symbolize for me their blind and rigid political fanaticism. Never, I had thought, would they get my sympathy.

But those people at the Sheraton, come from all over the land and Canada and Puerto Rico, too, just to read their papers and sell their books and rub shoulders with the extra-experts for three days, those people had in one afternoon chilled all my eagerness to pursue the Antis. They gave off disheartening signals of people who had spent too much time behind desks and podiums and clinic doors. They fairly oozed that dry and cerebral good will of clinicians or students of behavioral science. People who had their compassion and their anger all well under control and ready to be dealt out neatly in one-hour sessions at $50 apiece or in not-too-frank but not-too-vague-either health classes at considerably lower rates. Sprinkled in among them were a few hip-looking Afro-coifed blacks and long-haired young whites who must have been teachers or social workers or graduate students. But most of them were middle-aged or older, and you couldn't have told by looking at them whether they were John Birchers or psychiatrists. The women among them looked, for the most part, as tired and old as those Anti women in Chicago. Perhaps their skirts were a little shorter, but otherwise they would have passed for Middle Americans anywhere.

They were too diversified, of course, to accommodate themselves, 500 strong, to any easy generalizations. And yet, moving among them, reading the titles of their newest volumes of wisdom, listening to little snatches of their talk about so-and-so's study of hospital admissions and so-and-so's work with reality therapy, you could sense a sameness that ran through them all. It was their new faith in the power of the human relations professions. And whether they belonged to the sensitivity training sect or the strict Freudian school or some watered-down version of either of these, they were, all of them, members of that large and strangely humorless denomination whose priesthood dealt out the eucharist in small tablets. They had taken what was once considered sin and transformed it into something called neurotic behavior. They had taken the confessional and converted it into the cathartic soul-baring of the marathon group therapy session or the quieter, neater one-hour appointment on the couch or in the easy chair. They had, many of them, already forgotten Freud. For he had never argued for this new transcendentalism of the psyche. He had at least held out the possibility that civilization as we knew it was not merely something to suffer through with the help of palliatives, but perhaps something that individuals could also shape to their needs.

A good part of the struggles of mankind center round the single task of finding an expedient accommodation—one, that is, that will bring happiness between this claim of the individual and the cultural claims of the group; and one of the problems that touches the fate of humanity is whether such an accommodation can be reached by means of some particular form of civilization or whether this conflict is irreconcilable. . . . Happiness, in the reduced sense in which we recognize it as possible, is a problem of the economics of the individual's libido. There is no golden rule which applies to everyone: every man must find out for himself in what particular fashion he can be saved. All kinds of different factors will operate to direct his choice. It is a question of how much real satisfaction he can expect to get from the external world, how far he is led to make himself independent of it, and, finally, how much strength he feels he has for altering the world to suit his wishes.*

But, as Marcuse had pointed out, Freud's followers seemed to have absorbed only bits and pieces of his thoughts. They seemed to have heard him say that happiness was essentially subjective, that the truly unhappy could, if helped to certain insights, be eased of some of their pain, that unreasonable sexual taboos seemed to put unnecessary strains on the libido. But they seemed to have forgotten or ignored what he had written about there being "no golden rule which applies to everyone" as well as his careful avoidance of a final conclusion about whether the accommodation of the individual's needs to the "cultural claims of the group . . . can be reached by means of some particular form of civilization or whether this conflict is irreconcilable."

* *Civilization and Its Discontents*, James Strachey translation (New York: W. W. Norton, 1962).

If you listened to men like George Riemer, you got the impression that the "helping professionals" had indeed come to think that there was "a golden rule" for everyone's pursuit of happiness, which was, this year, at least, to be found in "communication." If you read the book titles in the display room, you would amend your previous conclusion, deciding instead that this year's golden rule existed for them in the new and better sexual methods being sold for a mere $8.75 per hard-cover volume. And if you read the program of events, you had to change your conclusion once again, for there the titles of the speeches and papers to be presented by earnest graduate students hinted of at least three or four different social panaceas—only one of which was sex education in the public schools.

Marcuse had called them Neo-Freudian revisionists, these modern social and individual therapists. In *Eros and Civilization* (Boston: Beacon, 1955) he had criticized them for having developed a new interpretation of Freud that "commits psychoanalysis to this society far more than Freud ever did." Discussing Erich Fromm's therapeutic goal ("optimal development of a person's potentialities and the realization of his individuality"), Marcuse had written:

Either one defines "personality" and "individuality" in terms of their possibilities *within* the established form of civilization, in which case their realization is for the vast majority tantamount to successful adjustment. Or one defines them in terms of their transcending content, including their socially denied potentialities beyond (and beneath) their actual existence; in this case, their realization would imply transgression, beyond the established form of civilization, to radically new modes of "personality" and "individuality" incompatible with the prevailing ones. Today, this would mean "curing" the patient to become a rebel or (which is saying the same thing) a martyr.*

If those NCFR conferees stood for anything, it was accommodation to the current culture. They said so themselves, right in one of the folders they had printed up especially for the convention. There, under a list of the organization's officers and beneath the capsule history of it, they had written, "Its purpose is to advance the cultural values now principally secured through family relations for personality development and the strength of the nation."

They stood for the kind of equivocation that, in my mind, was best exemplified by the ladies' magazine columns of the oh-so-popular 5-cent sage Dr. Haim Ginott, whom I had named Mr. Middle of the Road Psychic Manager. We had gotten heavy doses

* Marcuse, *Eros and Civilization* (New York: Vintage, 1962).

of Dr. Ginott in the *New York Post* after his new advice-to-parents book came out, and I had watched him one night on a TV talk-show. He offered an on-the-one-hand this, on-the-other-hand that, wisdom for the masses. A child needs some discipline, he would say, even wants it (on-the-one-hand), but parents should not be too rigid and should listen to his demands (on-the-other-hand).

And what haunted me, after that first dispiriting afternoon at the Sheraton, was the question that the Antis had raised so hysterically again and again and again. Which was: Who gave these people the right to tell us all how to raise our children? Who had conferred upon them their special qualifications for informing us of the best and latest sexual techniques? Among the Antis, I had always been able to tell myself that the helping professionals were better educated than the Commie-haters and could be expected to at least tell the facts straight to their children. But I could no longer rest easy on that assumption. For although I was prepared to accept the wisdom of certain social scientists—some of whom belonged to the NCFR—at least the wisdom of the ones who seemed to have no particular investment in the preservation of our culture, I was no longer able to trust the judgment of the considerably less objective health teachers and social workers and marriage counselors. I did not want to accommodate myself or my children to their particular standard of mental health. And if I didn't want to, why should the Antis want to? However frenziedly misled I might think them, and however much I condemned them for bringing in irrelevant arguments and for intimidating school boards, I could not avoid a small, uncomfortable sympathy for the Antis' hatred of the professionals who wrote them off as sick and therefore somehow incapable of speaking for themselves. Bruno Bettelheim, one of the most articulate and most respected psychiatrists of our time did the same thing to the young radical students. He called them neurotic and thereby subtly discredited all their indictments of social ills.

It all centered on the worship of normalcy. And we could not blame the helping professionals alone for that. We had ourselves to blame also, for we had given them their market. We ourselves had been gobbling up their books on happy human relations as readily as our forebears once gobbled up promises of transcendental ecstasy.

And if we were now getting sex education in the schools, it was not merely due to the demise of Victorian strictures but also to our fervent desire to produce normal, psychically healthy children. In a few days, Mary Calderone would tell me that her goal was "sexual sanity" for America. And that was it; that was what had put sex education into the schools. The desire for sanity, dear doctor, above anything. So you read in the Anaheim curriculum guide not of the wages of sin, but rather of the self-defeating (read masochistic) sexual patterns to be avoided through insights into your own and others' behavior (read the process of adjustment to the prevailing culture).

Although I could not find any argument against giving youngsters the facts, I was beginning to think that anything beyond the facts would be filtered to them through this new ethic of normalcy. Where they once feared hell-fire, they might now fear maladjustment.

Such were the thoughts that troubled me after that first afternoon among the clinicians. Not all of these thoughts were as clear at the time as they appear now in retrospect. And that evening I kept wishing that I had no book to write and need not feel compelled to return to the convention the following day.

*   *   *

Let us now take a little excursion to New York City, where we can observe one of the country's most recently developed sex education programs: "Family Living, Including Sex Education." Bearing in mind that we shall return to the National Council on Family Relations Convention just in time to sit in on that "theme section" on coping with the opposition, we will look at New York City's program to see what it is that those NCFR people may in the future be called upon to defend. We will see only certain snatches of the New York program, as well as snatches of the thoughts of various people who have a stake in it of some sort or another. I could call our interlude "The Case of the Condom," but that would not exactly sum it up, so I will name it instead "Looking at the Bottom of the Ostrich."

New York City, as the conscience-struck columnists have been telling us of late, is turning into a wasteland of unendurable housing. It's young men are killing themselves on heroin. Thirty-five of its teenagers died of heroin overdoses in the first two months of 1970. Many of New York City's ill-housed children learn about sex early, and some of them engage in it before they learn that the activity produces children. No one knows exactly how many conceive in ignorance, but, by 1969, the number of teenage girls who become pregnant every year had reached about 8,000. Unknown thousands of these and more contract venereal disease. Contrary to popular belief, the people who do all this copulating are not having, on the average, more fun than we of the guilt-ridden-but-now-also-orgasm-obsessed middle class. Lee Rainwater has done studies of lower-class black and white couples (one of which was published in the April, 1966, issue of *The Journal of Social Issues*), which quite puncture the myth of the feckless sensuality of the poor. The poor don't read marriage manuals, it is clear from Rainwater's studies, and, for several complicated reasons, which he discusses in his *Journal of Social Issues* essay, their women are not frequently treated to the long foreplay that is helping middle-class women achieve more and better orgasms. And if you ask any slum mother with seven children, or any young girl who has just dropped out of school to care for her infant, how much fun it is to play housewife on a welfare budget, you would quickly drop your notions about poor women having more babies to get more money from the state. The allotment is never enough to pay for the child's needs, and when you have small means you can't get any nice convenient little services to clean the baby's diapers or wash the family's sheets each week. Children mean work, hard or tedious menial tasks, for poor women.

In any event, the New York City School Board decided in 1967 to institute a sex education program in the public schools. They assembled all the local best minds in the field, Dr. Calderone among them, and they came up with a program, which was first put into the schools in the spring of 1968. It was started in a few schools, and with careful deference to the local PTA's, the city board has gradually expanded it. As of this writing, it is in about 10 per cent of the city's schools—kindergarten through twelfth grade.

The curriculum guide, which is sketchy, reads like something designed by the modernist Moral Rearmament Society. It is full of "concepts" about the importance of ethical and moral values. At frequent intervals, the guide reminds teachers: "When students ask questions using unacceptable terminology, answer these questions using the correct terminology. Encourage pupils to use correct terminology at all times."

The program does contain straightforward biology units and deals with masturbation in a matter-of-fact fashion. But about all that it offers adolescents in the area of contraceptive information is the teaching (in ninth grade) that the statement "The use of any precautionary measure is a guarantee against pregnancy" is one of the "common fallacies about sex."

And the teachers' "Resource Guide" on venereal disease, published by the Board of Education, tells them that prevention is only possible through "desirable standards of sex conduct to avoid contact with diseased persons."

Venereal disease, as all army trainees and Peace Corps Volunteers are told, can be avoided through the proper use of a condom.

Nevertheless, Herb Karp, the head of New York City's sex education program, will tell you that it is board policy to have all students' questions about contraception and prophylaxis answered thus: "There are ways of contraception, however, if you want to know more about this, you should speak with your parent or your clergyman."

Up at Columbia Teachers College, where he has been teaching courses on human sexuality for nearly twenty-five years, Professor James Malfetti, speaks about the lack of contraceptive information in most school sex education programs with gentle irony. Pointing to a rough diagram on which he has written:

VD	*condom*
out-of-wedlock pregnancy	*abstinence*

he will tell you:

"If I go into a community which says, 'Hey, we're very concerned about this' [he points to "VD" and "*out-of-wedlock pregnancy*"] and I say, 'Teach this,' [he points to "*condom*"] I'm likely not to have very many followers. I'm likely to be thought of as an extremist or radical of the sort to whom they would not like their children exposed. But if I go into a community and I say, 'Teach this, teach abstinence,' [he points to the word] Oh boy! they think I'm great! But, you see, if I'm a competent professional, I'm lying in my teeth—because I *know* I can't teach this. This [still pointing at "*abstinence*"] is something which is caught."

"The opposition, basically, is very much opposed to our teaching about contraception," says Karp. "And this is one of the main reasons it does not appear in the curriculum. It's too hot an area." And he hints darkly that teachers who give contraceptive information could get into trouble with the law—they might be accused of corrupting the morals of a minor, or some such ancient crime.

"There is no law relating to contraception and teenagers whatsoever," says Dr. Edwin Daily, the Director of Maternity and

Infant Care and Family Planning Projects in New York City's Department of Health. Legal problems only trouble doctors who wish to carry out pelvic examinations on female minors who are seeking contraception, Dr. Daily explains. Such patients must bring written parental consent just as minors in need of operations must obtain written parental or guardian consent in New York State.

"I've read that book [the Board of Education "Resource Guide" on venereal disease for teachers], and I was sick! I've been sick [with the thought] that it's been poorly done," Dr. Daily fairly groans. He nearly shouts when he is asked what he thinks of the "Family Living" curriculum guide:

"I think it's *terrible!* It was given to the Interagency Committee on Family Planning, who tore it to shreds, and nothing was done." And he quickly adds, "I think that teachers are scared out of their wits."

Dr. Adele Hofmann, who works with emotionally disturbed youngsters in Beth-Israel Hospital's adolescent clinic, is more charitable. She says that the New York City Family Living curriculum is at least "a first attempt, an honest attempt." She sees the psychological casualties of drugs up in the clinic, and she doesn't sound too alarmed about adolescent sexuality. Nevertheless, she says she has "psychiatric reasons [for thinking] that they [high-school-age youngsters] ought to abstain." She says she frequently tells girls, "First, keep your buttons buttoned, then, keep your legs crossed, and say no."

"But if somebody's doing it, anyway," she says, letting her voice trail off, as if to imply that any sensible person would then want them to know about contraception. It's interesting, she says adolescents seem to want to think that sex is "an impetuous thing that they can't help themselves about." She did a little survey up at the clinic, and she found that only one-third of the youngsters felt that doctors ought to discuss contraception with them. She thinks they feel that contraception is somehow separate from sex education.

A woman with a down-to-earth voice and a lively sense of humor, Dr. Hoffman offers no easy answers. She says that the trouble with the adolescent sexual relationships she hears about is that they are so often "exploitative." Yet she seems to think that that unhappy view of adolescent sexuality is no argument for depriving them of adequate contraceptive information.

On February 24, 1970, the City General Organization Council, the elected representatives of New York City's 275,000 high school students, made the front page of *The New York Times* with the announcement that they would be presenting a list of demands to the Board of Education, demands for what the *Times* reporter (Sylvan Fox) called "a major voice in determining policies and practices in their schools."

What the G.O. as the student government is familiarly called, wanted was the right to put some of their representatives on a committee with board members, a committee that would have binding power. And the G.O. listed a number of additional demands, among which were the following, as reported by Sylvan Fox:

All students should have the right to receive information from a personal counselor on abortion, contraception, drugs, and the draft, "without fear that it will be recorded on his record"; [and] there should be no "tracking systems in the school to direct minority groups into inferior occupations and women into traditional 'women's occupations.'"

"Take out-of-wedlock pregnancy," says Professor Malfetti, "big thing, very serious. And I don't regard it as serious *morally* in the usual framework. I regard it as serious because it can produce what I would call unwanted children. The morality which says, don't teach about how to prevent this . . . concerns me. Also we have this VD, biggest communicable disease problem in the United States. And the morality that says, don't teach about it, you know, let them suffer, concerns me, too."

Less than thirty years ago, the Surgeon General of the United States was not allowed to use the word syphilis on the radio. Today there is national television coverage of this and related areas. But our attitudes are still promoting what we dislike, to the extent that emphasis is placed on the shame or guilt one should feel if he or she contracts syphilis. The more we stress how shameful it is to contract syphilis, the more likely it is that an infected person will not go to public health authorities for treatment and will not report who his partner was. This situation encourages the spread of the disease and makes control impossible.—Ira L. Reiss, in his essay "The Sexual Renaissance: A Summary and Analysis," in the April, 1966, *Journal of Social Issues.*

The United Parents Association of New York City passed a resolution in support of sex education in the public schools at its October meeting in the Hotel Pennsylvania—in 1939.

In Kalamazoo, Michigan, a bogus newspaper story was being circulated among the followers of the local Antis during the fall of 1969. The gist of it was that seventeen male high school students had raped their twenty-five-year-old sex education teacher in New York City—inspired by a film on the " 'precautions' to be taken before introducing a virgin to sex." The film was supposed to have used live actors. And the harrowing rape story was allegedly told later by the pretty, young sex education teacher herself.

Needless to say, nothing that exciting ever went on in a New York City sex education class.

The United Parents Association had waited nearly thirty years for their sixth-graders (now their children's sixth-graders) to be told of "the importance of moral and ethical values as aspects of healthy social behavior" and to be treated to panel discussions on "Recreational Outlets as a Means for Emotional Release."

According to what I'd been reading in the mental health field (mostly Freud), there was some question as to whether "moral and ethical values" were always conducive to "healthy social behavior." In fact, there was so much doubt about the "healthiness" of certain ethical and moral values in certain situations, that one could argue that the New York City curriculum version of good health was not merely open to a good deal of scientific question, it was downright dishonest. At least, whoever had thought it up could be accused of dishonesty—if he had done a minimal amount of reading in the fields of psychology and sociology.

And if the sixth-graders were taught questionable science, the eighth-graders were drilled in "understanding the possible personal and social outcomes as well as the health hazards of indiscriminate relationships in any type of action with those of one's own or opposite sex."

As for that kind of teaching, well, Kinsey had long ago discovered that it didn't affect behavior to any significant extent.

"There is a tendency by parents, as well as by many who give professional advice, to overlook the pleasurable aspects of sex at all ages, especially for the young who are experiencing sexual pleasure for the first time," another of the April, 1966, *Journal of*

Social Issues contributors had observed (Robert Bell, in his essay, "Parent-Child Conflict in Sexual Values"), continuing:

Undoubtedly many girls engage in premarital sexual intimacy to "compensate" for some need and many may suffer some negative consequences. But it is foolish to state categorically that the "artificial" setting of premarital sex always makes it negative and unpleasant for the girl. We would be much more honest if we recognized that for many girls premarital coitus is enjoyable and the participants suffer no negative consequences. This was illustrated in the Kinsey research; it was found that "69 per cent of the still unmarried females in the sample who had had premarital coitus insisted they did not regret their experiences. Another 13 per cent recorded some minor regrets" (ALFRED C. KINSEY, *Sexual Behavior in the Human Female* [Philadelphia: Saunders, 1953] p. 316). Kinsey also found that "77 per cent of the married females, looking back from the vantage point of their more mature experience, saw no reason to regret their premarital coitus." (*Ibid.*, p. 316)

Herb Karp and the New York City Board of Education had been bothered by a few conservative Catholics from Queens. That group was predictably opposed to any and all sex education in the public schools. But then the New York City Family Living program was not being instituted in any school located in a neighborhood where there might be strong parent resistance. So what was Herb Karp afraid of? Wild stories in Kalamazoo, Michigan?

But then, New York City's sex education curriculum was quite radical compared to the kind of thing the State Board of Education was producing. Their "mental health" people had put out a teacher guide which included this statement: "Dating is a socially acceptable practice but necking, petting, and sexual intercourse may lead to physical, emotional, and social problems."

"If we agree that young people will continue to have premarital coitus—and the odds that this will occur are quite high—then the inescapable conclusion is that if we do not show them how to do it safely, they will do it without safety precautions," Ira Reiss had written in his *Journal of Social Issues* essay on "The Sexual Renaissance." And in a footnote on sex education courses, attached to the same essay he had stated, "Well trained individuals are needed if these courses are to become more than moralistic propaganda."

*   *   *

It was a chill morning in Washington, and something had gone wrong with the heating in the large chamber where the twenty-four "theme section" leaders were to assemble their groups. Perhaps the management had merely concluded prudently that no extra kilowatts or gallons of oil need be wasted on the NCFR conferees that Thursday morning. They were so dedicated, the management could have reasoned, they would start talking in their earnest little groups, and they would quickly forget the subnormal temperature in the large room. As it turned out, however, the "theme section" leaders lingered in the chilly hall only long enough to gather up their groups, being not only earnest but also resourceful and quick to think up contingency plans in the face of adversity.

I had come in a little late, having overslept, and I was desperately hoping that my group (I had chosen the section that was to talk about "Dealing with Opponents of Sex Education") would select for their contingency plan a move to the coffee shop. But, alas, my leader, an elderly physician with thick-lensed glasses, had already determined that we would all go up to his room. And he said he didn't want anybody to bring food up *there*.

So I stood in the great chilly ballroom called Sheraton Hall, waiting for our group to assemble and developing a quick theory about compulsively clean physicians. All over the room group leaders were holding up handmade signs with numbers on them. Each theme section had been numbered in the program, and the ever resourceful human relations experts had quickly realized that 500 strangers would never distinguish them from each other without the aid of clues. A few of the group leaders were without signs and these would shout out their names or their subjects at scattered intervals. It was a scene oddly like an auction, or perhaps an old-world market place. Up near the door Gerald Sanctuary, the Englishman who was soon to inherit Dr. Calderone's heavy mantle at SIECUS, called out his name in cheerful, brisk British syllables. Across the room, another voice, deeper and graver, announced another name, a name of no significance or value to anyone who had not memorized the list of twenty-four theme-section titles as well as all the names of their respective authors. And one poor man, who hadn't attracted any following at all, circulated around the chamber, stopping at little clusters of people to ask whether any of them wanted to discuss "a more useful definition of love" or "extramarital relations" or something-or-other of social significance, which I heard and immediately forgot. He wasn't having much luck, as there were considerably fewer than 500 people in the large room, and the ones who had risen early to make it there had come with their hearts already set on some topic other than his. Apparently, not everyone in the National Council on Family Relations was dedicated enough to make it to a 9:00 A.M. meeting in this their annual sojourn to the Big Convention, for the room was nowhere near to filling up.

Our group turned out to be one of the larger ones, the "opposition" having worried a good number of believers in the powers of mental prophylaxis. And when we finally settled in the cozy quarters of our leader, Dr. Bert Y. Glassberg, of the Washington University School of Medicine, we numbered, counting him, ten. We had among us: a grey-haired pediatrician who was working as a public health consultant in New Jersey and who had recently served as the president of the Tri-State (New Jersey, New York, and Connecticut) Council on Family Relations; a female health teacher; a bespectacled young man who said he was studying for his masters at "Penn State" and that he had himself taught sex education classes; a middle-aged woman from Puerto Rico who said she gave talks on sex education; a Canadian woman who said she was involved with a "Family Life" program in Toronto; a former social studies teacher who had recently been made coordinator of a "Family Life education" program in Minnesota; a man from the Association of Family Living in Chicago; and a sociologist from the Institute for Sex Research at Indiana University (the institute that Kinsey established) who had been doing research on college student and adolescent sexual behavior.

Dr. Glassberg started the session off with some general statements about the group's need to "discover effective means of combatting the opposition," adding at the end of this little exposition a magnanimous comment about his "hope that we can come to some kind of agreement that not everybody who opposes sex education is a kook, a Bircher, or a Hargis type."

That remark inspired the former social studies teacher to equal magnanimity. "I think we should welcome criticism," he grandly brought out. And the discussion was on. The New Jersey public health consultant observed that although, of course, some criticism was justified, "you cannot persuade superintendents of schools [to take that attitude]." The sociologist said that there had "always been criticism of sex education." Even psychiatrists criticized it, he said. Yes, well, "a physician's own background in sex education doesn't extend much beyond biology, physiology," said the public health consultant.

"I think the best people that can sell this program would be the parents themselves," suggested the female health teacher.

"Would it be fair to say that, despite the intentions of the parents, the argument is carried on in radical terms?" the Chicago Association of Family Living man tentatively brought out.

The Puerto Rican woman said she thought the trouble was that people expected too much from sex education, they expected something "that it will not be able to deliver."

The sociologist said he agreed with her. "We don't ask that of any other educational program," he added, "that" being apparently a behavioral outcome.

It was a meandering circuitous discussion that centered vaguely upon the public relations problems which the Antis had managed to create for nearly every sex educator in the country. It was clear throughout that the people in that room had never had to deal with the organized right wing before the emergence of this, their controversy. They seemed to feel that the right wing now constituted a clear and present threat to their respective human relations professions, and there was about them a genuine air of bafflement, a sort of befuddled indignation over the Antis' unscrupulous tactics. And though there was also a kind of unspoken understanding among them, a complacent agreement that most of their opponents *were*, in fact, kooks with unhappy sex lives or gargantuan sexual anxieties, they seemed quite bereft of ideas about ways to combat them en masse. "Who can you go to? The whole Birch Society of the United States?" the graduate student pleaded woefully at one point. And his questions went unanswered.

They were, most of them, at a loss for effective tactics. They could commiserate with one another and exchange stories of smear tactics they had suffered under. The sociologist, who seemed the least rattled, told them he had been accused of "teaching kids to copulate in the halls." His research team had put a stop to that kind of tale by telling their accusers "to be prepared to meet our attorneys in court," he said. And for a while the discussion centered upon legal tactics. The former social studies teacher gave a capsule summary of a libel case (involving a Communist smear) that he cherished. Then he launched into a kind of progress report on the Minneapolis sex education controversy. One of the local papers had taken a poll, he said, and it turned out that 82 per cent of the local adults "favored" sex education, and "of the adults under 50, 92 per cent favored it."

Dr. Glassberg then uttered something about the need for "effective relations with the communications media," after which he launched into his own progress report on the state of affairs in St. Cloud, Washington. When he had completed this, the Puerto Rican woman spoke up, changing the subject altogether.

"Maybe we are scared of the generation gap," she said. "I don't know. Maybe we try to become as if we were fifteen, sixteen. There's no reason to start [courses right out] with copulation or with four-letter words. We don't need to shock."

That brought a response from the graduate student. "I used four-letter words with my ninth-graders," he said. "I know darn well if I use the words 'sexual intercourse,' they wouldn't know what I meant. So I used the word 'fuck' once."

"Well, fuck's all right anyhow. It means freedom under Clark Kerr," said the former social studies teacher in a rare show of humor. But he quickly lapsed back into earnest pursuit of The Solution.

Soon the conversation shifted to a topic which was apparently of overriding concern to all of them: What's in a Course Title? Or: Is Sex by Any Other Name As Sexy?

"When you hear the term 'sex,' you think of one thing: intercourse," said the health teacher. "The term 'sex' just connotes those images to parents." Therefore, she said, she preferred the term "family life."

"Then you're going to be accused of trying to hide—" objected the former social studies teacher.

"But if we assume that people think just of the physical part [when they hear the term 'sex education'], then we should put some of the other topics in the title," the health teacher insisted.

"I've been collecting titles that the schools use," said the sociologist, looking faintly amused. "It comes under everything from driver education. . . . Nobody knows what to call it."

"I think 'human relations,'" the health teacher persisted.

"That has a civil rights ring to it," the cautious Chicago man observed.

"I wouldn't hide it under any name," said the Puerto Rican woman. "In the long run we have to really examine the content to see [what is appropriate]. . . . Will we be accused of using another name for evil purposes?"

"Do we define sex as an activity in the pelvis or [as an aspect of] the total personality?" Dr. Glassberg asked no one in particular.

"I think it's been brought out that you cannot deny anything," said the public health consultant. "Each person will put their own filter [on what they hear]. . . . There is, therefore, no suitable title for this. What you try to do is to define not a word but a concept in no more than a word or two."

But Dr. Glassberg was still interested in defining a word. "The dictionary definition of 'sex' is 'the sum total of the differences between male and female,' " he declared.

"Freud often used it to mean 'pleasure,' " said the sociologist. "Sex in the generic sense is whether you're a male or a female. But people equate sex with intercourse. The better term is 'sexuality.' "

There followed a series of digressions about the use of the term "sex" by doctors, doctors' poor training in sexual matters, and teachers' poor preparation for giving sex education courses.

Eventually Dr. Glassberg brought them back to the question of titles, saying, "The only term I have been able to accept is 'Education for Personal and Family Living.' . . . We do not allow with this terminology as many easy misinterpretations."

And that inspired the public health consultant to utter a remark which would have delighted every Anti in the country. For it fitted remarkably well into their conspiracy theories. "If you use a strange combination of words," he said happily, "then you've got the upper hand."

"When I went to medical school," said Dr. Glassberg, who was still pondering definitions, "the only thing I learned about sex was that you could get syphilis or gonorrhea from it."

And with that, the discussion ended. The theme sections had been scheduled to meet four times altogether, so Dr. Glassberg asked each member of his group to suggest topics for the future sessions before they left. The sociologist said he probably wouldn't be coming back, but he did want to emphasize that he was opposed to any course title that "uses the family" as a central focus. Single people have sex lives, too, he said, adding that he "opted" for the term "Human Sexuality." The Chicago man said he wanted some kind of "policy" statement to emerge from the group. The Family Life coordinator said he was interested in devising ways to "influence the public through effective organizations" like the NEA and the AMA. The Canadian woman wanted to discuss teacher training. The Puerto Rican woman simply said she thought they should "continue without fear." The graduate student wanted to talk about "what kinds of things should be avoided in classrooms." The health teacher wanted to discuss "moral questions." And the public health consultant said he

wanted to discuss just about every topic that had been mentioned
by the others. I said I wasn't coming back. I had to "circulate,"
I was sure they would understand.

* * *

Richard von Rueden, Harvard, class of '72, decided during his
freshman year to conduct a little survey on the students in his
"entry" in Hollis Hall. It was a special project that he thought up
all on his own for a writing class. He wanted to find out where
Harvard freshmen got their sex education. He came from a little
town (population, 1,400) in Wisconsin called East Troy, where
the only formal sex education you could get was offered by the
Catholic Church—one night a year. Von Rueden had heard something about the sex education controversies, and he thought it
might be interesting to find out how many of the people in his
dorm had been given any sex education in their schools. He asked
twenty boys, not a large enough number to qualify for any sociological journal, but his findings were still worth some consideration. Fifteen per cent of his sample had learned the essentials
from their parents; 55 per cent from their friends; 25 per cent
"from their own personal reading," and 5 per cent through organized instruction. And that last had been offered not by the school,
but by a church group.

The main source of sex education for most boys is the peer group—
friends and classmates. Nevertheless there are important differences,
depending on the child's social class (measured here as father's oc-
cupation). The peer group is overwhelmingly important as a source of
information for all boys from blue-collar homes: From 75 per cent to
88 per cent of them report other boys as their major source. The boys
of lower white-collar homes seem a transitional group, with 70 per cent
so reporting, while the boys whose fathers are lower white-collar men
find their mothers as important as their peers with respect to information. The boys from upper white-collar homes derive little from
their peers, most from their mothers, and a relatively large amount
from combined education efforts by both parents. . . .

When looking at the main source of sex knowledge for girls, we see
similar trends. Peers provide the main source of sex information for
35 per cent of the girls whose fathers are lower blue-collar men and
for 25 per cent of the girls whose fathers are upper blue-collar
workers. By contrast, only 9 per cent and 4 per cent, respectively, of the
girls whose fathers are white-collar men report the peer group as their
main source of sex education. The mother's importance as a source

of sex education increases with increased occupational status, being the major source for 10 per cent of the daughters of lower blue-collar workers [and] up to 75 per cent of those whose fathers are upper white-collar men. . . .

It is interesting to note that the teacher is not mentioned by any of the children as the main source of sex education.—JAMES ELIAS and PAUL GEBHARD in their essay entitled "Sexuality and Sexual Learning in Childhood," which appeared in the March, 1969, issue of the *Phi Delta Kappan*. (Their conclusions were based on the case histories of 432 prepubescent white boys and girls, gathered by Alfred Kinsey and his co-workers before 1955.)

*   *   *

James Elias, Associate Sociologist from the Institute for Sex research of Indiana University and the member of Dr. Glassberg's theme section who had said he objected to the use of the word "family" in the titles of sex education courses, did not look like a sex researcher. Sex researchers were supposed to bear some indelible mark of their trade. They were supposed to possess the blank, pale, impassive faces of men who had lost every last illusion and rash, unscientific trace of sentiment. Or if they showed any human frailty at all, it was supposed to manifest itself in perverse, unpleasant ways, in strange laughter or nervous, oddly patterned speech.

But James Elias fitted none of the popular illusions about the perverted cataloguers of orgasm rates. He looked like an English professor approaching middle age. And when he spoke, his eyes seemed to be laughing, their expression conferring upon everything he said a gentle irony. If he had acquired any peculiarity as a result of his work, it was a certain irreverent humor that caused him to look amused even as he spoke of the considerable resistance he had encountered in the community where he had done his research on adolescent sexual behavior. It was a "large midwestern suburb," he said, and securing the approval of its local school board had required considerable diplomacy.

In the random sample method that I had been using to "cover" the National Council on Family Relations Convention, I had selected Elias as a subject to be interviewed. He had displayed some knowledge of the history of sex education during that theme session, and I thought he might prove a good source. He proved a better source than I had bargained on. For it emerged that he had been doing research on the relationships between sex education and adolescent sexual behavior. I had not been able to find anyone who knew *anything* about relationships between sex education and sexual behavior—except for a sex education teacher in Keokuk, Iowa, who had kept track of the divorces and out-of-wedlock pregnancies among his former students. The Keokuk teacher (James Lockett) had found substantial differences between the divorce rates and illegitimacy rates of the students who had enrolled in his sex education class and those who had not, differences that might be proof of his effectiveness. But I had decided that his study didn't count because he had done it on his own students. Thus, I fairly leaped out of my chair when I learned about Elias's work.

Unfortunately, he said that he had not completed "analyzing the data," and hence had little to report as yet. But he did offer some useful tentative conclusions. And he seemed better informed about the literature on and history of sex education than any other source I had encountered.

He said that no one knew how many American school districts were offering sex education, that there were "no records" which would indicate how extensive it was. And he said that most of the research on the effects of sex education was superficial. ("They give them a questionnaire before the class and another questionnaire after the class is over.")

"Most of the kids are still learning most of their information from their peers," he said with some confidence.

What had obviously impressed him in the process of conducting his own study was the failure of the school administrations to consult the youngsters, to find out what they might want to know.

"The kids told us, 'You're the first person who's ever really asked us what we thought.' They're never consulted," he reiterated. "It's simply imposed on them."

The local Antis, who already know what the effects of sex education are and don't need any so-called intellectual to tell them different, hadn't taken kindly to Elias's research project. He said they had tried to find out from the youngsters themselves what sorts of questions he and his researchers had been asking them. "They had the school board to the point where the school board was about ready to throw the whole thing out. . . . Their impression was that we were subverting the kids."

Elias seemed to know a good deal about the subject of my book, and I decided to follow him to lunch, where he was to serve as the table expert for seven or eight fact-hungry souls. The luncheon was served in one of the innumerable vastnesses of the Sheraton, and all over the room people sat at round tables picking the brains of their designated experts. (Sally Williams was listed on the program as one of these. But the Anaheim trustees, some of whom at that time seemed to think they had unlimited powers, had said she would be fired if she attended the convention. She did not attend.)

Elias was to tell his group about how children get their "sexual information," and he was to be speaking about some of the results of his recent research.

Things got off to a jolly start. A woman from the Illinois State University quite unabashedly complained right off that "when you play with dolls you never have any organ there."

Elias began, in a conversational manner, giving them a kind of lecture. He was occasionally interrupted, usually by the woman from Illinois State University, but he managed to present them with a good amount of material.

"Early childhood is the period of peep and show," he began. "This is usually the first introduction, unless there is nudity in the home. . . . The higher up the educational ladder we go, the more permissive [we are] about nudity in the home."

Someone wanted to know whether the religion of the family had any special effect upon the child's sexual learning. Elias said he didn't know of any studies that might show the effects of the various religions, but he did know that in Jewish homes "you have somewhat of a different emphasis."

This prompted a man from Syracuse, who seemed quite eager to display his own command of the subject, to tell the luncheon party that his wife was an elementary school teacher in a Hebrew day school who had also taught in public elementary schools, and that she had noticed that the boys in the Hebrew school "draw a man with a large penis . . . not neutral as in public school." That reminded the woman from Illinois of a little experiment she'd conducted with her students. She had found a toy outhouse which contained a little male figure whose penis squirted you if you opened the door of the thing. She said she asked her students whether they would give it to children for Christmas. "Most of them said their friends wouldn't, but they would," the lady concluded.

Back to Elias. Fathers, he was saying, don't give their children any sex information, "and they never talk to daughters" about sexual matters, at least, not according to his research sample. Mothers in the sample talked to their daughters about menstruation and premarital intercourse. "Inner city" boys learned about prostitution and condoms by age eight or ten, said Elias, and by age fifteen, 80 per cent of the nonwhite, "delinquent" youngsters had had intercourse. Yet many of the "inner city" youngsters did not know the biology of conception. He said that researchers had found some girls who had become pregnant while still "ignorant of reproduction."

"I might say at this point that it's very difficult to do research on this age group. I had to spend most of my time on public relations," Elias went on, amusement again showing in his eyes.

The man from Syracuse wanted to know where most of the resistance came from. "From the school system," said Elias. "It even got to the point where I had teachers I had to throw out of our research rooms because they were trying to find out what students we were interviewing." The school staffs seemed to look upon his research team as "intruders," he said.

Briefly he explained the techniques his researchers had used, the kinds of questions they had asked, and the youngsters' comments about how no one consulted them.

At this point a man who said he was a representative of "the Mental Health Materials Center" passed each of his tablemates a little leaflet, which told them all about the wonderful new book his outfit had published. *Teach Us What We Want to Know*, it was called, and it had been put together from 8,000 pages of a Connecticut study of children's ideas about health education.

"I was accused of causing the kids to have intercourse in the hallways," Elias was saying. "I was called a perverted homosexual, and one letter accused me of being like a Nazi commandant of a breeding camp." Kinsey, too, had been credited with all kinds of sexual talents, and the people at the table reminded Elias of this as a kind of consolation. But Elias did not appear to have suffered much.

He was a veritable fund of information about the sexual practices and foibles of our society. He said that lower-class men tended to be polygamous when they were young ("His masculinity is based on the number of conquests he makes") and that they settled into fidelity after marriage. Middle-class males, on the other hand, started straying from the nest after a few years of marriage, he explained. "Females—especially through college—are more apt to maintain the attitudes they learn through the family." And he threw out this interesting tidbit; almost as an aside: "We find a large number of cases of incest in which children grow up to be normal adults." (So there, Sigmund.)

At one point a woman from the University of Maryland asked Elias whether he thought that "sex education about the physical aspects of sex is going to change people's attitudes."

"No!" he replied without hesitation. People's attitudes were affected by the society, the culture, he said. After all, children were not the consumers of pornography.

Well, weren't things changing? someone wanted to know. Vance Packard had done a study that showed that virginity rates among unmarried college females had gone down substantially.

Packard's data were inconsistent with all other studies, said Elias. "I think it's the result of using a mailed questionnaire.

"We had this question when we randomly selected high school kids," he went on, trying to illustrate how Packard might have gotten misleading figures. "They said, 'But we haven't done anything. Why do you ask me?' " His point was that sexually inexperienced people don't seem to realize that they are statistically important to researchers. And some of the prevailing misconceptions about sexual terms also create difficulties for researchers, he said. Females were under the impression that masturbation was "a male phenomenon." Thus, when his researchers asked the girls, "Do you masturbate?" and then asked them, "Have you ever put your hands between your legs and rubbed yourself until you felt very good?" they were much more apt to give an affirmative reply to the second question. "In taking a case history, masturbation is probably the most difficult area to get."

Elias knew a great deal, and it was clear as he talked that some of his observations were based on already published research. That April, 1966, issue of *The Journal of Social Issues* contained much of the general information he had been carefully reviewing for the people at the table. Reading over the sociology of American sexual behavior later, I realized that it would be impossible for me to glean from my notes of that luncheon just those aspects of Elias's informal talk that were based on his own research. But I found nothing in *The Journal of Social Issues* or *The Individual, Sex, and Society* (or in those parts of the voluminous Kinsey-Pomeroy *Sexual Behavior in the Human Female* that I studied) which contradicted Elias's statements. He knew his area thoroughly. And he seemed to have mastered it without any undue fondness for the prevailing culture—or for possible alternatives. He spoke calmly, easily, and without the condescension that knowledgeable men so frequently display among the relatively ignorant. He caused me to amend my easy conclusions about the National Council on Family Relations. (He and, also, Ira Reiss, who was one of the officers of the NCFR and whose writings contained criticisms directed at the kind of people who made up the membership of the organization.)

Toward the end of the lunch, Elias said, "What sex education is given is given too little and too late. . . . The time to answer questions is when kids are asking them—and not just the biological questions." In most schools, he said, it was offered in the tenth or eleventh grade.

This remark brought pleas for advice about fending off the Antis from all around the table. Elias told them to get the parents involved in planning their sex education programs, to show the parents the materials. But he didn't have any easy answers for them when they asked how they should handle the "context of marriage" question. However, he said he thought that "social responsibility" could be taught as something to be valued in all sexual relationships, in or out of marriage.

Just before everyone got up, a woman asked Elias whether he thought parent anxieties about school sex education would be eliminated "in a generation."

"In a generation, maybe the schools can give this up again," Elias said, looking as if, in the end, he stood bemusedly aloof from this creature, Homo sapiens, and all its odd history of religious wars.

*   *   *

Thursday afternoon was reserved for the "WASHINGTON D.C. TOUR," said the program. And later there was to be a "DUTCH TREAT SOCIAL HOUR," followed by a banquet featuring the "Grand Premier of a New Play for Living," calculated, apparently, to put you in the mood for all the speeches that were to come after it. And if the trip to the city on a bus full of human relations experts didn't appeal to you, you could always mosey on over to that little chamber behind the publications room to watch the uninterrupted series of films guaranteed to fill you full of healthy social attitudes.

It was another reprieve for me. I used the time to skim through a little blue pamphlet called "Annual Meeting Proceedings"— not to be confused with the 28-page glossy program. No, this little blue pamphlet was far more interesting. It contained a considerable number of capsule summaries of the myriad papers, speeches, and panel presentations that had been or would be delivered to the professional horde. It was a fine convenience for a young free-lance writer who, at the start of the session, had known next to nothing about the National Council on Family Relations. You could learn a lot about those people by just studying the language in that little pamphlet. They were the kind of people who would rather

say "utilize" than "use"; who always called the poor "the disadvantaged"; who described their more complex questionnaires
as "multidimensional instruments"; and who could seriously under-
take studies of "stress situations involving marital conflict" to
determine which ones were "functional" or "dysfunctional." Functional, was, in fact, one of their favorite words, for it was so nicely
sterile and suggestive of machinery; it carried just the proper
metallic tone for the detached and dispassionate inventory-takers
who had come to be called social scientists. They liked dispassionate words, for they were in the business of measuring intan-
gibles, and their language at least held forth the promise that
someday they would find the flawless "instrument"—another of
their favorite words—that would at last distill a ticking and exact
machinery out of that infinitely varied creature, man.

Reporters, who live always in terror of being fooled, regard social scientists with a cynical and superior sense of irony, mingled
with a grudging respect. This is because reporters seldom encounter the wisdom of social scientists outside the context of political debates. And within that context, science and language are
so often perverted, so often bent to the wishes of unscrupulous
men whose only ethic is success, that the poor scribes who are
asked to sort it all out for you, the public, come to doubt everything they hear.

And yet reporters eagerly hunt down the latest findings of social
science on any and all current social problems. Reporters are required to relay the news of catastrophic happenings as they occur,
and they have no adequate means by which to measure their effects. They have no teams of dedicated researchers (or not
usually) who can provide them with the incontestable percentages
of, say, blacks who gave up the faith two days after Martin Luther
King was killed, or squares who were transformed into hippies two
days after the end of the Woodstock Music Festival. In desperation, a scrupulous reporter will read back through the files after
these large events, searching for just those irrefutable facts and
figures that can *explain it all*. Inevitably, the facts and figures lag
behind the great events; and the journalists, who have to go into
print, there is no getting around it, are forced to fall back upon
their own theories. In just this desperate sociological poverty,
journalists had invented the notion of the Sexual Revolution of
the sixties. In similar desperation they had brought about the
Myth of the Idyllic Superpastorale, the Aquarian Age—just five
months before that same idyllic superpastoral crowd was to stand
impotently by as one of their young spaced-out members was dealt

an untimely end by the Hell's Angels. It had taken the passionless social scientists to establish the fact that there had been no Sexual Revolution, at least not as the term was popularly understood. And it would, no doubt, take another set of unfeeling researchers to discover for us that not all rock and drug fans were gentle, nature-loving souls. (The journalists were beginning to see dark and evil elements in the drug culture now that Altamont and Charlie Manson had embarrassed them out of their Woodstock visions, but there was now a danger that they would exaggerate the new Truth, the mythical Apocalypse.)

Thus, I had been banking on the hope that social science would provide the final elucidation of this odd controversy I had set out to chronicle. Social science would tell me whether sex education did, in fact, influence behavior. Social science would tell me why sex education had suddenly struck the hearts and minds of considerable numbers of parents with fear. Social science would tell me why, in Anaheim, California, where 92 per cent of the adults said they supported sex education, its opponents had, for the present, triumphed. Social science would tell me why, when 71 per cent of the American public said *they* supported sex education (according to George Gallup, June, 1969), cowardly foundations had stopped giving SIECUS money, the Birchers were saying that sex education "could be the greatest boost to recruiting" that they had ever had, and anti-sex education legislation was finding its way into nineteen state legislatures.

It turned out, of course, that social science was not in possession of all the answers, and those answers that it had were only fragmentary, only "instruments" for cautious speculations. In that little blue pamphlet, for example, where the summaries of the latest findings on the state of America's mind could be found, social science told you that 82 per cent of a representative group of "Caucasian" parents "approved of sex education," but:

"a slight majority preferred a teacher who believes in chastity while nearly half believed the teacher's values to be unimportant; slightly more than half wanted the teacher to give his or her own standards if asked by students."*

* Roger W. Libby, "Parental Attitudes Toward High School Sex Education," a study conducted on "125 randomly selected parental couples" and rated according to social class as: "6% upper, 24% upper-middle, 40% lower-middle, and 30% upper-lower." They were also of varied religions, "52% Protestant, 38% Catholic, 2% Jewish, 2% Unitarian or Humanist, and 2% agnostic or atheist." In *Annual Meeting Proceedings*, National Council on Family Relations.

If the results of this study were representative (applicable to the general public) then the Gallup poll was essentially meaningless. For it had not asked parents what *kind* of sex education they favored. In fact, if you asked them in the right way, you could probably get the "Hargis types" to say they favored some kind of sex education.

What's more, there were differences between the kind of sex education that the parents (in this study) favored and the kind that teachers favored. Another study, mentioned in that little blue book (and later sent to me by its author, James D. Greenberg, Ph.D. of the U.S. Office of Education),* showed that there were even substantial disagreements about what constituted proper sex education among the educators themselves. In that study, 38 per cent of the educators had said they agreed or strongly agreed that "students should be encouraged to develop their own standards regarding what is appropriate premarital sexual behavior." But 49 per cent said they generally or strongly disagreed with that statement. And 64 per cent were in favor of the school giving "guidelines to students regarding what is appropriate premarital sexual behavior."

In the study of parent attitudes, additional findings were that "the majority approved a wide range of discussion topics such as masturbation, homosexuality, and contraception." A majority of the educators, too, had approved these topics. But a large portion (48 per cent) of the educators thought that "boys and girls should be separated when certain delicate subjects in sex education are discussed." Among the parents (who may not have been asked as sophisticated a question), "mixed classes were favored by over 80 per cent." (In Anaheim, over two-thirds of the parents surveyed had said they thought the classes should be segregated according to sex.)

If you compared those two studies, you could get the impression that parents were generally more liberal about sex education than were educators. One nice little finding in the study of parents could give a clue to the sort of thing that was troubling the particular group that made up the Antis, however, this was that "parents with prepubescent children were more liberal than parents with postpubescent children." And Roger Libby, the young sociologist

* The study, entitled "Attitudes of Educators Toward Specific Issues in Sex Education," was conducted, by mailed questionnaires, on 250 teachers and administrators (only 72 per cent responded—hence, the percentages are tallied from that group) in Connecticut public schools.

who had conducted this study, was later to write an article for *The American School Board Journal*, in which he would discuss other findings that showed parents to be laboring under profound misconceptions about just who was qualified to plan a sex education program. (Libby's article, "Who Should Plan Your District's Sex Education Program?" appeared in the December, 1969, issue of the *Journal*. Jesse Potter, the scourge of Mrs. Westerfield, was a co-author of the piece.) Ninety-two per cent of his sample group thought doctors were best qualified to plan sex education programs; and after doctors they rated "family life and sex education consultants;" after them, ministers; after them, teachers.

Among the most firmly established principles in the entire sexual area is the finding that *guilt feelings* about masturbation rather than the *act* of masturbation lead to emotional distress. Yet as late as 1959, a study of medical students graduating from five Philadelphia medical schools revealed that half of them still thought—after three or four years in medical school—that masturbation itself is a frequent cause of mental illness. Worse yet, a fifth of the medical school faculty members shared the same misconception.

Thus wrote Harold Lief, M.D., (professor of Psychiatry, Director of the Division of Family Study at the University of Pennsylvania, and one of the founders of SIECUS) in his chapter on "Teaching Doctors About Sex," that was included in the little Signet paperback collection of essays analyzing "Human Sexual Response." That book had come out in 1966, and Roger Libby's subjects, who should have been reading it, were still laboring under the illusion that doctors knew just *everything* there was to know about the species.

This whole business of trying to discover who supported sex education and what kind of sex education they supported and why, although interesting, could produce some unintended results, it seemed to me. For school superintendents were essentially at the mercy of small-town politicians, and you could always count on politicians to read the results of surveys. They might read Roger Libby's material and say to themselves, if the *people* want doctors to plan the program, let them have doctors. In fact, if the politicians in Anaheim had been true Machiavellians, they would have insisted that the District Administration follow the suggestions in those survey results like the letter of the law. If the people want segregated classes, let them have segregated classes, they might have said, and James Townsend would probably have had considerably fewer supporters.

Of course, the educators themselves—as distinguished from the school boards—would try to get round the public if they thought they could. In New York City, if you asked Herb Karp why contraception had been left out of the sex education curriculum, he proudly told you, yeah, but we put masturbation in—adding later, not in so many words, but in effect, that you could get away with masturbation, but not with contraception. All you had to do was listen to those members of Dr. Glassberg's theme section trying to think up a noncontroversial title for sex education to become convinced once and for all that educators would try to get round the public on matters that they, the educators, thought themselves better equipped to judge.

But the controversy had scared them. They weren't quite sure what would get past the more conservative parents anymore. And even among their own ranks there were people who had conservative notions about just what ought to go on in a sex education class (if that study of Connecticut educators could be believed).

Roger Libby was to tell me that he thought one of the crucial mistakes made by the Anaheim District Administration was their failure to realize that the survey had revealed *qualified* support for sex education. Roger Libby's findings and his conclusions were getting wide exposure among educators. And although he himself deplored the restrictions that were later established by the Washington State Board of Education, his own research could be read as a warning to educators to establish such restrictions.

All this cataloguing of attitudes about sex education did not, in the end, explain the emergence of the controversy so well as it demonstrated the overanxiety of educators vis-à-vis that controversy. The controversy seemed to have generated the research. And, in turn, the research—on public attitudes about sex education—could begin to dictate the nature of the sex education programs that went into the schools. (Not that the schools had been exorbitantly adventuresome before the controversy broke out; John Kobler had concluded—prior to Drake's meteoric success—that the schools were being overly cautious and preachy about all the sensitive sexual areas. And he had so alarmed the *Saturday Evening Post* editors with his conclusions that they had written an editorial for the issue that carried his article in which they had said, "Basically, our schools do not just teach children what sex is, but also why they should abstain from it. In this, their function is not one of education but of propaganda.")

The crucial question was whether the public ought to have

the right to dictate what went into a sex education program—when the public didn't even know who was best qualified to give simple sexual information. But then, the educators themselves were not above turning sex education into a kind of quasiscientific propaganda for an updated version of virtue.

All this pondering over the cowardice of teachers and how the peculiar thing they called education was often merely a form of conventional wisdom derived by consensus had put me in an unhappy frame of mind. For it all kept leading me to the conclusion that public education was a noble but failing experiment. The very faith in democracy that sustained it as an institution also mitigated against the academic purity that was its rightful province. If educators were accountable, in the final analysis, to the public, then they could not—except in a community of superhuman, totally objective scholars—teach the whole truth, about sex or anything else.

But that conclusion depressed me no end because it led to impractical and highly undemocratic theories about how to educate our young. So I put it aside, and returned to the convention, nursing an aimless sense of disillusionment and looking for likely human relations types to blame it on. I found some, but before you meet them, we will take another excursion, this time through the Country of the Young and/or Disenchanted.

*   *   *

Last week, a weary Stockton (California) housewife and mother was told by her husband, "What in hell are you so tired about? You stay home all day—I'm the one who works like a dog," upon which she wigged out, calmly made herself a picket sign, and began walking up and down in front of their house. Most of her neighbors (women all) soon joined her, and the "homemakers" of the town are now attempting to organize themselves into a union of houseworkers. None of the women were involved in the Women's Liberation Movement. . . ."— an unsigned report in the Feb. 6–23, 1970, issue of the New York underground newspaper *Rat*, the first issue printed after the "Women's Collective" took over the paper.

"Guess who's keynote speaker at the Weatherman convention this month? Right on! I came up with this idea, that kids should assassinate their parents, and fuckin' Weatherman couldn't fuckin' top it. So they adopted me."—ABBIE HOFFMAN, December, 1969.

"Abbie took the stand Tuesday. 'My name is Abbie. I am an orphan of America,' he introduced himself.

" 'The defendant has a last name, I think he should state it for the record,' objected assistant prosecutor Richard Schultz.

" 'My slave name is Hoffman. My real name is Schlaboyzakoff. I can't spell it.'

"Defense attorney Leonard Weinglass asked him, 'Where do you reside?'

" 'I live in Woodstock Nation—a state of mind dedicated to co-operation rather than competition.'

" 'Where is it?'

" 'In my mind, the same way the Sioux Indians carried their nation around in their minds.'

"The Judge interrupted, 'I want your place of residence, if you have one, and nothing about philosophy or Indians. What state is Woodstock?'

" 'It's in my state of mind.'

" 'Where do you live?' asked Weinglass.

" 'Presently in the penitentiaries and institutions of our decaying system.'

" 'And when were you born?'

" 'Psychologically, in 1960.'

"Again Schultz interrupted, demanding the actual date.

" 'November 30, 1936.'

" 'Between that date and May 1, 1960,' continued Weinglass, 'what, if anything, happened to you?'

" 'Nothing.' "—from an article by Paul Glusman, entitled, "Schlaboyzakoff From Woodstock," in the Dec. 26, 1969–Jan. 2, 1970, issue of *The Berkeley Tribe*.

A little excerpt from the Conspiracy Trial transcript:

SCHULTZ: You said, did you not, Mr. Hoffman, that in your liberated zone you would have public fornication?

HOFFMAN: If that means 10,000 people, naked people, walking on Lake Michigan, yes.

KUNSTLER: I object to this because Mr. Schultz is acting like a dirty old man.

SCHULTZ: We are not going into dirty old men. If they wanted to have 500,000 people in the park and are telling the city officials they are going to have nude-ins and public fornication, the city officials react to that. . . . We are not litigating here, Your Honor, whether sexual intercourse is beautiful or not. We are litigating whether or not the city could permit tens of thousands of people to come in and do in their parks what this man said they were going to do.

. . . .

SCHULTZ: Mr. Hoffman, will you answer my question . . . you stated on direct examination people should fuck all the time?

"The sexual revolution is like most other things: it may or may not exist. If it does exist, it may be good or bad but will probably avail itself of the opportunity to be both. One thing is certain: sex is running rampant, unchecked, and spreading like wildfire.

"I am inclined to believe that this is pretty much as it has always been, but since I really know neither how it has always been nor how it is now, I am not especially qualified to make judgement. If pressed, however, I would probably say that there are indeed sexually revolutionary cadres, whose principal effect is to depress the hell out of everybody who is not in one."—James Kunen, in *The Strawberry Statement*.

"NEW HAVEN, March 3—The auditorium of the Yale Law School was the scene last night of an exchange between Russ Meyer, the filmmaker who is sometimes called the 'king of the nudies,' and two New York feminists.

"The women accused Mr. Meyer of having a 'breast fixation,' and said that his films showed sex as something 'sinful and evil.'

"Mr. Meyer, the featured guest during a two-day 'Russ Meyer Film Festival' at Yale, replied that the women appeared to be 'extremely insecure,' and suggested that he and the women 'compare our latest sexual experiences.'"—*The New York Times*, March 4, 1970.

"Parents don't explain sex to you and it's important that you find out somewhere."—eleventh-grader.

"Parents don't tell us. There's no place except the school to help us students."—twelfth-grader.

"Sex education should be taught in grade six to keep girls from getting into trouble."—tenth-grader.

"A girl might do wrong just out of curiosity and become pregnant, so they need sex education, and protection against sex relations with boys."—eighth-grader.

"Hire teachers who are not prudes, not teacher-like, who can handle kids without being authoritarian, and who are not ashamed to talk about things."—high school student.

"There should be free help for people who get into trouble with sex, dope, and other problems, and this help should be widely advertised so these teenagers can be sure of help and can be sure of where to go. Counseling and advice should be given *in confidence*. Not even their parents should be told."—high school student.

"Don't teach us what you want to teach; teach us what we want to know."—high school student.

Such were the thoughts elicited by the team of researchers who went into schools in four different areas of Connecticut to find out what the young wanted to know about health. The researchers were hired by the Connecticut State Board of Education, and they gathered their material among 5,000 students of varied economic and social backgrounds between November, 1967, and March, 1968. They compiled 8,000 pages of verbiage, and it was from this vast tome that the book *Teach Us What We Want to Know* was distilled. (It was published for the Connecticut Board by the Mental Health Materials Center, Inc., 419 Park Avenue South, New York, N.Y.)

Because of the special approach that was used in gathering the student opinions, the final book does not offer a hard and fast guide to general student health concerns. The researchers were instructed to avoid making suggestions to the students, and they were forbidden to use any standardized "check lists" of possible health topics—because these might make students think they *ought* to show an interest in the listed topics. Thus the opinions were gathered largely through discussions which the researchers stimulated with broad questions, such as "What would you like to know about your body?" And this approach apparently made systematic cataloguing of the answers quite difficult. For the book is merely a compilation of "typical" comments and concerns expressed by the students at each grade level. Beside some of the student comments, the editors put in parenthesis "many," but they never tell you just *how* many made such comments. Thus it is quite impossible for the reader to determine whether the book is an accurate summary of students' health concerns, or whether it is simply a selection of the student health concerns that interested, pleased, startled, or otherwise impressed the researchers. There are, for example, quite a number of student comments expressing the popular illusion that sex education can prevent sexual misfortunes. Such comments could easily be put to persuasive use by sex education proponents among Connecticut's educators (or by the nation's educators). And one wonders whether the editors were not motivated to select these and other such student comments for their eventual political utility.

Nevertheless, the book provides some startling revelations about the sexual curiosity of youngsters. Already in fifth grade, the youngsters in the sample wanted to know how birth control pills "stop birth." And one question, listed as coming from a fourth-grader, was, "Do you know what abortion means?" The seventh-grade section of the volume contains many questions about both abortion and the birth control pill. And one seventh-grader's question is, "What about premarital sex relations?" Another seventh-grader's question, which the editors have indicated to be a common one, is "Should we be afraid of sex?"

By eighth grade, judging from the selection of comments in the volume, students are already beginning to wonder whether conventional morality is "really important today." By tenth grade, they are wondering "what makes a good marriage." And by eleventh grade, their comments reflect a kind of resignation—they seem to feel by then that the schools have failed them, and they are more interested in giving advice about what should be done in the lower grades than in detailing their own concerns.

The students generally recommend that sex education begin at an earlier grade level than most educators have recommended. Of course, there are "family life and sex education" programs, like the one in New York City, which begin in kindergarten classes. But these programs don't usually include the detailed biography of reproduction or of physical changes during puberty until sixth or seventh grade. The students in the Connecticut study recommended that such teaching begin in fourth grade.

Teach Us What We Want to Know contains a good deal of additional non–sex related material, for the study was not merely focused on students' opinions about sex education. And reading through the whole thing, you could be impressed by the degree to which students worry about air pollution and the problems of the poor. You could even begin to think that the sex education controversy had gotten educators worried about young loins to an extent that was quite out of proportion to the youngsters' own concern with said loins. You could start to reflect that, to the young, the fears and shames and general furtiveness that plagued their sexual selves were surely no more devastating than the thought that perhaps incompetent adults were ruling their world, poisoning the very air they breathed, wasting innocent lives in their petty quarrels.

"All we think about is ourselves. We should try to get better living quarters for Puerto Ricans and Negroes," one of the fifth-graders had told the researchers. "Why don't people stop killing and start loving?" another fifth-grader had asked.

If you read such questions and then remembered what Jerry Stanley had said about the gradual disillusionment he had experienced during high school, when, as he put it, "you could say the truth was comine out" about America, you could begin to wonder whether that general political disillusionment had not far outweighed the peculiar sexual anxieties of the young in the late sixties. Of course, the political disillusionment of the young seemed in their underground newspapers to be intricately linked to the sexual disillusionings of adolescence, the period when they were discovering that their parents had not practiced what they preached. And their political statements were full of sexual metaphors that reflected this linkage. But at the heart of their anger was a concern for issues on which their very lives could turn. Sexual outrage seemed in their literature merely a microcosmic and particularized expression of that much larger outrage, the sense that they had been born into an age when youth itself was far more sinned against than sinning.

"What makes me mad is when people say that a word is obscene. How can something which is such a necessary part of this society (i.e., language, for meaningful communication) be 'disgusting?'

"What also angers me is when people become apathetic to things that *are* obscene. War and killing is certainly one of the most 'repulsive' things that man has invented. Yet how many people flinch or cry anymore when scenes from Vietnam or Biafra are flashed across the TV screen every night? The shape and smell of the Milwaukee River is certainly 'offensive.' Where is the public hue and cry over what man has done to this natural resource? I happen to think that any photograph of a nuclear bomb is about the most 'obscene' picture there could be, for it represents the final destruction of humanity."—Warner Bloomberg, in an article for *The Open Door*, a high school underground newspaper in Milwaukee, Wisconsin. (Reprinted in *How Old Will You Be In 1984?* [New York: Avon, 1969])

* * *

Friday morning, October 24th, in the Sheraton's Continental Room there was to be a triple-header. Three speeches in one session. Followed by comment from the floor. Starring: Donald S. Longworth of Texas Technological University (to talk about "Evaluation of Potential Family Life Teachers"), Richard K. Kerckhoff of Purdue University (to expound upon "Value

Stance Taken by Family Life and Sex Educators"), and Luther G. Baker, Jr., of Central Washington State College (whose topic was "The 'Who' of Sex Education in the Schools").

The room was quite full for this 9:00 A.M. multiple presentation, a promise I mistakenly assumed, that the three speeches would be interesting. Alas, they were woefully dull, and if I had not been slavishly taking notes, I would not have remembered a word of them—with the one exception of a disparity between the professors' and students' perceptions of each other's views on sexual mores that Kerckhoff had discovered at Purdue University.

Dr. Longworth, my notes tell me, suggested that school principals compile checklists of those qualities they think an ideal sex education teacher, sorry, "family life" teacher, ought to have.

Kerckhoff came next. He sounded rather woebegone because he had actually designed his study to determine whether "teachers who openly moralize in the classroom convey their opinions of, let us say, premarital chastity, better than do teachers who try *not* to inject their own moral positions." But it had turned out that the six professors used for the study employed such similar techniques that significant comparisons were not possible. Kerckhoff described his problem in dispiriting social sciences ("our data proved inadequate to test some of our hypotheses"), which did not exactly keep you on the edge of your seat. But at least he had discovered that one could use the "instruments" of social science to find out just how little professors knew about their students. Somehow his numerical rendering of professors' considerable ignorance of their students' views ("In all, the professors made correct estimates of student views on 52 per cent of our items, while students guessed correctly the views of their professors 71 per cent of the time") lent just the right amount of authoritative credence to my prejudices about professors. So I listened well for a while, and decided that Kerckhoff knew what he was talking about.

Luther Baker also kept my attention for a while. I had seen his piece "The Rising Furor Over Sex Education" in some of the SIECUS materials as well as the materials that the NEA had been handing out to reporters and, I assumed, worried school administrators. Baker's piece, in which he blamed the organized right wing for generating much of the resistance to sex education, had become a kind of Bible for sex education proponents. In it he had defended both SIECUS and *Sexology* magazine. And though he had also made some rather grand claims for the saving powers of sex education ("Sex education . . . tends to social solidarity"), he had by and large gotten his facts straight, correctly pointing out that the Antis had a few years ago opposed fluoridation and that nearly every large professional organization in medicine or education had come out in favor of sex education.

"This seems to have been the year of sex," this famous sex education proponent began. The year of *I Am Curious—Yellow*. The year of unprecedented pornography.

A gripping start. But soon he was offering generous platitudinous wisdom: "I think the current furor over sex education may prove to be an angel unaware. Theorists and practitioners are being forced to re-examine [sex education programs and sex education teachers]."

You bet, they're being forced to re-examine, I thought. And they're producing programs that are even worse than the ones they created before anyone was breathing down their necks. At least, Evelyn Duvall's books were only a few of some forty that had been available to the Anaheim youngsters before the controversy there. Mr. Baker lost my attention. And though I continued to take notes (He had launched into a progress report on the state of sex education in the state of Washington), I was sneaking glances around the room, making astute snap judgments about the membership of the National Council on Family Relations. They were middle-aged and conservatively dressed, the kind of people who, I noted once again, would have fit in at any bridge club or even a Republican convention.

But soon it was time for comments from the floor, and when these began, my theories were mercilessly shattered (as they had been temporarily with Elias) by the maddening variety of views expressed. There was the blond lady in the back of the room who said she found the NEA's code of ethics for teachers disturbing; it "presents a super square," she said, and she wasn't sure if she liked Dr. Longworth's idea of a checklist for rating "family life" educators. There was the ubiquitous Mr. Sanctuary from SIECUS who said that in Britain "for approximately the last twenty years we have been developing techniques for the selection of marriage counselors and sex educators" and that in America it would at least take "an extended workshop" to do the same. There was the man with very short hair who said that it would all "depend on how much influence we think the teacher has on the child. Somebody has to make that judgment. And I can't think of anybody better than the superintendent and the principal." (At which point substantial groans could be heard throughout the room.) There was the attractive grey-haired woman who said she thought the crucial question was "whether teaching is willing to grant students [the right] to have their own standards." There was Esther Schultz (also from SIECUS), who cheerfully said that sex education would soon be "incorporated" into health education "and health will be invading all curricula," thus, there would be no such thing as a specialized Family Life teacher. There was the large woman who said she was a sciologist from the University of Wisconsin and that she would "require all potential teachers to have many more units in sociology and social psychology." There was the balding man from New York in the back of the room who said he thought that "a value for Family Life educators" was "to be attuned to the students of today: What about our understanding of our own students' views and values?"

It was not an audience that accommodated itself to any one category. It contained liberals, and organization men, and SIECUS optimists, and one social scientist who was convinced that her field had been slighted in teacher education. It was an audience, in short, that was probably quite representative of the polyglot membership of the organization. They might be able to put themselves into neat categories (middle white-collar and upper white-collar), but they defied for me in the particular what it had been so easy to say about them in general and from afar. Yet they did have, apparently, a common investment in the American family. And they shared an eagerness to keep up with the professional styles. A good number of them had come to the convention to present their papers or sell their books, and though they had performed an educational function in doing so, it could not be denied that they had also advanced their own careers.

One of them, a marriage counselor from Brooklyn who had been doing some research for the New York City Board of Education, made a point of telling me several times that no one else in the country had done a study like his. He had been asking the New York students who had gone through one or more terms of the "Family Living" program various questions about how it had affected their attitudes. He had also asked their teachers how *they* thought the program had affected student attitudes. After all the counting and standard error tabulating, he had found that the students and teachers were generally in agreement and that what they agreed about was the fact that the class produced "attitudinal outcomes" that were of a "predominantly favorable variety." Of course, he (his name was Alan Schneider) had no record of what the students' attitudes had been *before* they were given their thirty-five minutes of Family Living once a week, and

I wasn't quite sure how you measured people's attitudes, anyway, so his study hadn't impressed me overly much. What had impressed me more was his reiteration of the fact that his was the *only* study of its kind in the country. And when I mentioned the work that Elias had been doing, Schneider had dismissed it with an "oh, he's not testing for attitude change," or something to that effect.

Schneider later proved quite helpful (and also a little less boastful) when I was trying to learn about the content of the New York City program. But he had left me with an unpleasant suspicion that even among the scholars in the National Council on Family Relations, there were those whose ambitions outweighed their concern for the social problems that had, after all, given them their careers. It even struck me that Schneider's study might serve the New York City Board of Education well should their Family Living program become the target of harsh criticisms.

But such reflections were probably uncharitable, and it was, in the end, the peculiarly passionless professionalism, not the darker greeds and ambitions, of the Council's members that stayed with me after their convention.

A few weeks later, I asked the people at their headquarters in Minneapolis to send me some literature on the organization. Along with their general material, they sent me the organization's November newsletter, which contained summaries of the position statements that various committees had been composing while I had been mingling among the rank and file. A group called the Family Action Committee, newly established at the 1969 convention, had put together a "Position Statement on Family Life and the Viet Nam War," which, it seemed to me, best revealed the passionless style of those professionals. The statement began with a lot of whereases about how the war was "concomitant with personal, social and family disorganization" and about how the organization was "gratified that the President has already committed himself to a partial withdrawal of troops from Vietnam and hopefully plans immediate termination of the war," which were followed by this message:

We as members of the National Council on Family Relations now recommend that the President of the United States, in cooperation with the Congress, appoint two Presidential Commissions:
   One to study the effects of the war on family life in Southeast Asia and to make recommendations on how our nation may best contribute to the rehabilitation of family life therein; and
   The second to study the effects of the war economy and military

losses on families in America, especially those of minority groups, and to make recommendations regarding the improvement of American family life.
It is further recommended that these commissions be recruited from recognized specialists in the family field.

Try to imagine those Presidential Commissions at work: "Excuse me, Ma'am, we'd just like to ask you a few questions about your family. What did it feel like when they burned down your hut?" Or: "Hello, Mrs. Jones, we're from the President's Commission on Family Life in Times of Adversity, and we'd like to talk with you. Would you say that your son's death has affected your family life: very much, somewhat, only slightly, not at all?"

These were truly people whose natures were subdued to what they worked in if the strongest joint statement that they could produce about warfare was simply that it was a matter that deserved careful study. No wonder the strident and vocal legions of the young were already further along that slow route than most school districts had traveled with all deliberate speed since 1954. No wonder the young were, in their rash and frequently impractical nations of defiance, already the keepers of a terrifying new vision of sexual freedom—not realized by most of them, but nevertheless bravely considered by them—while their elders were still worrying about ways to tell them the facts of life.

Oh! Sex Education!

A number of more prominent sex education proponents told me during the course of interviews that they thought SIECUS and its allies had helped to stimulate the sex education controversy. They did not want to be quoted saying so, but they would tell me "off the record" that they thought SIECUS had been too "militant" or too pushy or too pious and aggressively crusading. Or they would tell me that SIECUS should have handled the press better, that Mary Calderone had no sense of public relations, or that it was too bad SIECUS couldn't afford to hire a public relations specialist. (SIECUS *had* hired a public relations specialist for a time.)

They didn't want to be quoted, they would say, because SIECUS had already been so cruelly smeared. Mary Calderone had suffered through unjustified attacks, and they did not want to add to the artillery of her unsavory critics. And Professor James Malfetti told me that he thought a number of the sex education proponents had created their own troubles by raising "unrealistic expectations" about the saving powers of sex education (vis-à-vis VD and illegitimacy), which they were later unable to fulfill.

Nevertheless, it seemed to me that SIECUS had no more created the sex education controversy than the Civil Rights Movement had created America's racial troubles. And I considered those off-the-record comments to be evidence that some of the sex education proponents had already come to believe a little of the Antis' propaganda: that SIECUS *was* guilty of foisting sex education into the schools from the outside, and that without the organization, sex education would have been indigenous, local, and therefore uncontroversial.

The SIECUS people did push for support for school sex education programs among the large "helping profession" organizations. But SIECUS received, in its happier years before the battles, something like 1,000 letters a week, large numbers of which came from school districts that wanted help in establishing their own sex education programs. Now, it may have been that when Mary Calderone went into a community, she could have used a little more discretion with the local media—not saying in front of reporters, for instance, that she had very personal memories of the hazards of shotgun weddings. But sex education was obviously in vogue during the sixties, and it was my contention that if Mary Calderone hadn't been around, some other human relations expert would have been blamed for the vogue.

Because it just happened that while that vogue was developing, a great puritan frenzy was incubating on the shelves of that bookstore at Knott's Berry Farm and inside the slick sex-and-civil rights magazine that was first displayed on Alabama newspaper stands after the great Selma March of 1965. Sex education was a perfectly suited political issue for people who had long read political implications into pornography and interracial couplings, people whose fears of the mythical hippie love-making were intricately tied up with their fears of Communism or of anarchy.

And it didn't seem to matter in the least that no one involved in the debate at the start of it could *prove* that sex education would subvert the morals of Americans or teach them to make "responsible use of the sexual faculty." It seemed to matter even less in July of 1969, when two men at the University of Kansas Medical School in Kansas City published some findings that showed absolutely no relationship between sex education and "premarital petting and coital behavior." These two men, Gerald H. Wiechmann and Altis L. Ellis (respectively, Assistant Professor and Research Assistant in the Department of Preventive Medicine and Community Health), had questioned 545 students enrolled in a community health course at the University of Missouri about their exposure to sex education (including grade level) and their experiences with the two aforementioned pleasurable activities. They published their findings in the July, 1969, issue of *The Family Coordinator*.

Several months later John Steinbacher discovered their little article and said (in his column) that the thing disproved all the inflated claims of the sex education proponents. The more responsible sex education proponents told me they'd never made any inflated claims; they just thought sex education was a good thing. Mary Calderone went on saying that sex education could provide a "balancing force" against the terrible sex exploitation in the media.

It didn't matter what sex education could do because the argument was not about facts, it was about beliefs. H. L. Mencken knew about this kind of argument from the old Evolution debates, and he had summed it up this way:

No controversy to my knowledge has ever ended on the ground where it began. Even the historic one between Huxley and Wilberforce, two of the most eminent men of their time in England, ranged all over the landscape before the contestants had enough. It began with Huxley trying to prove that Darwin's *Origin of the Species* was a sound book; it ended with Bishop Wilberforce trying to prove that Huxley's grand-father was a gorilla. What was it's issue? Did Huxley convert Wilber-force? Did Wilberforce make any dent in the armor of Huxley? I apologize for wasting your time with silly-rhetorical questions. Did Luther convert Leo X? Did Grant convert Lee?*

And similarly the sex education controversy was an argument between two sets of believers, those who just *knew* that sexual enlightenment contributed to any number of socially commend-able attitudes ("sexual sanity" being only one), and those who just *knew* that such enlightenment created terrible and irresistible temptations that put a strain on every ounce of civilization in a child's mind. And though the two sides might be factionalized among themselves, disagreeing over fine psychological points, or religious styles, their battle always centered on this one question of faith: Was or was not knowledge of sexuality a good thing?

Professor James Malfetti, who was of all the proponents perhaps the least guilty of making unfounded claims about the saving powers of sex education, was still unable to relinquish the last central article of the educators' faith.

"You see, a course can be defended on—if it's built on an educational premise," he told me. "We assume, and we have a lot of capital invested in it here at Columbia, that there's a value in increasing the information base of an individual so that he's in a position to make a better decision. If an individual is acquainted with a wider information base, allowed an opportunity to discuss ramifications of potential behavior, get feedback from peers, get feedback from an instructor, it's reasonable to assume that for *him*, he will make a better decision for him[self] as a result of that experience than he would make without it.

"Now that's a premise on which *most* education is based."

Professor Malfetti used the phrase "better decision" instead of "rational decision" perhaps because he was a careful man and knew when he was speaking out of his own value system. But the fact remained that he *believed* education could help people to

* *Prejudices: A Selection*, James T. Farrell, ed. (New York: Vintage, 1958.)

live more rationally or more happily or whatever you call it when they are making "better decisions." And that was something no one could prove. Did James Joyce make "better decisions" for himself because he was perhaps the most educated man of his age? Did Edward Teller? Did Bertrand Russell? Who could judge? They had between them altered our literature and our philosophy and invented nuclear warfare, and surely, none could prove that their education alone had equipped them to make "better decisions" for themselves or for their fellow men.

"To me," the inspired Mrs. Pippinger had said, "higher education has become America's God. People are inclined to think that if you have a Ph.D., you're God. We don't have to know the answers to everything. Satan had to know everything, too. That's why he rebelled."

To her the yearning for knowledge was in the end something frightening and Faustian, a dangerous longing to venture forth upon the void, a terrible threat to a mythical, unself-conscious innocence that had been long ago set down in a folk tale about a place called the Garden of Eden.

She and her kindred spirits could no more demonstrate the outward and visible validity of her belief than could Professor Malfetti prove that knowledge made men rational. It was perhaps the greatest irony of the entire sex education battle that the man who had, in a sense started it, the man who startled the Western world with his revelations about infantile and childhood sexuality, had never held out the promise that enlightenment would render man more rational. Though he argued for sex education, Freud never promised that it would produce a race of happy and reasonable men or resolve all the conflicting claims of their civilizations and the individual genetics that propelled them toward that uncontrollable mystery on the bestial floor.

postscript

•

The Material Affects Its Messenger

". . . the irony of the whole battle was that it belonged to another age. . . ."

Postscript
The Material Affects Its Messenger

In the mail today (March 12, 1970) came an issue of *Homefront*, the Institute for American Democracy's newsletter, which has for the past several issues contained a page of small bulletins on the "Sex Education Battle Front." This one tells me that the American Medical Association is now sticking its fat neck out for sex education, through a saturation campaign in its magazine *Today's Health*. I also read that Billie James Hargis is starting a new crusade against pornography, which his devoted followers will soon read about in another Christian Crusade pamphlet, this one to be called "The Sex Revolution in the United States." Someone should send Hargis a copy of that April, 1966, *Journal of Social Issues*, I think. Maybe he's afraid the Infidels are getting something that he is not. A mean, ornery thought. Sorry, Billie. But I'm getting a little tired of you. You seem to be saying the same thing over and over again.

I'm getting tired of the whole issue, as a matter of fact. I may be a living refutation of the Antis' theories. I have read so much literature on sex that I ought, according to them, to be a hopeless, Communistic "prevert" with unbridleable desires and every ounce of Romantic illusion gone from my grey matter. Instead, I am thoroughly sick of dry sex studies and eager to get back to the novels that I always liked better than nonfiction, anyway. Russia seems drab to me, as it did even before I read excerpts from Masters and Johnson. Cuba seems a hopeful place, but I worry about the freedom of press question there, as I did before reading Masters and Johnson. Sex seems to be just about what it has been since I first discovered that my mother was right, although I wouldn't describe it exactly as she did. And Romance, well, Romance is just indomitable. If you were an English major, it positively hunts you down.

But I suppose I have changed. I have learned to fight off the strange resistance to that dry sexual material. It was a resistance that I noticed in myself when I picked up the first of the ten pamphlets (now there are more of them) that SIECUS published for teachers. It would emerge stubbornly each time I tackled something like Kinsey's material or the sections on human sexual response in *The Individual, Sex, & Society*. And each time I noticed it, I would tell myself that I was reacting exactly as Mrs. Westerfield would—or even John Rarick. I was really afraid all that clinical stuff *would* destroy my romantic illusions. And perhaps it did all work an imperceptible shift, a gentle shove toward reason. But you don't have much opportunity to test things like that out when you are writing a book. You hardly have time to spend a whole evening with someone, let alone Get Involved.

No, the big change in me came from my exposure to the right wing. I had imagined them to be terrible, evil people before I met them. And I can't say that I approved of their tactics, their late night phone calls to Sally Williams and Paul Cook, their belligerent behavior at school board meetings, or their curious ability to suspend democratic procedures when they needed to, as a group on a citizens advisory committee in West Milford, New Jersey, had done. I can't say that I liked their racism or their rabid anti-Communism. But I did learn to feel some sympathy for their fears. Mrs. Westerfield sometimes made sense when she tried to express what I would call the fear of dry sexual information's depersonalizing effects. I didn't think that the information alone would accomplish any deep numbing of the psyche. But I did find it disturbingly remote from the real problems of the passions. The sex education proponents had claimed that sex was too long partitioned off into a forbidden and furtive area, separate from the rest of our lives. But I wondered whether a special sex education course was not really a continuation of that partitioning. Mrs. Westerfield and I would part company here, for she just seemed to prefer the old kind of partitioning, a kind that would at least keep out the cold, clinical glare of the laboratory lights. But I was all for putting sex education into every part of the school curriculum that dealt with the human species.

I had complained to Professor Malfetti not long after the National Council on Family Relations Convention, telling him that I couldn't recall hearing the word "passion" being used at all during that affair. And he had said, yes, they were worried about that problem up at Columbia. He was even thinking of putting together a sex education textbook with some poetry and fiction

in it. Which was, I thought, doing it backwards. Why not put a
little more sexual material into the English classes? And the history classes. And the social studies classes. And the biology classes.
And the health classes. And so on.

The right-wingers had forced me to think about what it must
feel like to belong to a philosophical minority. And then, as I
examined the various sex education programs, I realized that I
belonged to a philosophical minority on the other end of the
spectrum. And if the schools weren't going to deal with sex the
way I thought they should, then I was almost willing to say they
should just leave it out. Almost.

What halted that dog-in-the-mangerish theory was the material
that the students wrote or told me. They *weren't* getting much
sex education from their parents, at least they weren't getting
answers to their questions—and most of them seemed to have
stopped asking them several years before puberty. But they wanted
to know. They wanted to know what made a good marriage. And
they wanted to know what made good sex. They wanted to know
whether they were normal and whether they would suffer if they
decided to try sleeping together. And whether anybody would fall
in love with them. And whether they would fall in love with anybody else. And whether their parents, friends, teachers, brothers,
sisters, ministers would hate them if any of these knew what they
were really doing.

For a time, after I decided that Mary Calderone, *et al.*, were
really for abstinence until marriage—or until something that was
going to lead to marriage—I went around telling all my friends that
I thought those sex educators couldn't be trusted to tell the truth
about anything other than the strictly biological material. I didn't
even think that their teachings on masturbation amounted to very
much because they seemed to be using those teachings as a subtle
method to keep the youngsters from trying things out with each
other. The sex educators seemed to have decided that masturbation was really a means for keeping the kids pure. It wasn't that
heterosexual goings on were exactly dirty to the sex educators; but
they weren't exactly clean, either. All that sober material about the
consequences of intercourse was just a little too close to the old
precepts to pass for enlightened and "realistic" sociological advice.
So I thought it was better that the youngsters just not hear it.

But later I decided that, since the students would bring up questions about consequences and social standards if they were given
the opportunity, someone had better write a textbook that told
them the truth. Someone had better take all that material in *The*

Individual, Sex, and Society and the *Journal of Social Issues* and rewrite it so that high school students could manage to get through it all. It wouldn't help them figure out ways to avoid getting hurt, which was what they all really seemed to want to know, but it would at least tell them that marriage wasn't successful just because you waited for it and that their own parents had been more liberal at age twenty than they were at age forty, that many of them had, in fact, done a bit of fooling around themselves.

Because the youngsters had a right to know those things. They had a right to know what we could call the truth for lack of a better term. And they had a right to know that the mythical Aquarian Age was really a myth, that there weren't hordes of ecstatic young nubiles cavorting away on the grass at every opportunity without a thought for the morrow. That everybody, even the most ambient of hippies, seemed to want one person's special attention, perhaps not till death did them part, but usually for more than an afternoon at a rock concert.

But I think it will be a long time before the high schools start telling their charges the whole truth. There is a good chance that this sex education controversy will die out soon. But even before it started, high school superintendents had a tendency to overestimate the conservatism of their communities. And now, it will take some persuading to convince them that they weren't right about it all along. So the young will go on being cheated out of the truth. But then, they're used to that.

And I suspect that they aren't really as stupid as their elders seem to assume. They don't seem to care as much about the precious sex education courses in existence now as their teachers do. They have other things to worry about, like the draft and the people who are ruining our water and our air. And overpopulation —as their incredible school administrations won't tell them about contraceptives. (Contraceptives would be included in my list of strictly biological facts, to be covered by all schools that are too cowardly to give their students any reliable sociological material about sex.)

Because the irony of the whole battle was that it belonged to another age, an age when contraception and abortion weren't needed and when women were mercilessly taught to abhor or pretend they abhorred the act that was so liberally necessary to the survival of the species, because so many of their infants died. But now, our scientists were predicting that we had only a few decades to go before the automobile and our industries wiped us out. And in New York City, the school board wouldn't allow its teachers to tell students about contraception. Never mind, in a few years, New York City's air pollution count would be so high that we might not have to worry about contraception anymore.

Dr. Albert Szent-Gyorgyi, the seventy-six-year-old Nobel Prize-winning biologist, said we were approaching a 50 per cent chance of survival, all of us on the whole planet, and he thought that by the end of the century, the odds would be lower. He had told *The New York Times* (in the February 20, 1970, edition) that youth was his only hope for the world. He had discovered Vitamin C in 1937. He seemed to be just the kind of person I would invite to my sex education class. What would he do if he were twenty today? the *Times* reporter had asked him.

"I would share with my classmates rejection of the whole world as it is—all of it. Is there any point in studying and work? Fornication—at least that is something good. What else is there to do? Fornicate and take drugs against this terrible strain of idiots who govern the world."

At least that was better than telling them to wait for the golden moments.

Index